BITTERSWEET

BITTERSWEET

The Clifford T. Ward Story

dave cartwright

Moonicorn Books

First published in Great Britain 1999
by Moonicorn Books,
Henwick Road,
Worcester WR2 5NP
e-mail: Lunacornis@aol.com

ISBN 0 9535388 0 X

A CIP catalogue record for this book
is available from the British Library

Book produced and designed by dave cartwright.
Printed in Great Britain by Ebenezer Baylis & Son Ltd
The Trinity Press, Worcester

Author's note

This has been an immensely enjoyable book to write, but it has not been an easy one.

Many difficulties have presented themselves, the most sensitive one being that although Clifford T. Ward has not written, sung, played or recorded a single note of music since 1986—13 years ago—he is still amongst us; a difficulty, I hasten to add, I am more than pleased to accept. But it has made some matters rather delicate in their telling.

Following diagnosis in 1985, the rapid onset of multiple sclerosis ended his career and life quality as effectively as a paralysing accident. There has been no remission, no opportunity for him to continue—to even touch upon—his musical past.

Away from the public eye, this ungracious patient shuns the wheelchair, or any other form of assistance; medicinal, physical, or practical. His innate stubbornness has created a being that is almost childlike in its refusal to accept or fight its predicament. At home his imminent approach is often heralded with the bangs and crashes of well-rehearsed exhibitionism. He enters the room on all fours like a bull in a china shop, and the atmosphere in that room will swing according to his mood. He can be obtuse, articulate, diffident, rude, hilarious, warm, sensitive, infuriating; he will smoke, joke, croak, choke, and drink a beer or two; he will opinionate, and dismiss any contradiction; but above all, he will not be ignored.

So in this book, I refer to him in past and in present, confusing and ungrammatical though it may seem. That is the only solution. He is here, now, his humour still remarkably intact, but his many diverse talents—sadly, cruelly—are forever locked away; gone.

david cartwright, February, 1999.

In loving and everlasting memory of
my father, James Noah,
and my mother,
Louisa Florence

CONTENTS

LAUGH IT OFF, GIRL

Laugh where we must, be candid where we can;
But vindicate the ways of God to man.

Alexander Pope: *An Essay on Man*

I walk over to the French windows. The unkempt lawn slopes down sharply, allowing a beautiful, unbroken view over the Teme Valley to where an early autumn mist snakes through the golden orchards and naked hop poles of Middle England. A view to be savoured and shared. Indeed, the rancid smell of cigarette smoke reminds me that I am not alone, so I turn back into the room to speak to my companion, the master of the house, but decide better of it.

He sits, legs stretched outwards, feet resting on a grey pouffe. He sighs, long and deep, almost ending with a curse, then inhales again, his hand shaking noticeably as it reaches his mouth. He is bored with me, my small talk and, much more important, he is bored with life.

It is over 25 years since this man was hailed by the music press as heir apparent to Paul McCartney, the Elgar of pop music, the saviour of intelligent, modern song; and, at first glance you would be forgiven for thinking that time, the magician, had been fairly kind to singer-songwriter Clifford T. Ward. The long, golden hair, though inevitably greying, still hangs curtain-like around the full-lipped mouth, and the once sculpted cheek bones have, like the rest of his body, filled out with the onset of middle age. Only the large, black sun-glasses—a permanent fixture—suggest anything is unnaturally wrong, and behind them, in the mirrors of the soul, lies confirmation of an awful truth. His blurred vision, his slurred, stumbling speech, his total lack of co-ordination and muscular control, are completely at odds with his ever fertile mind. He is trapped in a frame that cannot function; a victim not of accident, a feeble heart, or even stimulant abuse, but of that most cruel of illnesses, multiple sclerosis.

However, as death redeemed Elvis—oh, and many less deserving souls who fell before their time—there are those who suggest that the onset of MS has actually redeemed Clifford T. Ward, and were it not for the recent 'home-truth' press articles, the CD re-releases, the hastily conceived out-take albums, this man would have disappeared, like many other shooting stars, into the back catalogues and 'one-hit wonder' racks of musical history. To those who know only the one song, and the one all too frequently used picture, who remember the 'family-way' press cuttings, the eloquent, courteous interviews, he was Britain's, well, Barry Manilow…? Safe, wholesome, benign, many miles from the cutting edge of pop music.

Yet a surprisingly diverse collection of established performers quote him as their champion of sublime originality and unwavering self-belief. One of the most frequently requested artistes on BBC Radio 2, his recent compilation, *Gaye And Other Stories*, went gold in Ireland; a thriving appreciation society, The Friends of CTW, meets annually and *Waves,* an articulate, quarterly fanzine, has subscribers world-wide, from Argentina to Australia; his records eagerly sought out by fans and collectors alike.

So why? Is this pity? A morbid fascination in a once healthy hero? A rejoicing in sudden accessibility? Or is it, indeed, a long overdue recognition of a unique and once conspicuous talent, cut down in its prime?

Clifford T. Ward has always been a split vote, to anyone who remembers his comet-like success in the glum-rock 1970s. The national music critic who saw Clifford's pure, intelligent simplicity cutting through all the fabricated nonsense that called itself pop music; the local journalist, bombarded with the candy-floss and bubblegum, who recognized something astonishingly different; or that most endangered of species, the incurable romantic—all seem content to remain strangely at odds with the rest of the world.

Hopefully, in this book, I will go some way to redress the balance, and lift the man to his true position in the scheme of things. Whilst doing so however, I am acutely aware that disbelief—and even offence—may result from the many disclosures made and questions answered along the way. Yet whatever judgements are forthcoming, and no matter how many illusions become tarnished, nothing can possibly diminish the sheer beauty of his work. Anyhow, we are all no more than human.

Suppose he had not met Pat, his wife of 35 years. Would he have risen to earlier—and greater—heights? His 'overnight' success came courtesy of an unplanned teenage marriage and subsequent years of musical frustration, yet far from holding him back, I would submit that her strength held him together. Without her, he would have drifted, succumbed; probably have gone the way so many young, naïve and talented artistes went. Oh, he would have written 'Sympathy', 'Carrie',

'Coathanger', but he couldn't possibly have written 'Home Thoughts From Abroad', 'A Day To Myself', or—ironically—'The Best Is Yet To Come', without her, that's for sure.

Because one thing is certain. On my many visits to their home, and, after speaking to the many people who have known and worked with him over the years, it has become painfully apparent to me that coping with life and life's problems has never been Clifford's concern. He needed—*expected*—complete freedom from such matters, despite his inspiration depending absolutely on the family environment: wife, home, children, constancy. And with the tragic onset of MS, the burden again fell upon Pat, the girl-bride, the mother of his four children, the woman who, regardless of all that life has thrown at her, still 'oozes sex appeal'. She continues to manage his life; dressing, feeding and nursing her stricken husband, juggling their increasingly precarious financial situation with that impenetrable *sang-froid*; seemingly forever able—outwardly at least—to laugh it off.

Therefore, this story must also belong to her, and it all begins many years but not so many miles away, in what was once a quiet, pretty backwater town bordering the long, winding river the conquering Romans called 'Sabrina'.

Here, in what is now a chaos of hideously colour-uncoordinated amusement arcades, junk food franchises and fun pubs; on February 10th, 1944, as if voicing disapproval at the simultaneous birth of PAYE income tax, Clifford Thomas, the fifth child of Frank and Kathleen Ward, came roaring into a quiet corner of a war-torn world.

SPRING

WHEREWITHAL

Character is destiny — Heracleitus

Stourport-on-Severn lies 30 miles south-west of Birmingham. Behind the garish façade of the High Street, Georgian houses and lime-tree avenues serve as a sad reminder of this once thriving inland port on Britain's longest river. In a much darker age, the deep, swirling currents of the Severn brought Viking longboats inland to plague our Saxon forefathers; as the industrial revolution tore at the heart of the Midlands, it carried the first iron from Darby's furnaces down to the Bristol Channel and the sea. But now, in wasted days of state-subsidized leisure, it seems content to roll majestically through the hills and vales of Worcestershire, lapping the shaded haunts of the fishermen, the rotting landing stages, the caravan parks and the secret gardens.

In the post-war boom of the 1950s, before the blight of the family car, Stourport became a popular day-trip excursion from the sombre, stiff-lipped canal towns of the Black Country. The nearby carpet-makers of Kidderminster, the needle-makers of Redditch, the chain-makers of Cradley and the swarthy glass-blowers of Stourbridge, piled onto 'Midland Red' double-decker omnibuses and green Great Western locomotives, to descend in their happy hordes upon the beautiful Sabrina; hiring row-boats and canoes, queuing for 30 minute trips on pleasure steamers, or climbing the spiral steps to the road bridge, to stand gawping, laughing and pointing at the frantic activities of those below. A small funfair took root over the years, precariously balanced on the riverbank; a putting green and model railway were laid out on the flat land opposite, and, for the lifetime of my childhood at least, every August Bank Holiday Monday at high noon—the town overflowing with carnival revellers—a Tannoy-thin voice heralded the approach of a shadowy figure, weaving Pied Piper-like through the side-shows and carousels. Elbowing our way to the front, we would watch him climb the iron steps, leap onto the stone parapet and dive into the bright water, emerging to rapturous applause from the ice-creamed crowd.

The day rolled on, and as the trippers turned grudgingly back to the stations and bus-stops, the town assumed an air of almost Wild West apprehension. Local shadows tumbled from pub doorways, turned into the street and stumbled onto the bridge, where, fuelled by gallons of cheap cider—and at an almost mystically pre-ordained hour—the Nunns and the Pearce gypsy gangs would begin their traditional bloody battle, assaulting each other with '…fists and chains and unspeakable names…', high above the moonlit Severn.

Years before these carnival days, when the world was locked in war, and Stourport slumbered beside the river, Frank and Kathleen Ward lived a short distance from the seven-arched bridge, in a tiny, canalside cottage on Manor Road.

Frank, quiet, dark and wiry, was forty-one when Clifford was born. Too old for military service, he had laboured at the carpet factories, while his wife, thirteen years younger, was raising a demanding family with resigned desperation; the three boys and their sister, like all other children, constantly drawn to the water's edge: running out, falling in.

Kathleen Bishop smiles out of the sepia picture, taken when she was about seventeen; a vivacious round-faced country girl, with hair of spun gold. But even then, the camera could lie.

Her only daughter Kath, sitting in the deep-piled lounge of her tea-cosy bungalow, surrounded by family snaps and Constable prints, told me that canalside living was only one more problem:

"Mom was born with a withered left arm; nothing more than a short, handless stub. She grew up in a world that didn't condescend, yet which, in a way, made her determined to live a full, active, 'ordinary' life. After battling with the traumas of childhood and adolescence, well, getting married, having children, was a natural progression. Despite her impairment, there seemed to be nothing she couldn't do. She even rode a bicycle, with just one arm… The only thing to which she openly admitted defeat was not being able to manage her hair. She really needed help with that beautiful hair."

As the buds of peace blossomed, the nation's subsidized optimism, even in such rural communities, saw Utopian housing estates rising from the ashes, replacing the picturesque but dank Victorian homes and bringing hot water, electricity and therefore—surely—a better life to the poor. The Wards were moved to the Walshes Estate, nowadays a sad, decaying reflection of a world that has lost its way, but in those early dream days, a model of Brave New Worldliness.

Like waggons round a camp-fire, Ernley Close encircled a huge, lawned play area. Situated on a spacious corner plot, the whitewashed four-bedroomed house must have seemed like paradise; warm and dry, with all modern conveniences, and neighbours sharing an industrious, common bond. Kitchen doors stood open in welcome, hand-scrubbed washing danced and waved across the backyard, and no cars littered the pavements or gouged mud-ruts in the new grass.

Kathleen continued to rear her five children with quiet pride, refusing all offers of help from her new neighbours. Frank had now exchanged his job at the carpet factory in Kidderminster for a less distant—though more exacting—position, feeding the coal hoppers of the newly built power station in Stourport, and though always in regular employment, his labouring wage had to be supplemented by whatever means possible. Kathleen saw the potential in her young army. During summer holidays and autumn weekends, first-born Terry, brothers Barry and tubercular Melvin, Kath and young Clifford, were bundled onto the backs of clattering lorries laden with high-spirited fruit-pickers heading for the fields of bounty, where under their mother's diligent supervision, they would learn to earn their keep.

Well, that is how a romanticized Hollywood version would probably portray it. The actuality was less romantic.

Kath tells me: "We used to trudge over to Lewis's farm, just across the track, to join the other pickers, who were mostly gypsies, and spend all day in back-breaking toil. Fruit-picking is not for the faint-hearted, and though I would never say he was faint-of-heart, even at that tender age, Cliff let it be known: he hated working in the fields. It was all way beneath him. Mom and he were always at odds. Most of the time, if he didn't want to do something, he'd just say 'No!', face up to her, and that would be it.

"Obviously, he had to come along, but he'd soon disappear. We would work all day, then towards late afternoon, just before we packed up to go home, we'd stuff some fruit into our bags, as much as they could hold. That little bugger came running down the bank one day, shouting, 'Bulmer's comin! The farmer's 'ere. Bulmer's comin!...' We had to empty everything out, damn quick, spread it around. Up to our ankles in stolen fruit we were. He just rolled about on the grass, laughing like a madman. 'Fooled ya, gotcha all.' I could've killed him. Mom always stopped me. She ended up spoiling him rotten.

"Looking back though, and all things considered, I can't recall us going without. We had a television as early as 1953—I can remember watching the Coronation—and Mom somehow managed to buy a beautiful radiogram later on, which I commandeered for my Bill Haley 78s.

"When the American forces were stationed up at Burlish, Mom's sister latched onto an army officer. It must have got serious, 'cos he sent food and clothing parcels from America when he went home on leave. You can imagine the excitement: cutting the string and unwrapping that thick brown, greaseproof paper at the table. Inside, cans of corn, chocolate, comics and check shirts. We got chewing gum from the soldiers over at the camp. 'Got any gum, chum?' was *our* war-cry. And the things they threw away up there. We waited every Friday for the truck to come down to the tip. Real scavengers, we were."

Life offered a joyous freedom that any working-class child of the fifties would later remember with affection, and regret, that it all went so sadly wrong. If it was poor then it was likewise delightfully honest. Away from the home, the surrounding hedgerows, ancient oaks, abundant orchards and lush meadows instilled children in general, and Clifford in particular, with a love for the shades and sounds of nature that he would carry through all his days.

His formative years at Areley Kings Primary School—a rust-bricked Victorian building backing onto arable fields and thick, dark woodland—were as innocent as England before the war. For such children, in their still idyllic, pastoral surroundings, nothing, yet, had changed. They chattered along the empty lanes to and from their resonant, vaulted classrooms, through the yearly dance of the seasons, unconcerned with past or future, hardly noticing the small stone memorial that roll-called the names of young men lost in combat. Not so very long ago these brave but bewildered heroes had run through the very same lanes and fields, sat in the same desks, as did their mothers and fathers before them. They had helped win the glorious battle, but were never to see the golden peace.

I look at the school photograph, 1955. The fresh-faced classmates, arms folded, chins pointing up at the camera, gathered together on the yard fronting the small building. The names mean nothing to me as my eye runs along the list: J. Large, J. Evans, D. Chell, R. Hume... R. Hume?!!. Surely not *Ray* Hume, he's a friend of *mine*, has been for over thirty years... Good lord, it *is* him, sitting cross-legged, with that unmistakable grin, there on the front row, with Clifford at the back (for once in his life...) standing alongside their broody, bearded teacher.

All the times Ray and I have been together, through possibly every folk club in the Midlands—and possibly every bar—and he's never mentioned Clifford T. Ward. I wonder what memories he has of Areley Kings.

Best give him a ring, David.

Typical. The one time I try to make contact and he's moved house, left the area, and...he's missed me off his change-of-address list. So much for friendship. And where's he gone? Grimsby. *Grimsby*!!

But good old directory enquiries, and the fortunate situation that he is the only Grimsby-Hume in the book.

Yes, he remembers it well, and, as I expected, with great fondness.

Mr Walker, despite his Rasputin-like demeanour, was a great favourite. Both Ray and Clifford recall his stern but cordial approach. Misses Rimmer, Collings and Booton ran the other classes in their formidable spinsterly fashion, cycling to work along the winding lanes, blue-serged and hair-netted, like Dorothy's Aunt-Witch from Oz.

Ray talks about maths and music, birthday parties and holidays—when he and Cliff were close friends—and then, with great enthusiasm, tells of the proliferation of wildlife that lived in the hawthorn hedgerows surrounding the school: blackbirds, thrushes, gold and green finches, skylarks nesting on the uncut clumps of the playing-fields, and flocks of visiting lapwings in the cold, hard winters, when pale green ice crunched underfoot.

"We were avid bird-spotters, collecting eggs and checking nests, pastimes which now of course are strictly illegal." He justifies it, as we all do now—in our guilt—by emphasizing the abundance, and of course the unquestioning belief that it would be ever thus.

"We even had tree sparrows and spotted fly-catchers breeding in our front garden. It's hard to believe. As for collecting and pinning moths and butterflies, and pressing wildflowers…well, why not? We knew no better, no-one did."

Yes, we all did it, if we were fortunate to live in such beautiful parts, and now, thankfully—though maybe a little too late—we're all 'born again'…

For Clifford's family, with its strong male-bonding, rabbit-hunting was also a pleasurable diversion—or, speaking for the times, a 'sport'—in which he joined his elder brothers, though in his young excitement and fervour to impress, he is remembered for culling as many pursuing ferrets as he did fleeing rabbits.

Named after one of his two uncles (and fortunately the right one—Cyril T. Ward doesn't have quite the same flourish…) he grew confident and strong; an adventurous, opinionated child, forever chancing, arguing, questioning. At festive gatherings, fuelled by Mackeson stout and a captive audience, father Frank would settle back in his armchair, light a Woodbine, and elaborate on his Irish grandparents, music-hall artistes who he claimed had crossed the sea to Bristol, before moving up river to find work at the Kidderminster Playhouse. Cliff's early efforts to dress up and perform were 'in the blood', his father would say; "Our Cliff, he's a natural…"

This predilection and self-assurance for song-and-dance developed unchecked, making him an obvious frontman for school concerts at Areley Kings, scout gang shows at the decaying Playhouse, or youth club parties; indeed wherever possible. He wrote sketches, acted, sang and eagerly led his contemporaries—a more than capable exhibitionist.

Ray confirms such an instance. “One memory forever embedded in my addled brain is of a play we did in the cubs—of which Cliff and I were keen members; we both passed our Tenderfoot on the same evening, though I couldn’t do a fisherman’s knot now to save my life. Anyway, Cliff had to act an agonizing death from stabbing. I was probably Brutus…He took about twenty minutes, the longest ‘Aa-aaa-aargh’ in AmDrams I think. We all stood around watching him, bouncing off every wall, falling down, getting up, staggering across the room. Even Arthur Chance, the scout master, told him to hurry up and get it over with, his supper was in the oven.

“I guess that was a moment that—even at such a tender age—I felt summed up Cliff. He was determined to give his all. He was competitive and aggressive in the very best senses of the words. A very nice pal, but sort of larger-than-life with it.”

And Kath tells of his wolf-cub days, again in that hushed, ‘would-you-believe-it’ manner:

“When he was a sixer—leader of his little pack—before the meetings, he would call them all to the house and line them up, single-file in the back-yard. Then he’d walk along, inspecting them, like Montgomery and his troops: head to toe, back and front. Always had to be the best. Nothing else. He had have the best pack. He had to win. Poor old Roger Lewis, a little kid from along the street, he was always getting sent home by Cliff. ‘Lewis! Your shoes are dirty. Lewis! Your hair’s a mess. Go on home and tidy up!’ And little Roger would trudge off, back home and try to tidy up. His mother took as much as she could, until one night she came storming round. ‘You tell that bloody Cliff Ward to leave our Roger alone! He’s as good a cub as any of you lot!’”

“Where did he get all this competitiveness from?”

“I don’t know,” shrugs Kath. “Dad was very quiet. He lived for his work: punctual, conscientious. It was a dirty job, but he knew the alternative. Out of work was not a pleasant experience, so he made sure that he pulled his weight. He had no social life, pubs and such; his only vice, if you can call it that, was an occasional flutter on the horses, but he certainly wasn’t a competitive person. He adored Mom, absolutely adored her. He would often fill with emotion when he talked about her. Mom was loved by everyone. They had a happy marriage, the usual tiffs of course—which would upset Dad—but he doted on her.

“In fact, *every*body thought the world of Mom. All the children on the Walshes, all the locals, they looked on her like a queen,” says Kath. “She was an extraordinary woman.”

Extraordinary maybe, but as her daughter became a teenager, an increasing feeling of alienation in the matriarchal set-up—five males led by a dominant woman—induced her to leave home at seventeen.

"I didn't go far, just into Kidderminster. I could see Mom was encouraging—favouring—Cliff to strive for the best. He was the youngest, he had such spirit, and she obviously saw a lot of herself in his self-willed ways, though there were many times even she couldn't handle him. He wasn't exactly lazy, just single-minded. Errands to Badger's shop—a little stall set up in their front garden down the lane. I heard his 'No!' and I knew who would get the job: me.

"I had a laugh to myself when the vicar sent him home from the church choir auditions, saying he couldn't sing. Cliff was, well, shall we say… a little angry.

"He was a bit put out by that, particularly as Melvin, his elder brother, stayed in the choir for some years more, and then formed a skiffle group in his teens."

Beyond this life of sheltered, modernized tradition, great changes were taking place. Skiffle—with guitars at 4gns cash, or 22 fortnightly payments of 4/6d—was merely the precursor of a brand new, vibrant, popular culture that was slowly exploding, and, youth, not previously a world of collective excitement, was suddenly marketable. There was still the die-hard element of non-change: variety, pantomime, ABC Minors; all harmless, reliable, innocent…though in retrospect, sometimes quite audacious—the most popular show on radio for some years had been hosted by Archie Andrews, a ventriloquist's *dummy*, with novelty songs from the Hedley Ward Trio—but Elvis, Buddy and Eisenhower's America were beaming down from a planet beyond the sun, and Clifford, like any other developing adolescent, was soaking it all up. But, as he started to spend his pocket money on magazines and records, rather than *Last Of The Mohicans* and *Hotspur*, he also became aware of that terrifying slayer of pride, the opposite sex.

Five miles away, over the border, in the prosperous industrial town of Kidderminster, Patricia Beatrice, the only child of Charlie and Nancy Rollings was quickly outgrowing her china dolls and *Bunty* annuals. Charlie, a quiet, gentle-natured man, worked as a carpenter, the warm smell of wood permeating his very soul, whilst his wife, like most other aspiring women in the town, clocked in every day at the carpet factory, diligently 'setting', as she strained to hear—and pass—the daily gossip over the relentless roar of the satanic looms.

They had met in that sweet, old-fashioned way, walking home from Sunday school. Charlie had followed Nancy Hatton and Beatrice, her identical twin sister, back through the narrow terraced streets—an act of bravado born entirely of youth—and Nancy had won the day. Following a lengthy but acceptable period of courtship and engagement, during which time the twin sisters had caused quite a stir turning up at the carpet factory together for their first day's work,

Charlie had married his fiancée on her 22nd birthday. Beatrice, never in the best of health throughout her teenage years, had since died of rheumatic fever.

They bought their first house in 1938, a semi-detached, bay-windowed palace, on the Foley Park dream farm. It cost £540, and would be, according to Charlie's workmates, 'a millstone round his neck' for the rest of his life, but undaunted, they signed the mortgage, and with two regular salaries, settled into an aspiring middle-class existence. Come the war, Charlie joined the Army, and was posted to the foreign fields of Oswestry, before being exempted from further service, to assist as a carpenter in the war effort.

Their only child, christened Patricia Beatrice, was born in the autumn of 1944. She came into the world smiling, and, despite everything, has rarely stopped since…

A pretty, precocious child, she couldn't wait to start school—much to the relief of her busy parents—and after the few short, but happy primary years, joined the other erstwhile 49-ers at Foley Park Junior School, where, on her first day, she was lovingly, though unceremoniously, dumped alone by her parents as they rushed off to work, but where her talents at sport, and, by all accounts, attracting the boys, soon flourished. Despite having no sibling rivalry, she was never spoiled, and remembers, in her loneliness, looking forward to outings in her spinster aunt's car to the Black Country oasis of Wombourne, where a family friend had a small-holding. The flower-filled meadows and singing trees were a wonderland to her, but, back in the house, between cream teas and grown-up talk, staring longingly at the empty rocking-chair, she would sit in mannered silence.

On sun-filled August holidays in Barnstaple, again with family friends, she swam in the safe, warm waters of Bideford Bay and, stirred by the flushes of puberty, experienced those first moments of sexual initiation, whispering and giggling in the Edwardian bathing huts where she and cousin John, her older companion, hid from the world outside.

But home was always lonely:

"I was deep in dreams. I'd spent the afternoon at a fancy dress party, wearing a beautiful satin mandarin costume Mom had made from some pyjamas, when she burst into my room, shook me awake and told that I'd have to go and sleep downstairs. Gran had died, and Aunt Dot was moving in…"

She recalls the incident without any show of surprise, but it must have been a traumatic event, having to give up her warm bed in the middle of the night. But a death in the extended post-war family threw everyone into turmoil, though before long, it was as if life had ever been thus. Dot became a permanent fixture in the Rollings household, and her lively chat—plus a talent for dressmaking—helped compensate on a more regular level for Pat's empty life. During half-term, on Dot's Wednesday afternoon break from the sawdust and bacon Co-op, she would be taken in her aunt's black Morris 8 to explore the sandstone caves at Kinver or walk the dense woodlands of Cookley.

"She made such a difference to my life. I didn't make many friends at school; not because I didn't want to, but because I was painfully shy. I'd stand in a corner and watch the party. No brownies or guides for me. I would dress up for myself, glide about the house, but as for going out 'on parade...' no way. For as many childhood Christmases as I can remember, Dot made me a beautiful, flowered-cotton dress. I just couldn't puzzle out how she got every detail right. A perfect fit, every time. It was a wonderful, if predictable surprise—to wear in the house and in front of the bedroom mirror," and she rolls her eyes at the futility of it all.

Dot married, at the ripe old age of thirty-seven, and Pat became housekeeper to her busy parents, learning the art of cook and clean almost instinctively, though not without incident...

"I was always seeking approval, doing the dishes, the cleaning, and the ironing—using one of those little cast iron things that weighed half a ton and had to be heated at the fire—pressing all the shirts and blouses, and of course the socks and hankies, just waiting for Mom to come home and surprise her, get a big hug, a bar of Turkish Delight. No chance. What I got was a row for putting them into the airing cupboard when they were still damp..."

But Nancy and Charlie worked hard to get the comforts offered by the new age of consumerism. They were buying their house, they had a car and a television—one of the first families in the area to do so—and lived a comfortable, aspiring existence. They didn't drink a lot, though they both smoked: "Mom...when she was making the beds...," and socialized only with the 'select crowd' from the MEB Club.

Meanwhile, as she developed, Pat became more lonely; more shy, but so desperately lonely...

Stourport, with its fun-fair 'kiss-me-quick' image, its horse-fields and gypsy caravans, was very much the poor relation to the people of Kidderminster, and—to impressionable juveniles—where you lived, though not quite 'West Side Story', was most important when forming friendships. As in most rural areas, even today, the intense dislike for outsiders—to look down in contempt, or to look up in envy—decided your friends and lovers.

However, authority, as always, called the tune, and soon the bemused 11-plus failures, whatever their social alliance, found themselves reluctantly filing into the bright, airy classrooms of the new centres of learning. Lists were drawn up, and letters were posted, and the way forward was to Stourport Secondary Modern. It was here, down the chattering corridors, across the noisy playgrounds and behind the corrugated bike-sheds, that yet another love affair began, but one that would ride the dizzy heights of passion and fame, and plumb the dark depths of tragedy, as the two lives of Pat Rollings and Cliff Ward became inexorably entwined, like the rose and the briar.

Nothing happened for some time. They didn't mix socially; he was probably more aware of her than she of him, for her sporting abilities drew much attention. Despite her diminutive frame, she had a penchant for competitive games, and her motivation both on the field and in the classroom led her to captain her senior house team, Gardners, and become Head Girl. Intelligent, attractive, vivacious, she seemed destined for a promising future, but true-grit conformity left little room for such aspirations. Leave school, get a job, get married, get pregnant, raise a family. That was the expectation, that was the plan. That she was to get it slightly out of sequence was certainly not on the agenda...

Cliff was from the wrong side of the tracks, or, to be precise, the river; Stourport boys were out of bounds for a middle-class Kidderminster girl. Besides, he was brash, loud, showing off in the school plays, smoking, joking, shouting, striding his way through school, though, despite this outward irreverence, still displaying encouraging signs of academic potential.

His school report of June, 1956, shows him to be a great favourite with most, if not all, of his teachers. In English he receives A-minus for reading and written work, and a B-plus for spelling, '... a very high standard. Imaginative work is excellent.'; Drama: A, 'Excellent'; History B-plus, and Physical Education C-plus, 'Works hard and is keen on all aspects ...' His headmaster concludes: 'Probably the most capable and promising boy in the whole of this large first year.' In December, 1958, fourteen years old, he is B-plus in all written work, with French and Religious Instruction showing a new aptitude: B-plus in both. Here also, for the first time, we see his Music teacher, Gwen Adams-Davies, praising his 'Excellent practical ability. A member of the School Choir.' A-minus.

At Physical Education he is still C-plussing, playing soccer '... below his obvious capabilities'; otherwise, a fit and healthy teenager.

As a schoolboy, Dave Cole remembers Cliff—in that idolatrous way many younger pupils look up to their elders:

"He looked big and athletic, always running about, always in a hurry. We used to cheer on our teams after school. Cliff was senior house-captain of Woodward when I was a junior, and I have this image of him thumping off the football field after a match, wearing his yellow-quarter shirt, the sweat pouring off his face. I thought he was Superman."

School was a fact of life, and Cliff would do his best—as ever—but really, he was just waiting for the day.

However, unless I'm terribly mistaken, so was his Art teacher…

While I was looking through his school reports, two pieces of paper, handwritten—one in biro, the other in pencil—fell onto my desk. Just notes, afterthoughts, I presumed. I almost missed their content.

The first one is headed 'Homework', and, considering they were written to Clifford by his teacher, a female Art graduate, they are uncommonly personal in tone.

After a list of subject suggestions, addressing Cliff in the third person she continues:

> To be handed in Friday morning
> … should he be inclined to sketch other objects of interest it could only lead to an improvement in his drawing ability. (Full stop!!!) etc. etc.
> P.S. Classes on Monday morning & Friday All Day Visitors always welcome!!!'

Fine. Friendly, but fine.

Then comes the second letter, headed 'Letter to Clifford', in which, again, she occasionally spells out her punctuation—as if in some hidden emphasis—and voices her frustrations. Again, everything here is exactly as it was written:

> As last week's note has proved such an overwhelming success teacher decided that it was worth repeating.
> I cannot emphasize too strongly the importance of your sketch book, therefore … I would be pleased to see … anything else which would provide good background knowledge.
> Start Again!!!! Friday 24. Note No.3.
> After being very annoyed last week that above could not be handed to student—no Mon. visit. No Friday visit—most disappointing in fact—teacher is left sadly disillusioned after all the sincere and faithful promises made to her—what was it—a mere 3 weeks ago. Oh poor sad disappointed teacher.!!!!! (pause to sigh—and murmur—"Life is so hard") especially for teachers who believe and trust their students!!!! Perhaps she should adopt a completely different attitude towards this wayward boy? Maybe a growl here and there—a threat uttered from the side of a tight mean mouth and an even tighter meaner—glare!!! ouch. A few choice words at an opportune

> moment—such as—"I presume you would like to take your exam before you draw your pension," or "It's Now or Never"...!!!! Perhaps this would have the desired (repeat very much desired) effect of rocketing this wayward boy (hardworking in his other subjects he may be) into realizing that Miss still expects him to keep to the amount of time laid down for his work in Art otherwise—!!!! There. I hope you will take notice my lad—and don't cause me to growl—or glare—or tighten my lip—it's so unbecoming ... (Full stop)

She then suggests he '... spend a day [sketching] beside the river. I would like you to try the "Basin", [Stourport's boatyard and moorings] Have a good holiday,' and signs off.
Is it me, or is all that just a little...extra-curricular?

But Clifford's attention had already been drawn.
Pat Rollings remembers the playing fields, one sports afternoon. She was aware—as girls always are—of being watched. No smouldering eye contact was made, but she knew he was there, lying on the grass, joking with his friends, talking in loud whispers, her name floating across on the wind. Cliff's braggadocio, however, extended only to delegation. "Sometime later, he sent one of his mates to me with a note, asking me to go out with him. I said no." As she would. Wrong side of the river, Cliff. However, his intractability—no doubt exacerbated over the school years by continuous reprimands for being left-handed—refused to accept 'No' for an answer. An end of term party loomed and, almost as if by design, Pat was there. Come the inaugural kiss, something went 'boom!' They were 14 years old.
There followed a profoundly committed, and, for its time, an intensely physical relationship. The sap was indeed rising. Beauchamp Avenue front rooms, watched only by the ducks on the wall; Stagborough woodlands; the inevitable High School bike-sheds. They became inseparable, both in school and out.
Dave Cole again:
"I remember Cliff and Pat walking around the corridors and playing-fields together, satchels bulging with books. No-one else in the world as far as they were concerned."
Cliff's family had now moved to Barnfield Close, still in Stourport, but a council house of less substantial proportion. Pat would catch the bus into town, and call across in the early evening, as early as possible. This was some romance. The two of them would then walk as one over to Redstone caves, taking a couple of bottles of Woodpecker cider to sip along the way.
One of her many turbulent memories:

"We were both a little cidered, and I stormed off into the sunset. Of course, Cliff didn't come chasing after me pleading forgiveness and I so got a bit worried. I was completely alone, in this hinterland, and he was… well, he was back at the caves, or someplace. I went looking for him. He was nowhere to be seen. I stood on the spot, shouting his name. Suddenly he dropped right out of a tree, right there in front of me. Stark naked. Absolutely stark naked. It was not funny. [I was laughing.] He began cussing and swearing, then threw a few clods of earth at me, leaping around like a maniac. Dingly-dangly. He was quite drunk and, I thought at the time, quite mad. I was frightened."

They had a 'dangling conversation', kissed a few times, and of course, made up, but it was in danger of becoming a fragile, fairly one-sided relationship, in Cliff's favour, until, as in most things, the law of averages prevailed. One cold, grey Saturday morning in November, 1962, three years after they'd met, Pat realized she was pregnant. Some sixth sense—plus an obvious natural indication—told her so. Her mother screamed to the heavens and rushed her down to the family doctor, where the pregnancy was confirmed. A few days later, however, Pat started to bleed. Something must be wrong. Her mother, in that matter-of-fact post war manner, this time brushed her off to the doctor alone. She was told to rest, and, as the symptoms subsided, felt well enough to go out with Cliff on one of his gigs. Cliff wasted no time telling the band that his girlfriend had '… gone and got bloody well pregnant.'

"I remember them coming over to me, saying how sorry they were," she recalls. "I couldn't understand it! I wasn't elated, but it certainly wasn't something to be sorry about, a baby on the way."

But with Cliff, the usual 'young-trapped-male' reaction followed: "I don't want to get married, Mom. I'm too young."

Kath remembers her mother telling him, "…you don't have to, if you don't want to, Cliff …' He was obviously in love, but he didn't want marriage. What boy of eighteen does? There was certainly no pressure from Mom or Dad, but Pat's parents insisted."

There were many heated family 'conferences', but conformity at last forced his hand; the social stigma was too great an issue. They married at St John's Registry Office, Kidderminster, on December 29th, 1962, the very week The Beatles wound up their Hamburg days to prepare for world-recognition.

Besuited and button-holed, Cliff's brother Melvin, and Charlie Rollings acted as witnesses for the brief, cold ceremony, and the newly-weds rushed out, to move in with Pat's parents and 'celebrate' the New Year, fully aware that a little apprehension from both parties tinged the festive streamers.

But Cliff and Pat were now both working. There were jobs a-plenty in those heady days: we'd 'never had it so good,' and there seemed no compulsion to hang around being further-educated. Money and freedom beckoned, or so it seemed. Cliff, after a half-hearted attempt at A-level study, dropped out of sixth form at King Charles Grammar, and began working for local auctioneer G. Herbert Banks, recording cattle sales at market, which he found 'fairly tolerable', until he was seconded to monitoring their time in the pens.

Pat, meanwhile, had applied for a secretarial position at the amply-named Kidderminster Permanent Benefit Building Society. She was interviewed, along with eight other school-leavers, where it became apparent that typing skills, of some order, would be necessary. Single-minded even then, she immediately found a tutor, an elderly spinster in the next street, and started a crash course before the second interview came along. However, Patrick Bradley, the interviewer, had sensed something quite special, so he paid a personal visit to Beauchamp Avenue—parking his bicycle at the gate—and offered her the job on the spot, typist or not. She started the following Monday, seated, almost hidden, at an enormous mahogany desk in the large, dusty rooms tucked behind Church Street's imposing Edwardian façade. Within a fortnight she was virtually running the office single-handed, distracted only by occasional. wordy intimidation from solicitor Colonel Painter, her war-veteran employer.

Life, however, was to change much sooner than anyone could have foreseen. Their first child, Deborah, (named after the Sonny Curtis-Jerry Allison song) was born prematurely in March 1963. The suddenness of the birth took them all by surprise. Assuming a normal pregnancy, Pat had been provisionally booked into the Lucy Baldwin Maternity Hospital for July. She woke in the early hours of March 21st with severe pain. Cliff had nonchalantly finished his bacon and eggs and bussed off to another dreary day at the office—he was now a desk-bound civil servant for the Ministry Of Pensions—but Pat's mother, realizing something was wrong, had decided to stay at home; the factory would, on this one occasion, have to wait. Things then moved quickly. Too quickly. In a bizarre scene reminiscent of an Ealing black comedy, with people running about like headless chickens, a nearby neighbour was called upon to telephone for an ambulance. Pat, groaning upstairs, remembers the woman shouting, "It's okay, she's only 18, there's plenty of time to have some more…!" But by the time help did arrive, Nancy, capable, instinctive Nancy, had delivered the baby herself. Cliff, meanwhile, nonchalantly strolling back to the house for lunch, rehearsing a song in his head, was more than a little surprised to see an ambulance outside. He rushed upstairs only to see his exhausted bride of four months, a lot of blood, a doctor, his mother-in-law and a midwife, holding a tiny bundle, which was quickly whipped away, down the stairs and into the waiting ambulance. Neither he nor Pat saw the child until a week later, when they went by bus all the way up to the Sorrento Children's Hospital in Birmingham. There, because it had been the only incubator available in the whole area, they were able at last to view their baby daughter for the first time. She weighed just over three pounds. The midwife later told Pat that, not knowing, or having the time to ask their chosen name, she had considered baptizing the tiny child in the ambulance, her chances of survival were considered that slim. Debbie was confined to hospital for almost three months, closely monitored, and Pat frankly admits that she initially felt no bonding with her daughter.

"She was so tiny, I couldn't accept or identify with this strange thing lying there. When she was allowed home, well, it was just like having another doll." But as she developed, naturally, the mother and child instincts blossomed. "She became a happy, responsive baby. I quickly began to love her dearly." But of course, no-one knew at this time, though it must have been suspected by their worldly-wise grandparents, that anything was seriously wrong.

And home life, as in most cases, soon became strained. Pat's parents, though disapproving of Cliff right from the start, offered love and support, but were in no way prepared for trauma, and the situation quickly became traumatic. After almost a year, with Pat pregnant again, Nancy and Charlie, with their tolerance at breaking point, decided the only way out…was out. They decided to move to a smaller home. They weren't actually putting daughter and family onto the street, but it was quite obvious that their new bungalow, in Caldwell Crescent, was, to use Jerome Kern's lovely phrase, simply '… a cottage that two can fill.' Nothing more.

So, Cliff and Pat had to quickly locate some rented accommodation. They found a room in Kidderminster's notorious Horsefair, with its gloomy, flickering gas-light alleys of Victorian tenements. There, as the Beatles told the nation that '… money can't buy me love …', the very lack of it meant sharing a wash-house, backyard and basic toilet facilities—amid the town's *demi-monde*—for 18 shillings a week, all inclusive. Amazingly, despite all this dazed confusion, they still found the time—and the inclination—for in March 1964, in the safe haven of The Croft Maternity Home, Pat gave birth to a bouncing 6lb 5oz boy, a brother for Debbie, whom they christened Martin.

And it was at this time, almost twelve months after Debbie's birth, and with a second child, that the young, bewildered mother was summoned to the hospital to be told that her daughter had cerebral palsy. The prematurity, the possible trauma at birth, something had caused and dealt a terrible blow to Pat and Cliff. Even now, it's not hard to imagine their feelings, thrown together, like many others, as victims of the 'reap what you sow' social mores of the day; poor and desperate, suddenly confronted with the added complication of a first-born child that, in the opinion of their doctor, was destined for a short life of tragic isolation.

Two bewildered teenagers, the mother barely 18 years old, with two children, one severely disabled, having to cope with a life that had, almost overnight, turned turtle. It begs the obvious question: If they had known of Debbie's condition earlier, would they have tried for another child so soon? Pragmatic as ever, Pat gives an unequivocal "Yes." In her typically disarming, stoical manner, she speaks of them "... just having to get on with it ..." Life would be difficult, but life would be lived.

In 1965, the Horsefair slums were put under a long overdue demolition order, and, obviously concerned with their situation, the council found them a house on the Habberley Estate.

"There we were, pleased as Punch, moving in to our new home. We were knee deep in lino when Cliff's mom answered a knock at the door. She came back looking a bit anxious. 'It's somebody for you, Pat', which we all thought was strange as we hadn't yet told anyone our address. I went to the door. A woman, red-haired, about twenty-ish, blocked the light, a man standing behind her. They both had bicycles at their side. They looked like gypsies As soon as she saw me, she pointed, shouting, *'There she is, the bitch! That's the woman that's been playing around with my husband!! That's her!'* I took a quick step back into the hall, Cliff came out and told them to well, clear off ... and slammed the door shut. I was flabbergasted. They hung around a while, then we watched them ride away. After a few minutes, Cliff and I walked down to the police station—quite a distance—and reported the incident. They knew of her, saying that she was a notorious trouble-maker, but until anyone was harmed, physically, there was nothing they could do. Great. I saw her a couple of times more in town, once where she sneaked up behind me in a queue and hissed into the back of my neck as I stood there trembling..."

For that brief moment the Horsefair, with its honest poverty, seemed positively idyllic. But the matter was a soon forgotten—once Pat had convinced Cliff of the stupidity of such a suggestion.

"That's when I first saw the jealous side of his nature. For one short moment, I think he actually believed it. I would think about that often in times to come, his reaction, when he tried to explain his own behaviour away."

They settled in. It was a modern home, though without the modern conveniences they desperately needed. "A washing machine ... what I would have given for a washing machine," says Pat. "The house was forever steamed up with hand-washed nappies drying over an economically low gas fire. The coal fire was for Christmas. Debbie and

Martin saw me from the back most of their waking hours, standing over the sink. They were visibly surprised when I turned around, sat down, talked to them. I never understood why my parents didn't offer to buy us something, they could see my predicament, they could easily afford a machine, even if it was second-hand. But no, I had made my bed...and Cliff wasn't their ideal son-in-law, by any stretch of the imagination."

But at least it was their own home, via the council tenancy. Cliff, after his brief flirtation with the civil service (where his time-keeping had led to an irreconcilable breakdown), was now working as a clerk at the solid fuel office on Comberton Hill—a long uphill walk for Pat, and even longer on the way back, with her hand on the brake of a pram full of purloined coal—but again, only for a while. There was no future in solid fuel...especially for a musician, so he handed in his notice and went home to write some more songs. Nancy was still at the carpet factory, and devoted mother that she was, used her lunch break to rush over to Habberley with some desperately needed rations, innocently assuming Cliff was at work. These mother and daughter tête-à-têtes were thus a little uneasy for Pat, as her husband hid upstairs, searching for rhymes, and "... bloody well *star-ving* to death..."

Nevertheless, such family crises, no matter how severe, or comical, did little to lessen his obsession with music. Marriage, babies, homes, whilst he never outwardly considered them as incidentals, were dealt with admirably, though always by Pat. He merely pursued his ambition.

When their relationship had started, she recalls his music as being one thing that set him apart from most of the other boys.

There were other boys obsessed by pop music. Of course there were, it was a mania that had spiralled almost out of control to equal, if not supersede, the appeal of girls, but whilst all other aspiring pop stars around him were using Bert Weedon's *Play In a Day* for bedtime reading, Clifford showed no interest in learning the guitar. So how did he write those early songs? There was no piano in those early days; not until well into their marriage, when the Rollings family heirloom was unceremoniously transported across town into their first real home, would he begin learning keyboard. Whenever I questioned the Old Devil about this lack of interest in playing the guitar, it was impossible to get a serious reply, so one can only suppose that, not being the most tolerant person, Clifford, assuming he did pick up a guitar at one time, being left-handed, and impatient, probably found difficulty with the 'cack-handed' string arrangement: "... this bloody book's all over the place." He also undoubtedly saw himself as a front man, singer-songwriter—somebody else could do the playing—so he bought a tape recorder instead, singing whatever tune came into his head *a cappella*, in the good old oral tradition. This gave him freedom to compose melodies away from the pre-determined structures of a musical instrument, and obviously honed his melodic and rhythmic vision for the future years. Even in those early days, some of his first attempts at writing show him experimenting in a kind of 'free-form' style that was quite alien to the AABA-format compositions then dominating the charts.

But of course, like most self-reliant musical aspirers, he soon fell into debt over what*ever* equipment he had. Besides the tape recorder, he had hire-purchased a top quality microphone and amplifier from Wilsons in Kidderminster.

This huge, two-storey Art Deco music shop, for years stocked with mahogany uprights and dance-band sheet music, was now trying desperately to join the second half of the 20th century by selling electric guitars and amplification alongside Jew's harps and recorders, and weekly payment cards were being handed out like gift vouchers; no credit check necessary. Cliff exuded charm, a silver-tongued devil, so it didn't take much to acquire a lot, even without proof of employment, and he walked out of Wilsons suitably equipped, though fully aware that any regular financial commitment would be too much. He knew he wouldn't—couldn't—maintain payments, but, so what? 'Non-functional' household items could be sold off; his music was all that mattered; a good microphone was essential for the coming years.

Back in his schooldays, during that brief incarceration at King Charles', he had formed his first group. Bob Newton, Bob Spencer and Cliff called themselves The Senators, in true adoptive-American tradition. They were only a threesome—drummers were thin on the ground in the Stourport-Kidderminster locale—with just the basic equipment and Cliff's vocal set-up, which they augmented with a home made amplifier built by close friend Tony Furness. After weekly practices, usually at the Methodist Hall in Stourport's Prospect Road, early on Friday evenings, Cliff would rush up to 'John & Patty's', a venue run by two local ballroom dancing instructors who, notwithstanding their middle-age and musical leanings, had the business acumen to realize some extra money could be made. Here, mid-week, brylcreamed bus-drivers and perfumed school-dinner ladies would swirl to Latin-American rhythms and sensuous tangos hissing from Dansette amplified 78s, but come the weekend, the hall would reverberate to '...some of that rock'n'roll music.' Cliff would pay his 1s.3d at the door and, after checking his quiff in the Victorian oak mirror adorning the gents, would edge down to the side of the stage. Bringing rock'n'roll to town, two indigenous combos, The Crestas and The Victors, alternated weekly, fuelling his magnificent obsession. He stood, a-slappin' his thigh, drop-jawed, mesmerized by their raw sounds and slick, confident performance. Dave Arnold, the bass player from The Victors, had ingeniously adapted his Hofner Brunette, fitting a long metal spike at the bottom, to enable him—on less complicated numbers—to stand it on end, simulating hero Bill Black's upright. It was a wonderland, and Cliff wanted to be part of it all.

The Senators, though no-one could doubt their enthusiasm, were well aware of their limitations. Mixed feelings of excitement and trepidation coursed their veins as they shuffled into the Walshes Tenants Hall—a community centre for adults—one Saturday evening in July, 1962, to play support to another group of local heroes, The Strangers. Singer Ray Percy, guitarists Graham Drew and John Wainwright, plus that rarest of species, a drummer, all dressed entirely in black and exuding the false but desirably glamorous image of menace, had the lot: Vox amplifiers, Watkins Copycat echo-unit, Fender Stratocaster, Gibson bass, oh, and the drums. The full monty. After the gig, Cliff struck up conversation with Eden Kane look-alike Graham, the friendliest of the bunch, who, surprisingly, expressed that he was unhappy in the group and wanted to form one of his own. He knew of a rhythm guitarist and, well, would Cliff be interested? Loyalty didn't come in to it. Come Saturday morning, Cliff met Graham, they hopped on and off a Kidderminster omnibus, swung open the glass door of The Coventry café and strode across to the table in the corner, where, over a cup of swirling espresso, Cliff was introduced to Rodney Simmonds.

In contemporary pictures, with his heavy-rimmed glasses, chiselled features and slicked back hair, Rodney resembles a young Roy Orbison, laughing out with the nonchalance of youth, but, unbeknown to either of the others (for it certainly didn't affect his socializing or, indeed his competence), he was already in the early stages—and consequently the first in a line of tragic victims—of the illness that would weave like a poisonous snake throughout this story: multiple sclerosis.

The threesome clicked immediately. After swopping opinions on favourite records, aspirations and, almost certainly, a name for this new band, the search went out for bass and drums. They started practising at Rodney's house, with encouragement from proud father Fred. Graham knew someone who had recently bought a bass guitar—he couldn't *play* it yet, but that was incidental—he had an amplifier, and so, come Saturday afternoon, Cliff, Graham and Rodney trooped up to the other café, on Lion Hill, where soft, gentle, flint-eyed Trevor Jones was assaulting the pinball. "At first he wasn't really interested," recalls Cliff. "He wanted to learn guitar, but not in a group … he hadn't thought that far ahead. Huh." But, after prising him off the machine and enticing him with promises of wealth and fame—and a possible residency at John & Patty's—they won through. Well, it became too good an offer to refuse. Rodney meanwhile had dreamed up a name, so that, when they *did* find someone to do the drum solos, they would hit the waiting world as Cliff Ward and The Cruisers.

With Trevor in tow, they began rehearsing in the back room of yet another café—long since gone—in Stourport's High Street. Between the Midland Bank and The Wheatsheaf public house there is now a gap, like a missing tooth, in the row of plastic-fronted shops. Today it serves as a parking space, but back then, a small, lace-curtained, slightly faded coffee-bar leaned out to the pavement, struggling to satisfy the growing demands for faster food and alcohol. There was always plenty of room inside, not too many customers, and of course, without drums, the boys made very little noise. Here they got together and honed their act. "Cliff was always practice, practice. It had to be right, *dead* right," recalls Trevor. "Over and over. He'd have made a good pinballer. " At the end of the sessions, as Rodney and Graham made their way to the bus stop, Cliff and Trevor would slog it back on foot to the Walshes Estate, each taking turns to carry the bulky bass amplifier, Cliff talking animatedly of songs, arrangements, gigs, the future.

Rodney's father Fred was a carpet salesman, small, bespectacled, tenacious; dashing around the county with samples of Axminster and Wilton weave spilling all across the plastic seats of his company car, a red Ford Anglia. He relished the idea of his son being in a pop group and suggested he manage them. His influential client database provided contacts way above the usual village hall venues, and following completion of a carpet deal, out would come the Cruiser file. "Look at my boys," he'd smile. "Why don't you book them for your do-o? They'll give you a great night..." And so The Cruisers found themselves performing at imposing country houses, Round Table dinners, State Openings of Parliament...prestigious and well paid gigs, but still without so much as a snare drum.

The musicians, and occasionally Pat, squeezed sardine-like into the state-of-the-ark Anglia, always dreading the wild journey home, with Fred—regularly under the influence—at the wheel. Pat recalls Rodney often telling his father to slow down as the bends became more and more angular, as the tyres screamed louder... "You bloody-well shudd-up!!" Fred would shout, foaming at the mouth, "I'm old enough to be your father!" "But...you *are* my father!" squeaked Rodney. "Bloody 'ell..."

As the venues got larger and more prestigious, Fred's habit of a lifetime—together with an obsessive devotion to the band—would manifest itself in feats of almost superhuman strength, as he humped the ever-expanding PA system up and down marbled ballroom steps.

"You just leave it all to me, lads. You look after your instruments," he

would insist, and, remembering his army training—knees bend, back straight—would huff and puff his way down to the van.
Very occasionally they would find him crumpled in a heap, or spread-eagled in the lobby, arms, legs and glasses akimbo, but with the AC30 safely positioned across his string-vested chest.
"Fred? You all right, mate? Fred?!!" And Cliff—or Graham, or Trevor—would kneel down at his side, checking for pulse or breathing but more likely than not, giving the amplifier a quick visual.
Expensive things, amplifiers.
And when those 'musical differences'—that generic term for a personality clash—rose to the surface, and tempers flared, the situation was quickly diffused by the appearance in the doorway of Rodney's mother, Vee.
"Don't you raise your voice like that, Cliff Ward. This is my house, and that's my son you're shouting at."
"Sorry, Mrs Simmonds."
But as they took a break, sitting around the oak drop-leaf table, he would eat the fish paste sandwiches she had brought in, drink the Vimto, and seethe quietly inside.
"We never actually abandoned a practice," maintains Cliff. "I did chase Rodney around the garden once or twice…[Rodney's garden, remember], when Vee was out shopping, to give him a slap on the head maybe, but we always made it up. We were just kids. No real aggression, just little disagreements." For the moment, anyway…

But, they still had no drummer.

The Wharf at Holt Fleet was a popular, albeit somewhat notorious, venue. Beautifully situated on the banks of the Severn, in the shadow of Holt Bridge, it was a rustic, ramshackle watering hole for caravanners, boaties and Sunday night Teddy boys. Approached from the road by a long, gravelled drive, it is now surrounded on three sides by caravans. In the mid-fifties, in its idyllic isolation, an ambitious landlord had added a rectangular, large-windowed dance-hall to the side, and almost overnight, the *crème de la crème* of Worcestershire's beat groups found a perfect venue. Many of them first trod the boards here, hunched together on the tiny corner stage, almost knee to face with their audience. The landlord, the mighty Quinn, 'curly-collars Quinn', was an ex-policeman, dealing out his no-nonsense fare with an ever-watchful eye.
Fronting Kidderminster's original rock'n'rollers, The Clippers, I had played regular Friday night gigs there throughout 1960-62. It was a night where, as you performed, you watched. Not your guitar, not your drums, not your shadow. You waited for that first shuffle, that first

swell in the crowd, that Holt Fleet 'wave' that would roll across the crowded room, invariably toward the stage. This wasn't audience participation, well, not with the band; it was altercation. Someone was not 'appy…

A circle would then form, surrounding the thrashing, drunken shapes of the two be-suited brawlers, each trying to get the best punch in, before, as they well knew, Quinn would come Moses-like through the crowd, grabbing one, or both, and throw them outside onto the cold, grey car park, where, if they so chose, they could bloody themselves to oblivion. And, as soon as the eventual and magical reappearance of the landlord behind the bar signified all was well, the evening would continue.

But it was here also, on Sunday evenings, in a somewhat more congenial atmosphere, that The Rebel Rousers played their regular country and western spot.

A different crowd entirely, more inclined towards Faron Young, Marty Robbins and Hank Locklin than Eddie Cochran, The Coasters or Chuck Berry: they danced but didn't fight. Maybe because it was a Sunday.

One night, well into a three-year residency, their drummer, Roger 'Butch' Bowen, became aware of "… three blokes standing near the front, watching me … They didn't look threatening, just interested, more so than your normal punter."

Rodney, Graham and Trevor had come looking for a drummer.

Roger had been a stalwart on the Kidderminster scene for some years. Prior to The Rebel Rousers, he had played with The Zodiacs, an early rock'n'roll band, featuring Keith Hubbard, Mick Birch, Nick Miller and Roger Jackson. These last two musicians were each to eventually achieve notoriety of a sort, but in quite disparate fields of fame.

"When I first joined The Zodiacs, after a few really good gigs, we decided it would lift our standing even more if we added a pianist. Not Jerry Lee stuff, more Floyd Cramer; 'On The Rebound' type of thing. I met Roger Jackson on the steps of Kidderminster Retail Market," he recalls. "He was preaching the gospel. A Jehovah's Witness. A good looking bloke, in the Russ Conway mould, just right for us. I knew he played keyboards, and gave him a bit of smooth talk, so that, despite his strong religious beliefs, he joined. We even gigged in his church, to show willing; it was a disaster. But Roger seemed keen to continue; he even got to partaking the odd drink or three, and started smoking. We continued playing in pubs and other various dens of iniquity around Stourport and Kidderminster, until The Zodiacs split. However, Roger and I carried on playing as a duo for about six months before also calling it quits, leaving a good residency at The Hope & Anchor, Stourport. He and Nick Miller then went off to London in search of the streets of gold, and, in quite different ways, found them. Roger met

Jack Good, changed his surname to LaVern, and, in September 1962, fronted The Tornadoes to the top of the charts with 'Telstar', a world-wide hit. He came back to Stourport, via the newly opened M1, driving a bronze Rolls-Royce. But of course, he hadn't read the small print. They were world-famous, but living on cloud-money. It was all gone, over, within a couple of years. Back to the cabaret, the 'chicken-in-a-basket circuit.' Last I heard, he became a male model. That was over thirty years ago.

"Nick, on the other hand, well, he just hit the skids, became an alcoholic and very nearly died. He was, literally, just one step away from the crematorium. But something, or someone—and it wasn't Jehovah—saved him. He now runs one of the most successful alcohol treatment clinics in London and was recently awarded the MBE for his work. Incidentally," continues Roger, scarcely pausing for breath, "he tells a lovely story, concerning Cliff. Apparently he was stumbling around the gutters of London, ragged and desperate as usual, when he saw the name Clifford T. Ward on a billboard outside the Queen Elizabeth Hall. He remembered Cliff Ward from the early days, but, in his situation, didn't see it as a chance to renew a friendship, merely an opportunity to get some money for the next desperately needed round. He decided to get in and tap up Cliff for some cash. He remembers approaching the box office, dressed in his best tramp's outfit, lice-ridden, quite inebriated, mumbling Cliff's name, before slowly passing out, sliding down the side of the glass screen, vomiting over the carpet."

Good heavens. Where were we?

Rodney, Trevor and Graham, The Wharf, Holt Fleet. Right.

He apologizes, though we're both laughing. A Sauvignon is opened. This could get serious…

"We had some great nights down there," he continues, "especially when the river flooded. The Wharf was built on a high part of the embankment, high in the sense that whenever the river rose, which it frequently did in the winter, the pub itself was up there, surrounded by water, like an island. We had a dedicated following, and Quinn, not to be beaten, used to get a flat-back artic lorry to collect us and our equipment from the top of the drive, off-load us, so we could set up, then do a shuttle service throughout the evening for the punters, bringing them down. There we were, up on stage, looking out onto swirling water. A strange, eerie feeling. They wouldn't allow that now. Such days."

Rodney, Graham, and Trevor…?

"Oh, right. Sorry," he laughs. "*Any*way, at the end of this particular night, as I dismantled, packed and loaded away my drums, they got talking to me.

"I was quite happy with The Rousers, but these lads mentioned this great singer they'd got, even writing some songs he was, so I agreed to meet them for a practice at The Crown. I remember the first time I met Cliff. As I had my own car—an added bonus as far as they were concerned—I'd arranged to collect him from the bottom of the Walshes Estate. It was raining, light drizzly stuff, and there was this kid, sitting on the pavement steps with a load of records under one arm and a Dansette on his knee. He got into the car; shy, timid, unassuming and damp, and to me, instantly likeable. I couldn't for a minute imagine him singing in front of a crowd, and I became quite protective towards him. As we progressed, he began to look up to me, not out of respect or admiration, but, I suppose, because I was older, outspoken, worldly-wise. He'd never been *anywhere* Cliff. He was a loner, even in his own family, even though he had wonderfully hard-working parents, true socialists—as Cliff has always remained, whatever happened—but he was, well, timid. He had his room where he would study, play records, whatever, and until the group thing, he kept himself very much to himself. *We* became Cliff's family. I think I probably ended up knowing Cliff better than anybody at home. He confided in me, trusted me, and I could see he was special, and also that he was after something far beyond our small-town, blinkered rock'n'roll vision."

And so, they practised, at The Crown or down at the café, but this time a little bit louder, until, on a warm night in October, Graham, Trevor, Rodney, Cliff and Roger met up for their first gig, at the Roman Catholic Hall in Kidderminster's Birchen Coppice. Cliff Ward and The Cruisers were now complete.

And where was Pat when such a momentous event was taking place? Well, since you ask, she was also enjoying a heavy session—musical not, but heavy certainly—on a bench, in Brintons Park.

Phil Smith, a good-looking, intelligent, sensitive sixth-former had often questioned Cliff about the pretty girl he used to meet at the bus-stop on his way home from school. Cliff—in what we now recognize as one of his most 'endearing' mannerisms—out of devilment or design, told Phil that she was his sister!… and passed on her telephone number. Pat, well, "Why not?" she thought. And so, as the Cruisers rocked the Catholic Hall, she and Phil sat on a dimly lit park bench and got to know each other.

"Phil was beautiful," she remembers. "I was emotional [as ever], but rational [as ever]. As passion soared, I told him, quite truthfully, that I thought I was pregnant. By Cliff of course! It didn't deter him in the slightest. He insisted that it didn't matter; he would take care of us, my baby and me." Such chivalry. Such innocence. He walked her to her door, they kissed goodnight, and she never saw him again. But the night was still young for Pat. She crept into the lounge, only to face her mother's anger and disbelief at such barefaced duplicity. Those old social mores again…

Roger Bowen continued reminiscing at great length about those early times. I just sat back and listened. A friendly, solid, athletic 57-year-old, he lives, as he has done for the last 28 years, with his wife Gill, and a thousand cats, in a beautiful period farmhouse, set in a lovely secluded Worcestershire backwater. The long sweeping drive leads up to the imposing Georgian façade, surrounded by rich, green lawns studded with mature willow, birch and conifer trees. I remark on their beauty. "Cliff did it," he nods. ['Bloody 'ell,' I muse. 'Capability Ward…'] "He didn't *plant* them of course, he just pulled up a deckchair, a glass of red wine in one hand and pointed where to position them with the other."

"What, after you'd left the band?"

"Oh, yes, we remained very close friends. Cliff and Pat used to come here a lot. Gill did his hair! Lovely times."

He then talked lucidly of The Fountain, The Golden Cross at Alcester, The Black Horse in town, the country houses—frequently fuelled by 60 per cent punch, and big paper-money overtime—the incessant gigging.

"I loved it. A night out, playing, having a few bevvies, chatting up the girls. I could pick up Graham and Trevor, whilst Fred, with Rodney, would collect Cliff, and sometimes Pat. Sometimes I'd cuss Fred for being late. I'd have my drums set up, with Trevor and Graham running through a Shadows number, the punters would be filing in, but no Cliff or Rodney. They'd arrive just in time. 'Come on Fred, where've you bloody well been?' I'd say. 'We start in ten bloody minutes!'

"'Tain't my bloody fault!' he'd whine, 'It's that bloody sex-maniac,' pointing to Cliff. 'He's been down in Brintons Park with that bloody woman, down in the shelter for hours. I kept on shouting to him, "Cliff! come *on*!" But he was going at it, wouldn't let her go [or maybe she wouldn't let *him* go …]. 'Tain't my bloody fault!'

"He told me to have a word with Cliff. 'That woman's ruining this group!' he'd say. I did speak to Cliff, and he didn't know what to do. He'd look at me, like a big soft puppy, and in that low, throaty burr, asking for advice. 'She's always coming round the house, Roger, chasing me, not letting me out of her sight. What can I do?'

"So I told him. Not that he took a scrap of notice, or maybe she kissed him just that little bit harder when he tried to break away … I told him that the group had to come first. Y'see, I didn't know her then. To me (and forgive me here, Pat) she was just another girl. But now I realize that they were passionately in love. Two teenagers, with no other real friends of their own, just absolutely mad about each other. So, well ... I think if it hadn't been for Pat, Cliff would have *really* gone for it. She didn't consciously hold him back," he protests quickly, "but her demands, and his desires; well, we never stood a chance..."

Pat was indeed, whenever possible, at Cliff's side. She became almost the fifth member of the band, sitting it out at whatever gigs she could manage, watching her man.

Cliff, considering his high profile image at the front of the band, singing the hits of the day to dreamy-eyed teenage girls, didn't seem to bother too much about actually *chasing* them. He didn't need to: if anyone was to make the first move, it was usually the predatory female. But despite his *hauteur*, his single-minded pursuit of stardom, and the presence of his wife, things occasionally got out of hand.

"There was some girl in at a gig we played regularly in Redditch, in the very early days," Roger whispers, almost conspiratorially. "Funnily enough she was the spitting image of Pat, could have taken them for sisters. Anyhow, Cliff was pretty keen, and I remember him coming to me, like a son almost, asking *me* which one he should go for...! Oh, that got pretty close, but of course, deep down I think he knew, or he wanted me to say, that it would be Pat."

Pat however, recalls Roger many times playing his own mischievous part in trying to entice Cliff away. "We were walking down Stourport High Street, Cliff and me, hand in hand, when Roger drove past in his big car. He tooted his horn, pulling in a bit further up the road, calling Cliff by name. Cliff, of course, immediately ran up to the car. They were going to a party at Redditch. I knew that girl would be there, so did Cliff, that's why he wanted to go. I told him he couldn't, astonished at his audacity. We started to row there in the High Street, with Roger leaning out of the car shouting for him to come on. I started pulling, Cliff started pushing, until he just lashed out at me, across the face, splitting my lip. A woman came running out of a house to see if I was all right."

And did he go to the party?

She had her chin resting on her hands, almost as if in prayer. She shot me one of her infamous, penetrating sidelong glances.

"He went," she said.

"We had a few fights like that," she continues. "I suppose I was very possessive—after all, he was my husband—and Cliff, since the very beginning, had always been flippant, to say the least, about relationships. Though Roger, bless him, wasn't immune from chancing it where possible. But that's men. They played Brintons Canteen, alongside every other group in the world. It was a great gig, Friday evenings, which meant I could go along. Cliff and I had a row about something; probably that Sylvie dancing at the front, making cow's eyes at him. We'd both had a few drinks and I ran outside into the car park, leaning against the wall, crying. Roger—not Cliff—came out after a couple of minutes and started to comfort me, and typical man, began to…er, take advantage. Next thing, we were in his car snogging. Nothing serious, you understand [I understand…]. After a while, there was this knocking on the car window. 'Rog, come on, we'm on in five minutes.' It wasn't me Cliff was worried about, it was his bloody band."

But they were all young and, in their own way, quite lovable, as the young always are. Pat herself tells of another incident, this time *not* a domestic, featuring Graham. Lovely, dreamy Graham, who had to be hauled out of bed—in the evening—for gigs.

They had arrived at a venue one night, in Shipston-on-Stour. Fred, Rodney, Cliff and Pat were there first, for a change. Strange… Twenty minutes or so later, Roger, Terry and Graham had come shuffling in, Graham looking decidedly sheepish. After raising Graham from his slumbers, they had quickly loaded up, jumped in the car and charged out into the night. A couple of miles down the road, tanking along, talking music, Graham had suddenly voiced serious sounds of panic:

"Ode on a tick, weer's me gitarr?"

Roger, incredulous, slammed on the brakes. "What y'mean, Graham?"

"Well, I cor see me gitarr anywhere."

"Well you bought it out the house, I saw it. Where'd you put it?"

"I pud it on the roof 'uv the car when we was loadin' up," he moaned.

They drove back to the house in silence, to where, twenty minutes later, they found the lonely blue Strat, sticking out of the privet hedge in Graham's drive, a little more out of tune, but otherwise okay.

Nevertheless, whilst such humours prevailed, Cliff was finding it increasingly difficult to tolerate father Simmonds, and not just because Fred wanted Pat off the scene. Probably having read the Larry Parnes 'Do-it-yourself Guide to Management', Fred had tried to instil a false sense of respect and authority in his boys. Roger recalls: "He told everyone to call him Mr Simmonds, except me, that is. He was a bit wary of my reputation, thought I might put one on him. Cliff ended up not speaking to Fred at all, only communicating through me. 'Tell that silly old pompous bastard … etc.' He disliked the family anyhow, and this only made matters worse.

"It wasn't their middle-class affluence that he despised, though Cliff was, and has remained, a committed socialist. What he hated was the arrogance. He hated arrogance.

"Fred did work hard for us though. He even got the Mecca chain, who owned ballrooms the length and breadth of Britain, to come and see us at The Fountain. That was our first real dilemma. The contract was there, waiting to be signed. We were immediately offered a 12-month residency through the chain, which would mean us turning professional. Trevor wanted to sign, Rodney obviously, Graham, although he loved his job with the council, would have been persuaded, me, well I don't know. The family business was very important, I was enjoying myself, with a well-paid job, it's hard to say what I'd have done if it had come to the crunch. But it didn't. Cliff, he just refused point blank. 'Get that bugger to sign!' Fred pleaded with me. But Cliff was adamant: 'No.'

"Looking back, I can't honestly say if it was Pat, his fear of fame [which contradicted his fierce ambition], or whether he felt that something better would come along. I really don't know."

So, The Cruisers continued cruising locally. They trawled the charts, copying hits which were chosen democratically, though somewhat indiscriminately. "The charts governed our repertoire," says Cliff, "but the playing of such songs obviously influenced us as a band. It was fine if we copied something good, but when we copied something bad, and there were many bad records in the charts, well, of course, it made *us* sound bad…"

It is indeed hard to imagine the Clifford T. Ward that we all know singing 'Jezebel' and, er… 'Eso Beso' (in pidgin Spanish), giving the obligatory pop singer whoops and yelps, and in phrasing and mannerisms sounding remarkably like Sir HeathCliff of Esher, but to his credit, he does them well. In a rare, almost exclusive tape recorded by Leon Tipler at The Fountain, Habberley, in April 1963, The Cruisers sound a terrifically tight band. Note for note instrumentals such as 'Kon-Tiki', 'Blue Moon' and, of course the standard rock'n'rollers, 'Johnny B. Goode' and 'C'mon Everybody', even Gene Vincent's 'Lotta Lovin', all pepper a selection of early Tamla-Motown and rarer B-sides, and all done with skilful, if not original, talent. But of course, in the early 1960s, that was the way to impress. They weren't exactly tribute bands, other than paying tribute to pop music *per se*, they were mimics, though only because any deviation from the original, any improvisation, was scorned by the cloth-eared punters. The old 'Hank-didn't-play-it-like-that' syndrome.

"But we *were* that little bit different," Roger emphasized. "Cliff's wide musical interests, American Soul, Tamla, Jackie De Shannon, and so on, put us that little bit ahead of the others. The combination of familiarity and obscurity created extra interest."

Something better *should* have come along, and then, for a moment, it seemed something had.

Through their contact—and hire-purchase contracts—with Jones & Crossland, in Birmingham, the meeting place for all ambitious musicians, The Cruisers had formed a friendship with the proprietor,

Cyril Jones. He suggested they enter the Locarno Ballroom 'Midland Band Of The Year' contest, a high-profile annual event that obviously attracted a lot of media attention, and would guarantee lots of work to any finalists. They didn't just make the final, they won. "We were up against some stiff competition," says Roger. "Shane Fenton and many other notables of the time were after the prize, and we went through them like a scythe. They weren't very happy about it either. Every heat, every round, the ballroom was packed. Somebody suggested we dressed up for 'La Bamba', which was our *tour de force*, so, with Cliff fronting us in his lamé suit, pointed shoes and lacquered quiff—just about condescending to play maracas—we, the lads, donned ten-gallon sombreros and coloured siesta-cloaks. The crowd loved it. We were on a roll."

Roger rolled so much that, the week before the final, he fractured his cheek playing football, and was hospitalized.

"That made me bloody sick, but, when they did win, using drummer Tim Jackson, [Roger LaVern-Jackson's brother] on loan, they came to see me in hospital, carrying the winner's cup like the FA Trophy. A wonderful gesture, a great bunch of lads."

But, despite this triumph, again, nothing really changed. The Fountain, The Black Horse, The Golden Cross, The Park Attwood, The Crown, an endless succession of one-nighters. Cliff started writing more songs about this time, pale Tamla-Motown/Soul imitations, but certainly confirming a blossoming talent. The others still wanted rock'n'roll, pop, singalongs, but Cliff persevered, and an uneasy compromise ensued, consequently the practices grew more arduous, the atmosphere more strained. Father Fred decided to call it a day. He couldn't see the sense in fighting resentment, apathy, whatever. Roger is quite definite. "All Fred was interested in was getting the gigs. He wasn't enterprising in a professional way; I suppose his age made it impossible to see the potential outside the area, records were something only Frankie Laine or Londoners did. We had to get someone more ambitious."

Roger knew a much younger carpet worker (you'd be forgiven for thinking there was no other profession in this town ...), with the wonderful name of Finlay Tinker. He was a Scot, knew nothing about pop group management, but he was keen. A dapper 20-year-old, pin-striped suit, with matching tie and pocket-handkerchief, he loved music, and used to come and watch The Cruisers at the Black Horse, while Fred was still in charge. He lived with his parents in a fine Georgian house out at Chaddesley Corbett, a pretty chocolate-box village, surrounded by verdant meadows and dense woodland, five miles east of the town. As soon as Fred pulled out, Finlay moved in. They started rehearsing at the Tinkers' house (fast-talking Roger addressing Finlay's mother as 'Mrstinker'. It became a standing joke,

Cliff in convulsions, hiding behind him).

But it was here that the simmering Simmonds-Ward feud reached its climax.

"Cliff was a taskmaster, a perfectionist," says Roger. "Nobody, even in later years, was quite good enough. He had to get every note, every beat *his* way. I'd spend hours trying to get a drum roll, until, often quite by accident, I'd succeed. 'That's it!!' he'd shout. 'Now just remember it, *and* where to put it!' Of course I didn't, but the mistakes *I* made didn't annoy him half as much as those Rodney made. Maybe it was left-over resentment from father Fred, but I could see it brewing, week after week, until one time they started *really* arguing. Then, much to everyone's surprise, Cliff challenged Rodney to step outside into the garden, and settle it with fisticuffs.

"I'll never forget that day," he continues. "I was asked to referee. We went out onto the lawn. I know it sounds silly, but I'm sure that night is when Cliff's MS started. It was a late evening in July, sultry, oppressive, threatening. There wasn't even the whisper of a breeze, but, as they fought, and I stood on the sidelines, something seemed to come down and envelop us." Roger is not one prone to flights of fancy. "I actually thought I was having a heart attack, the feeling was so intense. It was like a visitation. I swear, there was even a strange, well, kind of deep humming sound. I actually felt a tingling sensation. I kid you not, David. No music, no heavenly choirs, but I felt something decidedly...spooky. Then there was the blood. They both drew blood. Cliff's often asked me over the years, 'Why me Roger? Why? Where? How?' and I always think back to that fight. Something definitely happened that night."

Of course, despite the argument, nothing was resolved. Well, not immediately, but within a couple of days, Rodney announced that he was leaving the group to join his brother in The Simonals, a rival outfit on the other side of town. Exit one rhythm guitarist.

Finlay immediately placed an advert in the local rag and...enter Terry Clarke.

Terry was, and still is, a very likeable individual. He is now also a multi-millionaire, having founded, in the mid-70s, with his brother Philip, the recording equipment empire Clarke-Technik, but he came into the story by a circuitous route, though well qualified within the geographical and musical area.

The Clarke family ran a thriving wholesale grocery business in Kidderminster, and lived in an imposing mansion, secreted away behind the leafy lanes of Wolverley. They were established and financially successful enough to have sent their three children, Terry, Philip and sister Jane, to a private school in nearby Droitwich. Also attending this school for privileged children had been another local businessman's daughter, Heather Williams, who had formed and maintained a close friendship with Jane Clarke, Terry's sister. Years later, when Terry held his 21st birthday bash at the family home, he invited Heather, who, by then—much to Terry's chagrin—was jazz guitarist Bev Pegg's steady girlfriend. Bev, who in the years to come would have considerable impact on the recording career of Clifford T. Ward, remembers driving to the party in his red Sunbeam Alpine, cruising along the autumn country lanes and up the sweeping gravel drive, to join in the celebrations, where Terry and two musical friends, the *fait accompli* house band, were playing the Buddy Holly, Eddie Cochran hits of the day. Fronted by a Gene Vincent impersonator, they called themselves Alfie Knott & the AKs (I kid you knott...) and featured Dave Pugh on bass guitar, with Terry playing lead.

Despite having his destiny securely mapped out with the family business, Terry was yet another teenager hooked on pop music, although family financial security—in those early days at least—allowed him the advantage to indulge in his passion without sacrifice. The AKs had been together for about a year when he saw the advert in the carpet town weekly, the *Kidderminster Shuttle,* and he felt it would be a nice step up the local musical ladder. An audition was arranged; he played, he impressed, he joined.

Cliff and Terry hit it off immediately. Here was a very competent, malleable guitarist, willing and able to do what was required, without fuss or furore. The tensions within the group quickly receded, and, as they started to divide practice sessions between Chaddesley and Wolverley over the summer of 1963, the definitive Cliff Ward and The Cruisers sound began to take shape.

THE TRAVELLER

The calm confidence of a Christian with four aces. Mark Twain

Leon Tipler lives in a quiet, bottle-necked cul-de-sac half-way between Kidderminster police station and Doolittle & Dalley, the wonderfully Dickensian-sounding estate agent. On one side of the street stand red-bricked, terraced, Victorian cottages, originally built in their hundreds for the loom-weavers and shuttlers of Brintons, Grosvenor Carpets, Gilt Edge and CMCo. Now, those few that remain house first-time buyers or pensioners, and survive only because of the town's somewhat belated, guilty recognition of its industrial heritage.

In the last of the post-war semi-detached houses opposite, edging the church graveyard, lies the home of the legendary—though entirely fictitious—commercial radio station, Radio G-LTK. Up the narrow, winding stairs of this outwardly normal home, with its clipped front garden, gilded mirrors, mahogany barometer and English-seaside mementoes, in a tiny, sound-proofed, airless bedroom, stand tired racks of steel shelving, bowed by the weight of LPs and tape reels, fighting for space between record decks, recording decks, microphones, huge Ferguson speakers and literally thousands of cassettes that line the walls and litter the floors. A Sheffield tram destination roll hangs limply against the far wall, a locomotive name plate serves as a partition, and assorted groups of, yes, garden gnomes, look down, and smile. Such artefacts and containers indicate an enduring love for times gone by, for times and occupations of labour and creative recreation: an obsession for dance band days, steam trains and test match cricket. In one corner, near the double window, stands the one concession to creature comfort; an oak drop-leaf table, with a narrow cushioned bench, onto which you can squeeze, just as long as you leave your legs somewhere else…

These days, these media-accessible days, Leon finds somewhat puzzling. Not out of ignorance; he is remarkably intelligent and, despite being a man of few words, has an extraordinary imagination. He just doesn't see where it's all leading. He won't invest in the digital age, he says, until it has sorted itself, if it ever will. But back then, well those

were the times 'BeforeThe World Was Round'...
His father, a carpet factory engineer, was a keen radio ham, and built a crystal set in the early days, which he kept, like all married enthusiasts, in the wardrobe. Leon grew up listening to the golden age of radio on a giant Philips valve-set, reception of which was much improved by the huge aerial rigged up in the garden, with wires trailing in through the attic window and down to the set in the parlour.
"Oh, 'twas all radio in those days," he mocks, in his perfect Robb Wilton voice. Leon is a lean, outwardly serious 54-year-old, his life revolving around recorded sound. He still tapes test matches, movies (on audio cassette...), idiosyncratic radio shows ('The One-armed Bagpipe Player'), anything that appeals to his wonderfully controlled eccentricity, and, it seems, 'twas ever thus:
"How my mother put up with it, I'll never know. Father and son, messing about with the wireless. One instance. I was about 11, she was taking in the washing [as she still does, in her mid-eighties]. It was grey, overcast, blustery. The aerial insulators were glowing eerily along the garden, as the wire swung in the wind. Mother turned back to the house and saw a big orange ball, hovering over the attic. Rather like St Elmo's fire, I suppose. Static build up. Quite shook her, it did."
The radio itself stood on a small table at one side of the black leaded fire-grate. From the back of the set, alongside the aerial wire, ran a screened cable which looped over the mantelpiece, into one of the tall, panelled side cupboards, where it was connected to a wind-up gramophone, complete with a magnetic pick-up.
"I discovered how to work that, playing my folks' 78 rpm records through the wireless speaker, generally amusing myself and without any objection. I don't remember breaking any of them: things would have been quite different if I had. Then they generously bought me my very own wind-up, one Christmas, a Decca portable, which I still have somewhere. It was decorated with comic-cartoon characters, obviously a ploy by the industry to off-load the last of the 'acoustic' record-players onto schoolchildren, who, about that time, 1953, were beginning to become a market force."
He subsequently developed an almost encyclopædic knowledge of labels and artistes from the pre-pop days, and supplemented his parents' collection with anything that appealed. Roy Fox, David Whitfield, Gigli, Ambrose, Cy Laurie, Jimmy Shand (Jimmy *Shand*...?), and eventually, of course, good old rock'n'roll.
"The thing is, I've got a wide, mixed taste," he says proudly (well, he must have, if he likes Jimmy Shand...), "because the radio was so well equipped. I could pick up Radio Scotland, Luxembourg, Rome, wherever. It was an education in itself."
And so, unbeknown to his teachers, and most probably his classmates,

he coasted through school, accumulating this specialized knowledge in his own time, playing old records and 'dial-surfing' for new ones.

Encouraged by an elder cousin, he bought his first tape-recorder in 1958, a big, heavy, grey thing, 'built like a battleship.' German obviously.

"We'd record anything: cuckoo clocks, whistling kettles, anything. My cousin, who lived near the engine sheds, once stuck a microphone out through his letter box, to capture the sound of the steam trains blowing their whistles at midnight on New Year's Eve. *That* kind of thing. Those pieces of history, all those long-gone traditions."

Influenced by those early radio broadcasts, he developed an affinity with the spoken word, with the wit and wisdom of voices and accents and began to mimic, to write and to construct his own shows, purely for his own amusement, shutting himself away in the tiny spare room upstairs. He started writing make-believe documentaries, inventing fictitious countries, radio stations.

"But things drift on, don't they?" he suggests. "I never actually sat down and focused on one particular thing, and said 'That's what I'm going to do.' Then you realize it's all, well…building up."

I looked around the room. Was that wallpaper peeping through? It had built up all right…

He subsequently bought a Ferrograph. A 3-motor machine, hire-purchased from F. W. Long in Mill Street, then built a mixing desk from a kit, before later splashing out further on a Vortexian valve-desk. The professional's choice.

"I loved editing, cutting those 1/4" tapes, re-arranging phrases, sounds and suchlike, making nonsense out of sense," he recalls. "Then I discovered the limitless possibilities of over-dubbing, but those early machines had very little scope, so I decided to buy another, so I could bounce tracks." With two state-of-the-art mono Ferrograph recorders, he began looking around for new projects.

He was working at the time in the pattern shop of Gilt Edge Carpets, another of the carpet giants dominating the Kidderminster skyline, but inexplicably razed to the ground a few years ago to make way for that modern consumer scourge, the supermarket. Over one hundred years of tradition, not to mention over 1000 jobs, gone. The burghers of Kidderminster are no different from anyone else, when money shouts.

Sorry. Where was I?

There, at Gilt Edge, he also knew the young Finlay Tinker, and, during one of their afternoon tea-chats, Finlay mentioned a group he was following around called Cliff Ward and The Cruisers. Though Leon was no musician, he had by then, via his records and his radio, developed an excellent ear for sounds, and felt confident enough to suggest recording the group. After sure-fire agreement with the others,

it was organized for the coming Wednesday evening and, though well within walking distance, Finlay collected Leon in his car [you don't carry a 3-motor-valve-driven-metal-encased-Ferrograph by hand], and they motored around to Fred Simmonds's house in St John's Avenue.
Roger Bowen, for some reason wasn't present on that occasion, but the end results impressed everyone enough for further recording sessions to be arranged, which inevitably led to Leon taping some live gigs, first at The Fountain, then at The Crown. To be able to listen to themselves in playback mode was a luxury in itself: they were able to criticize, analyse and subsequently become an even tighter, more polished outfit. Leon enjoyed the sessions and his membership of the clan was secured, though his ultimate contribution to the story was still some years away.

With the prestigious Locarno prize safely under their belt, the workload had increased significantly, though they still maintained that local profile. Finlay lost interest, so Terry's brother Philip took over and began securing bookings further afield. This, in turn, led to another, and more significant, change in personnel.
In the excitement of the beat boom, holiday camps and caravan parks were offering residencies, or 'working holidays'—though on somewhat loaded terms—to whoever seemed available, capable and keen. If you were prepared to share a caravan, or a chalet—all five of you—for a week, and play until midnight, for a few pounds each, plus second sitting meals and a putting green, well, you were in. So in they were...
But Roger Bowen had his family business, working as a butcher in Stourport, and if it was impracticable, which it increasingly proved to be, then his loyalty lay with his father. Hence another vacancy, another advertisement, another respondent.
Enter Kenny Wright.

If you were an aspiring drummer (or, better still, an aspiring musician...) in the mid-fifties, there were Boys' Brigades a-plenty. Marching down Stourport High Street in uniform and rat-tat-tatting his snare drum, Ken doesn't look that much different to how he is today. A neat, handsome man, a very sharp dresser, straight off a 1960s 'Avengers' TV set, he progressed quickly to become a sought after drummer in the vanishing days of the local dance bands, before finding his forte with the burgeoning traditional jazz scene, where his steady rhythm drove trumpeter Alan Worrall's Apex Jazz Band. Jazz and pop were never soul-mates, and in those young days there was an unspoken, but quite definite, social divide between the two. Apart from education and family background, jazz always emphasized the sports car, rugby and brogues set, whilst pop, or rock'n'roll as it was then, was very much public transport, football and slip-ons, with white socks... All this came to an end with The Beatles. The Liverpool sound cut scythe-like through class prejudice. Suddenly everyone wanted to dance to, listen to, or even to be part of, a pop group. The sonorous jazz clubs, with their mystical beatnik skip-jivers, their MG 'taxis' and their songs of Indiana, began a sad, steady decline, and, as the white-haired men of the old guard turned and walked away, shaking their heads at the decay of society, bold, brash working-class came swaggering in, loud and surprisingly all-embracing.

The Cruisers were pop, and to a talented jazz drummer like Ken, it was easy. Once he'd played a couple of songs, all he had to do, as bassist Bill Black once said of Elvis, was to '… watch the singer's arse.' Cliff Ward didn't exactly gyrate, didn't even strut, but he froze for the gaps. Stop when the singer stopped. It was a cinch. And again, musical ability apart, there was a personality fusion between the two, and that was enough. In May 1963, after his first rehearsal with the Cruisers, Ken appeared with them at Studio 1 (taking home 60/-), backed The Vernon Girls at Stourbridge Town Hall—a disaster, according to his diary—before joining them again for an ATV audition in July, which they failed. A working holiday in South Wales followed—the first of many—at such then-glamorous venues as De Valence Ballroom, Tenby, the Fountain Café, Milford Haven, the Tower Ballroom, Swansea; during which times Terry Clarke, keen but conscientious, drove home each evening to be at his father's grocery business for the morning. On the final journey home, his luck ran out as he spun off the road, wrecking his beloved Austin-Healey Sprite, and breaking poor Graham Drew's nose.

Further gigs, including backing boxer-turned-singer Mike Preston at Kidderminster Town Hall, consolidated his position, until it became obvious to everyone that this line-up worked, and worked well. As ever with Cliff's dreams, loyalty never entered into it. Fortunately, Roger, with his worldly-wise perception and devil-may-care attitude, assessed the situation, and it bothered him not one jot.

"Looking back, I wouldn't have changed a thing," he assures me. "I knew my limitations, Ken was a much better drummer, certainly more sensitive. I was a basher. If I'd have wanted more out of the business, then I would have had to work for it, and I didn't want it that much. To me it was a hobby, a good way of socializing, getting out, oh, and meeting the girls…"

Cliff was clearly taking things a lot more seriously than that and so, in September 1963, and on perfectly amicable terms, Ken Wright once again turned up, but this time he stepped in, sat down, and stayed.

About this time, Pat became pregnant again. Debbie was six months old, and though still very small, was a delightful baby, giving little indication of the condition that was soon to be diagnosed and thus affect them all so deeply.

They were still living in the Horsefair, Cliff supplementing his Ministry of Pensions salary with whatever The Cruisers earned from their gig schedule, although sometimes even this prospect was not enough to ensure reliability. Ken remembers instances where Cliff didn't even bother turning up, family pressures probably having got the better of him, or maybe he was having a bad hair day…

And the rehearsing, oh, the rehearsing.

"The songs were all chosen by Cliff," Ken told me. "They were invariably American artistes no-one else in the group had heard of, and, to our cloth-ears, not particularly commercial. When he started writing his own stuff, well, then we spent at least 90 per cent of practice time on *those* songs, even though we, the band, were expected to open the show and, when he didn't turn up, or walked off and went home in a sulk [!!!], carry the night."

"Cliff actually used to walk out on the group, for the rest of the night?"

"If the gig wasn't going well, in Cliff's view, he would quickly lose his temper, usually with poor old Graham, and frequently leave the stage. We wouldn't know how long he'd be, or even if he was coming back at all. He actually went *home* on many occasions, when he'd driven himself to the gig. That left us with a measly 10 per cent repertoire; instrumentals, 12-bar blues, whatever."

"And did no-one ever take issue with him?"

"No. Cliff was the boss. He knew it, we knew it."

And Ken then threw a perceptive viewpoint on the reason for this prima donna behaviour.

"I don't think Cliff ever really liked performing live, as one of a travelling band of musicians. I rarely saw any joy in his output or in his reaction to the audience. He certainly wasn't relaxed on stage, in fact he very often would retch before a gig. He never shared any humour with the crowd, even though he could be very funny in private, out of the spotlight. I don't know if he felt it was beneath him, or whether he was genuinely shy; it's a strange business to be in if you've got a complex. [Or is it?]

"This became more apparent even after he had made his mark with *Home Thoughts*. Absolutely refusing to tour, despite the wonderful offers we had. Brazil, for heaven's sake! But he refused point blank."

Whether he liked it or not, Cliff put his all into performing. He'd done it as a child, those many years ago at Areley Kings, and he still gave his everything, taking it very, very seriously, to the point where some people felt embarrassed, even amazed, at his stage persona.

School pal Ray Hume turned up at a dance at the Stone Manor about this time, to see his old primary school classmate.

"I would have been a hopelessly spotty, blushing 18-year-old. The band was Cliff Ward and The Cruisers. I'd been watching and dancing to them for about half-an-hour, thinking all the time that the bloke doing the singing was Cliff, but that he looked a bit different—despite the years—from how I remembered him. Suddenly, there was an announcement from the drummer, a brief *'da-da-ra'* from the group, and the *real* Cliff Ward bounced out from the wings, silk-jacketed and super-quiffed, grabbed the microphone and launched into 'Kansas City'! It was, for me, then at my most unconfident and neurotic, a mind-boggling display of outgoing, larger-than-life bravado, the likes of which I had never seen. I was impressed, but I was also *de*pressed. How come he could do that without feeling self-conscious, and, more to the point, why wasn't *I* doing that?"

Back to Ken:
"Rehearsals were damn hard work. Trying to get vocal harmonies from of a bunch of non-singing musicians was a 'blood out of a stone' affair. Cliff, of course, could sing all the lines—but only one at a time—so it was me, then Graham, then Trevor, or whoever came along later. All to be sung whilst we played. And even what we *played* was taught by the note; Graham having to substitute melodic brass or string lines with his Fender, Trevor having to remember bass lines he'd learned by playing his 45s at 33 rpm and my off-beats, well, they were never quite loud enough. Murder, sheer bloody murder.
"What also puzzled me is that Cliff often used to pitch the key too high for his voice. You could hear him really straining away on '... Tulsa' and '... Loving Feeling'. I used to suggest dropping it down just a key, but he wouldn't have it. That couldn't have done his throat much good, especially as the gigs increased."

Even so, the group continued to continue, entering local competitions, substituting players whenever shift-work intervened, and then as the year-end approached, they confidently entered the Locarno Band Of The Year event, but this time defending their title from the previous year. Ken Wright, in the first of his many financial contributions to Cliff's career, took them all into Birmingham to buy black leather waistcoats from Loo Blooms, and thus suitably attired, sporting the obligatory black trousers, black shoes, and whatever coloured quiff nature had blessed upon them, they played their way triumphantly through the heats, to be chosen for the quarter-finals to be held in January 1964.
Despite the numerous venues at which they held residencies, The Cruisers were at this time also drawn into the musical-mafia circuit run by the legendary Ma Regan, who owned the equally legendary Old Hill

Plaza and Handsworth Plaza ballrooms. About 10 miles apart, as the Transit van flies, these two Art Deco-style dance halls played host to the double-billers—a spot at Handsworth, then, quickly, *very* quickly, into the van through the roller-coaster back streets of the Black Country to 'Ode 'ill'—that every celebrity band of the time endured. A gig at The Plaza—as support to the famous—though not particularly well-paid, was a shot in the arm for a local group. The Beatles had headlined, The Rolling Stones, The Dave Clark Five, The Ronettes (who ran off the stage in fright as the whole male population of Old Hill moved *en masse* toward them, salivating), The Swinging Blue Jeans: everybody who was anybody did the Saturday night relay, and local combos, of which there were literally hundreds, fought for the regular spots. Ma Regan could take her pick.

Where she came from is shrouded in mystery, legend. A large, Ma Larkin-type, with a quiet, authoritative manner, she ran both venues virtually single-handed, hiring and firing with ruthless charm. Auditions were carried out mid-week under her watchful ear; her eyes were invariably reading a contract for the following Saturday, or maybe even *The Sporting Life*, but, just when you thought it was safe to go back to the beginning, she would walk across and, almost Cæsar-like give you the 'yes-nod'—or, you poor souls, the 'no-nod'…

The Plazas, and the less prestigious Ritz at Kings Heath, were converted cinemas, strategically and conveniently placed for the street-wise youth of Birmingham or, in the case of Old Hill, their country cousins from the Black Country, and gave many music fans their first real experience of seeing their heroes live, on stage, in a convivial atmosphere. It was of course, a time of great change: the past was refusing to just lay down and die, irrespective of the force of the present, and the Saturday evening's entertainment reflected this. The Cruisers, The Corvettes, Tony King and The Olympics, The Crestas, any of the token locals, would start the night, give it all they'd got, whip their fans into a well-rehearsed frenzy, until, at a pre-determined minute, encores *verboten*, the stage would slowly revolve—*à la* Sunday Night At The London Palladium—to reveal Dennis and his eight-piece Dance Band, wearing their faded, jaded dance-hall jackets, pressed slacks and sad shoes, who, against all odds, would try to entice the punters to stay on the floor and indulge in 30 minutes of 'strict-tempo'. This die-hard act of defiance merely prompted a mass exodus to the downstairs bar by anyone under 25, leaving the mirror-globe to pick out the whale-boned factory-girls and the Burton-tailored sharks, still desperately seeking a soul-mate to brighten their ageing, lonely lives.

Down in the red-carpeted lounge, the images reflected in the gilt-edged glass, chrome and brass fittings and the cloakroom vanity mirrors couldn't have been more opposite. Car salesmen and apprentices, with their mop-tops, Beatle-jackets and cuban-heels, chatted to Mary Quant secretaries, panda-eyed and perfumed, all of them drinking and hoping for a real taste of this wonderful revolution, whilst David Frost, with his Nero-fringe and clip-board, recounted the week that was on the monochrome television sets dotted around the room. It was New Youth all right, and pop music was the catalyst.

The Cruisers were up there with the best of them, though still with a guarded reticence to commit themselves to contract or obligation over and above their numerous gigs. They were asked to—and did—audition for the *Brum Beat* LP, a Regan sponsored compilation album, containing, as its name suggests, Birmingham's answers to the Mersey Sound, but because this would inevitably involve a contractual commitment, they, or most probably Cliff on their behalf, declined.

Even so, for some inexplicable reason, though Cliff obviously had his sights set very high, he still didn't look further afield than his home town for management. He had rejected both Mecca and Plaza deals, which would have taken them into prestigious venues nationwide, yet continually reverted to local entrepreneurs for career guidance. There had been Fred Simmonds, Finlay Tinker, current road-manager Philip Clarke, who was under fire—all is never enough in management of *any* kind—and now, two more Kidderminster boys appeared on the scene; Carl Hasdell and Roy Northover, promising the world, in a grain of sand…

They had just started the Mercian Agency, based in Coventry Street, Kidderminster and were building a roster of local talent and naturally saw Cliff Ward and The Cruisers as a potential main act. Carl had even deputized for bass-man Trevor Jones on occasion, though not under any circumstance was he considered a musician. Mercian waved a few documents at The Cruisers, and a period of lengthy consideration ensued, though without commitment, as two *other* would-be aspirers, Nigel Reece and Peter Phillips, began to work hard on their behalf, and would continue to do so—on and off, between others, for almost a year—as Epstein-mania began to explode throughout the nation's non-musicians.

A potential Decca recording contract was also discussed, but found to be pie-in-the-sky; why would Decca want anybody else? They'd closed the door on those Beatle chappies in favour of Brian Poole and The Tremeloes…, and the Locarno semi-final loomed large on the horizon.

On January 13th, 1964, The Cruisers came joint first with The Plainsmen, beating off Guitars Incorporated, Mark Raymond and The Cyclones, The Top Cats, and old Stourport-on-Severn rivals, Tommy and The Crestas; though the euphoria of the evening was tempered somewhat when Cliff's personal microphone and Graham's guitar and pre-amp were stolen from the dressing room. Terry Clarke's Gretsch, which was insured against such incidents, was left alone. Obviously a Fender fan.

Ken felt a strange sensation. His wallet was vibrating in resigned anticipation…

He put up the money once again. Cliff got his new microphone and Graham chose a Fender Jaguar, then it was time for their next booking at the old home-from-home watering hole on the outskirts of town, where, in true and seasonal Kidderminster tradition, the evening ended early with a fight in the crowd.

"I remember two things about The Fountain," Cliff recalled, in a 1977 interview at his home in Lyonshall. "It was always snowing [?], and there was always a fight [The Good Old Days, we call them], and when we came out at the end of the night, you could see the blood in the snow."

Nice place, Kidderminster.

Two nights later, The Cruisers were back at The Locarno, in the finals of the 1964 'Band Of The Year' competition, but this time, despite some more theatricals from Terry and Trevor, who donned animal-face masks for their version of Big Dee Irwin's 'Swingin On A Star', they were unplaced. The Plainsmen romped home, followed by The New Cyclones, and—offering a touch of irony to the proceedings—Rodney Simmonds's group, The Simonals, with The Kingsford Four and, yes, I'm afraid it's true, the courageously named Mark Thyme and The Offbeats pulling up the rear.

And so, like a bunch of bad workmen, they blamed it all on their manager, not that Philip was unduly concerned. He told them, as they pinned him against the back of the van, that he was emigrating. "I'm off to the Antipodes," he said, blocking a left hook. They spoke not a word all the way home.

But the gigs still lay a-waiting.

They played word-games to keep awake or relieve the boredom during the journeys home. Ken, as always, was driver. Cliff sat next to him at the front, the others strewn around the back of the van, snoring or breaking wind (in Graham's case, often both at the same time…) in the darkness.

Ken smiles:

"When the tired silence became uncomfortable, Cliff would challenge me, and one of his silly games would begin:

'I bet I can tell you, by the shape of his head, whether the next driver in front has got a moustache.'

"Okay, you're on!" I'd say. Anything to keep awake.

"So we continue, both of us looking across out of the corner of our eye as we pull out to overtake. Yes, no, yes, no. Sometimes right, sometimes wrong. Wrong again. 'Right,' says Cliff. 'Definite this time. This one's got a moustache. Definitely a 'ed for a moustache.' I started to pull out, waiting for the chance to look down at the poor unsuspecting driver. 'Told you!' he shouted. I glanced towards the passenger window, trying to see down into the car. There was Cliff, holding his hairbrush horizontally across the glass. I nearly left the road in hysterics."

Around this time, they were playing—or practising—virtually every night. Regular bookings at Bromsgrove's beautiful Perry Hall Hotel (still functioning today), Hartlebury Village Hall (now used for playschools, Womens Institute meetings and Antique Fairs), The Mare & Colt (the dance-hall now a Steak-and-Chips eatery), The Nautical William and The Park Attwood Hotel (both now numbered among the ubiquitous 'Rest Homes'), and the fairy-tale Chateau Impney Hotel, where young blades with sports cars took impressionable mini-skirted, bee-hived hairdressers, leading them downstairs to the delightfully tacky '007 Bar', where they plied them with dry Martinis, and later drove them the long way home, through the dark and winding back lanes of Droitwich…

Whilst they still pondered over the Mercian contract, another local man tried his hand as group manager. 'Carpet-bagger' Roger Rowe, a long, dark, son-of-the-town, whose father owned Rowe's Carpets and socialized as Master of The Hounds, stepped into Philip Clarke's shoes, but only for a while. It was tough at the bottom.

Roger had grown up with Terry Clarke, both attending the same school, their families holidaying together, horse-riding around the ancestral Rowe farmland in Trimpley; y'know the everyday activities of simple country folk.

He had been on the local music scene for some time. Whilst still at school, he and Terry had formed Coral Agency—named after the record company of their idol, Buddy Holly—and began booking bands at such quaint post-war venues as Hartlebury Village Hall, charging 1/6d admission, soft drinks extra… Then, of course it had started to snowball; the successful groups asked Coral to get them more work, and so on. It was happening all over the country.

After Terry had joined The Cruisers, Roger had continued running the agency alone, helping them find work and following them around, eventually rising to manager-designate. He had already been instrumental in raising their profile by starting—and featuring them at—Kidderminster's first 'out of town' venue, the Park Attwood Hotel. This stood on the periphery of the Rowe family land in Trimpley, and

Roger had persuaded the proprietor to replace the prehistoric Saturday dance band trio with a pop group, initially for once a month. While the dance band drew a regular dozen, Cliff Ward and The Cruisers, the first group to appear there, sold out. Marge, the proprietor was dutifully impressed, wise enough to recognize the potential, and thus began the Thursday night hops, with Nigel Reece and Peter Phillips on the door, drawing teenagers from all over the county, their Triumph Heralds (and my blue-black Vitesse convertible; such glorious times…), Healey Sprites and Minis lining the long tree-lined drive, as music—pop music—reverberated off the oak-panelled walls and spilled out onto the warm, shadowed lawns… Absolute Heaven. (I wonder whatever happened to the beautiful Diane…? Oops, sorry. Silly me. Off at a tangent there…).

The South Wales venues were still a draw. They were booked for a five- night tour of the coastal ballrooms, sleeping on the stage or in a beach café at Tenby, or, when things got better, a caravan just off the beach.

Ken Wright recounts a salutary lesson:

"We had a few followers who came to see who they could meet at gigs, in the way of girls. One of the gang [who shall be nameless, but it wasn't a Cruiser…] came back to the caravan really late one night, after a dalliance with one of the local girls. He'd had a good, er…time, but was a bit worried about, well, the consequences. Not of her becoming pregnant mind you, but of him becoming…infected. We were a bit far from a clinic," Ken laughs, "so Carl [oops, I've said his name…] decided to wash his parts with TCP… We had to peel him off the ceiling. He didn't stop screaming for a good twenty minutes."

During his spell as manager, despite some of the distances, Roger went everywhere with them.

"Dedication," I suggested.

"Well, you had to." he laughs. "With Cliff, if the acoustics were bad, if the PA wasn't up to scratch, he just wouldn't sing, no matter how far we'd travelled. On more than one occasion, when his voice amplifier was in for repair, say, and we'd borrowed one until his was fixed, if that started being temperamental, crackling, whatever, well he'd just walk off stage. The rest of the band would just have to continue until someone, somehow, coaxed him back on.

"And the rehearsals…"

Oh, God, here we go again.

"We hired The Crown in Stourport every Tuesday for practice. It would start off okay, then something snapped and Cliff would go absolutely raving mad at the lads. 'C'mon, you lot, naah, naaah, *naaaaah*, that's how it bloody well goes!!'" and Roger plays air-guitar, sitting behind his mahogany desk in the company office, high above the trading estate car park. "Absolute tunnel vision," he continues, "no variations whatsoever. It had to be just right. But that's why they were so popular. And the girls thought the world of Cliff. He was quite aloof on stage, no picking out members of the audience for jokes and such, but they recognized his talent. And he really gave it everything he'd got. It was his life. Sometimes he'd come off-stage and could hardly talk, he was that hoarse, and audiences loved that commitment. There are loads of instances, but one that springs to mind is good old Hartlebury Village Hall. He started singing 'Anyone Who Had A Heart' and the crowd just stopped dancing, talking, whatever and just stood watching him, swaying. Just like the movies it was." He gives a gentle laugh, almost embarrassed at what he'd just said. "He seemed, well, he *was*, a very shy person. When you talked to him off-stage, he'd listen, while looking down picking his little fingernail, a kind of nervous habit, and as soon as they'd finished playing, usually with 'La Bamba', he'd be up at the back of the stage, putting his stuff away, couldn't be bothered talking to the hangers-on. Just wanted to get home. He had his stage gear as well as his equipment. I'd encouraged them to maintain their smart appearance because around that time, a few of the groups were beginning to dress more casually, jeans and things, but The Cruisers always stayed immaculate.

"Pat used to come along some of the times, they were quite inseparable, but he still gave her a hard time if something didn't go right. Everything had to be just perfect.

"Musically, I think he was ahead of his time. Even when he started writing, he wouldn't just write something simple. I used to plead with him to make it simple, catchy, but no, not Cliff. Anybody could do that, and yet ironically, when he made it big, the first ones to take off were the simple ones…"

Roger, like a few others in this story, soon realized that he'd have to make a choice between family obligations and pop music. He actually chose pop, but Pop just upped his pay overnight, more than matching what he was earning handling The Cruisers. A good way to get a pay rise in the family business.

So he moved. On, and up, and though even the carpet business would see its fair share of world change, it was always certain to be a more secure place to be than the shaky world of pop music.

Ken Wright, when he wasn't playing pop'n'roll, still maintained his jazz contacts and was able to continue his regular Wednesday night session with The New Orleans Jazz Band in Birmingham, whilst also working full-time in the day as an accountant at a large steel works in Brierley Hill, in those days a spirited market town at the heartland of

British industry, now sadly known only for that glass-and-chromium edifice to the great god Mammon, the Merry Hill Shopping Centre.

He had, by now, developed an almost protective and proprietorial relationship with Cliff, absolutely convinced of the man's talent, and feeling it was only a matter of time before they would indeed turn professional.

But it was a long time coming. The Cruisers bade an 'all-is-forgiven' farewell to Philip, playing until the wee wee hours at his going away party, just a few days before Pat gave birth to second child, Martin. Then again, it was on the treadmill of gigs and practices, with a few music-based interludes. In May, Ken and Cliff, with Pat and Ken's girlfriend Maggie, went to see Chuck Berry at Birmingham Town Hall; a week later The Cruisers supported Little Richard at Wolverhampton Civic, (Ken: "They used our gear; walked on, plugged in and beat the crap out of my drums!") and in flaming June, they had their first good publicity photos taken, at the good old Crown Hotel, Stourport. But publicity is as publicity does. A week later their impressive PA system, the envy of many a local outfit, was stolen from outside the Crown, after yet another intense practice session. Standing around the bar, Cliff was as usual holding forth, under landlady Renee Bell's motherly eye. "It should have gone 'Boom-boom-boom-b-boom …" as Graham and Trevor, with strength in numbers, mildly protested that *their* interpretation, 'Boom-b-b-boom-b-boom …' was correct, and Ken, ever the diplomat, nodded at both parties, sipping a pint of shandy. His van, however, sat out on the car-park; lonely, loaded and unlocked…

Two weeks later, the local press reported that two locals had been arrested and charged with stealing '… musical instruments and equipment worth £450, belonging to Mr K. Wright …'

Re-equipped, The Cruisers were ready once again for the Mare & Colt, The Nautical William, Droitwich Winter Gardens. Lawdy, lawdy.

It was time to take things a little more seriously. Gigs are fine, but fame is better.

Cliff had been writing with a vengeance, honing his songs, and subsequently re-acquainting himself with tape enthusiast Leon Tipler, who had moved a little nearer to Cliff's home in The Oaklands. Apart from producing some impressive demos in Leon's bedroom-studio, he began indulging in some slapstick 'radio-comedy', written with painstaking attention to detail by that man of many voices…

"He started coming around to the house about March 1964," remembers Leon. "We'd talked a few times on the telephone over the couple years since I'd taped The Cruisers live and I suppose he felt ready to do some demos. He brought Rodney along; how they'd got together again I don't know, but there was no animosity between them, considering the troubles they'd been through. Just Rodney, his guitar, Cliff and his songs, me and my machines. Cliff would sing his tunes, Rodney would fit chords around them and they'd be off. He always double-tracked his vocals, which, with my primitive [though accurate] set-up, meant a lot of work. Then he'd decide on a harmony—or two, or even three—so you can imagine the 'bouncing' I had to do, and if a mistake was made, back to square one. Rodney got a lovely, full sound on his acoustic, double-tracking that where possible, and slowly, gradually, we built up some good sounds. Cliff was a perfectionist, he knew what he wanted, that sound in his head, and, more often than not, he found it. But, being human, and a non-musician, I found it all bit wearing, all that strumming. The folks downstairs said that was all they could hear, jingle-jangle, jingle-jangle... One night, after a brief session, I suggested to Cliff we try some comedy, spoken word stuff. He was all for it! I pulled out a script I'd written [as you do...] and we all picked a name, a character, from a list I'd drawn up [as you do...] and we just read it onto tape, from scratch. I didn't realize what I'd started, but I'm glad I did it."

Leon became Jack Powdermonkey, and Rodney became, well, anything with a cultured voice, whilst Cliff became Tom Crite, gradually developing a shy, low-voiced street-cleaner, with a broad Kidderminster accent into a loud, blaspheming son-of-Satan.

They also managed to recruit a girl into this strange, make-believe land of buffoonery.

Teresa Oakley, a tall, willowy blonde, with fashionable mascara-eyes and long, long legs, had been drawn into The Cruisers circle following her brief spell working for Mercian Agency. She was one of the many girls who flocked to the Park Attwood and other local venues, to watch the group, but in Teresa's case, to watch one man in particular.

"I was about seventeen, obviously very impressionable and given to the flights of fancy such beings take. Ken Wright was the love of my life," she speaks, without any embarrassment or regret. "He was about six or seven years older than me, [nine, actually, Teresa, but I won't tell anyone...], and I worshipped him, but it was never reciprocated, other than an occasional kiss or maybe even a quick snog, if I was lucky...

"I actually used to walk through Kidderminster, in the morning, an *hour* before I was due at work, just so that I could see Ken driving by in his Mini-van. When he smiled ... oh, it would make my day. My diary entry would read something like 'Heaven! Ken smiled at me today.' I can still remember his car registration number, thirty years on. And indeed, she quotes it.

I asked her about Cliff.

"Oh, he was a terrific singer." She draws on her cigarette. "There was always a gang of girls standing up at the front, watching him. I'm certainly not saying anything about affairs and such, though he certainly played up to the image. Tell me a musician that doesn't! But he seemed to treat his music and his family as two separate entities, and in that way he really, honestly believed that he could justify anything...

"Musically, I think Cliff set his own goals, and, if he achieved them, which he invariably did, well, then in his eyes, everything else was incidental. He didn't respond, or react to audiences, because he felt no need to. He did his bit and it was usually—no *always*—spot on. The reaction was not his concern. His aim was to do it well. He was very nervous, and quite shy, but he was determined, in everything he did."

And the tapes?

"I was asked, by either Cliff or Leon, to come along to the tape sessions, probably because of my accent, which, I suppose, was very public school, ahem ... in comparison. I went along because I knew, or assumed, Ken would be there. He was, the first once or twice, but seemed to drift out of it soon after. He had a steady girlfriend at the time, so I just lived my teenage life of unrequited desire, doe-eyed and love-struck.

"Leon invented a character for me, whom he christened Gloria Bosom, and every Friday, for a couple of years, I would turn up at his house, climb the stairs into his bedroom, and ... record the G-LTK shows. Leon would hand us a script, tell us *not* to read it before recording commenced, and away we'd go. He had an incredible talent, witty, flowing scripts, with one-liners thrown in quite unexpectedly, catching us completely off-guard and generally reducing the whole thing to giggling, hysterical shambles. It was, for me, a gauche, seventeen-year-old, a world beyond my comprehension, but I loved it."

Those tapes, of which I have heard most, also show another quite remarkable side to Clifford T. Ward. Incredible vocal inflections, read straight off the sheet with impeccable timing, together with gems of occasionally spontaneous humour, all thrown into a radio-show format, complete with commercial breaks, local news, weather checks and a signature tune. Blimey, they even conceded an audience research item, indicating listening figures throughout the county, and Rodney, an extremely competent draughtsman, drew amazing cartoons of the characters, which, along with the many hours of broadcasting, survive to this day, thanks to Leon. Radio G-LTK was a piece of English eccentricity, boys at play, but to those who know only of the serious, committed musician, these tapes are a revelation. No, you certainly wouldn't listen to them for their beauty, their play with words, their gentle reflections on the world around us, but, for certain hours in his life, singer-songwriter Clifford T. Ward would become stinky, flea-ridden, big-bellied Tom Crite, working-class commentator.

"Were you surprised at Cliff's ability to mimic?" I asked Leon, as we

listened to yet another wonderful G-LTK special.
"Not at all. Y'see he was an observer," Leon gave one of his non-eye-contact smiles, his admiration apparent.
And so it seemed. A loner he might have been, but Cliff noticed everything around him, the idiosyncrasies of life, the absurdity of it all. A vocal cartoonist, I suppose.
I listen to another tape. Tom Crite, in full flight, spoofing with 'Sweet Little Sixteen': that broad, guttural accent, adroitly missing the beat, losing the words, flustering and blustering his way through Chuck's classic paean to teenage years, and I remember Eccles, Rambling Sid Rumpo, Benny Hill, and all those years of innocent goonery that we have now so sadly lost.
"Ah, yes," nods Leon slowly, surrounded by his miles of memory, "we had some good times in this room..."

But Cliff could only be side-tracked for so long, and so, when the time came for him to record professionally, he was well and truly ready.
In August, after a summer of serious practice, they booked in at Hollick & Taylors, a small recording studio housed inside the back room of an electrical retailers in Birmingham, staffed by serious, white-coated technicians. Over a couple of confident sessions, they produced an acetate of four songs: Marvin Gaye's 'You're A Wonderful One', a Cliff and Graham joint composition, 'Ooh-we Baby', Cliff's own 'Rachel' and a surprising cover of Chuck Berry's broody, Johnny-wanna-be, 'No Money Down'.
To hear Cliff singing the blues, rolling out those street-wise Berry-isms with a Stourport burr, is a delight, though before actually entrusting his version to tape, like every other pop singer in the land—before and since—he sang what he *thought* he heard, not what had been written. Ken recalls them substituting their own words or sounds—phonetics took precedence—then comparing notes to find the most acceptable version; "... a full mess of ale in my back seat ..." Have a listen to Chuck. Can *you* make it out?
Pat also remembers that song, only too well:
"He just couldn't get some of the words, hadn't got a clue what the singer was saying in some places. We spent hours playing the record on the radiogram, slowing it down, speeding it up, trying to make sense—interpret—what was being sung."
Ken also remembers Cliff's dogged desire for simplicity in later years.
"Although he was a Beatles fan, like the rest of us, some of their lyrics confused him. He was genuinely puzzled by some of their street-wise lines, though he didn't have any qualms at all about singing Sam Cooke's '...Yo-oo-ou Send Me...' phrase twenty-five times..."

Following the demo, things really started to move. Ken moved as well, into Trevor Jones's flat on the Walshes Estate, which Trevor had shared with his sister since their mother had died. Here there was more room for his drum kit, and, at the beginning of 1965, he handed in his notice at one of the last great British Steel outposts, Richard, Thomas & Baldwin, Brierley Hill (where I was serving out my slave-labour apprenticeship—and I didn't even miss him in the dinner queue...).

EMI-Columbia had shown interest in the demo, so Cliff began looking around for some female backing singers, someone he could take down with them to record, well-primed and obedient. The Park Attwood was the obvious source, there were girls a-plenty shimmying up at the front; all it needed was a little announcement, spread the word. They auditioned the hopefuls at Terry Clarke's house.

Not the casting couch, surely?

No, this was Kidderminster. It was a cup of tea and a ginger nut, *if* they were any good...

On 1st February The Cruisers motored down to Abbey Road, where 'them Beatles...' were just about to record their next number one. Whether or not The Cruisers realized they were treading such hallowed ground is uncertain, but the session was quickly completed in the time-honoured tradition of the production line. They packed their equipment away, signed the job sheet, and were handed their Musicians Union fees in the legendary brown envelopes. They weren't exactly rich and famous, but The Cruisers could now at least consider themselves truly professional.

The recording contract arrived, duly signed, in March. Columbia were satisfied with the recording, but were belatedly expressing doubts as to the viability of the name that Rodney and Cliff had chosen in that tiny espresso café nearly three years ago. Cliff had to think fast, for on the 26th it was down to London for group photos and press interviews, following which a Radio Luxembourg 'Friday Spectacular' spot was pre-recorded at EMI Studios in Manchester Square, for transmission on 30th April.

'Ticket To Ride' was now at pole position and Bob Dylan had two singles in the Top Twenty, but Cliff Ward and The Cruisers were no more. Seemingly overnight, without warning, they had become Martin Raynor and The Secrets, '... to avoid confusion with Mancunian Dave Berry's group', currently chart-climbing with 'Little Things'.

But names do not a hit record make, and the Secrets' Columbia single, 'Candy To Me'—which Cliff would later describe as possibly the worst Holland-Dozier-Holland song ever—disappeared without trace; except in Kidderminster, where, as the town's first home-grown pop single, it held the number one spot in the local Top Ten for two weeks in May.

Hypothetically, things *could* have turned out differently if Cliff had taken Roger Rowe's earlier advice on one matter.

"When they were talking of making that first single, I suggested they record 'La Bamba', and make *that* the A-side. No-one else was doing it as well as them, and I don't think many people had recorded it, despite its popularity on the live circuit. Nowadays, of course, everybody's done it, even the Boston Philharmonic, but Cliff wouldn't hear of it. 'They'll think I can't sing anything else,' he said. He was so stubborn, and because of his talent, no-one liked to upset him, he always got his own way. 'Candy To Me' was awful. He was so good, and he did make it eventually," concludes Roger, "but he should have been bigger than he was. Who knows what might have happened with 'La Bamba'?"

Indeed, but then, there most certainly wouldn't have been any 'Home Thoughts From Abroad'…

But they had work to do elsewhere. Now that they had taken the plunge and turned professional, they had to work the circuit. Mercian Agency, having finally secured a contract with them in March, had asked for some time to arrange better paying UK gigs, but meanwhile a two-month 'continental tour' had been offered, via an Evesham agent, to work various US bases in Europe. Great deliberation ensued, but the prospect of money *and* adventure overcame any real doubts, and so on 29th June, after Ken had part-exchanged his mini-van for a road-and-room-worthy yellow Commer Transit (reg: 271 LNP—Let's Not Panic?…), and with insurance cover arranged via Clarkes Wholesale Grocers, the Secret-Cruisers set off for the green fields of France.

It was doomed from the start, but they had started, so there would have to be some attempt made to finish…

Ken collected each member in turn, with their luggage, instruments and, in Cliff's case, plentiful stage-gear: suit and shirts on hangers, freshly ironed handkerchiefs and a copious supply of hair-lacquer, 'which he used by the gallon', and, after ensuring Graham's guitar was on board, and inside, they set off down the road.

They had to travel via Belgium, owing to some complication with the French authorities [yes, even then…] concerning band—or was it banned?—equipment, but the point of departure was still Dover, seemingly a few thousand miles from the country pubs and hotels of Worcestershire.

The financial arrangement was, as ever, decidedly shaky. They were to be paid locally, but in arrears, via the French poste restante system, whereby monies were collected at pre-arranged post offices, *en route*. This meant, in effect, that for the first two or three weeks at least, all petrol, food and accommodation costs would have to be met by the band themselves.

Ken takes up the story:
"On the way down to the docks at Dover I suggested that a float should be started to cover petrol for my van. At this point Cliff announced that he had absolutely no money at all, having left what little he had back home with Pat."
It's not hard to imagine the scene.
A long, loud silence. Everybody staring straight ahead at the road, thinking, "Oh, shit, here we go…"
Terry had already experienced Cliff's financial juggling. Two days previous, when the question of him being unable to raise cash for the trip had prompted Cliff to suggest selling one of his treasured microphones, Terry had given him the £12.00 asking price against an I.O.U., only to find that he had then sold it anyway!
"I've still got the piece of paper," he laughs, "signed by Cliff Ward. 'I.O.U. Terry Clarke, £12.00.' Dated 27th June, 1965."
"But Terry, who always had a little more than the little we others had, volunteered to 'grubstake' Cliff again," continues Ken, "on the understanding that he would be repaid as and when. The *coup de grace* came when we actually collected our first payment. After sharing it out, Terry was amazed to find that Cliff had immediately posted his complete share back home to Pat!"
[Okay. Not exactly cricket, but I remember being in similar positions myself, accused of meanness by single or gainfully employed musician friends, when I had first turned professional, and 'all' I was doing was desperately trying to maintain a house, a wife and two children. It's not cricket, but it's not easy, either…]

Fontainebleau is a pretty name; it rolls off the tongue, making even the untutored linguist sound fluent in French. A beautiful town, famous for its palace and its pottery, it was here, in the not-so-beautiful US Army camp that The Secrets commenced their tour.
Ken continued:
"When we arrived at the first base in Fontainebleau, the manager, a 'Spec 7' sergeant, greeted us with the immortal words, 'Where's the broad?'"
Apparently they had been booked on the premise that the band was fronted by a sexy blonde singer. Female, that is. Several phone calls later, Spec 7 reluctantly allowed them to set up and play. Things didn't improve. After a couple of unnerving performances, during which the audience drunkenly overpowered their Tamla and soul renditions, hitting higher and stronger notes during 'That Loving Feeling', they realized that this particular base was a topping up camp for Vietnam and was thus full of US boys living in fear and dread of the Nam posting. One request note handed to Terry reads 'How about something

slow & easy before I have to fight this goldurned woman?' Another one asks them to '...play 'Apache' for SP/4 Jones who is a full-blood Chipawa Indian.'

There were at least two suicide attempts whilst they were on the site, though, Ken hastens to add, it wasn't because of the music...

Lodgings for the stopover were in the Hotel Launoy, Boulevard De Magenta, a weary, though once-elegant hotel, *en face le Château*, where Cliff, using his seductive charm, negotiated two shared rooms for the five of them, but included in the tariff, at no extra charge and unbeknown to the guests, were resident horseshoe bats.

"They didn't come in every night," laughed Ken, "only when we were *really* tired. It was too hot to close the windows; not that we could—they seemed to be nailed open; but on more than one occasion, we wondered exactly where we were: France or Transylvania."

Obvious jokes abounded, mainly directed at Graham, who hid terrified beneath the bed clothes, as the others swiped hopelessly at the intruders, using their 'grey' rolled up bath-towels.

The forests of Fontainebleau offered an oasis of calm during the day. They could drive out to secluded spots and relax, when Cliff wasn't insisting on a run-through of material, and when they weren't chasing the beautiful indigenous green lizards. Such breaks also kept their mind off food, which they couldn't afford, and made the one meal a day, eaten at the base commissary, seem almost *haute cuisine*.

Playing six nights a week, from seven until midnight, to bored, worried GIs, must have made the Park Attwood seem positively romantic. Whatever breaks they could wangle, they wangled, and, because Cliff was continually losing his voice, whatever instrumentals they knew they adapted on the hoof, speeding them up or slowing them down to avoid noticeable repetition. Terry Clarke's handwritten set list (which includes 'Tchakila'—a scholarly interpretation no doubt...), shows him taking some of the pressure off Cliff for 'Twist And Shout', 'I'm Into Something Good' and 'I'm Walkin''; duetting with Graham down 'Tobacco Road', and Ken helping out on 'Pretty Woman', but the majority of vocals were Cliff's, through choice and natural ability.

Morale was low with the troops, but even lower with the group. This interminable workload, coupled with the being away from home, didn't appeal at all to Cliff. It was certainly not what he, or they, had imagined. Whilst many other musicians would have treated this all as an exercise in career development, or better still, a paid holiday, a chance to maybe sow some wild oats, he really was homesick.

Seeds *were* sown here, however, but in the innermost reaches of his mind, as he sometimes walked the woods of Fontainebleau alone, listening to 'cick-cick' of the yellow-hammers, the 'tap-tap' of the woodpecker, the soft wind in the trees. Or sometimes, on choosing 'a day to myself', he would wander the graveyards of war, now tended by weathered French peasants, and read the names of those who lay beneath the rich soil. He would remember these wanderings years later: the loneliness, the sadness, the desperation; the home thoughts from abroad...

The others, including poor old Graham, who had now taken to wearing garlic necklaces...(sorry, that's a poor joke), had befriended a French student, who worked on the base during summer vacation. One afternoon he journeyed the 50 kilometres or so with them into Paris, then conducted a guided tour of the city whilst expressing his dislike of the bold, brash American visitors, although from what the musicians saw of the UN soldiers, also based in Fontainebleau, there seemed little difference in behaviour. Even in those days, drink, boredom and lack of female company combined to shape a rude, rough soldier.

The following Sunday the student took them to his family home, where a meal was prepared—on that grand French scale—by his bemused parents, and where Cliff, Ken, Terry, Trevor and Graham watched each other nervously as they dined *en famille.*

And so on to the next venue.

Saint-Dizier is situated in the heart of the countryside, on the River Marne, just south-west of Bar-De-Luc, and was once a prosperous industrial town, with iron, steel and copper works, but, following the second world war it became another yet another US Army base, though mainly for storage and maintenance purposes.

With a few week's work under their collective and tightened belts, financially they could now afford a slightly more civilized life-style. An old hotel in the heart of Saint-Dizier, Le Deauville, was used for lodgings, enabling afternoon strolls about town, even coffee at a café for heaven's sake, and the mood generally began to improve, though poor old Graham's lovesick pining for his girlfriend did little to help.

Security at the camp was, for some reason, a lot tighter than at Fontainebleau. The Military Police at the gate insisted upon searching the van at each entry, but in a manner relaxed enough to allow some Marx Brother-type humour from the occupants, as they lined up alongside, 'assuming the position'.

Back at the lodgings, the *maîtresse d'hôtel* took a shine to the innocents abroad and allowed them to use the basement café/club for daytime rehearsals ("Rehearsals??!! Did you say re-*hearsals*?? ...!!"), eventually letting them stage a gig down there on their next night off. Photos and flyers of the hotel were passed around the town, overwritten, in Cliff's scholarly French, '*Nous jouons ici ce soir.*' It was a great success and a bit of extra cash. (Meanwhile, in one of those since-realized coincidences, I was singing 'This Little Bird' on a camp site in Bandol. In the dark, and to myself...)

Two weeks into their residency at the base, they encountered one of those spectacular, though terrifying electric storms. Terry Clarke, the electrical guru, refused to play, citing the decidedly dodgy French power system, fearing electrocution. But there was already an underlying current. The mood of optimism had given way to one of melancholy; they all wanted just to go home. The site manager threatened them with a 'play or be fired' ultimatum: Terry maintained his 'play and be fried' stance, so they quit.

This act of defiance cost them dearly, as the agent's contract allowed him to withhold payment for work already done, which he naturally did. They left for Belgium and the nearest port, the following day. The cruising Secrets were heading for home, somewhat bruised.

"Everyone except Cliff telephoned home to inform relatives of our expected [or unexpected] arrival," said Ken, his manner intimating a shrewd observation. "Maybe he just wanted to walk in on Pat, make sure everything was...as it should be..."

By mid-August they were back home, though somehow still finding the wherewithal to arrange an intensive practice session, over three consecutive nights, at the Mare & Colt.

But the experience of being a professional musician, the 'glamour' of life on the road, had soured Graham's and Trevor's enthusiasm. They continued for a while, recording another single—a cover of the Quotations 1962 Verve/HMV radio-hit 'Imagination'—at EMI (which was never released), until, towards the end of the year, both musicians informed Cliff and Ken that they were leaving.

Various local players were auditioned; Kevin Gammond, a young, precocious guitarist, then fronting Kidderminster's bluesy Shakedown Sounds with vocalist Jess Roden, made an impressive though totally alien appearance; bassist Paul Turner began to alternate with Trevor; organist Dave Floyd made a brief showing; but it was all ifs, buts and maybes.

Well into 1966, Ken received a letter from 'Zep-to-be' Jimmy Page—at that time working for Andrew Loog Oldham's ill-fated Immediate Records—expressing some interest in a demo of 'Infatuation' that he had received. Jimmy had his own in-house production set-up, Freeway Music, albeit run under the Immediate umbrella.

The group were back down to London before the phone was back on the hook, recording at London's historic IBC Studios, with Bill Wyman, Jimmy and producer Glyn Johns in attendance. But despite a contract being offered to Cliff, in his guise as Martin Raynor, the recordings—including the up-front satire 'The Gloria Bosom Show'—never saw the light of day; only a note-for-note cover version by The

Sundowners of the Bosom Song, on Southern Music's low-key Spark label, made the shops. Cliff received a cheque payment of £15 for his contributions, signed by the Rolling Stone Svengali, and seriously contemplated whether to frame it for posterity, that famous signature sprawled across the bottom, but the rent was due...

So. Jimmy Page also enters the frame. I wonder what he remembers of those young heady days?

I was talking to his partner-in-time Robert Plant, the Wolverhampton Wanderer, and just in passing enquired whether he could ask if Jimmy would like to contribute something to the book. I thought no more of it. Robert is always a busy man, his head is forever filled with ideas; recording projects, vintage vinyl, football...which he invariably carries through with such enthusiasm and seemingly boundless energy.

It was 8.45, Monday morning. I'd just spoken to my vet—or should I say my *cat's* vet—and I was waiting for him to call me back.

The phone rang, I picked it up (as you do).

"Is that Dave?" Not Dave Cartwright, mark you—this was a friendly, personal call, though I didn't know the voice.

"This is Jimmy Page."

Stay cool, David. (He doesn't call me very often...)

"I tried to get you yesterday," he continued, "but you weren't answering." (Sunday...)

So this guy didn't give up, he tried me again.

"Robert asked me to give you a ring about Clifford T. Ward." (Robert. What a star.)

"I can't remember too much about those days, it was a long time ago, and a lot of other things have happened since then..."

(Er, yes Jimmy, I believe they have...)

But he continued, in his laid back, laconic, London drawl, as I, ever-ready, scrambled around for a piece of paper, oh, and a pen.

"Anyway, when I was working for Immediate records, as a kind of in-house producer, I had my own publishing company and Cliff Ward sent down this home demo of a song called 'Infatuation'. It just knocked me out. It was so confident, professional, powerful; girls on backing vocals, the works, everything. I went rushing in to see Tony Caulder, who was Andrew's administration guy. I was really excited. But he wasn't interested. Not because he didn't like it, he just wasn't into signing unknowns. He'd got this arrangement in the States with Bob Crewe, who was handling the Four Seasons, whereby he'd bring over backing tracks to hand on to established UK artistes. Apart from The Faces—for obvious reasons—he just wasn't interested in newcomers. I managed to sorted out a little publishing deal for Cliff, we did a bit of recording, but that was about it. And we all got swindled anyway, so

maybe it was a good thing nothing big happened along.
"I thought he was a wonderfully original pop writer. I'd like to have given him a bigger break than I did, but in those days my hands were well and truly tied. His talent had to come through somewhere, and even though I was on top of the world myself when it did happen, I was really pleased for him."
And here's the contract, right in front of me. A standard form courtesy of The Solicitors' Law Stationery Office, headed in super-scroll print, 'An Agreement'—no doubt purchased from the corner shop in their hundreds by hopeful entrepreneurs during the sixties music boom—and completed by the typist-receptionist. It was something else to do between filing royalty statements and fingernails.
Officially it ran for five years, commencing 1st July, 1966. Clifford's address at Habberley and young Jimmy's Epsom home location precede the statement that 'The Artiste is desirous of performing as a professional singer/musician under the name of Martin Raynor…' then follow the usual forms of contract; the promises, the exclusions, the royalty rates (halved for all records sold outside of Great Britain) the traditional 'hereunders' and 'notwithstandings', and then Jimmy's bold signature, over a sixpenny stamp.
The agreement, however, was never fully consummated, despite his obvious belief in the artiste.
For a few lucky people, things were to move faster than anyone could have imagined over the coming years, but sadly, not for Martin Raynor.

And so it went on. Trevor finally called it a day, and went back on the night shift, more musicians were checked out, there was a rather heated 'discussion' between Cliff and the Mercian Agency boys, Ray Northover and Carl Hasdell and another fruitless London meeting with Jimmy Page. Lead guitarist Graham Drew unplugged himself, putting rhythm player Terry Clarke into the front seat, and substitute bassist Paul Turner decided to concentrate more fully on his sewing machines (should have been a Singer then…), prompting a cautiously worded advertisement in *Brum Beat*—Ma Regan's all-powerful tabloid newsheet of the local music scene—whereupon Malcolm Russell, a Smethwick-based bassman, stepped into the vacant slot, just in time for a summer tour of coastal resorts, along the 'English Riviera'.
All through September, this line-up—seemingly now and forever to be in a state of flux—practised rigorously at Terry's house in Wolverley, with record companies still showing interest enough for Cliff to be constantly urging the band on and on and on, '…it's got to be right…' He thought they were almost there when, after another arduous three-hour rehearsal, Terry let it be known that he was off to join brother Phil in Australia; er, next week. The practice was quickly terminated…

Taking it well in their stride, Cliff and Ken ran around like headless chickens. With London bookings and another tour lined up, who could save them? Casually, in his dry, nasal accent, Malcolm mentioned a friend of his from Birmingham, Fred Nash. Fred was brought along and found to be a more than competent lead, quickly picking his way through the band's repertoire in time for a mid-October gig in London, where they played The Flamingo night-spot, sharing the newcomers' fee of £10 between them...

Further publicity came in the glamorous frame of Gloria Bosom herself, as Teresa Oakley, now embarking on a modelling career, began a brief, but quite fictitious spell as road-manager to the boys, ensuring newspaper coverage quite beyond the call of duty. In the dear old *Daily Sketch*, Saturday December 3rd, on Shirley Flack's Boy/Girl page, she stands in front of the group—who are precariously perched atop the old van, drums and all—Avenger-like, wearing '... a gold trouser suit in pure wool, by Ivan Goujon, with a long feather boa she bought at Biba.' A great piece of promotion for all concerned: it was a national daily, the newly-released single was mentioned, and Cliff and the boys were seen by millions. Similar pictures of Teresa, in Radio Luxembourg's very own *Fab 208* magazine, Dennis Detheridge's *Midland Beat* and various other musical weeklies—besides prompting the formation of her very own fan club, via 'Sig. S. Green, 1st Royal Scots, in BFPO 36, Germany'—ensured maximum exposure, whilst also bringing her frequently within the arms of her drummer boy, though only for the camera.

This was to be the final line-up of any Cliff Ward group, and hence the last-gasp attempt by the singer to break into the highly competitive beat-group scene. Dropping his alter-ego Martin Raynor, and instead using the collective name The Secrets, he enlisted Cornishman Eddie Trevett—whom he had met whilst on tour of the south-west—to produce a first single for CBS, having signed the publishing rights of 'I Suppose' to Terry Oates, a one-desk, one-phone set-up off Denmark Street. Working from his office above IBC Studios, where he ran his own publishing company, Eddie was one of popland's early freelance record producers. Under the clever pseudonym of T. V. Music—implying media connections—he recorded, and subsequently took, whatever publishing was available from those struggling artistes who passed through the swing doors below.

'I Suppose' was released on December 2nd, with another of Cliff's songs, 'Such A Pity' (assigned to T. V. Music...), becoming Cliff's first record bearing his name as songwriter, before they set out on a cold, dreary mini-tour of South Wales.

Fred Nash's brief introduction to fame and fortune was made all the more nerve-shattering with Ken crashing the van on one of the dimly lit hairpins, in a well-meaning but foolhardy attempt to reach London overnight for a publicity event next morning at the Russian Embassy no less. Mercian had amazingly managed a dream promotion based on a cold-war 'Secret's Out' angle to promote the record. They didn't make it, what with Cliff's bloodied nose and well-fired temper, and Moscow probably breathed a sigh of relief.

Between March and December The Secrets had played over 150 bookings, without any particular route-plan. Tenby one night, Stourbridge the next; Chateau Impney, Droitwich, another night, Llandrindod Wells the next; scattered between the other famous, but now long-gone venues that roll off the tongue of memory: Brum's Rum Runner, Cedar Club, Silver Blades and the Adelphi; The Chalet, Rednal; Three Men In A Boat, Walsall—where fame would call on Robert Plant a few years later—Oldbury's Hen & Chickens, Walsall Town Hall. They were a great band, but they weren't rich…and they weren't famous.

Thank goodness it was time for the festivities.

GIVE ME ONE MORE CHANCE

O sacred hunger of ambitious minds.

Edmund Spenser: *The Faerie Queene*

And so another year.

But 1967 became Sergeant Pepper's year, and as the flag of psychedelia waved above the streets of London, great changes rolled across the world. The musical *Hair* hit the stage in East Greenwich, New York; de-segregation became law in Alabama; Great Britain—despite being vetoed by France—made a successful application to join the EEC, and, as if a failing career wasn't enough to upset Cliff Ward, the Conservative party enjoyed massive gains in the borough elections.

The Secrets had started the year determined to break their run of, well, not bad luck, more *no* luck. For the January edition of *Midland Beat* they were given the whole front page, serious and stylistic, dressed in their Brummel jackets (borrowed from Bob Tansley's Mr Casual Boutique), telling the world—well the Midlands—of Cliff's developing prowess as a songwriter, advertising the new single and also mentioning drummer Ken Wright's novelty routine, '...performing an intriguing Lennon-McCartney routine on gazoo [*sic*]'. Nice one, Ken.
They were undoubtedly as good as, if not better, than many others who *had* succeeded; it was just a matter of time...
Before what though?
January 13th found The Secrets once again at IBC, for their next CBS single 'Infatuation', assigned in yet another one-off deal to Kassner Associated Publishers Ltd, with Eddie Trevett once more picking up rights to the B-side, 'She's Dangerous', then as the month ended, in a year that would see the world wearing flowers in its hair, gentle, smiling blond-haired Simon Ward was born at home. With three children cramped into a small council house, it was time to think about moving. They did think about it, but of course it was an impossible task. The local council was actually debating the issues of offering cheap mortgages for first time buyers, but with what little Cliff was earning—though briefly supplemented by a Saturday job at the

boutique, where, apparently, he was an excellent salesman—the stigma of being a self-employed musician relegated them to the bottom of the heap; they would have to stay put for the moment.

In February, yet another two tracks, 'I Intend To Please', coupled with the appropriately titled 'I Think I Need The Cash', were recorded, both songs on this occasion published by T. V. Music. 'Infatuation' was released within the scheduled five weeks, but CBS held back on this next single until 23rd June, but by then, of course, the music world was preoccupied with other things.

Looking back at these records, it is possible to understand why the media, and thus the public, ignored The Secrets' singles. The recordings themselves stand up extremely well, as assured as all Cliff's previous recordings—demos or otherwise—but the songs, though good and capable, are too off-beat, too erudite. None of Cliff's early, pre-Dandelion efforts were instantly appealing enough to give any real indication of the singular talent he was to become, when he did at last find simplicity and his own, true sound.

And if that isn't enough reason, just take a look at the competition:

February-March saw amongst many others: 'Let's Spend The Night Together', 'I'm A Believer', 'Hey Joe', 'Penny Lane'/'Strawberry Fields' and 'Mellow Yellow'; June-July only got better, with: 'Whiter Shade Of Pale', 'Waterloo Sunset', 'Paper Sun', 'San Francisco' and 'All You Need Is Love'. Really, what chance was there? 'Twas the Summer Of Love, and it wasn't just the gonads that were in full swing.

The once-healthy optimism had now soured, and they split from the Kidderminster Mercian Agency in February. It had been a difficult partnership, exacerbated by an ambitious contract guaranteeing a minimum of £1000 within the first six months and £5000 after 18 months: this at a time when groups were commanding only £30-50 per night. Ken traded the Transit war-horse for a Mini-van, then took up an offer to deputize with Jimmy Cliff at Nottingham's Beachcomber night-spot in March, joining former acolyte Kevin Gammond, who had rightly fulfilled his potential as a young guitarist.

Nevertheless, Ken remained on loyal standby. Eddie's agency arm, T. V. Management, based in Seaton, East Devon, secured a couple more gigs for The Secrets, one at London's Tiles Nightclub, the other at the Purple Fez, in Plymouth ('Smart dress at all times, please—and take that stupid 'at off...') and, as the multi-coloured summer began, they were offered a second BBC audition. Nothing, however, clouded his pragmatism. Despite having no financial responsibilities other than to himself, he joined a firm of chartered accountants in Bromsgrove, before moving to Steel Stampings in Cookley, where he enlisted Pat as his secretary...

Then, just as all around seemed to be fading, they were advised that the audition had been successful, and almost immediately The Secrets were booked for a coveted radio spot: a 'Monday, Monday' special for the BBC, to be recorded at London's Paris Studios on 7th August, hosted by Dave Cash, with Cat Stevens headlining.

It was only Cliff's second broadcast, and he wanted it to be right. Almost eighteen months had passed since The Cruisers had promoted 'Candy To Me' on Radio Luxembourg, but here they were being asked to perform *three* songs, on national radio. It meant practice…

Worcester organist Tony Scriven was enlisted to augment the group, and they spent a couple of long nights rehearsing at Pete King's café in Stourport, until all seemed to be to Cliff's satisfaction. The evening before they were due to go down to London, he and Pat arranged to meet Ken and his girlfriend Maggie, plus a few friends, at the Running Horse in Bewdley for a celebratory drink, a rare occurrence indeed.

"We had parked the car and were heading for the doorway, when Cliff started to retch," Pat recalls. "At first I wasn't too alarmed, he'd done it once or twice before. He hated socializing, this fear of being on show, having to be just right, but this time he was quite sick. I stood helplessly by for about ten minutes, then it was all over."

Ken drove the group down next morning, guiding the small convoy into the Paris car-park. Cliff seemed in fine spirits, occasionally joking, but obviously on edge. A quick sound-check, a coffee, and they were ready to roll.

Theme tune, a few words from Dave Cash, then, in front of the polite, cue-card audience, as Cat Stevens finishes 'Matthew and Son', they are ushered onto the stage, to sing their new single, 'I Intend To Please'.

The song itself, with stuttering rhythm and eloquent lyric, comes over well, but though Ken's drumming is as assured as ever, Cliff's vocal is pitched much too low. The courteous 'Workers' Playtime' applause—backs upright, radio-smiles, no cheering—brings back Dave Cash to make some biting remark about first-timers (Cliff had nervously replaced the microphone back to front), before The County Set launch into sing-along-a-Woody, with 'This Land Is Your Land'.

Originally booked to perform three numbers, the hazards of live broadcasting then become only too apparent for them. As Joe Tex and the Ray McVay Sound overrun, The Secrets have to drop 'Sympathy', a forthcoming B-side, in favour of their third choice.

And here begins a mystery. They launch into a song musically equal to the first, and easily more commercial than the chosen second; the wonderfully catchy 'Two People':

> One thing I can say for her she tries;
> Though she knows he's not worth any tears, she cries…

A great, bouncy 4/4 song, it is nevertheless hopelessly under-rehearsed, with the organist stabbing in the dark towards the end, the performance is saved by Cliff's marvellous vocal and the band's tight harmonies; but whence cometh the song?
Cliff insists he wrote it: "...Why else would I have sung it, David ?" though neither Pat nor Ken Wright believe this. I found the lyrics written on one of Ken's lead sheets, and he remembers Tony learning the organ riffs from a recording, yet where the song came from, no-one knows. PRS have 45 songs entitled 'Two People', none of them credited to Cliff—or Clifford—T. Ward. Maybe it came from the T. V. Music catalogue, but nowadays, in his secret retreat in the New Forest, Eddie Trevett is in retirement, a millionaire property magnate. He owns the masters to all his productions, including the Secrets recordings, and must have a wealth of unreleased demos, but is reluctant to talk of such times, letting his wife—ex-'Golden Shot' hostess Ann Aston—intercept all calls and enquiries in her overtly insouciant manner.
So it could have been an IBC demo Ken remembers. With his prodigious output at that time, Cliff Ward was Eddie Trevett's 'in-house' songwriter, and dozens of his numbers would have passed over to T. V. Music, only to disappear into the shadowland that was Eddie's domain. There, other hopefuls: Peter and The Wolf, with lead singer (the now) Rev. John Pantry (aka Norman Conquest...); The Factory, and one Ray Carlson, who recorded a Cliff Ward throwaway, 'It's Getting Me Down Girl', as the B-side to his MGM single 'Speak No Sorrow', stood in line, waiting to be produced by—with rights assigned to—Eddie Trevett.
Starmakers and Svengalis indeed...
'Monday, Monday' was broadcast at 1.00 p.m. on 28th August, by which time the music world was totally preoccupied with the news of Brian Epstein's death. (The music world, that is, apart from Ken, who was smelling the roses at a Woburn Abbey flower festival, and Cliff, who, after sitting with the family at home critically analysing his performance, had slammed the door, and trounced upstairs to fret.)
And so this was to be his last group appearance. What had been seen as the big media break—Radio One no less—only served to exacerbate his growing disillusionment with the music business. He had given it a fair crack of the whip, had felt confident that he would make it, only to find, like the thousands of others out there who still held on to their childhood dreams, that it was nothing but a minefield of disappointments and despair. His pride, his upbringing, his duty as a father; signing on the dole just wasn't right. And so, whilst still convinced of his potential—and thus certainly not throwing in the towel—but with a wife and family to consider, he took a deep breath

and filled out an application form. With his love of language and books, and a market demand for new teachers, there was an open opportunity. He was going back to school.

Worcester Teacher Training Centre—now re-named 'University College', and accepting all manner of academia—is on the west side of the 'Faithful City', facing the river and the famous racecourse. Clifford was accepted for the September 1967 intake, to read English and Divinity.

Back home, after dressing the children and hoovering the rug, Pat continued her compliant but increasingly essential role—as bedmaker, breadmaker *and* breadwinner—working the twilight shift at Naylor's Carpets. Her brief spell with Ken Wright at Cookley had ended.

Throughout that seemingly fruitless autumn, Cliff's brain went into top gear. His studies were important, but the pop-muse would not relent. More demos were arranged, this time using the Worcester Cross public house, a big Edwardian mausoleum situated at the bottom of Comberton Hill, and, on Sunday mornings, Leon's little bedroom set-up. These were not group demos as such—though further releases were planned—but consisted mainly of Ken, Cliff and Ken's old jazz guitarist-friend, Bev Pegg, who over-dubbed 12-string guitar, lead and bass on these sessions, for more new songs 'Naughty Boy' and 'Coathanger'. They had met before, when Bev had gone to see The Cruisers perform at The Black Horse, but these demo sessions were his first workings with Cliff in the musical sense, and prompted Bev to step even more strongly into the picture, offering his state-of-the-art garage studio, where he would subsequently combine his talents further, as producer.

The year 1968 saw Cliff turning up for lectures, laden with books, and spending hours in the library, poring over Thomas Hardy, Nathaniel Hawthorne and Laurie Lee, reading the classical poetry of Keats and Wordsworth, plus modernists such as Philip Larkin and Thom Gunn. Despite his distinct aversion towards employment—other than music related—he settled remarkably well into teacher-training, accepting student life, and its consequences of work within the profession, as an image-honourable compromise. The literary side was of particular appeal—he had always enjoyed reading—and would no doubt help sharpen his already well-developed aptitude for musical word-play, and there were indeed irons still resting in the fire…

Blue Mountain Music, Island Record's publishing arm, after showing mild interest, eventually signed him to contract and, in April of the 'new term', Cliff Ward and his not-so-merry band, this time under the *nom de vinyl* of Simon's Secrets, again on the CBS label, released probably the most commercial of his beat-group songs, 'Naughty Boy' b/w 'Sympathy' (here strangely credited to Pat Rollings, and which would blossom many years later on Dandelion).

But there was also a subtle and, indeed, very secretive change in line-up for this newly named group.

After the positive negativity shown to their last three singles, The Secrets had decided to take a rest. Well, in fact, disband. Malcolm and Fred went back to Birmingham and were not heard of again, musically speaking, whilst Ken, with a characteristic shrug of his shoulders, continued with his dance-band drumming by night and his numeracy by day.

Cliff, though seemingly immersed in his teacher-training, still dreamed of pop success and so, unbeknown to Ken (??!!)—still living and working in the area *and* helping with the occasional demos—he had enlisted Ian Simmonds, brother of erstwhile rhythm guitarist Rodney, and *his* group, the Bridge St. Jump Band: Dave Holder on bass, Davie Conway on rhythm and Rob Elcock on drums. A ready-made unit. All they had to do was learn the songs, which they did.

Ken, astonishingly, knew nothing of the singles until their release, reading a preview of 'Naughty Boy' on April 5th, in the music section of the *Shuttle*. [On the very same page, tucked away in the right hand corner, Dave Cartwright makes a guest appearance at the Worcester Cross 'Folk Evening', never to recover…]

By the time the second single, 'Keeping My Head Above Water', appeared, some eight months later, though somewhat bemused, he was only too glad to disassociate himself from the '… wasp in a tin can' drum sound.

Demo activity at Bev's house continued as if nothing untoward had happened. Again, true to his colours, Cliff felt obliged to explain nothing. And no-one dared ask.

Tucked away in that garage-studio in Kinver, they put down more songs and more demos, including a couple of frantic sessions recording Indigo Set vocalist, Colin Youngjohns, Kidderminster's answer to P. J. Proby. (I tell you, Kidderminster had an answer for everything…)

But where exactly had Bev Pegg come from? Well, it's a slight diversion, but it's relevant.

In 1971, after almost four years of endless but, admittedly, very enjoyable gigging throughout the country, playing in virtually every folk club and university in the land, I signed my first recording contract. A keen, but ineffective management company, with impressive, but top-floor 'attic' offices in the London Haymarket, had failed, despite encouraging noises, to sign me to, amongst others showing interest, the CBS giant. So, after a prolonged, though low-key dispute, I ran away and found myself a much less prestigious—but acceptable—deal with Nathan Joseph's friendly little folk label, Transatlantic.

I was living in Bewdley at the time with my wife Carole and our two young children, having turned professional at the end of 1970, after abandoning a 'promising' suit-bedecked career with Sandvik Swedish Steels. Many, many years earlier, I had become totally obsessed (but, as time would tell, not committed or confident enough) with rock'n'roll. I could quote singers, songs, labels, dates, birthdays, charts, third lines, whatever; but, despite forming and fronting precocious local groups, including the instantly forgettable 'Downbeats' and 'Crossfires', and, finally, between 1960-62, Kidderminster's own raw rock'n'rollers, 'The Clippers', I had not found musical compatibility. Then came Dylan and the folk boom. Suddenly, pubs and clubs throughout the land became meeting places for self-contained singer-songwriter-guitarists. There were folk festivals, folk circuits and folk media opportunities a-plenty, and the record industry, with its ever-present opportunism, saw gold. Solo albums became viable, introspection became the key. A man with a guitar (oh, yes there were women too, but not so many…) could play to hushed audiences hanging on every word, *and* make a damn good living. Having already been through rock'n'roll, country, even a brief flirtation with jazz, I had at last found my niche. And it was so easy…except that it was, in retrospect, almost underground, an acquired taste, what today we call Specialized Music.

But all this development in *my* career had been made possible, in no small a way, because of the help and encouragement received from Bev Pegg, an old-time acquaintance. A prosperous Black Country industrialist's son, Bev had now married and moved to the picture-book village of Kinver, with its sandstone cliffs, rolling heaths and acres of National Trust woodland, where most of his spare time, away from managing his father's business in smoke-stained Cradley, was spent running a small recording set-up from his garage adjoining the wonderfully appointed home in which he lived with his vivacious wife, Heather. An extremely talented and respected guitarist, he had initially learnt classical piano, via his parents' semi-professional status in the world of light operetta, before turning to boogie-woogie, rock'n'roll and then discovering the fast, technical guitar styles of Eddie Lang and Django Reinhardt. His speed, expertise and, infectious enthusiasm stand undiminished to this day. At that time, Bev was also becoming attracted to the newly blossoming post-Woodstock singer-songwriter scene, supplementing his extensive and remarkably catholic record collection with the sounds of the New Americans, whose laid-back, hypnotic style appealed to his love for guitar-based music. He never made it to Woodstock…but had managed the Isle Of Wight, where the now-legendary stage performances further fuelled his obsession. From his earlier jazz days, he had maintained a close friendship with Ken Wright, whom he'd met via clarinettist Rick Vaughan (Rick's house was later used for the inner-sleeve pictures on *Home Thoughts*. Trivial?…moi?).

This was way back in the heady, halcyon days of Stourport Jazz Club, where the Three Counties' well-heeled teenagers gathered every Saturday evening, spilling out onto the balcony overlooking the shining Severn and where, Bev recalls, somewhat ruefully, he had first met his future wife…

"After a succession of keen drummers, we [The Blue Blood Jazzmen] decided that, with Rick, myself and trombonist Duncan Swift, a fairly good band would, with a tighter rhythm section, become an exceptional band. Rick was keen to get Ken into the line-up." So Duncan drew the short straw and matter-of-factly told the current drummer and double-bass player that they were to be replaced forthwith. Exit two unhappy musicians. Bev and Ken hit it off immediately. "We developed a rapport that, to me, was wonderful. Up until that time, I'd never played with a drummer who listened; to words, phrasing, mood, whatever. He was, and still is, an incredibly intelligent musician, I regard him as one of the best jazz drummers of his time. We also shared the same sense of humour, which is always a bonus."

Around that time—early 1963—far ahead of almost everyone else, Bev had started home recording, purely for his own amusement, experimenting with overdubbing on a Cossor two-track, one of the earliest affordable domestic machines available in this country. It was mainly instrumental jazz standards, Les Paul, Wout Steinhous overlay technique, no other musicians required. Simultaneously, The Blue Bloods flowed on quite happily, until, one weekend, via local entrepreneur Carl Hasdell, Ken was asked if he would play for Kidderminster pop group, Cliff Ward and The Cruisers. Their drummer, Roger 'Butch' Bowen, was indisposed, so Ken went along. It was a few quid, and it would add another line, or drum-roll, to his CV.

The Blue Bloods carried on with a new drummer, but Bev felt that the best times were over. With the advent of the beat-group sound, the jazz club lost its impetus, and, though bravely struggling on through 1964, it eventually folded.

Times indeed, were a-changing. The Beatles had levelled the teenage social scene virtually overnight, removing the 'us-and-them' traditional snobbery that for so long had symbolized the class strata, and local pop groups began to replace jazz bands at rugby club dances and pig roasts. Bev moved upmarket and further afield, backing jazz legend Ken Rattenbury for the next couple of years on a part-time, three- evenings-a-week basis, whilst remaining true to *his* tradition, the family foundry.

In whatever spare time he could find, however, he continued to expand his studio set-up, helped by ex-Cruiser and electrical guru Terry Clarke, who had since returned from Australia, with dreams of breaking into the studio recording business.

The Antipodean Adventure had run its course. The niche in the down-under market that brother Philip had spotted for discos had blossomed into a small empire. Terry had joined him and together they enjoyed a successful two years, opening a chain of dance clubs and clothes shops, before Philip got homesick. Terry, considering his earlier experiences with The Cruisers, stayed over, joined a rock group and spent another year travelling through the outback playing to the cork-hat boozers at joints and halls, whilst spending all his spare time—of which there seemed to be plenty, with two weeks on, two weeks off each month—utilizing his ex-Decca electrical skills, repairing amplifiers, record decks, anything he could lay his hands on. But after a while, even this became a 'one step forward, two steps back' situation. Beset by insecurity and financial hardship, the nadir of which caused him to throw his prized Rickenbacker 360-12 into dear old Botany Bay for an insurance claim, he came home in 1969, determined to set himself up as a recording engineer, but found this virtually a closed shop. So he turned to audio equipment, initially approaching Bev with a view to investment and partnership. To his everlasting regret, Bev didn't see a future in it.

"I was ploughing whatever profits I could from the family business into re-investment or steel stockholding. I thought the recording game, not the steel industry, was on a downward path. I subsequently lost a fortune…But…" grinning resignedly, "that's life, Dave…"

Terry and his first wife Angela were then living in a poky flat in Wribbenhall, Bewdley (which CTW guitarist Derek Thomas moved into some years later), and finding life a bit hard, to say the least. But at least it was home territory. He somehow persuaded Lloyds Bank to put up the financial assistance he needed, and once again went into business with his brother Philip. This time they succeeded, both eventually becoming multi-millionaires, as their truly innovative company, Clarke-Technik, swept the field in the recording industry, supplying quality hardware to international artistes and major recording studios world-wide.

But back then, he was installing machinery for Bev, who, after splashing out further on a couple of 'state-of-the-art' Bang & Olufsen reel-to-reel tape recorders, various BBC quality microphones and other exorbitantly expensive (for their day) pieces of equipment, *and* making a few demos himself, felt confident enough to start recording other people. Still being in touch with Ken Wright, Cliff had been an obvious first choice, and 'twas so, dear reader, that they came together.

But again, Cliff could be persuaded—though always on his terms—to indulge in schoolboy humours. Bev has always been a natural joker; an early incarnation being his one-man mime act, dressed in bowler hat and pin-stripe suit, miming to Johnny Bond country and western 78s, or Stan Freberg's wonderful pop-parodies. So, whenever a session seemed to lose direction, Bev would be 'in like Flynn', and music would, for that half-hour or so, play second fiddle. There were also plenty of amateur musicians that could be called upon to help with the demos, and thus assist in the juvenilia. When Ken wasn't available—maybe taking a well-earned break from it all—builder-drummer Pete Burke, arch-goon-pianist Adrian Fenwick and lovable guitarist Harry Rowlands would be only too eager to play the fool, and Cliff, naturally, was not to be outdone, bless him.

'Now I am a man, I will cast off childish things'…

Not quite.

December soon came in, her cold wind blowing, freezing the roads, dampening the spirit, as Cliff continued his studies, homeworking and babywatching at night, whilst Pat shuttled her loom (if you'll pardon the expression).

In the dying days of the year, with Lily in the pink (after holding off stiff competition from Des O'Connor and Hugo Montenegro…), his last pop single was released. Simon's Secrets and 'I Know What Her Name Is'; a vain attempt at raising the decibels—literally ringing them out for the season of goodwill—coupled with the whimsically appropriate 'Keeping My Head Above Water', sank into the unfathomable depths, and, though perplexed, but probably breathing a quiet sigh of relief, Cliff accepted that his beat-group days, together with yet another year, had finally come to an unremarkable end.

But suddenly January blows in and there is other work to be done.

In his final year as a student, Cliff wanted to do well. There was much at stake; a growing family and maybe, if all went well, they could move into their own house. And, again, who knows? Maybe one of his songs would click.

He wasn't the only one thinking this way, although his persistence was admirable, considering his misfortune thus far.

I started recording demos with a vengeance about this time, at Bev's house during the spring of 1969, and Ken was there to back me up, musically speaking. I didn't know him until the sessions began, and I certainly hadn't met Cliff, nor was I aware of his connection with these two, but we seemed to get along, though I was never an easy mixer. Through March, April and May, we recorded, and Bev ran Cliff and me in parallel, keeping his cards close to his chest, although I have to admit, I never showed interest in anything other than what *I* was doing at the time. I'd become, like everyone else, totally single-minded, and for me, if it didn't have acoustic guitars and harmonica, I wasn't in.

I knew Bev from those privileged Stourbridge 'jazz-circle' days of the late 50s, and had, quite coincidentally, bumped into him recently during a lunch-break in Halesowen. Having only recently—and thus very lately in life—broken through the 'first-song' barrier, I was now writing them by the dozen and couldn't wait to run round and record.

Despite living so close to him (Bewdley was equidistant from Stourport and Kidderminster) it was not until arriving here, in that welcoming haven of sound, one night a little earlier than usual, that I was first introduced to Cliff Ward. Unbeknown to me (and not that I would have minded at all), Bev had asked Cliff to try some backing vocals for one of my songs, but for some technical reason it wasn't used. Crashing into the studio, 12-string guitar in tow, I found this sad, serious looking bloke sitting at the piano. Bev introduced us. All I remember, after the initial handshake, was Clifford asking me something about songs and inspiration. Did I just make them up, or were they based on particular happenings, etc.? As I was writing mostly about fairies, goblins and unicorns at the time, I told him, quite sheepishly, to draw his own conclusions…

"Dave was a terrific performer and writer," says Bev, "though in no way could you say he was writing 'pop' songs. I'm sure if he'd tried there would have been absolutely no problem, but he'd seen Peter, Paul and Mary [especially Mary…], The Springfields, Bob Dylan and actually sung with Tom Paxton, and that was it. He was smitten by the folk bug. He'd swopped his Harmony electric guitar for a 12-string acoustic and quickly, *very* quickly, learned harmonica, seeing himself as, well, I dunno, Dave-Sebastian-Dylan-Cartwright. I thought he really was wonderful. We eventually completed an album of Dave's songs, with Ken on some tracks, called *In The Middle Of The Road*, which I suppose was exactly where he was; Dave's cry for guidance. A push either way would have convinced him where to go, he was that indecisive. Cliff, on the other hand, knew *exactly* where *he* was going. He didn't have Dave's lyrical precision, the superbly well-metered 'poem-music', which was Dave's forte, but his voice, melodic structure, word-form—and single-mindedness—was very, very Pop. He would never say, as Dave did all the time, 'Oh, that'll do. On to the next!' No, with Cliff, it was always, 'Let's try it again,' or, '*You* play this note, Bev, *you* play that. Ken, *you* do *this* on the snare. Bev I want more … (whatever) in the mix. Come on, let's do it again.' Also, to be quite honest, Dave wasn't the natural recording artiste that Clifford was, and subsequently developed a positive hatred for recording. Dave was a born entertainer, his reputation being deservedly built on his live performances *par excellence.* I remember him doing Glasgow Apollo—a notorious graveyard for solo acts—supporting Irish folk-rock group Horslips, on St Patrick's night!! He bought the place down. Incredible. But he didn't take anything seriously enough, especially his recordings. He wasn't assertive like Cliff. He would go home, leave me his stuff, '... do what you want with it ...' You couldn't touch anything of Cliff's without him being there. Though they had many similar characteristics, they were also complete opposites. Cliff on record exuded confidence, yet he wouldn't play live; Dave, as soon as the red light came on, lost his nerve. He always sounded uncertain on record, yet put him in front of 15,000 people, and he'd set the place alight. When it came to recording, Cliff was the Master; Dave was always the Slave..."

One of the many vignettes committed to tape, in Bev's collection, illustrates, even at this early stage, the CTW session atmosphere for which he was to become so notorious. Here after numerous attempts at a take, Ken and Bev, as a result of some off-mike childish comment from one or the other, can be heard giggling childishly. Cliff, after a few more tries, shouts, "What the bloody hell's the matter! Don't you like the bloody song?!" reprimanding them as if they were a couple of mischievous schoolboys. Needless to say, the take *was* completed, and to Clifford's satisfaction. Again, that is *not* to say he was without humour, very far from it, but it was always on his terms, when *he* was ready. "He was *very* hard to work with," concludes Bev, "a perfectionist to the extreme, a natural, a born studio musician, and that's why, of course, it paid off. People buy records."

And so it continued throughout the summer, demos and more demos, both at the Kinver studio and, in Cliff's case, also at Leon Tipler's Radio G-LTK set-up in Kidderminster, interrupted only by the council agreeing to advance Cliff and Pat a mortgage for their first house. The forms were duly completed, following numerous grillings by the housing department regarding Pat's possible loss of income should she become pregnant again (to which she had calmly replied, 'I can't *have* any more children. Honest.'), and the Ward clan, seven-year-old Debbie, six-year-old Martin (?Raynor) and two-year-old Simon (as in Secrets?), with their young, outwardly conventional parents, moved into their first proper home, a new development just off Kidderminster's Land Oak crossroads. The bright and shiny Oaklands.

Here, with a little more space, was where the songs began to develop. The piano Pat had used since childhood—a quality mahogany upright—was installed in the lounge and Cliff began experimenting. Before long, however, other needs took precedence; he needed a better microphone, a larger amplifier and so, without any real considerations, he advertised the instrument for sale. A local school paid the asking price, and so began the task of finding something a lot less ornate, but still playable. He was subsequently offered, free-of-charge, on condition that he collected it, an old upright 'joanna' by Ken Wright's brother, David, landlord of The Green Man, a notorious Kidderminster watering hole, where Cliff had sometimes worked as a barman, serving, for sure, many old school friends, including, on one occasion, Ray Hume.

"He didn't waste much time talking," laughs Ray. "Just a 'Hi, Ray', and he was gone. Considering all those times we had as kids, fishing, bonfires, nesting…"

But, back to the piano. Together with Kevin Gammond and a few public-house-spirited helpers, they transported the iron-framed machine up to Cliff's new house, where, after just one look, it was left to stand in silence in the garage until taken *away* again by Kevin. Another upright was found via the local rag, and eventually positioned in the tiny lounge-cum-dining room, where, within a week, Cliff had painted it a lovely shade of green.

Ken, meanwhile, took a step that was to prove rewarding to all concerned. He applied for a position with the BBC in London, er…as an accountant. But not just any accountant. He was quite obviously ready for promotion on the ladder of er…accountancy and so, after two rigorous interviews, conducted within the hushed corridors of Portland Place, he was deservedly offered the post, to commence on October 1st, 1969. This man was definitely going places.

Not so long after he'd put his feet under the desk, Cliff, together with Terry Clarke, went down to visit him, and they all went to see *The Wild Bunch* (*re*ally…) at the Odeon, Leicester Square, where, on a warm October evening, for one of the few occasions, they acted normally; no musical business discussions pending.

But within a month, Ken was on holiday, albeit back at Bev's, doing some demos for me, which resulted in my going down—all dressed up—to London on 28th November for a chat with publisher Andrew Heath, after which I later met Ken for a drink. Ken doesn't miss a trick. As I walked towards him, feeling conspicuously smart, he greeted me:

'Jeans in the wash, David?'

Simultaneously, Cliff had completed his training course at Worcester, after submitting an impressive thesis on Theodore Dreiser, a little known American author, whose work had actually been introduced to him by… Ken Wright.

After seeing *A Place In The Sun*—the powerful screen adaptation of Dreiser's *An American Tragedy*, starring Montgomery Clift, Elizabeth Taylor, and Shelley Winters as the unfortunate wife—Ken had bought a complete set of his works—which incidentally includes *Sister Carrie*—before recommending, and passing, them on to Cliff, who read and

immediately entered the obscure Dreiser for his main college thesis.
Even then, away from the music, Ken Wright had been there, dependable as ever, pointing the way from *his* place in the shadows, as he would continue to do, so many times, in the glory years ahead.
"Cliff had absorbed the intellectual life-style like a sponge," Ken remarks. "His whole outlook, appearance, even his accent, became noticeably refined. His letters to me, in London, were full of literary references and clichés. I thought they were rather pretentious. He was trying very hard to impress."
Be that as it may—for education is the whole idea of going to college—there is one part of a letter, written 19th January, 1970, during his final year, which I find personally quite touching.
Here is man, having resorted to teaching, after temporarily failing as a pop musician, corresponding about Kidderminster, local politics and, inevitably, forthcoming demo recordings. He is still pursuing his dream, and yet, upon hearing that someone else (i.e. me—at that time in the process of signing a publishing contract) is seeming to succeed writes, "… I've heard nothing from Immediate and am undecided about what to do. What is the situation with Dave [Cartwright]? I do hope it materialises …"
I find that a genuinely surprising emotion. Not because it's Cliff, I didn't know him personally then. But for a musician who is having very little luck to wish well of one who is—albeit fleetingly—shows to me a great generosity of spirit, and one which I wish I'd been aware of at the time; I would have made a greater effort to befriend him.
Interestingly, the letter ends:

> I am making an application, meanwhile, for the Open University, about which, you've no doubt heard. I forwarded your name also, so you will be receiving prospectus and application form; I thought you might be interested.
> Well, I will close and go about my business; or is it pleasure?
>
> See you soon, Cliff.

On the 24th March he enthuses, with his neat, flowing hand, about involvement in school and the completion of his studies:

> … How is everything with you? And, as everything that could possibly follow up that clichét [*sic*] question could only be even more clichét I will once again become the Freudian egotist and resume talking about myself.
> Teaching practice has ended, and I have enjoyed it enormously! My morning assembly, which I told you about, was

> tumultously [*sic*] successful and the hall was filled with spontaneous applause.
> The dance was even more successful with The Reflections [ex-bassist Trevor Jones's new group] playing very well and impressing everyone—including the headmaster! We raised £25 for the Spastics. I even danced with the kids and had a most unusually good time ...

Almost Victorian in its phrasing, but more noticeable—and more so to those who saw him only occasionally—was the way his speech had changed. Gone: the rough Stourport vernacular; in: the well-spoken, lucid, gentle manner that suggested an education far beyond teacher training college. It was a metamorphosis that he pulled off with unbelievable skill and self-control. A transition that he would maintain for the rest of his life. He had learned, found self-fulfilment and become a man—a master—of words.

But though his training was complete, Cliff chose not to stay on another year for his degree. He had cruised through the requisite spells of teaching practice, including one at Bewdley Secondary (now High) School, where he inspired, amongst many others, a young guitar-dreamer, Karl Hyde, who in later years was to become the woolly-hatted guitarist-singer in the phenomenally successful techno-dance outfit, Underworld.

I telephoned Karl. He offered to come up from London and talk to me, despite his hectic work schedule. Underworld were on the crest of a wave: nine albums, tracks on the multi-million selling *Trainspotting* soundtrack, interviews, recordings, oh, and a recent concert at the top of Mount Fuji.

I collected him from Shrub Hill Station. He looked like a second-year student. Close-cropped hair, flawless complexion, chiselled, handsome face, bright eyes, American teeth. This was the man from Underworld?

He'd been born in Bewdley, remembered the cherry orchards on Wyre Hill, before they were chopped down to build my first house, and certainly had a love of the area, regretting his work needed him now, more than ever, to live in London.

We found a nice country pub—as you do—one of those unpretentious little places where the beermats still proclaim 'Keep cool this summer' at the end of November, and, over a nice roast, he told me about Bewdley schooldays and Cliff Ward.

"He took us for English, R.I. and P.E., which, I have to say was an absolute disaster ... for *him*. He was there in his shorts, tee-shirt, whistle and fairly long hair, trying to control a class of 20-odd, *very* odd, 12- year-olds, who just did not want to know. He'd blow away on his whistle, threatening us all with cold showers, or to even call an end

to the lesson if we didn't behave and of course we knew, as kids do, that he was fair game. We pushed him to the limit, took a rise out of him at every opportunity. He must have dreaded P.E. on the time-table.
"But then, one day, in English, he came in with a bag full of records. I was learning guitar. Paul Simon was my hero, 'Scarboro' Fair' my anthem [this is the singer from Underworld??]. 'I've got something to show you lot,' he said, almost triumphantly, and out came these 45s. The first thing *I* noticed was the colour of the labels. Orange. CBS. Which meant Simon and Garfunkel to me. But *his* name was on these records. Under each song title was the name 'Cliff Ward'. There was a group's name as the artiste, but he was the writer. Then he brought out these pictures, and there he was, posing with three other guys; he was the singer. I remember thinking the photos were dreadful, a bit, well…cheesy, but that's what they did in the sixties, fingers on cheeks, hands on chin, hair immaculate, striped blazers, all gazing into the distance; reflective. But the records and his name, well that really knocked me out. It was as if someone had opened a door for me, I'd suddenly been shown the way to all that I dreamed about, all those TV pop shows I drooled over, those magazines I bought every week, thinking it was something far beyond a mere mortal like me. And yet, here was my English teacher. *He'd* done it.
"He really encouraged me from then on. I began to respect him, and he obviously noticed, and began to spur me on. I was taking guitar lessons from someone up the Birmingham Road, every Saturday morning. It was just round the corner from Cliff's house. When he found out, he told me to drop in on my way back. I couldn't wait to finish my lesson. I took my best friend along, just to impress him. Cliff and Pat made us really welcome."
Pat did make them welcome, but under duress.
"I remember seeing them come round the top of the road and saying to Cliff, 'Oh, bloody 'ell, here come those kids with their guitars again. Quick, let's go out the back door !' But Cliff wouldn't have it…"
Karl continued:
"The first thing I noticed was his tape-recorder. A reel-to-reel Revox. Not a Philips, a *Re*vox. It was like NASA to me! I sat down on one of these huge orange leather sofas, that seemed to fill the room. Pat came in with a cup of tea, and just sat there smiling at the floor, for the rest of my visit, not saying one single word, while Cliff asked me about my lesson, then asked me to play something, and he really gave me encouragement. As I left, I remember noticing a beat up old Ford Anglia on the drive and thinking, 'Well, *I'd* rather have a Revox than a flashy car, any day.'
"We carried on visiting him, even sometimes took a few of our favourite records along. He didn't like 'Lola', though *we* both idolized

The Kinks; he liked Joni Mitchell's 'Big Yellow Taxi', of course, but he wasn't too sure about 'Love The One You're With' from the Stephen Stills solo album. But he only indulged us for so long. 'Have a listen to this,' he'd say, then play us something of his. The Revox whirred into life. I just sat there watching it, the VUs bouncing around, the silver tape-reels turning, it was wonderful. But we weren't too struck on his music ... though neither of us had the nerve to say so ...

"Then I wrote a song for some competition organized by Shelter, the words went something like '... oo-ooh, they're building too many houses, man, digging up our pleasant land, oo-ooh ...' which wasn't exactly going along with Shelter's policy, but Cliff loved it and he took me around to this friend of his who had a *proper* recording set-up, in a little bedroom in his parents' house. Cliff showed me the best way to record my voice, my guitar, and we put it down. The school eventually took me to Birmingham, the University I think, to make an acetate of the song, but it wasn't anywhere nearly as good as that bedroom tape."

We spent the rest of the afternoon talking about, well, almost everything. The music business, naturally, and, most important, his later memories of the man who became Clifford T. Ward. I took him back to the station, via Pratley's Emporium in Worcester, where he was under strict instructions to buy a brown teapot to replace the one that had just been broken back home.

"Best tea cums owt a brown teapot," he said, mimicking the Tetley man. "Tra, Dave."

Back at the house, settled in front of The Word Distresser, I was rewinding our conversation when the phone rang.

"Hi, Dave? It's Karl. I forgot to thank you for the lunch. Really enjoyed today. Keep in touch."

Astonishing. Think I'll get one of those woollen hats...

I called Leon next day:

"Do you remember a young kid coming to your place with Cliff to record a song he, the kid, had just written? Around 1970-ish?"

The lazy, sonorous tone came back down the line without a moment's hesitation:

"Karl Hyde."

I couldn't believe it. We're talking 25 years ago. Then, as we talked, I heard him leafing through some ancient log-books. After about two minutes up came the date.

"15th May, 1971," and Karl's parents' address.

What a star.

"Do you know who he is now?" I laughed. "He's the singer out of Underworld. *Underworld*," I repeated. "The techno-dance outfit."

"Never 'eard of 'em," came his curmudgeonly reply. Then, in a shaky, Bloodnok voice: "Da-nce? Da-nce did you say? Have you heard Jack

Hylton's version of 'When My Dreamboat Comes Home'...?" and he was off again. It was Robb Wilton, Arnold Gruntbucket, Jack Powdermonkey ...

Cliff wanted to get a job, start earning some regular money. He didn't want to fall behind on their first mortgage. After all those crazy years of fighting conformity, life seemed as though it was taking a straight course at last. He must get a job. Oh, and he might just make some more records...

Alan Holden was Cliff's Head Of Department at North Bromsgrove High School. Apart from the professional connection in those brief, far-off days, their lives today share a sad, common bond, which neither could have foreseen way back in 1970, when the newly qualified, disillusioned musician first joined the staff.

Now 70 years old, Alan maintains a wonderful enthusiasm for life, past and present. A member of the local Madrigal Society—which, he assures me, sings anything from 'Jesu, Joy of Man's Desiring' to 'Ole Man River'—he still lives in Bromsgrove, in the house he once shared with his wife, the poet Molly Holden, who died in 1985 from pneumonia, after suffering, for over 20 years, from multiple sclerosis.

He remembers fondly those days at Bromsgrove High:

"We were changing from an 11-18 co-educational grammar school to an 13-18 co-ed comprehensive and needed extra staff to cover the modifications in the new academic structure. Cliff had completed his training at Worcester College, although he hadn't stayed on to complete his degree; he needed to work. We interviewed and liked him, the Headmaster made the final choice (this was well before our days of elected Boards of Governors), and took him on. He proved to be a capable, conscientious member of staff, forming an immediate bond with the pupils, and indeed, they with him, mainly, I suppose, because it soon became known of his past (or so *we* thought...) involvement in the pop business. He taught English with a passion," recalls Alan, "and, as we had stipulated in his interview, subsequently took on producing various plays via the drama class which we had recently introduced into the curriculum. For his first venture, he produced a commendable interpretation of Act One of Thornton Wilder's *Our Town* (with, in the cast, one Trudie Styler, who went on to become Mrs Sting...)." he emphasizes, almost proudly. This evidently boosted his confidence, for in the school play, December 1972, he then produced Anouilh's *Antigone*, "... which was very well received." *The Boar*, Bromsgrove High School's provocatively named magazine, comments on Mr Ward's '... refreshing approach and wholehearted involvement ...' in the production, whilst Trudie thanks 'Mr Ward for...invaluable help

and advice, from which I am sure we all benefited.' [Too true, Trudie…]
There is also, within the pages of the magazine, a brief biography of the star-teacher, entitled 'Grilling Mr Ward', in which pupil Julian Cairns does an exemplary piece of junior-hack writing on Cliff's background to date, succinctly quoting his political and religious beliefs thus:

> Politically I am on the left, but I am sickened by party politics. I am more interested in people than political dogma. I cannot accept the Christian doctrine of life after death. I don't belong to any church. It seems we are moving further away from Christ, and I believe in him. I read the Gospels from time to time and am always fascinated, encouraged and saddened by his life and teaching. I love reading *Pilgrim's Progress*. Sometimes I feel like Christian when Evangelist says, 'Do you see yonder light?' And he replies 'I think I do…' I feel there is something, but I suppose I lack faith. I've written a song which is included on my album and based on Bunyan's work. It's called 'A Dream', and expresses my doubts and hopes.

The article then concludes, summing him up as '… a shy, tolerant person who considers and gives reappraisals of his surroundings, not merely accepting them …', and '…if you want to find out more about him, buy his LP,' referring to the *Singer-Songwriter* album. The Dandelion singles, 'Carrie' and 'Coathanger' had also been released by this time, so, to the pupils of a rural comprehensive school in the early 1970s, Mr Ward most certainly appeared as something of a celebrity.
But now, for the moment riding the wave as school drama producer, Cliff threw a party, for friends and pupils, at his home in the Oaklands. Alan's son, Gerard, who had also been in the productions, had a ' fairly uproarious time'. "No details were disclosed," laughs Alan, "but he and Cliff obviously got on well together; they respected each other."
Impressed by *Antigone*—the performance, the performers and the producer—Alan excitedly implemented a sixth-form course for drama and theatre arts into the time-table, with Cliff as tutor. "He seemed very pleased," smiles Alan. "It was a brand new 'O' level, incorporating academic and practical sections, and it showed that his efforts were being noticed and rewarded." But all concerned didn't reckon on the still powerful draw of that Old Devil Music. "The only trouble was, it was planned to start September term '73," continues Alan, this time with that 'shrug' of the voice that indicates a well-remembered aggravation, "and on May 31st—the last day on which it was possible to recruit a replacement member of staff for the next term—Cliff handed in his notice. The headmaster wasn't too pleased, and I did in

fact give Cliff a piece of my mind. I was very, very angry. We were left well and truly in the lurch. I realize now that he was doing what was best for him, but there was no sense of loyalty whatsoever [i-yup…], no hanging on until such times as …" He raises his hands in despair. "I hadn't even been aware—until the very last minute, that sudden surge of publicity—of his continuing, well his *escalating* involvement with pop; the cutting of more records…"

"Well he certainly wasn't cutting his hair…" I interrupted. "Was that ever a problem?"

"No!" he laughed. "But that didn't bother me, never has done. He dressed adequately; he was presentable. The hair was getting a *bit* long…The headmaster did mention it once or twice (well in fact quite often) and I had to mention it to Cliff, not that it made much difference."

Though, for the benefit of Mr Kyte—Ernest Kyte, Headmaster of North Bromsgrove High—Cliff did toe the line, up to a point, but as he was '… a brilliant drama teacher, who manages to get very close to [the] children …', his unorthodox appearance was treated with unusual tolerance. But then, he was playing his cards close to his chest.

So, almost as surprisingly as they had begun, the schooldays were over. With the clandestine new album completed, 'Gaye' started its slow climb up the charts, and of course, the 'Teacher turns pop-singer' headlines became ideal copy for the dailies. He was the PR man's dream, bringing intelligence and unadulterated glamour to a shallow, vacuous industry. Even the *Daily Express*, still a broadsheet in 1973, published an attention-grabbing article showing him reclining on the grassy slopes of the school playing fields, surrounded by his pupils, his books and the ubiquitous photo-prop—a Spanish guitar [!] ; his long, blond mane signifying triumph over convention. Far beyond the confines of the local press, the world saw at long last, Clifford T. Ward, pop star.

But how, after all the years of struggle, the hopes, disappointments and capitulation, how had it finally happened? How had defeated pop singer Cliff Ward metamorphosed into 'overnight' success, singer-songwriter Clifford T. Ward?

Well, firstly—and this is an observation, not advice, kiddie-winkies—he had never, for one second, given up either hope, or belief in his own talent.

Secondly, he had been fortunate in finally meeting—through the determined efforts of his faithful Sancho Panza, Ken Wright—someone who, whilst also recognizing his talent, was in a wonderful position to help.

The commitment of Ken Wright cannot be too strongly emphasized here. Holding down a newly-appointed and demanding position at the BBC, he still somehow found time and energy enough to dedicate hours and miles to Cliff's cause, helped by a sympathetic boss, who allowed Ken to work flexible hours to suit his needs; quite a luxury and certainly an innovation in such times.

The year 1970 had been a year of change, but only outwardly. Cliff had taken to teaching with enthusiasm, yet whenever he could, he was back at Bev's, or Leon's, or, when it needed a more professional end-product, at Johnny Haynes's Zella Studios, housed in a converted chapel in the back streets of Birmingham, little more than a boundary from Edgbaston cricket ground.

Johnny, a bubbly Brummie, was one of the first accessible studio owners, in terms of price and attitude, and his modest, though spacious studio lent itself easily to demos, but with the bonus of an in-house engineer and superb mastering facilities. I last saw him at Ken's 50th birthday party, probably 17 years after we'd last met. He hadn't changed one bit, but, he told me, "... times have ... Everybody's got a home-recording set-up now. Anyone can do what I used to do, but do it in the space of a bathroom, on a machine the size of a briefcase."

And of course, he was right, but it hadn't altered his outlook on life. He was a survivor, adapting his client database to include the hundreds of non-technical ethnic bands now springing up around Birmingham. Still friendly, laughing Johnny Haynes, and, if I wasn't mistaken, still wearing the same jacket...

Cliff's publishing contract with Blue Mountain Music had thrown up a song or two co-written with Kevin Gammond, on Kidderminster-based Bronco's debut album, *Country Home*. Even a single was released, on one side the Clifford T. wordy, 'A Matter Of Perspective', produced by front man Jess Roden, on the other side, 'Lazy Now', written by Jess and ex-Yardbird Paul Samwell-Smith, at that time forging a reputation *par excellence* producing Cat Stevens. Bronco had secured a deal with Island records on the basis of their in-vogue West Coast sound, a far cry from the much earlier—though at that time equally vogue-ish—blues wailing of their Shakedown Sounds. Vocalist Jess Roden, after a spell in London with the Alan Bown Set, had returned home disillusioned; an immense talent never to achieve his rightful position in pop history. With guitarists Robbie Blunt and Kevin helping on harmonies, Johnny Pasternak on bass and Pete Robinson on drums, Bronco had become fairly hot property.

Kevin talks about those earlier days:

"What attracted me to Cliff Ward and The Cruisers, way back in 1965-66, was the black artiste material they played; we looked upon them as a sort of 'walking jukebox', those tight harmonies, the solid soul feel.

At that time we were very young, having just left school, and very much into black music, but of a different kind, the desolation of Charlie Patton and Robert Johnson. We had a good agent, Malcolm Rose, and were managed by Mick Walker, of The Redcaps, so, a lot of excitement for such youngsters; supporting Buddy Guy, the Stones.

"Cliff's lot were just a little bit older than we were, and they kind of looked down on us as mutant offsprings, punk rebels, liable to blow the fuse box with our economical free-wiring approach. Not welcomed as a support band…

"But there was an amazing 'feel' around at that time, that we all stood a chance of making it big, and so when Cliff's band actually secured a recording deal, the first in the area to do so, well, he became more of a god. He did some stuff for Immediate, when Jimmy Page was an in-house producer, and came back with wonderful tales of those sessions; how Graham would spend hours trying to tune his guitar, until Jimmy, sitting up in the control room, would finally lose his patience, come down, take the guitar, go 'ping-ping-ping' … hand it back, perfectly in tune. On with the red light.

"The Shakedowns disbanded when Jess went off to join the Alan Bown Set. He asked me if I wanted to go down with him, but my parents didn't think much of the idea, so I wandered around Kidderminster until Cliff generously offered me a few gigs [The Cruisers were having staff-stability problems around that time]. My jagged blues style didn't go down too well at the Hen & Chickens and the Park Attwood…so I ended up doing the interval spot. Eventually I joined Jimmy Cliff, persuading my folks that I *could* make a living as a working musician, and moved down to London; then of course Robert [Plant] started Band Of Joy.

"But then Bronco came along, with Jess having come back from London, and the set-up became a great trading of ideas. Cliff was without a recording deal at that time—he was at teacher-training college—but still writing, of course. We would meet up and he would ask me what kind of approach I wanted on a particular tune, I'd say, "Oh, make it cosmic…" or we'd try a Hoagy Carmichael pastiche; I was even into Charlie Byrd, so there would be a Latin-American spoof, anything to confuse or amuse the Bronco fan. Kid Jensen was a great supporter of both Cliff and us, so we'd go out to Luxembourg occasionally, plugging the product."

On the Bronco album *Country Home* Cliff is credited with 'Tonic vocal' on his joint composition, 'Misfit On Your Stair', a billing that must have brought great pride to Kevin—having been the great follower in his younger, less hirsute days—and one that was to appear on their two further albums, *Ace Of Sunlight* in 1971, and the heady *Smoking Mixture* in 1973.

The slightly extended name, Clifford Ward, thus began appearing on record labels, though not as a solo artiste, merely as a writer (which, if the truth be known, is really all he ever wanted to be).

Through 1970 and into 1971 he demoed, Bronco-ed and taught, with Ken ever on call. In the spring of 1971, Kevin introduced Cliff to a young, keen staff reporter working on the *Shuttle*. Derek Thomas, a tall, gentle, blond-haired home town boy, had glowingly reviewed Bronco albums in his music column, and was himself, already, a competent guitarist.

A long way down the line, Derek recalls the genesis:

"I was doing the semi-pro bit with various local bands, belting out 'Yellow River' at Droitwich Winter Gardens, lots of fun, but little ambition. Then I stumbled onto—or was it into?—the vibrant folk club scene, where I was drawn to the acoustic folk styles of Bert Jansch and John Renbourn; country blues, ragtime and so on.

"Paul MacReath was an acquaintance. He drummed for The Reflections, and was also somehow on hand for the demo sessions with Bev Pegg when Ken couldn't make it. He mentioned my name, Cliff seemed to like my style, so I joined the gang."

So they rehearsed. On 3rd June, Cliff, Ken, Bev, Terry Clarke and Derek travelled down to Marquee Studios, where they met up with session-pianist Dave Skinner, to record the wonderful 'You Knock (When You Should Come In)'. Ken also remembers another session pianist trying to add 'some fucking fairy-dust', as Reg (Troggs) Presley called it:

"We were listening to the playback, when in wanders this little guy, with glasses, wearing tennis gear. The producer introduced him to us, then he sat down at the piano, headphones on, playing along to the backing track. After a while—about five minutes—he got up, shrugged his shoulders, said there was nothing he could add to it, and wiggles off. Exit Reggie Dwight."

This was where it really began to happen, and the man who made it all possible enters the frame.

It was part talent, part commitment, part luck, part timing; almost the complete list of prerequisites for success. All it needed was the backing of a music entrepreneur…

Yet it was with some apprehension that I telephoned Clive Selwood.

Although he had been Cliff's mentor, things had gone terribly wrong and I wasn't sure what reaction would be forthcoming.

"Clive Selwood? My name is Dave Cartwright. I'm writing a book about Clifford T. Ward."

"Yeah," in a very 'so what?' tone. My fears were seemingly confirmed.

A somewhat stilted conversation ensued, but an appointment was made to meet and interview him the following week at his home. I put the phone down, realizing I'd made a real pig's ear of *that* one and noted in my diary, 'Thursday, 7th August. Clive Selwood'.

So I left Worcester-on-Severn for Sussex-by-the-Sea with slight trepidation, though the journey, initially, was pleasant enough; through the bountiful Vale of Evesham, with its roadside fruit stalls, on to chocolate-box-Broadway, then Chipping Norton, right past the studios where Cliff, Gerry Rafferty, Beverley Craven, The Proclaimers (!) and that nervous Dave Cartwright chappie had recorded; thankfully skipping round congested Oxford, queuing at Newbury—and nodding, sadly, at the necessity for the by-pass (but then, the whole world needs a by-pass)—down through grey, grim Basingstoke, before joining the once-familiar winding roads of Hampshire. Everywhere they were building. Everywhere. Places that not so very long ago had probably boasted six houses and a woman with a cow, were now being Barratt-ed, Wimpey-ed and supermarket-ed, with motorways to the front door and red Ford Mondeos on the drive. I drove on, wondering where it was all going to end, and eventually came into beautiful West Sussex, er...where I got lost.

I telephoned Clive from a real red call box, my foot wedging the door open in the stifling heat. His wife Shurley (honest; it's an affectation, he assures me...) gave me precise directions—to which I never, ever listen—saying it would take me about 15 minutes to the house.

About 45 minutes later, after my usual run of u-turns, questionings, reversings and cursings, I turned into the gravelled courtyard of Clive's cottage, to find an outstretched hand and a beaming smile bidding me welcome. This was not what I had expected.

Voices never match faces, and Clive was no exception. A tall, distinguished looking man, with a fine head of Grecian-greying hair and a charming Zapata-cum-Prince Albert moustache, he joked about me getting lost (they knew my talents, even down here...?) then showed me into the house, introducing me to Shurley, who sat at a desk, shuffling through a pile of terrifyingly official looking documents.

He started talking immediately—before I had time to set up the tape machine—and didn't stop for six hours. I kid you not. But, it transpired, we had a lot in common.

Clive had been head of Elektra Records in the UK and, after expressing my delight at such information, I dropped a few names of my still highly treasured albums from that label: Tom Rush (with whom I'd shared—well, not exactly *shared*—billing at my first Cambridge Folk Festival in 1972), Spider John Koerner, Tim Buckley, The Incredible String Band, Tom Paxton, Judy Collins; prompting him to launch into a dozen anecdotes of life on the road and in concert with these legendary performers. This was heaven.

But eventually, what about Clifford T. Ward? This is when I remembered to plug in and switch on … *and* get him to sit down.

"I started Dandelion Records with John Peel in 1971," he started, in his warm Home Counties drawl. "I'd met John through my Elektra days, when he was on pirate Radio London. Peely was the only disc-jockey in the country who'd play Elektra stuff; in fact when the Incredibles released *5000 Spirits...*, he played the whole album, all the way through, on his show. I mean, what a star.

"Anyway, when the pirates were closed down by the government [who are the *real* pirates…], he was out of a job, so I used a bit of my influence elsewhere, and actually landed him his job at the Beeb. They hated him, still do. Not as a person—you couldn't hate John as a person—but his image, all that long hair, hippie clothes. The bosses at the BBC, whenever his name was bought up in conversation, used to make the old druggie sign, y'know… [he fakes the 'needle-in-the-arm' movement]. John's never touched drugs in his life! Anyhow, they took him on, but were always moaning about his music, his show content, and I remember telling the then Head of Light Entertainment to look after John Peel 'cos he was playing to the future leaders of our country, and Tony Blair has proved me absolutely right, citing John as one of his early influences. I'm proud of that," he nods with a contented smile.

"John has always been a mover-shaker, hated music that stood still, and around that time there were a lot of bands, musicians, whom he admired but who couldn't get a record deal, so one day, over lunch, we decided to start our own label. As simple as that. We wouldn't have the budget of the biggies, but at least we could offer a bit of hope to the hundreds out there who were being neglected. Our first signing was Bridget St. John, whom John knew personally and who was also a popular act on the folk scene—which at that time was flourishing—then we had a couple of very successful singles from Medicine Head, and various others; Kevin Coyne, Stackwaddy, a duo called Tractor. We also released a record by Gene Vincent, one of John's idols, including a re-make of his fifties mega-hit, 'Be-Bop-A-Lula'. Now there's a story." [And forgive me, dear reader, if I diversify a while…]

"We recorded a whole album with Gene, who was really weird, and I mean *really* weird. He'd phone us up in the wee small hours from America, Shurley would answer the phone, Gene would be on line from, ooh I dunno—Norfolk, Virginia—in his thin, Virginian Civil War accent. 'Missus Selwuud, mairm, noibedie's tallkin tue mei…' This is three o'clock in the morning," emphasizes Clive, "and we'd have to spend the next forty minutes listening to the reasons why. But that's showbiz," and he leans forward, with an almost conspiratorial smile in his voice. “Anyhow, sometime later, I get a phone call from...Don Arden...[Clive adopts a wonderful Reggie Kray accent] ‘Clive, eye ’ere that yew ’ave dun an album wiv Gene Vincent.’ Affirmative. ‘We-ell, eye fink yew shud no that Gene ’as bene under hexclusiv contract wiv us for thee parst firteen ye-arss. I fink whee gotta tork...’ [Don Arden was a legendary, or I should say, notoriously proprietorial, manager, and definitely not a member of the softly-softly school...]

“Next day, there I was, in Don Arden’s office, shaking all over. Don sat in the middle, with two heavies, *really* heavies, on either side, like gorgons at the Gates of Hell. ‘Eye’ve got a contract ’ere, sined by Gene.’ He opens a drawer; I stand up to look, leaning over the desk as he quickly slams the drawer shut. ‘Oh, yes, I wasn’t aware...’ I humble-mumble, really just wondering how I was going to get out in one piece. The phone rings. Don picks it up, listens, then speaks. ‘Kill ’im.’ Puts down the phone, end of conversation. We talk some more. The phone rings again. Don picks it up, he listens, then, ‘Knee-cap the bar-stad’... End of conversation. It’s all a set-up, I know, but I’m frightened, really frightened, so I say, ‘Lo-oo-ok, Don, you take the album, with my, with *our* compliments. Oh, and by the way, Shurley send her regards.’ ‘Shairley? Shairley oo?’ He looks puzzled. Now it so happened that my wife, Shurley, once played and sang in a band with Don Arden, way, way, back, and, for just that brief, but seemingly endless moment, his guise dropped, and he became almost human. ‘Aaah, Shairley. Larvely lady. She your wife?’ I nodded, quickly, almost idiotically. ‘Aaah.’ Long pause. ‘We-ell. Tell yew wot, Clive. Go a-ed wiv de album. If it sells a millyon, yew o me wan...’ I got out of that office so damn quick, you’d have thought my bum was on fire. But of course, we didn’t sell a million, and I never heard from Don Arden again.”

And within a short while, sad old Gene, still racing with the devil, died from an alcohol related seizure.

“But the label’s success continued unabated, though on a very low-key, cultish level. Yet, as it flourished, so John’s enthusiasm diminished. Typical. Then, in the dying days of Dandelion, around October, 1971, Ken Wright passed a demo tape of Cliff Ward on to John Walters, John’s producer, who passed it on to me.” [Songs included on this tape were ‘Sam’ and ‘God Help Me’, recorded at Johnny Haynes’s Zella Studios, with Bev Pegg—whose wife Heather had walked out on him that very night; God help *him*—Terry Clarke and Big Adrian Fenwick on piano.]

“Contrary to popular belief, Peely was never very keen on Cliff; it wasn’t ground breaking enough for him. He could see the talent there, but it wasn’t that ‘moving forward music’. However, when *I* heard it, well, I was knocked out. And Shurley. We loved it.”

"Exactly why?"

"Oh the songs. He had a pleasant enough voice, but we thought the songs were extraordinary, so much to say. We wanted to capture that. So, after numerous telephone chats, I eventually arranged to meet up with Ken [21st and 22nd December, 1971]. He was wonderful to deal with, very unsophisticated in music world terms—and by that I mean he was dead straight—a real pleasure to talk business with. So, after the festive break Ken brought Cliff over to my offices at Polydor. I was surprised when I first saw him, all that hair. Don't know how he got away with it, being a schoolteacher, but he was an affable bloke, charming, polite, a bit bandy…[?]," he laughs, "but I could see the potential, so we signed him up. Incidentally, that's where his star-name came from. He signed the contract 'Clifford T. Ward' and I just remarked how good it looked, why not use it? So Cliff became *my* baby on Dandelion.

"Considering what was to come, that first album was recorded fairly smoothly, mainly, I suppose because he used his friends from home as the musicians; the guys who had actually done the demos and they, literally, knew the score. They could also give as good as they got—for the time being…"

They started recording almost straightaway, 16th January, 1972, at The Marquee, with Phil Dunne engineering, but it went on into a long spring. Cliff wanted strings, brass, orchestration, so Clive gave him a couple of telephone numbers. In one of those simple twists of fate, he called Robert Kirby, who was first on the list. Kirby had recently arranged fellow Cambridge scholar Nick Drake's *Bryter Layter* album, and was much in demand with the current singer-songwriter vogue. Cliff called him once, twice, three times; always engaged, so he went to number two.

Richard Hewson, with his interpretative ear and subtle scoring, was to play a major role in the Clifford T. Ward success story, yet even in those early days, Hewson still had an awesome pedigree, having worked from James Taylor on his first Apple album, to The Beatles on 'Long And Winding Road'. Although, as he told me, his very first foray into the music business had resulted in a very acute learning curve:

"My first job after leaving college was on Mary Hopkin's 'Those Were The Days', produced, as you know, by Paul McCartney, the melody of which is a traditional Russian folk song. The new lyrics were written by Gene Raskin.

"In copyright law," says Richard, "—and I didn't find this out until it was much too late—the arranger of any traditional melody becomes the composer. Raskin, the lyricist, claimed all the royalties, the full 100 per cent, and did a runner. I was paid £25 session fee, for what would ultimately become a world-wide number one, a multi-million seller.

"Shook me a bit, that."
As it would.

For the album, Clifford insisted on doing his own production, "… which was okay by us," shrugs Clive, "though we saw him lean increasingly on Richard's expertise as the recording progressed."

"I thought his stuff was quite unique, the unusual subject matter, the zany syllabics," remembers Richard. "He wouldn't admit to any influences, in fact he was difficult to talk to off-camera, but I certainly heard Jimmy Webb in there, and Harry Nilsson. If Cliff had played guitar, I'm sure Paul Simon would have been discernible."

Clive himself actually rejected the first album mix, and they then moved on to mixing at the now legendary Sound Techniques Studio, deep in the heart of Chelsea, with Jerry Boys engineering. Here—tucked away in Old Church Street—Cat Stevens, Nick Drake and many other *nouveau* artistes had already recorded what were to become classic albums.

Clive was pleased with the subsequent results. He truly felt there was something special happening here, but he also knew, with his industry experience, the importance of promotion. Nothing would sell without it. He talked the distribution men at Polydor into funding a small concert, and, after he decided the ICA in The Mall was not the most suitable venue, a launch reception was held at London's Speakeasy Club in Margaret Street. Gold-edged invitations were printed and circulated amongst the media: 'Clifford T. Ward invites you to luncheon and brief recital … on August 10th at 12.30 p.m.' It was all too much, too quick. Clifford sang at—rather than to—the music men, with a hurriedly rehearsed session band comprising Ken, pianist Paul Davenport, Derek Thomas, and Bronco men, Johnny Pasternak on bass and Kevin Gammond, '… rampant on guitar, as usual …' remembers Ken.

Bev Pegg went down to watch, on Ken's invitation. He and Terry Clarke had long since dropped out of the all-consuming session work, for which they, like all around, were receiving no payments—though Cliff himself was, according to one source, '… covertly being paid considerable expenses by Clive'—and besides which, family business commitments were becoming very demanding. Bev freely admits he was glad not to be playing that night, "… Cliff was *very* nervous, very uptight, and it all seemed somewhat unrehearsed …"

Bev and Terry—from the material world of commerce—were the 'businessmen' in the outfit, hence their waiving of the loyalty clause, but payment for *anything* had become a non-confrontational issue with all the musicians.

Derek confirms—but only when coaxed—that financially, nobody saw any rewards, even in the heady days of success that were to come:

"We weren't on a percentage, or any sort of contract; neither were we paid session rates. The arrangements were, I suppose, informal, and they got more informal over the years ... We should have held out for a more professional set-up, but we didn't. [But] I'm [definitely] not nursing any grudges ... I would hate to appear to be. It doesn't matter to me now."

Clive Selwood sweeps his hand across the table, leans back and recalls the promotion for that first record:

"I thought the album, which we called *Singer-Songwriter*, was great—still do—and we spent a lot more money pushing it. We were one of the first labels to utilize advertising on the sides of buses; a banner saying 'Who Is Clifford T. Ward?' There's a lovely picture somewhere of Clifford standing in front of a London double-decker with his name and picture plastered all over it. We also fly-posted half the city, then put out two singles. ['Carrie'/ 'Sidetrack', the first Clifford T. Ward single, was released on 11th August, 1972.] Followed up with whole pages in *Music Week* and such, thanking the disc-jockeys for their support, which they most certainly gave. Plug, plug, plug, but...nothing."

But Clive's faith in Clifford remained strong, and he continued to finance recordings, which were now all being done at the Chelsea studios, even though by this time there had developed a growing uncertainty within Dandelion. But Cliff wasn't aware of this, and he fell into the scheme of things with great intent. He was recording—at someone else's expense—in an almost professional capacity, with promises of glory abounding, and he was in demand for the obligatory, but nevertheless prestigious, radio spots.

Despite the impact of the pop-revolution, archaic practices still ran rife throughout the BBC. Radio One had fallen victim to its own success, and the Musicians Union, acting in the interests of its older members and those who were not prepared to join the pop-arena, had drawn up an agreement stipulating that only so many hours per day could be used for actually playing records, the so called 'needle-time'. The remainder of any pop-time would consequently be padded out with orchestral arrangements of the hits of the day; hence the continuing high profile of Ray McVay's Big Band, Sounds Orchestral, The Squadronaires—with Pete Townshend's father—even Joe Loss. Victor Sylvester had by this time, thank goodness, retired to that great strict-tempo orchestra pit in the sky.

This agreement was still in force in the 1970s, despite the spectacular rise of the disc-jockey. Tony Blackburn was free to play records, but inevitably used up most, if not all, of the total allocated time. So a compromise was reached, whereby those groups who were able to play, who were an actual 'unit', were actually auditioned by a frighteningly

serious BBC panel, and, if successful, listed for potential slots.
Antediluvian though it now may seem, this method of selection enabled many young musicians to experience 'live' performing (the spots were always pre-recorded) and also to see the inside of those hallowed halls of the BBC: the Aeolian, the Langham, The Playhouse and the legendary Maida Vale.
Cliff and his merry band recorded in all of these over the period July, '72 - April, '73. On the Johnnie Walker Show of 21st August 1972, he was heard singing four songs: his recent single, plus 'Coathanger', 'God Help Me' and 'Sam', all recorded a week earlier at Aeolian Hall, again with Bev Pegg and Ken on backing vocals. A Langham Studio 'Sounds Of The 70s' slot for Anne Nightingale had been canned on the 16th, and on October 26th a pre-recorded John Peel Show session was transmitted—on which Clifford sang his now second, but subsequently last, Dandelion single, 'Coathanger', which had been released 13th October. He likewise previewed 'Gaye', in a gentle, acoustic setting; the song that would become his first Charisma single.
Ken reminds me, when I question the extra musicians listed on these sessions, of Cliff's total disregard for institutional authority, i.e. the BBC's strict and miserly code of payment, and how they picked up a few extra pounds as a result:
"We just added a couple of names here and there to the session invoice. No-one ever cross-checked who was actually present, or even the number of players; they paid, in cash, per person submitted. I went to school with Paul Booton; it seemed a credible name for a guitarist. Paul Lockey was a mate of Cliff's from Bronco—he wasn't there, except in spirit—we just filled in the details. We even used a C. Cope—as in 'can't...Cliff pocketed their session fees.
"'Why not, Kenny?' he'd say. 'They'm a-makin' millions out uv us...'
Ken smiles: "It was a nice little earner."
Precisely. The Beeb weren't exactly remiss at milking the golden calf. All recordings done on their premises, or at their instigation, immediately became BBC copyright, which allowed them complete freedom as to the subsequent use of the tapes, in perpetuity.
Brian Matthew, the staid, personable honey-voiced compere, even had his own radio version of Top Of The Pops, which was transmitted world-wide, using segments of these sessions. During the show, he would present the artiste(s) as if they were there in the studio, supposedly moving from one act to the other 'across the floor'. On one of the few surviving tape copies, with Brian introducing 'an unusual young man, schoolmaster Clifford T. Ward...', we hear 'Coathanger', 'Gaye', 'Where Would That Leave Me', a delightful string quartet version of 'Wherewithal', 'Home Thoughts...', and an obviously much later session previewing 'Scullery'—judiciously described by Brian as

'a love song with a difference'. Impeccably performed by Cliff and his band, with Richard Hewson conducting his BBC-allowance orchestra, there is a wonderful intimacy in these recordings, almost Beatle-esque. Cliff sounds quite relaxed, happily utilizing his years of studio experience. Acrobatic vocal trills slip delightfully into certain lines. The end result must have augmented the belief held by all those around Clifford T. Ward, apart from the man himself, that he could have—*should* have—capitalized on the demand for concert performances; they would have been an unqualified success.

These radio dates were squeezed in between the Sound Techniques sessions, with Vic Gamm now engineering alongside Jerry Boys. Clive had an experienced crew overseeing production. Life was busy, and life was looking good, though, as the year drew to a close, a major change was imminent.

Clive draws a breath:

"*Singer-Songwriter* was probably Dandelion's 'last hurrah', for not long afterwards Peely and I decided to call it quits. I felt it incumbent on me to try and get deals elsewhere for whoever I could. [Times have indeed changed…] Virgin took Kevin Coyne, Chrysalis took Bridget and, after doing the rounds, in January, 1973, I managed to place Clifford—already well into his second album, which would, ironically, be his *Meisterwerk*—with Charisma, who, thank goodness, appeared very, very keen."

Clifford showed little outward emotion, but deep inside he knew it was a great career move. From a small, independent set-up to an established, gregarious label, situated in Soho Square, deep in the heart of London.

SUMMER

THE DUBIOUS CIRCUS COMPANY

He's full of alteration, and self-reproving. King Lear V.i.

I saw your pictures in the magazines,
I heard your songs on the radio,
I thumbed your records in the music stores;
I knew you were doing so well...

The Author: 'Old Friends'

In effect, Charisma was a grown-up Dandelion. Born of the same autonomous spirit, many years earlier, it had built a healthy reputation in the business for integrity and energy, allowing artistic freedom amongst its free-thinking artistes; an attitude that reaped just reward with the company's first single in 1968, Rare Bird's 'Sympathy', which became an international hit.

Tony Stratton-Smith started Charisma after a high profile career in sports journalism, graduating from his home town of Birmingham, where he worked on the *Daily Gazette* with cricket legend Len Hutton, through the *Daily Sketch*, the *Daily Express* [miraculously missing the Manchester United Munich air crash by choosing instead to cover a World Cup qualifier with Wales...], before entering the music publishing world via his friendship with Brian Epstein. After a brief spell at pop management, handling The Nice and The Bonzo Dogs—who reached the top five via 'Urban Spaceman', with a little help from their friend Paul McCartney—his frustration with record company incompetence led him to start his very own label.

Tales abound of his passion for life, his generosity of spirit (and spirits...) a man who, according to Creation's Kenny 'Grandad' Pickett, you could actually enjoy getting drunk with, even whilst knowing that he had just pocketed your Ready Steady Go!, fee. He drank, cursed, joked, and filled the air with cigar smoke, but a patriotic, romantic soul was always just below the surface, waiting. And so, sure enough, the pure English romanticism in the new songs of Clifford T. Ward touched that raw nerve. *Melody Maker* writer Roy Hollingworth wrote of seeing "... tears in [Strat's] eyes," after listening to a demo of 'Home Thoughts From Abroad'. With such emotion involved, there was no doubt that the Charisma bandwagon would be right behind the album, as and when it was released.

"Tony had sunk a *lot* of money into Genesis without too much reward," continued Clive, "but I knew he had this tenacity. If he believed in an artiste—which is why he would have signed them in the first place—he would stick with them as long as was commercially possible."

The tracks that had been played to Strat showed a great maturity, both in content and presentation, over the previous album, as if Clifford had consciously decided to move right away from pop and create his own, inimitable style. He had also bought in another local boy—Terry Edwards—again introduced to Clifford by Kevin Gammond—to replace Bev Pegg on bass guitar, the backing track line-up now reading: Ken Wright on drums, Derek Thomas on guitars, Terry on Bass, with Clifford and Richard Hewson on strings; oh, and Roy Rogers on Trigger. (Sorry, couldn't resist that ...)

And, possibly because of his new style, Clifford had started feeling more confident in his producer's role. Sure enough, it proved a precursor of things to come...

Clive remembers little instances, little niggles that would gradually develop into '... such awful time wasters.'

"He had this thing about drums. We spent *hours* getting—or trying to get—a drum sound that Clifford was happy with. Ken was so patient, we *all* were, and, from what other people have said, working in similar situations, the first or second take/sound/mix, whatever, show very little difference to the final one. It is all in the mind, and it was certainly in Clifford's mind."

In the twilight world of recording studios, as on the Starship Enterprise, (one presumes...) time does well and truly warp. Evening sessions become overnight sessions, there is no sunrise, no sunset, nothing but initial excitement giving way to the terminal boredom of repetition. Tempers fray, friends fall out and music, that wonderful catalyst, becomes a bother. And even when it is all completed, just when you think it's safe to go back into the water, it bloomin' well isn't...

The album was declared finished on February 25th. Everybody was er...happy. On February 26th, Clifford, back home by now, telephoned Ken to say his copy was no good, "... the mixes are doubtful." Ken drove up to Worcestershire the following day with alternative copies and then on March 1st, Clifford decided to re-mix and subsequently re-cut the album. This dragged on for a couple more weeks, with Ken tearing up and down main roads and country lanes in his Mini-Cooper.

A further John Peel session, where 'Gaye' was reprised, and appetisers from the album were aired, went out—with perfect timing—on 19th April, the day before the timeless Clifford T. Ward album *Home Thoughts* escaped from his clutches and was released, to an ecstatic world: April 20th, 1973. His time had come. At long last.

And what a reception it received. I sit here tonight, as I write, surrounded by piles of newspaper cuttings; yellowed, curled and torn, all adorned with pictures of that almost angelic, very English face, hair sweeping back, full-lipped and half-smiling, looking out in a kind of acceptance, assurance even; a gaze that says, modestly but confidently, "It was just a matter of time…"

The reviewers went to town, using every superlative imaginable. *Melody Maker*'s Roy Hollingworth said the songs were '… the finest… I've heard since James Paul McCartney wrote 'Yesterday' … real songs, written because they were felt …', and about Clifford's '… cleansing, English voice …'; *NME*'s Steve Clarke, in a questionable but well-meaning comparison, cited the song 'Home Thoughts from Abroad' as

'… possibly the best ballad since 'Eleanor Rigby', and remarked on the '… haunting, frail … clear …' voice. Not surprisingly—but surely a first—the August 17th edition of *The Teacher*, a magazine for the profession, did an in-depth interview, quoting the singer's almost reactionary views on teaching, but also shrewdly noting '… satirical inclinations …in the … 'soft and gentle … songs …'

Almost as if trying to impress their subject with their own schoolmasterly eloquence, they were virtually unanimous in their praise, creating an almost hysterical reaction to this beautiful, gentle album. There was one isolated exception, a strangely uncredited—*Disc* review, citing '… overkill … omnipresent cellos … gooey strings,' which, considering the important part the brilliant orchestrations played in the album's success, shows an amazing ignorance of ideals.

And even in bed-sit land, where aspiring songwriters by the dozen were watching and waiting their turn, the influence of the record was incalculable.

One such person, just out of university, was Chris De Burgh.

I rang Chris, early one Monday morning. He had no idea of the impending book, or that I was trying to contact him; yet, when he answered the phone, he spoke with great passion and affection—without hesitation or question—quoting titles and complete lines out of the Clifford T. Ward songbook as if he'd just taken the albums off his music centre:

"About the time of 'Gaye', I'd left university and was living in London, virtually on the breadline … trying hard to get into the music business. The singer-songwriter thing was very much in vogue, Al Stewart, Jackson Browne, and when I heard that song, saw Clifford singing it on TV, with his long, blond hair—and he sang it so well—I liked it even more. He seemed so unpretentious. I went out and bought the album, loved the gatefold sleeve, the family snaps, the whole concept and the songs. Some of those lines: '… You're the tray of nice things I upset yesterday …', 'Our love is just another broken down motor car …', such original angles for such an everyday theme.

"But 'The Traveller' actually moved me to tears, with the children singing 'Yes, Jesus loves you' against Clifford's 'God so loved the world …'. It truly made me cry. I wrote a song many years later, 'Just Another Poor Boy', which I suppose, subconsciously, was inspired by 'The Traveller'; 'Be kind to strangers, for it might be Christ himself …' that kind of thing.

"I think, about that time, he was really giving McCartney—who was then into his *Ram* period—a run for his money. Apart from the fact that Robert Browning—alongside W. B. Yeats—was my favourite poet, Clifford's lovely turns of phrase, the analogies, the whole feel, it had a simple beauty and startling originality. *Home Thoughts* is certainly in my top ten favourite albums of all time."

"Did you ever meet him?" I asked.

"We met once, over late breakfast at BBC Pebblemill Studios, and he was exactly how I expected him to be, how I *wanted* him to be. Polite, articulate, attentive and with a wonderful, gentle sense of humour; in fact, everything his records portrayed.

"Give them both my love, from the heart."

[*Home Thoughts* arranger Richard Hewson would later join up with Chris on his breakthrough album, *Spanish Train…and Other Stories*, in 1975, and is still working with him, all these many years later.]

Pete Frame, founder of *Zig-Zag* magazine, and now writer-historian of *Rock Family Trees*, was a young punter at Friars Club in Aylesbury, held at the Civic Centre. With a full-to-capacity crowd of 1200 most weeks, the club, run by Dave Stopps, played host to the hip bands of the era, everyone from Roxy Music, Eurythmics and Blondie to The Stranglers.

"Stopsy used to play records between the support act and the headliner, preceding the top act very week with Clifford's rousing, 'Would you like to see, would you like to see, would you like to see our show…' from 'Dubious Circus Company'. This would be a signal for the bar to empty and the audience to flock into the hall. That went on for ten years, until Stopsy went off to manage Howard Jones."

I'm not so sure Clifford would have approved of such 'exploitation', but it was a sure sign of his acceptance by connoisseurs of pop.

Even old friends Bronco, though now in a slightly different form—having lost singer Jess Roden and guitarist Robbie Blunt—were releasing Clifford T. songs.

With Paul Lockey on vocals and guitarist Dan Fone, the final Bronco album *Smoking Mixture*, released in August, 1973, at the height of Clifford's popularity, contained yet two more songs written in collaboration with Kevin Gammond, the '...Ipanema'-inspired 'Attraction', and 'Southbound Express', but, as a B-side to their single 'Steal That Gold', they had generously recorded 'The Traveller', with a full 20-piece orchestra, conducted and arranged by Richard Hewson.

So it had worked, the time and energy, the angst and the expense. Hopes were high.

Clive Selwood sighs:

"'Gaye', which had preceded the album by almost three weeks, didn't take off straight away by any means; it was a long, hard haul but, as I'd expected, but Charisma stuck by it. Tony was determined to break it, and he paid his pluggers to pursue it until it did. Peter Thompson, whom I consider the best PR man in the country, possibly the *world*—and who had previously worked on Laurence Olivier, Liz and Richard, oh, and Genesis—was brought in to work on Clifford. He naturally picked up on the 'schoolteacher turns pop singer' angle, and ensured every newspaper in the country took up the story in some shape or another, air play increased dramatically until finally, around about June, three *months* after its release, 'Gaye' entered the top 50.

But, despite all this media coverage, and their undeniable quality, neither the single nor the album made a truly significant impact on the British record-buying public. Depending on which source of reference used, the single spent between 11 and 15 weeks in the charts, finally peaking at number eight in July, 1973, in a list sprinkled with discs by Peters and Lee (honest...), the Osmonds (cross-my-heart...), Gary Glitter and hero Paul Simon; whilst the album *Home Thoughts*—with its gatefold cover of timepieces and trinkets surrounding Clifford's framed face (photographed by Bromsgrove workmate, art teacher Tony Bell), and literary liner notes underpinning sombre family portraits—unbelievably hovered around the bottom end of the top 40 for two weeks before mysteriously disappearing into the past.

The actual sales figures, meticulously noted by Ken in his managerial-accountant capacity, also serve as a sad reminder of the once-healthy state of the recording industry. UK figures alone, between 16th July and 30th July, show that 'Gaye' sold 70,000 copies (compared with, in total, 'Carrie': 131, and 'Coathanger': 364), whilst the *Home Thoughts* album was turning over a steady 700 copies a week during the period 30th July - 31st December, totalling *26,000* copies by end January, 1974 (*Singer-Songwriter*: 550...). Yet, due to enormous record sales per se, it had only dented the bottom rung. The impetus was there; why wasn't it sustained?

Even I couldn't understand it. I was touring, sorry, *gigging*—believe me, there is an enormous difference—five nights a week at that time,

up and down the country, at folk clubs, colleges and suchlike. Everywhere I played, inevitably, during the interval, someone would sidle up to me and, firstly confirming what I had said during a song preamble—that I did indeed come from Kidderminster—would then ask excitedly, whether I knew Clifford T. Ward. His name seemed to be everywhere, on everyone's lips. Lawdy, I was in Holland promoting one of my singles, appearing on the 'Eddy-Go-Round TV Spectacular'; I was in Germany playing a shadowy, highly aromatic club near the Russian border; I was in Jersey, playing St Helier Folk Club. Could I find any of my records in the shops? Could I 'eck, but I tell you, *Home Thoughts* was on the shelves in Holland, Germany, Jersey and probably every other country in the world. Those were also the wonderful but simple days, when you could sometimes ascertain the sales of an album by removing the shop insert and checking the assistant's sales markings on the card; '2, 5, 8, 15. Re-order'. Boy, was it moving off the shelves. But why wasn't it climbing?
I mentioned this to Clive.
"Well, it's a strange business. You can sell an awful lot of records, but that doesn't necessarily make it a chart hit," and he gave me a keen glance, "but Clifford *did* do well out of it all, though he—*we*—also must have missed out on a few bob...
"I mean, just to emphasize the nature of the business, for some inexplicable reason, 'Gaye' made Top Five in Brazil. Top *Five*. Sold an *awful* lot of copies in Brazil [there's a song in there somewhere Clive...]. An extraordinary amount. We never saw a penny of it."

I couldn't believe what I was hearing, so I made a note to definitely check that one out...

Astonishing. Though Brazil, in those days, was one of those countries where:
"It's one of those things," Clive shrugs. "Y'know. 'It's coming, it takes a while to go through the system, we'll check it out'...then you get other things on your mind, until, one day, when you're scratching around for some spare change, you think, 'Whatever happened to that money from Brazil?' by which time things have moved on, Charisma has been sold to Virgin, fat chance of getting that now... Ha!" His voice trails off ...
"So that could have been a lot, an extraordinary amount of money for Cliff?" I suggested.
"Oh, yeah, an *awful* lot, but it's lost. Somebody picked it up, somewhere..."

A little too late now for audits.

Life was now 'maelstroming'. Ken—whilst nonchalantly playing some Bridget St. John sessions—fought off a management take-over for Clifford, successfully negotiated a MAM Agency deal (almost securing the coveted regular slot on Lulu's TV series after David Essex pulled out), and, as if to prove his faith, transported or accompanied his charge on a relentless round of personal appearances, slotted in between the next bout of recording.

From spring through to October, '73, Cliff and he joined the media circus, now in full flight, recording again with Johnny Walker on the 19th April—this time being allowed the luxury of a string section: six violins, two violas and two cellos, for 'Home Thoughts From Abroad'; Annie the Nightingale's 'Sounds of the 70s'; 'Today' for Radio 4; Michael Aspel; guest reviewer on 'Rosko's Round Table': Radio 1; 'Start The Week', and, after a slight hiccough, the 'Brian Matthew Show'.

"The first Brian Matthew session was a disaster," Ken tells me. "My fault entirely. We were so busy, rushing here, there and everywhere. The recording was at Maida Vale Studios, 21st June, just as we were sensing the sweet smell of success. I tried to pull the wool over the eyes of experienced session men; fudging the rhythm charts, using my primitive, self-taught transcriptions. They just shook heads in unison. 'Can't use these, mate, they're unreadable.' *I* could read them, but I wasn't in the Union, where they have an unshakeable code. So," a deep breath, "the recording was cancelled. They simply packed up and cleared off. Like a union walk-out. I wrote personally to Brian Matthew the next day, a grovelling apology: '… If you still feel that we warrant another try … I will certainly have the rhythm section charts prepared in an acceptable form …' It worked, thank goodness. Cliff went spare, of course."

But the battle was being won. In his office at Charisma, Tony Stratton-Smith was beginning to see the fruits of his labours. He put down the phone and poured himself a large vodka. Surely, now, it was indeed just a matter of time.

On 12th July, they secured a Russell Harty TV appearance. Anxious not to repeat the manuscript fiasco, Ken had the score copied out and set about delivering them personally to the musical director of Harty's show, living deep down in the wilds of Sussex.

"I left London with the transcript about two o'clock, his address pinned on my dashboard. After about two hours of country lanes, cul-de-sacs and ploughed fields, I turned into his drive and rang the bell. Eventually, this dishevelled figure came to the door, listened, looked at me over his pince-nez, and, after saying something to the effect of 'Oh, you needn't have bothered, mate …', shut the door in my face."

On July 13th, 1973, 'Gaye' had jumped eight places in the BBC chart, to number 24, and Clifford T. Ward finally appeared on the 'Top Of The Pops'. The world saw a humble, nervous talent, shying his hair like a pony, sitting alone, high on a stool—no piano—puzzling even the most dedicated follower as to his apparent lack of euphoria at having achieved, literally, the fulfilment of his dreams. No smiles, no winks at camera, no nod of acceptance. Notwithstanding all this, 'Gaye' climbed steadily for the next two weeks—bringing him a second 'TOTP' appearance on the 27th, slotted between First Choice, with 'Smarty Pants', and Pan's People hot-panting to Free's 'All Right Now'—but then it stopped at number eight, as Gary Glitter headed a Top Ten family assortment that included Peters and Lee, David Bowie, Slade, Elton John and The Osmonds.

It was to be Clifford T. Ward's first and finest moment as a chart-breaking recording artiste. He was now rubbing shoulders with Paul Simon, just as ex-Dandelion stablemates Medicine Head were enjoying a somewhat higher—but equally brief—flush of success on Polydor, whilst Stratton-Smith's original protégés, Genesis, were quite literally, only at the beginning of theirs. His days as a song*writer*, however—his great, silent ambition—were only just beginning.

The follow-up album, *Mantle Pieces* (a perfect example of Ward word-play), was in progress even before 'Gaye' had charted. It was a creative peak. The songs were in the air, just waiting to be plucked out and captured, so they had block-booked into Chipping Norton Studios, a pleasant 40-mile, 90-minute journey from Worcester, and, at that time—along with The Manor, and Rockfield Studios in Monmouth—one of the only three 'stay-over' studios in Britain. Theoretically, irrespective of time-warp, things would progress smoothly.

But here, insidiously, the pressure began to show.

Up until now, although he had always been a perfectionist in his approach to recording, Clifford had ultimately accepted the inevitability of the *status quo*; that there comes a time when a track is as good as it will ever be, and that even so, time and money dictate the terms of such acceptability. With a hit record *and* an unprecedented reception to his talent, he subsequently became unprepared to let anything go.

The line-up was the same; the songs had been run through countless times, some were even overflows from *Home Thoughts*—fairly normal practice—and so familiarity and interpretation were no problem; it should go easy, after all, there are only so many ways to cook an omelette…

Young engineer Barry Hammond had just then entered the big, wide world of recording:

"I was dead keen, it was one of my very first sessions, so I got in early, cleaned the heads, set up the tape [such days …], then the drummer arrived and we got to getting a sound balance. I'd never met Clifford. I was a little in awe, he'd had a sizeable hit, so I wanted it to go well. The others trickled in, then about an hour later in he came. He wafted up the stairs, hair flowing, into the control room; we probably shook hands, but the first thing I remember him saying was, 'That's a good tom-tom sound'. I was really chuffed, but then, after a few run-throughs, we spent the rest of the afternoon trying to change it...

"A couple of days in, word came to me that Clifford didn't feel that I was experienced enough, which of course was true. He'd discovered that I was a beginner—not that I remember making a fool of myself—and that just wasn't good enough for him. I suppose he wanted the best available, so my boss, Dave Grinstead took over from then on."

Ken Wright had been with Clifford almost from the beginning, knew his approach, but even he could see changes:

"Derek Thomas had translated many of Cliff's simple ideas into the beautiful songs you hear on record. Cliff would come into the studio saying what a great song he'd got, 'Just listen to this!'. We'd listen to the plodding piano, wince a little (behind his back, of course), and then set to work making it listenable. It happened on *Home Thoughts* as well, although not to such an extent. That lovely intro to 'Gaye', for instance. Derek replaced the strident piano chords with that beautiful guitar work—which sets the tone for the whole song—virtually transforming it, and Terry Edwards, that [greatly] overlooked talent, continually produced some of the finest bass lines and harmonics on any of Cliff's records."

Derek puts it a little more modestly:

"I thought Cliff was a tremendously nice bloke and his songs were very strong. It was obvious right from the start that he took himself seriously and was determined to get somewhere. But [at the beginning] he was also good fun to be with, and the demo sessions at Bev's I remember as being a real laugh. Bev was the main joker, of course, but Clifford used to enjoy himself just as much.

"I think I helped quite a bit in getting the songs together in the early days. Clifford would start with his piano chords—which he didn't always know the names of, and I'd create a chord chart...

"Sometimes I'd embellish his simple shapes for the guitar and he'd like it; sometimes not.

"As we progressed from demos to records, there tended to be fewer laughs.

Clifford was always very self-disciplined and concentrated hard all the time he was in the studio. Although there was rarely any real aggravation, the atmosphere was sometimes terribly tense, and of course, Bev wasn't there to crack the jokes after the first album. The sessions [soon became] something to be endured rather than enjoyed for me."

Back to Ken:

"'Scullery', his second-biggest seller, wouldn't have even come to fruition without the studio band. Cliff walked out on it, left Chipping Norton, went home. We stayed behind and, in between breakfast and playing pool, put together the backing track that you hear on the record. I even ran the studio taps and clattered a few dishes; Cliff loved it in the end. But oh, those recording sessions. Over and over and over again."

"So, are you also saying they were tense, difficult, strained? There was an atmosphere?"

"Oh, fuck me, *ye*-eah." He stretches the last word, surprised at my apparent incredulity. "I became an expert at peacemaking. I'd been all through the early days with Cliff and it became second nature to me to spot a storm brewing and to try my best to prevent it happening. My catchphrase became, 'Time for a cup of tea and a Garibaldi…'

"And it didn't end with the recording," Ken goes on. "It was a 'performance' from inception to fruition. Mixing, re-mixing, cutting, re-cutting, and as for running order…hell's bells…!" His voice tails off, but he hands me one of his note-pads which shows the shuffling of tracks, not just once or twice—as would be normal—but half-a-dozen times or more, and, on a trivia note, shows that *Mantle Pieces* originally included 'That's The Way Our Love Goes' and 'Cellophane', but these tracks were dropped, only to re-surface much later, "… by which time the original players didn't get a credit !"

Bassist Terry Edwards, however, tells a slightly different story.

A slight, shy country boy, he was, like Derek Thomas, plucked from obscurity and transported almost overnight into the dream-world of the recording studio by Clifford, for which he is eternally grateful:

"Cliff had such a musical ear. He wrote his songs almost like a classical composer. He couldn't *write* music—the notes and dots manuscript thing—but he knew precisely how and what every instrument should play. He would sing me the bass lines, and I would learn them parrot fashion. Take it from me, every one of my best notes was out of Cliff's head."

But surely there must have been *some* musical input. Justin Hayward, a great CTW admirer, remarked on the 'root notes' that made Cliff's music so distinctive, and, listening to the songs, even as recently as the last convention, when Terry appeared once again—with Derek Thomas and Ken Wright—to recreate the past, you could see him stretching his bass lines to unimaginable limits.

Ken Wright insists that Cliff only intervened when something was played that jarred his preconceptions. I suggested this to Terry, that perhaps his musicians played what they felt, until something Cliff

didn't like happened to bounce off the wall, then he was in like Flynn.
Terry's modesty—or reverence—remains unshakeable.

"Well, yes," agreed Terry. "But once he moved in, he generally rewrote everything I'd been playing.

"My favourite, without question, is 'For Debbie and Her Friends'. Even now, when I put that track on, I cry. Not only because of the sentiment, but because of the sheer beauty of the recording.

"I remember going up to the house, at the Oaklands, for a rehearsal, and saying to Cliff that I hadn't got a *clue* what to play behind the song. He just quietly took me to one side and sang me, note for note, that simple, understated line that pins the whole thing together. It's absolutely beautiful."

Most creative artistes are notoriously difficult in the studio. There are exceptions, of course, but generally speaking, they give their musicians a hard time. It was probably more so in Clifford's case because of his lack of expertise on any instrument. He did teach himself basic piano, adopting a very self-taught technique—which helps to explain some of his wonderful chord inversions—but also, as Terry so rightly tells, he could hear things in his head that he struggled to describe or illustrate to others. This, with his intolerance of anything other than the best, obviously created tensions. Listen to songwriter Reg Presley on the infamous Troggs tape, as he tries vainly to explain a drum roll that not even his drummer can understand. It's there in the writer's head, but because Reg can't play the drums, he can't communicate his vision. It's absolutely hilarious to the distant listener, maybe, but hell for the musician—sorry—*drummer*. So it must have been with Clifford.

But time and again, whenever I question musicians, engineers, producers, about Clifford T. Ward in the studio, there is invariably a sharp intake of breath, a shaking of the head, a look that says, "Bloody 'ell…"

I was recording my third album at Chipping Norton Studios early in 1974, about six months after Clifford had finished *Mantle Pieces*. During a lull in proceedings, I got talking to engineer Dave Grinstead, a highly proficient, affable man, who had an impressive recording pedigree. As always in my life, talk came round to Cliff. We both lived in the Kidderminster area, we both sang our own songs, but I had made the mistake of being enticed into the subterranean world of the folk circuit, where they look to half-talents for their heroes, blah, blah.

"We'd completed the album," Dave was telling us. "Cliff was lying on the couch, listening to the playbacks, behind the speakers. It was probably the first time he'd listened in, or from, that position. Suddenly he sat up, said that his singing sounded flat, the mix was wrong, *everything* was wrong and, despite all assertions to the contrary, insisted on re-doing the whole lot again. Every vocal on every track. Astonishing. We couldn't understand what he was on about. But, because he was paying for it, well, you know, the piper calls the tune…" There were times, it seems, when even Clifford was not good enough for Clifford.

I met Dave again, 25 years later, passing through Oxford. We met for a lunchtime drink at a hostelry in Begbroke, where he now works for Solid State Logic, utilizing his wonderful years of recording experience to instruct world-wide clients in the usage of those fabulous recording desks.

He was still the same, recognizable man. Warm, friendly, but sadly lacking in recall about Clifford T. But then, he's been very busy over all that time. It is equatable, I suppose, with the pupil expecting to be remembered by the teacher: we pass through those hallowed portals, our lives changed forever by someone who, let's face it, is just doing a job, and, unless something quite traumatic, or truly inspirational, occurs whilst under their wing, then individuals are forgotten in the magnitude and time scale of it all. Insultingly so. He'd also forgotten me…

Dave did, however, acknowledge the incident concerning Clifford re-recording the vocals, only because it was such an event, and, in his opinion, quite unnecessary; but most of the lunch was spent talking about how the industry had changed, and not for the better.

"I got out of Chipping Norton just in time," he said. "There is no challenge, no real talent that needs a studio like that any more. It's a case of doing the demos at home, then the recordings—if you're lucky enough to get through the impenetrable wall of sign-up hype—are done in some extortionately expensive complex somewhere that just reads good on the sleeve. I'm generalizing here, of course, but it just isn't the same any more. Times have changed."

"Too true," I replied, looking around the spotless, but soulless bar. "They've got Rentokil *soap* in the toilets…"

The end of July saw Cliff in Monte Carlo for a TV promotion, then in August, Tony Stratton-Smith, aglow with his new success, threw a lavish party at his country retreat in Sussex. Ken, sensing the justified excitement and aware of the demands of show business etiquette, turned up to enjoy the night. Clifford, however, made no such appearance, and sent no apologies. His innate dislike of socializing, particularly on a grand scale, was not yet recognized amongst his business contemporaries, and the gesture was interpreted as far more than mere artistic temperament. Here, maybe, word began to fuel discontent within the company as to the marketability of Clifford T. Ward.

He was being nationally—almost internationally—acknowledged, yet he was only prepared to conform so far. *Home Thoughts* had lifted him to where he believed he rightfully belonged, but, it seemed, he wasn't prepared to play the game now that he was there. Show business is about show.

A month later, a vocally enhanced version of 'Wherewithal'—adding extra harmonies to, and re-mixing, the album version—was released as a follow-up to 'Gaye'. During Emperor Rosko's Round Table review programme on 15th September, Ray Davies, head Kink and one of England's most innovative writers, praised its eloquent originality, also justifiably complimenting Derek's wonderfully phased guitar solo, but, despite this and other regular airplay, of a far superior record, it failed to make any impact.

At the end of September, overlooking the party incident, Cliff and Ken—and Lufthansa—flew to Germany, for a short media tour…

They were met at Frankfurt Airport by Jurgen Schmeisser.

"He was the [record] company minder," smiles Ken. "An efficient click-heels German; firm handshake, curt, polite, no-nonsense. We were just country boys, out on the town, enjoying our first real taste of the pop star lifestyle. He ushered us into the back of the car—a big limo, then, as we sat admiring the plush leather upholstery, making small talk, he put on a crash helmet…In a car. You can imagine our faces. We turned to each other, open-jawed, then slid slowly down the seat, cowering. He lane-hopped the autobahn all the way to Baden-Baden; in, out, in, out. I actually felt like grabbing Cliff's hand, to comfort him, or to reassure *me*, as we sat there sliding from side to side, looking at the back of this steel-clad head, which occasionally spoke, pointing out various landmarks, at 120 kph…"

The tour went well, and a little less terrifyingly, with a television appearance on 'Hits-a-Go-Go', miming to 'Gaye'—before heading, pack-like, with the other British bands on the show, to a slap-up restaurant meal—paid for by, well, somebody, then radio interviews, then a video recording at a fairground in Saarbrücken, before a brandy-soaked evening at Otto's Bar—hosted by the wonderfully named York Prettiwitz—and stumbling back to a badly organized double-bedroom ('The first and last time I slept with him!,' jokes Ken). Next day, on by train to Brussels, another TV spot, miming 'Gaye' once more, and then, thankfully, back home and down to earth, at Chipping Norton Studios to finalise the third album…

About this time there had also been some other home thoughts happening: Clifford and Pat decided to move house. They bought The Spinney at Pensax, a large, red-bricked bungalow overlooking open farmland at the back and The Bell public house at the front; the move planned just towards the end of the school summer holidays but—and again, a sign of things to come—also coinciding with another long recording session, meaning Clifford would not be at home.

It's up to you, Pat:

"Debbie was due to start at the Thomas Delarue School, Tonbridge, in August. The local authority had suggested various local places, but we had done some extensive research, looking for a school that could offer the very best facilities and settled on this one. Deb, thankfully, was quite thrilled with the idea."

But as with all children, the novelty soon wore off. Debbie didn't always look forward to Monday mornings.

Ken offered to collect her from Charing Cross Station on his way up to one of the weekend sessions. Experience should have warned him. The recording overran—his diary records that it was 'not a happy session'—and at the eleventh hour he had to race Debbie back to London to re-connect for her journey on to Tonbridge. She didn't want to go back, so she made him suffer, letting loose some heavy verbal objections all the way down.

Poor old Ken.

Meanwhile ten-year-old Martin and six-year-old Sam had been accepted at the local village school, a charming Victorian building situated deep in the heart of the ancient woodland, no more than half-a-mile away. But for the moment they were all still on holiday, they had to move house, and Dad was far too busy, even though he was merely 'down the road'.

To be fair, it was one of the studio's block booking arrangements; the musicians could work throughout the night and sleep on the premises, resuming work as and when they felt fit; an agreeable arrangement—if the muse was flowing.

The move went well, of course, completed on 1st September, 1973. Pat was more than capable of handling children and a house full of furniture. She even found time to appear on BRMB, as the first female guest on Birmingham's newly opened independent radio station, and conduct an interview for the Wolverhampton-based tabloid, the *Sunday Mercury*, who chose her as their 'Woman Of The Week'. By the time Clifford returned, before flying off to Germany with Ken, everything was neatly in place, everything was just tea-cosy.

All through October, interrupted only by another promotional appearance—this time in Zurich—they continued mixing, re-mixing, cutting, re-cutting. Then came the appearance on the BBC 2 late-night music showcase, 'Old Grey Whistle Test'.

Sergeant Pepper's Band had ignited an explosion of creative talent unsurpassed in the history of pop music, and now, those few years later, the writer-performer was centre stage, though the media had been slow to acknowledge the demand for something other than chart shows and personality comperes.

Producer Mike Appleton was brought in to fill this void, and with *Melody Maker*'s Richard Williams as anchor man, the 'Old Grey Whistle Test' was launched in September 1971, using Charlie McCoy's Area Code 615 track, 'Stone Fox Chase' over stuttering star-kicker graphics as its leitmotif.

The programme took its name from the golden days of 'Tin Pan Alley', and the Brill song-writing factory of the late 50s, when, at the end of a busy working week, in-house writers would often 'audition' their most promising songs in front of the domestic staff, who were lovingly known as 'The Old Greys'. In the era of the two-and-a-half minute single, immediacy was the keyword: if the cleaner or doorman could hum, whistle or, better still, sing any of the new songs after perhaps two hearings, that number was deemed a potential hit—'The Old Grey Whistle Test'.

The show soon achieved enviable cult status. Whispering Bob Harris, co-founder of the London gig guide *Time Out*, took over the chair in 1972, and enticed the world's greatest pop musicians into the tiny Presentation B studio on the fourth floor of Television Centre—hereto used only for weather forecasts—to perform live, on camera. With these performances, and subsequent concert specials, Harris's eloquent enthusiasm, and many classic album tracks played against backdrops of archive film footage or Betty Boop-era cartoons, it was a pot-pourri of vibrant, intelligent pop music, welcomed into our homes every Thursday for 42 weeks of the year. I remember sitting spellbound, for seven whole minutes, as Janis Ian sang 'Stars', right at me; Queen's 'Keep Yourself Alive' over a Tugboat Annie short; the magical Cat Stevens coloured animation of his own 'Moonshadow'; marvelling at the utter tranquility of Martha's Vineyard, where whispering Bob, in that serene, seductive way, interviewed James and Carly; and watching—in naughty-schoolboy disbelief—Debbie Harry's mini-skirt inching unbelievably floorwards, as she shimmied through 'Heart Of Glass'...

The studio acoustic section often showcased the solo singer-songwriter, though Clifford T. Ward, living in his self-imposed artistic seclusion, was probably never even aware of the programme's dazzling pedigree; it was left to Clive Selwood to advise his golden boy that this was indeed an enviable opportunity, whilst capitalizing on his recent chart-success, to reach out to a more discerning public.

Maybe Clive should have treated it as just another show, for the pressure became only too apparent. Pre-recorded on the evening of November 20th, Clifford performed two songs, sitting at a grand piano. With Ken astride the drums, Derek playing a gleaming Martin D-28,

Terry holding his Fender bass at the obligatory 45-degree angle, and new boy, but old hand Dan Fone (or is it Jerry Garcia…?), playing an unidentifiable guitar with *two* holes in it, the band and Clifford exude an aura of intense fear rather than ultra-hip coolness. Opening with 'All Modern Conveniences', his acutely observed comment on re-housing, Clifford then flicks the hair from his face and softly introduces '…another song from my new album'—not mentioning it is in fact the next single—before they glide into 'Scullery'. Here, because of the Moog solo, Clifford insisted on singing to a backing track, strictly against house-rules, but somehow it was agreed. Even so, on a video copy of the producer's cut, after a seemingly faultless run, a voice-off requests another take, blaming camera angle. This is done without question, but then comes another, by which time Cliff is noticeably seizing up with the tension. He begins humming. Nothing in particular, just a few nervous notes. Clive Selwood is heard. "Don't worry about the hair, Cliff, it looks fine," to which Cliff replies, via Tom Crite, "…'taint me Clive, it'sa Kenny, he keeps on at me … Huh."

The vocals are impeccable, but, barely peeping out from behind that curtain of hair, he gives the impression of it all being perfunctory. Nothing could be further from the truth: he is scared witless. He never once acknowledges the camera, as if fearing it will move in and bite him. In the transmitted version of 'Scullery'—the *third* and final take—he doesn't even bother miming piano; he just sits, hands on lap, moving only to reach and 'play' the Moog solo.

It is a heartbreakingly beautiful vignette of five talented but absolutely petrified musicians. They probably of him, he of the occasion. You can almost hear the collective sigh of relief when it is all over.

Introspection—navel-gazing self-indulgence—was an art perfected by the solo singer-guitarist, and accepted as such, but this newcomer, sitting at a grand piano, motionless, distant, mechanical, would not have impressed OGWT viewers. His appearance that night did little to further his career.

But certain enclaves of the media were still entranced by his placid public persona. Acknowledging the high profile and eloquent spirituality, Tony Jasper, the respected Religious Affairs producer for the BBC, brought a film unit up to The Spinney to feature Clifford on his Sunday evening programme, during which the family man was strongly portrayed; his views and beliefs given impressive exposure in the lovely, tranquil setting of Pensax school playground and back at his home. A gentle half-hour of persuasive broadcasting.

The press were clamouring for at-home interviews, besieging the house, sometimes without invitation, but Mr and Mrs Clifford T. Ward handled the inconvenience without murmur.

"We had one amusing insight into the journalist life-style," recalls Pat. "A female reporter came to the house, floating around the place, gushing, flirting with Cliff, trying hard for an in-depth interview, with very little success. Cliff could handle anybody when it came to words...

"Then, about a month later, Ken, Cliff and I were having supper when the phone rang. It was the Lygon Arms [a five-star hotel in Broadway]."

Ken takes up the tale:

"Cliff answered the phone, listened for a few minutes, then handed it '... to my manager, he's here with me now.' I took the call, without even a glance or a hasty warning from Cliff. It transpired that this lady journalist and her boyfriend had spent a luxury weekend at the hotel, had a slight *contretemps*—in that he'd upped and left her to pay the bill—and she was left without adequate funds. They wouldn't accept credit, she had no cash, and had consequently given Cliff's name as surety. Would we vouch for her? Well, would you?"

November 1st had seen the 'final' cut, 5th November the re-programming and final *final* cut, which received Clifford's reluctant nod of approval—to everyone's relief, for there were rumblings in the land.

Ken Wright, in his duty as 'personal manager' to Clifford, had noticed a significant lack of enthusiasm in the Charisma camp for the new release, prompting him to write to Tony Stratton-Smith.

In a letter dated 8th November, he outlines his concerns, '... bearing in mind ... the type of artist that [Clifford] is ... that the pattern and dynamics should have automatically continued—if not improved.' Then duly acknowledging '... setbacks over tasteless sleeve design...lateness of the record's completion ...', he notes, referring to the meeting that very day, '... important members of your staff had not heard the album or the single, no acetates of 'Scullery' had been cut to gauge reaction (as had been agreed) etc...' and continues, '...In short then, there seems to be a very worrying lack of impetus, enthusiasm, teamwork, call it what you may ... it is particularly important that the promotion and marketing be scheduled precisely and effectively.'

There was little positive response; a phone call assuring him all was being done that needed to be done, a few placatory gestures, until, on 1st December, 1973, came the release of the eagerly awaited follow-up to *Home Thoughts*, the third Clifford T. Ward album, *Mantle Pieces*.

Meanwhile, as if his career wasn't worrying enough, Cliff had throat trouble. A continuation of earlier discomfort had been finally diagnosed as tonsillitis—to his neurotic satisfaction—and he entered an Edgbaston nursing home for the operation. The date clashed with his long awaited—and thus never-to-be—'Jackanory' audition, but priorities prevailed, though in true Ward fashion he quickly discharged himself—*too* quickly, some suggest—and launched himself grudgingly into the round of press interviews and public appearances. Tony Blackburn—in those lovely days when it mattered—had chosen 'Scullery' as his Record Of The Week; a 'David Hamilton Show' was recorded at the Aeolian Hall, and on 18th December he recorded another—to be his final—'Top Of The Pops', transmitted on the 20th, bringing 1973, Clifford T. Ward's finest year, to a fitting climax.

We had seen the last American troops leave Vietnam, the birth of legal commercial radio, a three-day working week imposed on industry as a result of the miners' strike, and a violent Christmas bombing campaign from the IRA; all this within the 12 months since the children had sung, 'Yes, Jesus loves me, the Bible tells me so ...', in a song inspired by John Bunyan, for an album inspired by Robert Browning's love of England, performed by a school teacher who himself had found inspiration, initially, in the black soul music of America.

It seemed, to all concerned, that talent and dedication, despite, or together with, sheer bloody-mindedness, cussedness, stubbornness—call it what you will—had finally won the day. From here, the only way was up...

Home Thoughts was released in America on January 3rd, 1974. This would be the year of Watergate, Lord Lucan and the World Cup, and, indeed, it even began musically with us all at odds with each other. As The New Seekers, Sweet and Slade faced Barbra Streisand, Barry White and Donny Osmond across the water, and with the beautiful James Taylor days of melody and sweet introspection already fading, Great Britain—which had given hope to the universe with John, Paul, George and Richard—was now exporting the kitsch excesses of Elton John and the wild, sensual pleasures of Led Zeppelin.

It is little wonder, therefore, with so very little advance publicity, and, from the artiste himself, a positive unwillingness to promote, that this oh-so-English record was totally ignored.

He had become a celebrity at home by record sales only. No concert appearances were forthcoming, though plenty of offers were. Just at the very time when he should have been capitalizing on his success, something was holding him back.

The Great Easton Arts Centre Group, in Essex—a charity boasting such luminaries as Cliff Richard and the then-Settler Cindy Kent on their committee—almost pulled off a coup arranging a concert around Clifford for 25th February, even to the point of costing a '... modest orchestra. ... at £15 per head inclusive of four hours work...a budget of around £150 ...', but Ken, in his letter of January 8th—wearing the heavy mantle of manager—tactfully suggested that the Arts Centre had jumped the gun a little, merely quoting '...several [unspecified] reasons...' for it '...not being appropriate at this time ...' The concert was cancelled.

And about this time, it becomes clear just what impact 'Gaye' had made on some of the world charts. It had hit big in Australia and Spain, and Cliff had flown to Rome for an Italian TV appearance at the beginning of March. Clive had mentioned Brazil, '... an awful lot of copies ...'

Sure enough, 'Gaye' had hit it big in Brazil, but even bigger than Clive had realized.

In a letter dated March 11th, 1974, promoter Malcolm Kigar, based in Sao Paulo, writes endearingly to 'Dear Person' at Charisma:

> Enclosed please find a best selling records poster chart ... for the week Jan 15th/74 to Jan 22/74.
> As you notice, your artist Clifford T. Ward is scoring with a solid number one position. The record remained first for more than three weeks. My guess is that the single sold about *300,000* copies ... [The italics are mine.] There is, however, bad vinyl supply and some companies are unable to manufacture records according to demand. The number one EP by Demis Roussos was also unobtainable from retailers once it peeked into Brazil's top ten.

Perhaps 'Gaye' had taken all the vinyl on the market...

He continues:

> ... I am seriously interested in bringing Clifford ... to Brazil for a few concerts ...

Then the startling comment:

> ...I gather there isn't an album out ... Please contact your licensee and instruct it to provide [such a] release ...

Once he had established a contact name, he continued to pressurize Ken Wright, but with little joy. Ken intimated interest in a tour—even to the point of checking whether Cliff had a valid passport—which brought an exclusive 'Foreign Management Agreement' almost by return of post, seemingly an honourable agreement, tactfully reminding Ken that his suggested dates for June/July would not be suitable as '...it is winter vacation time in Brazil ...'

However, this time the boys did not reply, which prompted a delightful 'Speed Letter', this time from Kigar's Los Angeles address:

> I am still awaiting word from you ... Do you also manage Genesis? I am looking for a rock group [like] Alice Cooper for a film production beginning in June ... Please reply!

They didn't, and in a final missive dated April 17th, Malcolm Kigar, still polite and hoping, bows out. Whether he was ever as successful in other ventures as his opportunism deserved is not known.

Clive Selwood, meanwhile, was still doing his bit for the cause.

He had written to Jerry Greenberg at Warners, New York on 21st January, enclosing UK reviews of *Home Thoughts*, and expressing pleasure at Jerry's '... enthusiasm for Clifford ...', but went on:

> ... I was more than a little disappointed that you did not have any concrete marketing plans beyond giving the single a shot on radio. I was even more disturbed when I was unable to obtain a copy of Clifford's album in any of the New York or Los Angeles stores including Sam Goody's which is not a hundred yards from your office ...
>
> I do believe that Clifford in person will be your best means of promotion.

And then, confident as ever with his belief in the talent, he thus concludes:

> As I said to you at our meeting, there is no doubt in my mind whatsoever that Clifford will become an enormous star in America, with a very lengthy career ahead of him ...

A copy of the letter was sent to Ken and Tony Stratton-Smith.

But across the sea in Ireland, things were going well. In a country known for its beauty, its friendliness and its love of family, the music of Clifford T. Ward had touched many a heart.

Peter Grogan, a young schoolteacher, and his wife-to-be, Eileen, were among the many new converts to this English songwriter.

In those days he was a long-haired, wide-flared student. Today, his wiry locks—that Irish shade of yellow sand—are shorter, his clothes are Pringled for comfort, but his eyes still have the sparkle of youth.

"I was about 21 when I bought *Home Thoughts*," he tells me, in his warm Dublin brogue. "I was just starting my own record collection, and the main reason I bought Clifford's album"—and the slightest hint of a smile crosses his face—"is that it was a gatefold sleeve, and up on my shelf it looked like two albums, giving me a total of four...

"But apart from that, it was the whole presentation: the family snaps, the intelligent under-stated sleeve-notes and, of course 'Gaye', which had received considerable air play over here the previous autumn.

"You know, that song—and I've been fortunate to hear the original studio version, the song stripped of its beautiful string section—well, it's very much like Pinter-ism, the art of the unsaid. 'Gaye', to me, is a typical example of such an art, which shows how far ahead Clifford was in his songwriting. The whole album conveys the art of understatement. Terry Wogan, bless him, considered 'Gaye' to be a trite song, on first hearing—with which I suppose many people would agree—but he is now a great fan of the man's music, because, as he listened more he became aware of the nuances, the subtleties. Clifford never said more than he had to. Some songs were maybe two minutes long, some, like 'The Traveller', were five minutes plus, but nothing was wasted. He treated songwriting as a craft, rather than churning out a three minute pop song.

"After I'd bought the next album, *Mantle Pieces*, I read an article by Shea Healey [who later went on to Eurovision fame, writing 'Just Another Year' for Johnny Logan]. Shea ran a magazine called *Spotlight*, a fortnightly look at the music scene, and here was this schoolteacher-turned-pop star (a fact that I hadn't been aware of, although it should have been obvious, with such poetic references in his work), who was coming over to Ireland in April, four or five months ahead. Well, that weekend, Eileen and I were in a record shop in Henry Street and the guy behind the counter, knowing we were great fans of Clifford T., tells us that he's in town that very night to do Gay Byrne's 'Late, Late Show' [Ireland's equivalent to Terry Wogan's UK peak-viewing television programme]. I told him he had to be joking, 'cos I'd read in *Spotlight* (the Irish pop bible) that Clifford wasn't due over until next April. 'I'm telling you, I heard him doing an interview from Dublin Airport this morning,' says y'man. 'He's definitely in town, for the RTE show tonight.' So, that was it. Eileen and I got over there for about seven o'clock. We'd no tickets, but we just stood around, with both albums tucked under my ... army surplus coat (which I'd bought for one pound from a desperate friend). It was pouring down, and I mean *lashing*. We stood there, me in my trench coat, hair well and truly frizzed, Eileen looking her cool, beautiful self ..., until about nine o'clock, by which time the 'Late, Late Show' was well under way. I thought, 'This guy has really sold us a dummy.' Suddenly a taxi pulls up, out steps this tall figure, long hair blowing in the wind. 'That's him,' I says. We run up. 'Clifford, can you sign these for us please?' He signs willingly, then asks us if we're coming in. 'We've no tickets, it's an all-ticket show,' says I. 'Well, you're friends of mine then, come along,' says he. End of story."

They were ushered in, wide-eyed and helpless, "... into that bright,

precious wonderland, the Mecca of Irish Showbiz.
"I hate that term, 'showbiz'", he protests, "but you have to realize …"
Peter and Eileen stood there, side-stage, transfixed, as Clifford sang to a backing track.
"I just couldn't believe it. Here I was, suddenly standing in the wings of RTE Studios, holding the jacket of my idol, as he performed to the nation! I'd learned every song on his albums, knew them off by heart, and he'd suddenly materialised as if out of nowhere, walked toward us as we stood there gob-smacked, and treated us, a couple of young, ridiculously wet, star-struck strangers, as if we were old friends. It was just beyond belief.
"As I stood there watching him, I remember feeling in his coat pocket, checking his cigarettes. I was smoking some cheap brand. Clifford had Rothmans in his pocket. I thought, 'Jeez, that's it from now on. Rothmans for me …'When he came off, we chatted, he spoke glowingly of his wife and family, then he wrote his address on the back of a publicity photo and *insisted* that, should we ever get to England, to make sure we dropped in."
They did make that trip—itself a valuable insight into the open-house, indeed open-hearted attitude that Clifford and Pat always showed to his fans—and went on to forge a strong friendship with the Wards that lasts even to this day, with Peter, as we shall see, playing a strong part in Clifford's subsequent popularity in Ireland.

But in the meantime, back at the ranch, it was on with the show.
'The difficult third album'—a media cliché—did not exactly dazzle the reviewers, but, because of the plaudits *Home Thoughts* had rightfully received, *Mantle Pieces* received an obligatory amount of press coverage, though it was noticeably less enthusiastic. The schoolteacher story was now old hat, and so, without an equivalent angle on which to work, reviews were confined purely to the music sections of the papers, and the critics, in attempting to justify their position, appeared to indulge in criticism for its own sake; nit-picking, over-analysing, just being that little too clever for the simple, genuine emotion displayed on the album. There could never be another 'Home Thoughts From Abroad', that was Clifford T. Ward's *magnum opus*, but the songs were still worthy, were still unique, and yet, sadly, that is probably where they began to fail in their appeal; they were not commercial.
A lot of hard work had gone into this album, really hard work; times where, as Clifford had said, he 'could upset … [them] but they wouldn't get upset with me …' referring to his tenuous relationship with his dedicated musicians Ken, Derek and Terry. The songs were decidedly more personal, perhaps *too* intimate for most reviewers, but oh, the angst that went into their completion.

Kathleen Bishop, aged 17

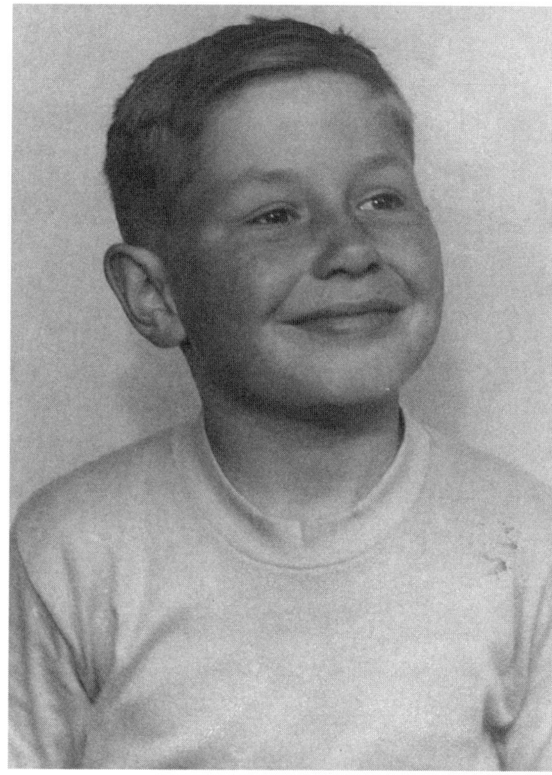

Clifford, aged 10

The Ward 'Cosa Nostra'. A family wedding, with father Frank third from left, daughter Kath, mother Kathleen, sons Barry and Melvin, Clifford centre stage

Charlie and Nancy Rollings at the beginning of their marriage

Pat as Head Girl

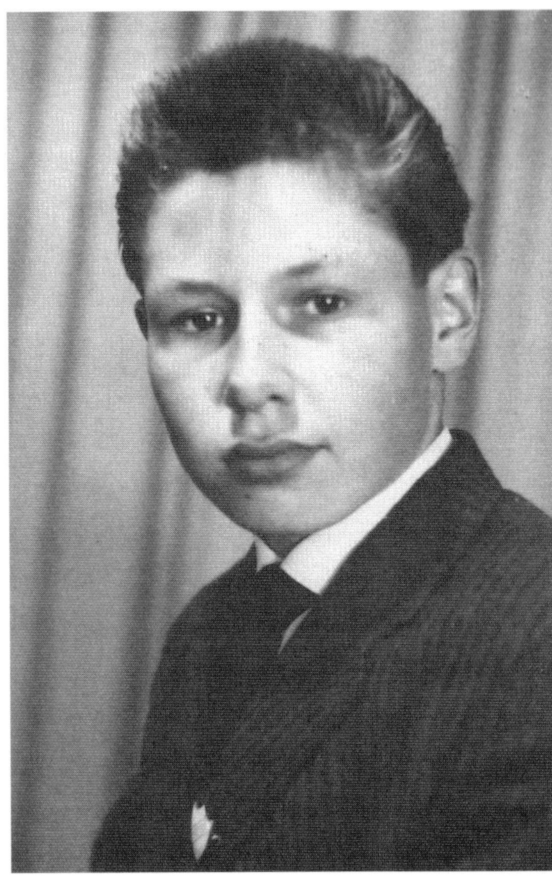

Clifford as a prefect, aged 14

Vox humana

'and I was your big hello'

Poseur? Moi?

A rare guitar picture; a rare guitar

Stourport Bridge. Cliff, Ken, Trevor, Graham and Terry

Leon Tipler, Zella Studios

Left: The original Cruisers, with Roger Bowen and Rodney Simmonds

Right: The Locarno 'Band of the Year' winners 1963. Fred Simmonds holds the cup, substitute drummer Tim Jackson at rear

Left: The Cruisers, ready to take on the world

Right: The Lavender Hill Mob planning their next heist (© Express & Star)

The track 'A Sad Cliche', for instance, with its '…awkwardly contrived snatch of supposed court room … magistrate's [voices] …', as one reviewer put it, was a prime example of Clifford's developing behind-the-scenes obsession with perfection way beyond the call of duty.

Clive and Shurley Selwood, in their role as executive producers, remember it all too well, as Clive tells me:

"That's us doing the magistrates. It took nearly *six* hours to do those few lines. And we spoke them the same way *every* time, the only way we *could* speak them …" he groans. "Cliff would insist, in his wonderfully charming manner, that gentle smile, that soft voice over the intercom: 'Perfect! Clive/Shurley, but can we just try it one more time …' *Six* hours! I tell you, my patience was sorely tried. Little did I know what was to come… [*Escalator*, the next album] "

Mantle Pieces did not shake the charts, barely touching the bottom fifty, and the much under-rated 'Scullery', with its '… pots and pans … soapy water, washing machines …' made an all too brief appearance in the Top 40, then went down the plughole. At the end of February, Polydor reissued *Singer-Songwriter*, trying to capitalize on what had seemed to be a promising career, but that only aggravated or confused the situation. Both sold poorly.

It was back to the drawing board, which of course meant, in effect, back to the studios.

At Chipping Norton, the engineers probably breathed a sigh of relief as Clifford started recording his fourth album …at Chelsea's Sound Techniques Studios, with Jerry Boys and Vic Gamm—now affectionately known as Tweedledum and Tweedledee—again on the flight deck.

Work began on 7th February, 1974, and it is worth pointing out here that it would be over a year before *Escalator*—which was to be the final Clifford T. Ward on the Charisma label—would be completed. The machine that had grabbed, polished and pressed two albums in six months was running out of enthusiasm, whilst the architect himself was beginning to question even his own judgement. It was becoming a precarious partnership within a dubious circus company.

Ken Wright was becoming only too aware of this. Following his letter to Charisma in November, 1973, he had realized the way things were going and felt an obvious need to keep on top of the situation. Through the following spring, besides continuing to rehearse at Bob Tansley's Hundred House Hotel in Great Witley (two miles from Pensax, 130 miles from London), and late-night recording sessions—oh, and working full-time at The Beeb—he had at least eight business meetings with the record company, trying desperately to recapture the enthusiasm they had shown towards Clifford at the time of signing him, only 15 months previous. Whether as a diversion is not known, but on two occasions Ken was asked whether Clifford would be interested in writing an album of hymns, obviously with 'The Traveller' in mind, and Strat's tangential thought process sensing a niche in the market. [Charisma did follow this idea through, in part, with the release of a collective artiste compilation, entitled *Beyond An Empty Dream* in 1975].

There had been numerous local radio interviews, including Marsha Hunt's Capital show on 4th January, a 'Pebblemill At One' session in February—singing 'Gaye' rather than the new single, which desperately needed a shot in the arm—and many other promotional appearances, but Clifford was not responding with gratitude.

"By the time we got to this fourth album, Cliff was really at full gallop in the studio," Clive Selwood told me. "As I've said, he just wouldn't let anything go. Over and over and over again. Like a dog with a bone, and he was just as hard on everybody else as he was on himself. Cliff can be the nicest, most charming of people, when he wants to be, but nothing ever seemed right. To Cliff, and Cliff only, there was always room for improvement. Then, because he couldn't find the perfection he wanted he started switching musicians. Ken, who'd been with him from day one, was suddenly out of favour, his capacity as manager was virtually put on the sidelines. Cliff even suggested I should manage him, as a kind of interim affair. Things were becoming desperate.

"I tried to side-track him a bit, take his mind off it all. It was the pressure. Before a recording, Cliff was *so* apprehensive. I used to see his temples throbbing, he was so tense, and the slightest thing would spark it off. After an album was finished there was a visible change in him, such *relief.*

"So, during a lull in recording sessions, I called Mick Robertson, whom I was handling and who was then fronting 'Magpie', a great and very popular children's TV show. Mick was quite a heart-throb in those days, and I thought it would be a good idea for him to make an album of Cliff's songs, or at least record some of them, with Cliff producing. We did about five, maybe six songs, to what I considered was a fairly good standard. Mick wasn't the world's best singer, but they sounded okay to me. But of course, okay was never good enough for Cliff. He let it get so far, then just walked off with the masters and vetoed the whole project."

Such incidents, though suggested by associates with the best of intentions, did little to help. Things were indeed becoming desperate, and the relationship between Clifford and Ken Wright, the two friends who had seen, been through and achieved so much together since The Cruisers, was now reaching breaking point.

March and April saw the plod of recording, practice, recording, practice, with Ken arranging those meetings at Charisma with whoever condescended to 'spare the time'. String sessions were conducted at Kingsway Studios, with Richard Hewson still producing his beautiful arrangements (John Mealing deputizing where needed), but Clifford was still unable to be at peace. Clive, in his role as executive producer, popped into the studios now and then, bringing royalty statements and, on one visit, surprising news of his impending resignation from his lofty post as Marketing Director at CBS.

Throughout all this mayhem, sessions being cancelled, sessions being unproductive, Charisma being uncharismatic, Ken, Clive and Clifford had been in deep discussion concerning a new management agreement and a revised publishing deal with Island Music.

Then, towards the end of May, came the straw that broke the drummer's back.

"We'd been doing an all-night mixing session at Sound Techniques. I think that was the only time we took pills, just to keep awake," confesses Ken, sheepishly. "Anyway, come the dawn, we called it a night and went off to yet another pre-arranged meeting with Lionel Conway at Island. Cliff, like most musicians, hated the idea of anyone making money out of his music except him, and saw Island as complete parasites, taking their 50 per cent, whilst he (and I quite naturally thought that meant '*us*'... and Charisma, just about...) was doing all the work. My input from the start had been considerable, in fact, enormous. I felt, quite rightly, that Cliff's success had been helped, in no small part, by my endeavours. I'd negotiated the deals, organized the press, the media showcases, spent a lot of hours on the phone, business meetings, dashing all over London at the drop of a hat, basically working as Cliff's manager-designate, and I must admit my patience was tried on more than one occasion. I was even approached by The Hollies, and Cliff Richard, via their managers, enquiring whether Clifford T. Ward would be interested in supporting them on tour. Naturally, I jumped at it, but Cliff refused point blank. We were offered good money, orchestras, whatever; they were ideal promotion vehicles, but, because he wouldn't, *couldn't*, be in control, he shied off. It hurt and it puzzled me. I, *and* the other musicians, felt cheated out of a great career opportunity. Here I was, working for the man, and he wasn't responding. To Cliff, it was studio, home, studio, home. He was only interested when he had full and total oversee. He hated London, whereas I was working down there, so it was delegation by situation, and, although I didn't think about it too often, I assumed—rather foolishly as it turned out—that some form of reimbursement, either in a professional capacity, or financially, would follow.

"The frustration had set in. Cliff wanted to off-load Island, I wanted a bit more certainty and recognition as to my role. We'd talked it over and arranged to see Lionel. Naïvely, we assumed he would just let us go. Really. I'd suggested forming something with just Cliff, Mooncrest (the Charisma publishing arm), and myself, to which Cliff had wholeheartedly agreed. I'd even gone to the expense of buying an offshore company, and, after some protracted negotiations, we had agreed on a name: Clifford T Music.

"So there we were, stumbling up the stairs at Island, tired, weary but, I believed, determined. We went in, sat down and were immediately hurled a tirade of, well, not exactly abuse, but Lionel certainly let us know, in words of legal and moral significance, that we were a couple of ungrateful chancers. Cliff then turned to me, in the office, in front of our accuser and said, more or less, 'Yeah, Ken, why'd you want to do all this?' I couldn't believe my ears. The blame was laid fully upon my shoulders. We left with our tails firmly between our legs and Cliff reiterated his turncoat feelings down there in the street. Oxford Street, London. May 24th 1974. I turned, without so much as a shake of the hand, not even a goodbye, and walked out of his life. I didn't see or speak to him again face to face, for nearly four years..."

The incident must have played on Cliff's mind, for he made an attempt to re-establish relationships in a letter dated August 3rd, though the tone of his letter was almost as if nothing had happened:

> Dear Ken,
> Hope you are well.
> The album is now finally finished and due for release in a few weeks. I have just come back from Portugal where I did television and radio. The weather was very hot and the whole trip very enjoyable. 'Scullery' is number three there!
> I have instructed Clive to pay all monies due to you and the others so that should be with you fairly soon. Please keep in touch and let me know how you are.
> Sincerely,
> Cliff.

Then, on September 3rd, by recorded delivery to his Dorset Street flat, Ken received the following note:

> I have now studied the accounts in detail and in view of the total amount earned I am able to offer you ten percent for drumming and ten percent for your efforts in management.
> I am enclosing a cheque for £1657. 36 which I hope you will find acceptable.
> If you want to discuss any aspect of the earnings further please give me a ring or 'drop in' for coffee.
> I would be grateful if you would return all documents relating

to my earnings, such as BBC cheque counterfoils etc., as I shall shortly be handing everything over to an accountant for tax purposes.

Sincerely,
Cliff.

The olive branch was ignored and the silence, apart from what few account papers were requested, continued to be deafening, until many years later, when contact was re-established as a necessity, for in 1979, completely out of the blue, the jolly old taxman wrote to Ken, asking him why he hadn't declared the payment of £1657.36 he'd received—in 1974—from Clifford T. Ward.
"This was the last straw as far as I was concerned", he shrugs. "Apart from the fact that it was referring to something five years previous, it re-opened the old wound. None of the money I had put into helping Cliff's career had ever been repaid—and there was quite a lot," his tone suggesting that he might have been an slightly understating the case. There followed a lengthy correspondence, but his letter dated July 24th, 1979, (reproduced verbatim here, after my five hours spent deciphering his writing—he is a drummer after all, *and* an accountant...) explains his frustration perfectly, if not too succinctly:

Dear Sir,
I refer to your letter dated July 4th, which I received on July 11th, 1979.
I was surprised to receive your letter, concerning [*sic*] that it refers to a period of five years ago, but also because it refers to the receipt of fees by me from Clifford T. Ward.
For several years prior to the one mentioned in your letter I was involved in trying to help Clifford to establish a career in the recording and publishing industry—in the capacity of a friend.
In this, I believe that I was quite successful, primarily because

a) I believed in his talent and ability

b) because I played drums and percussion instruments quite well for free, and

c) because I lived and worked in London, had certain contacts, and anyway Clifford hated even visiting London!

I have never received any fees from Clifford although from time to time, when he was able, he did give me nominal reimbursements for my considerable out-of-pocket expenses.
There was never any contractual arrangement between us because I regarded this activity as a hobby—although it proved

to be an expensive and exhausting one at times. I had, and still have, an excellent job with the BBC, as you will be aware.

There was of course always the thought that if Clifford's career were to become successful and lucrative (on the pop musician scale) that I would have been keen to play a professional role and to share in the fruits of success.

In response to your letter I have been reading diaries of the period and looking into various files and memorabilia and I have listed the sums of money that I received in the attached schedule. The final item is, I accept, significant and my explanation of how it arose follows:

As I have explained there was no contractual relationship between us but nevertheless I devoted a great deal of time and trouble to help further his career. I had known him and his family for nearly 10 years and so it was a close and happy friendship.

My assistance involved extensive travelling between London and Worcestershire attending rehearsals, demo recordings sessions, professional recording sessions, publicity and recording company meetings, meeting contacts, attending TV and Radio recording etc. During the period we recorded four LP albums and several singles and for several years my annual leave from the BBC was spent in the darkness of recording studios—for which I received no fee.

In 1973 there was some success with recordings and income generated more successfully. Unfortunately the success also damaged our relationship mainly because it brought pressure from professional agents and managers to sign Clifford. he was of course a prime target since his only contractual commitment was for publishing.

This worsening in our relationship plus the obvious problems of my career with the BBC competing for time and energy, persuaded me to have nothing further to do with Clifford.

This was at the end of May, 1974 and my only contact since has been the receipt of the cheque for £1657.36 at the beginning of September 1974 and, perhaps one or two telephone calls.

The cheque came as a considerable surprise, particularly as our 'parting' had been a little acrimonious, and I accepted it gratefully as going some way to reimburse me for my considerable out of pocket expenses during the previous four years. Clifford's career at that time did look exceptionally bright having had three top 30 singles and two good album releases.

> I am sorry if this has been a lengthy explanation, but I hope you appreciate my difficulty in getting across to you the nature of our relationship and why I took the view that I did of the repayment of expenses. They were certainly not fees.
>
> Yours sincerely,
> K. F. Wright.

"This incident only reminded me of how unfairly I had been treated," he told me. "The cars, the moving up of houses, the swimming pool he installed at Lower Hollin; they had all been financed by American release advances and other deals that *I* had negotiated for him.

"I'd spent a fortune subsidizing his career from the day I joined. Okay, I wasn't *forced* to, but the implication, as I've said, was that whenever it happened, as it surely would…

"Crikey, I even bought his outfit for 'Top Of The Pops', *and* paid for his hairdressing in London.

"He did actually have the grace to look embarrassed on one occasion whilst showing me a shining new Reliant Scimitar, sitting in his garage, knowing how much a 'normal' manager would have taken from his income, and how I had received nothing. And I mean, nothing."

Pat was surprised at these revelations from Ken's correspondence and his account of the bust-up. She had always believed—because she had been told so—that Ken had tried to sign Cliff's publishing away, and that Cliff had prevented him from doing so, hence the argument, the fall-out, and the walk-out.

Months later, when the Island royalties started coming in—and at a much greater level—Cliff was triumphantly striding around the kitchen, waving the PRS payment advice.

"If Ken had got his way, we wouldn't be seeing anything like this money coming in," she remembers him saying.

But the payments were larger because they were now covering the most successful period of his career, not because he had thwarted a rogue deal; there was no justification whatsoever in accusing Ken of attempted malpractice. And Cliff knew it.

I mentioned this to Ken. Not that it really mattered, twenty-four years later, but I was curious. Of course I was.

"Cliff told Pat that you were the baddie in that little episode."

Ken just looked at me.

Was that a twinkle in his eye?

The words of Mandy Rice-Davies floated across the table, and landed straight in my chicken bhuna.

"Well he would, wouldn't he?"

It was the end of a long and successful partnership. Very sad, and, one would feel, totally unnecessary.
Despite Ken Wright's valiant attempts at rekindling enthusiasm for Clifford in the Charisma camp before he left the field, an ongoing lethargy within the company seemed to be willing them on to self-destruct, and despite Clive—with his years of corporate dealings—taking the reins as Cliff's manager, there seemed to be little that could change Charisma's attitude.
In correspondence towards the end of 1974, he replies to Tony Stratton-Smith:

> I must confess to a sense of disappointment at the personal tone of your letter…If I may take your points in order:-
> You appear to be content with your efforts on Clifford's behalf over the past twelve months. In that period you have released one single—'Jayne' [From Andromeda Spiral]—*which was recorded entirely at your request and released over the objections of both Clifford and myself.* [My italics. This helps to explain the recording, but not the song's eventual and mysterious inclusion, on *No More Rock'n'Roll.*] I did see two 2-inch strip advertisements for the single.
> Ken Wright ceased to be Clifford's manager only two [?] months ago and I am but a phone call away. Gail [Colson—Stratton-Smith's PA] will confirm that at no time have I failed to keep an appointment … The only [ones] I have failed to keep are the four which you recently arranged and then cancelled [at short notice].

Clive then goes on to compliment Charisma's handling of *Home Thoughts* and 'Gaye', but then queries:

> … your reference to A & R problems and failed singles, when Clifford's second album sold in excess of 30,000 copies and featured a single 'Scullery' which sold 50,000 copies in the UK alone. If '… rushing into albums …' means the third album [*Escalator*], which we have only completed in the past twelve months, then I can only refer you to our contract which calls for two albums a year, which Clifford has always been able and willing to provide. I was present when you informed Clifford that you had put back the release of Escalator to November [1974], but the news that it had been further postponed to February 1975—a total of fifteen months between album releases—was a unilateral decision, gleaned from Gail during one of my many attempts to meet with you.

Clive then concludes with a couple of financial ultimatums, implying—quite within his rights—that refusing such will be in breach of, and will thus terminate, any existing contract.
That was October. In November, things seem to have calmed, and everybody was smiling and meeting for drinkie-poos, as Clive writes:

> … It was good to hear you reaffirm your faith in Clifford and, though I still believe that, owing to the past accounting problems, Clifford is technically out of contract [ouch …], his heart is with Charisma and nothing would please him more than to be even more successful with you.

The plan, as Clive saw it, was then outlined: Clifford would begin recording a new album in December, and a single from the current album, either 'Jigsaw Girl' or 'We Could Be Talking', would be released in early January, 1975. This would then be followed by a February release of *Escalator*, '…with a truly massive launch and promotional push as if Clifford were being re-launched.'

Emphasizing his belief in the future releases, Clive then suggests organizing top video producer Mike Mansfield to shoot a promotional film for the single, as soon as possible, and that '… a promotional visit to America to tour the radio stations is a priority.' He continues:

> … I'm sure that Tamla (if that is our new label) could arrange this without much trouble. Both the singles are strong and I will bring maximum pressure … on Clifford's agency to obtain television coverage.
> Clifford is very happy with his new band [??!] and should give a much more convincing performance.

Regarding the cover of *Escalator*, which had obviously been causing concern […], he suggests '… we should go for a new, simple portrait … and leave the back as it is.'
In what was to be the final written exchange, and in a professional attempt to maintain and encourage the current situation, Clive concludes:

> Once again, I'm glad that we had the opportunity to shout at each other, if the end result is of benefit to Clifford …
> [I] am ready and willing to co-operate in any way to this end.

That was November 1974. 'Jigsaw Girl' *was* released—in March 1975—two months late, and *Escalator* in April, again two months late, but, apart from its being chosen as Johnny Walker's Record Of The Week, no conspicuous attempt was made to 're-launch' the career of Clifford T. Ward.

I know. There can't be an artiste, manager or record company in the land, in the *world*, that hasn't seen letters like those. I've got about two hundred in *my* drawer... Promises, promises. People will tell you that it's a business, just like any other business, but it's not. This is a business where you create and deliver a highly personal and emotionally charged finished product, but then have to leave it to the air-heads, the no-talent wafflers, the 'I'm-in-the-record-business-but-I'm-tone-deaf' poseurs, to handle; and if they fail, *you* fail. And if *you* fail, the whole world knows...

I'm sorry.

Did I go on a bit there?

The Seventies. Well, 'tis true, the music business was then permeated with such souls. It isn't like that any more, is it?...

And so, fourteen months after recording had begun, *Escalator* appeared in the shops. Apart from the incredible amount of time and money spent in and out of the studios—a whole Sunday morning hiring and firing flashlights at London departmental store Bourne & Hollingworth had produced two pictures of Clifford on that moving staircase—it had then been re-cut *seven* times, plus the usual last minute running order changes and cast-offs, then re-scheduled; all this and more had produced an uneven album. With drummers Andrew Steele and Glen Lefleur replacing Ken on certain tracks, and ex-Bronco Dan Fone supplementing Derek Thomas's guitar work, it did, nevertheless, contain some of Clifford's finest moments. A fine fourth album, with the assurance and quality of a major-league songwriter. Alongside his confident chart-stabber, 'Jigsaw Girl'; a majestic, Elgar-ish song, 'The Way Of Love'; and arguably, his greatest neo-classical work since 'Home Thoughts ...', the politico-love song, 'A Day To Myself'; the record saw the Ward-Hewson magic again at work, recalling all those wonderful moments that had the music press applauding his first Charisma album. Yet they virtually ignored *Escalator*. In a time of photo-art profusion, the bold, idealistic cover portrait by Joe Petagno—capturing Clifford perfectly as the pastoral, Byronic writer against a backdrop of his beloved Worcestershire fields—may have affected sales, again a portent of things to come, but we all know that music critics don't buy, so why, despite the promises and expectations, such low media interest?

Well, as we know, success is the goal constantly aimed for yet totally dependant on an all-important combination, and if things are falling down all around, what chance is there for him who is standing?

There were good people at Charisma—of course there were—but invariably they were distracted, or without the enormous influence that was needed.

At the beginning of May, Steve Wood, at the Charisma Press Office, arranged for Clifford to record a series of local BBC radio station 'idents'—personal messages that could be slotted into music programmes to give a little conversational lift to the humdrum days of the parochial DJs— which he dutifully did; his warm voice was heard welcoming listeners to Radios Bristol, Medway, Oxford, Solent, Swansea, Plymouth and the newly opened Orwell 257. Theoretically, it helped sell records, kept the name abroad, but really, it was just cheap station promotion.

Pete Frame had joined the label in October 1974 as A&R man. He confirms the strange situation there, and that it wasn't necessarily a slight to Clifford. Other events were overtaking the company:

"I was … at Charisma … until June 1975, but the company was up shit creek financially and my job was only notional. Waste of time really … Stratton-Smith wanted to break Clifford bigger and suggested getting in John Lissauer as producer. Lissauer had a Leonard Cohen connection, and Strat was in cahoots with Cohen's manager, Marty Machat.

"Clifford met Lissauer for lunch, but decided he'd rather continue producing his own albums, as he had been doing until then. Quite right … His albums had a charm … Even Dave Robinson, later to form Stiff records … came into the office to blag a copy of 'Jigsaw Girl' for the jukebox at the Hope & Anchor, where he used to run gigs. He liked the record so much and was convinced it would take off big. Give Strat his due—he loved good songs and he loved Clifford's work—but I'm not sure that anyone else in the company [that mattered] shared his vision. He was an odd contradiction was Strat. A wistful romantic frustrated by a [strange] genetic impulse…

"I thought … Clifford was brilliant. *Home Thoughts* was one of the great albums of the period. And Joe Petagno's sleeve for *Escalator* really caught the essence of [the man]—the concerned romantic rural idyllic poet."

Back to Clive Selwood. The master plan had failed:

"Charisma were losing the plot. Somebody didn't feel *Escalator* was up to scratch—whatever marker they were using—so they began to concentrate on frying other fish. Naturally, without promotion and with the lukewarm response, irrespective of who was to blame, things *really* began to cool off, on both sides of the fence. The album wasn't a success and so a chicken-and-egg situation developed with Clifford and his songs. He would tell Pat, whenever she *dared* to ask about anything new, that he wasn't writing because he just couldn't see the point …"

Clifford's plans depended, actually, on his state of mind at any given point in time. In an interview with *Melody Maker* journalist Colin Irwin in the April 19th copy, he spoke of the future.

Irwin was a great CTW fan, citing *Mantle Pieces* as the album that should be '... locked away in a glass case along with the best china and played only as a special treat ...', but he too was disappointed in *Escalator*, and, by the time of the interview, it was quite obvious that Clifford was also having serious misgivings:

"... I'm much more enthusiastic about [my] new songs [for the *next* album] because I've [gone] back to a more rhythmic feel and a more simplified presentation ... because I do feel that my songs, in the way they've been presented, have tended to limit their appeal ... I think [I] have become very establishment, which is not what I set out to do ..."

He continues: "Mistakes have been made for sure ... You don't have to prostitute yourself to get commercial success," then referring to Paul Simon's admirable track record of artistic integrity and public recognition.

"A hit single is important to me financially ... but that's all ... one's life in pop music is only finally good as long as you sell records."

Then, no doubt to the amusement of his fellow studio musicians—past and present—he states: "... I still think I haven't found my level yet in the recording studios ..."

"He kept on *promising* new material," says Clive. "Oh, he could talk up a storm. 'I've got some *great* songs, you *must* hear them.' But the only way we could hear them was to drive up to Worcestershire. He'd never send us a tape, just maybe hum a few bars over the phone—honestly—and just keep us believing...

"And to make matters worse, about this time, Tony Stratton-Smith started getting interested in horses..."

"Oh 'eck," I responded, a sharp intake of breath.

"We'd turn up for a meeting—when we could get Cliff down to London, that is—and there would be Tony, on the phone to his trainer ... *horse* trainer, that is. He was a *lovely* man, Tony, but his interest had to be fed to keep him interested, and we obviously weren't feeding him. It was a bit disconcerting, sitting there in the office, the phone would ring. 'Oh, injured a fetlock? ...Hmmm ... yes, okay... Ring me back.' Down goes the phone. 'Now, about the next album...' Phone rings again. 'Oh, nag's off her *food*, eh? ... Oh dear...'

We both laughed, but I could see the implications.

Pete Frame also remembers the horses:

"We were all turning up for work one morning and Gail Colson was meeting us at the door, one by one, whispering furtively, 'Whatever you do, don't mention the horses. Tony's ... [horse] died yesterday.'"

Clive Selwood also remembers that Charisma were becoming financially precarious. He told me that following our conversation, he had found, amongst some ancient correspondence, a few B&C [Charisma's holding company] cheques marked 'Please re-present.'
'I'd forgotten their parlous … situation, which was another good reason to move…"
Clive concludes:
"Tony wasn't a rude man, but it just showed where his interests lay. It was a waste of time. I also heard Gail Colson say—well within earshot of Clifford—that the only good song he'd ever written was 'Home Thoughts From Abroad.'
"It really was time to get out."

WHERE WOULD THAT LEAVE ME?

The toughest thing about success is that you've got to keep on being a success. Talent is only the starting point in this business.

Irving Berlin

And so they did. All of them.

The domestic scene, apart from providing inspiration, also served as a barometer for Cliff's state of mind. Bored with the music, bored with the business, he became bored with the house, and with the help of a healthy bank account, Cliff and Pat decided to up roots and have a change of surroundings, or at least, a different *view*-point of their surroundings. They bought Lower Hollin, which was literally one mile down the road, but on the other side.

Knowing first-hand—like most of us—the upheaval of moving house, I put the obvious question to Clifford one lunchtime recently, whilst snapping open some cans of bitter. [He is now a 'born again' beer drinker; the red wine comes out only very occasionally.]

"Why did you move so many times?"

"We were behind with the rent...," he teases. "No-o-o-o, David, we just got *bored* and wanted to move on."

Pat said nothing.

"Yes, I can understand that, but I would understand it even more if, when you moved, you bought a house in, say, Surrey...or Norfolk...All that upheaval just to go as little as one mile down the road, on some occasions. Doesn't make sense to me."

"We didn't consider moving house an upheaval."

I caught Pat's eye, remembering the conversations I'd had with her about The Spinney, where she had been left to handle the move, and, later on, Castle Weir, the beautiful 14-bedroomed country mansion they had purchased at Lyonshall, deep in the heart of neighbouring Herefordshire, in 1977. There, the day after moving in, Cliff had flown off to America, leaving Pat, Debbie and the two boys—I should imagine—well and truly upheaved...

But Lower Hollin was worth every bit of it.

"That was my favourite," smiles Pat. "I have my happiest memories of that place, our best years, I think. We did an awful lot of work renovating the place. It was really buedieful," her slight Kidderminster accent adding poignancy to her words.

And it is easy to see why they were so happy. Clifford was at home, money was still coming in from his earlier successes and there was the house itself. The rustic, red-bricked Georgian farmhouse, set at right angles on the main road from Abberley to Clows Top—one of G. K. Chesterton's drunken, rolling roads—commands sweeping views over Clifford's beloved Worcestershire, stretching from the front and side, way across open fields and onto distant woodland, like Bestall's drawings of Rupert Bear's Nutwood, whilst, to the rear, two large ancient barns, oh…and the smell of pigs…

"That was the only disadvantage," she laughs. "We bought the house and the barns, but right next door, in a purpose-built bungalow, was the working farmer."

When the wind blew from the west, it was pigs all the way…

But that was of little consequence. After all, this was country life, and the house was a dream. The warm brickwork, the imposing Regency doorway—where many CTW publicity shots were taken—the large rambling stairway; it is easy to see why anyone that lived there could be happy.

It also had, along the way, and well within stumbling distance, the wonderful Bell Inn, a true English pub, with a snug, barrelled ale, a twisted oaken floor and a collection of resident countryfolk that made the Archers seem like townies. Harry Knott, whose picture now smiles down from the refurbished panelling alongside Stan Abberley, the bowler-hatted accordion player; pictures that you see today in many town pubs and even some country pubs, where they would have been hung as part of a job-lot 'theme'. Here, however, they testify to a genuine past, and not so very long ago, when men came in from the fields and drank to quench a thirst—not to fuel an anger—or when newly wealthy pop stars played darts and pool, for Cliff and Pat were not alone in this haven of escapism.

ELO leader, songwriter extraordinaire, Traveling Wilbury, Beatle re-union producer…and real ale lover, Jeff Lynne told me of those days:

"It would have been, yes, about 1973-74. I'd just moved from Birmingham to a little hamlet in west Worcestershire, so of course I went checking out the country pubs.

"There were lots of nice ones, but the one I fancied was The Bell. That's where I first met Clifford T. Ward.

"The Bell at Pensax was a wonderful little pub which at that time seemed as if nothing had changed for a hundred years or more. It was always filled with farmers, which I loved, having just become a 'landowner' myself—all ten acres of it—in a valley a couple of miles away.

“Then one night, into The Bell came Clifford T. Ward. He was on the crest of a wave at that time, having just had ‘the Big One’ and all that press about *Home Thoughts*, but he was easy to talk to, if a bit intense…”

A grimace:

“We started hanging out at each other’s houses for a while. He played me some great songs he had written on his big upright piano, I played him some of my songs on my guitar.

“He was always expounding the virtues of communism, so one day I asked him the big question. How come you’ve got a brand new GT Scimitar if you’re a communist? Quick as a flash he said, ‘It’s not that *I* shouldn’t have a GT Scimitar, it’s that *everyone* should have a GT Scimitar.’

“It was a brilliant bit of reasoning, so I just said, ‘Well, let’s go down the pub in it then.’”

Pat tells of parties over at Jeff’s house in Shelsley Kings, ‘…silly, embarrassing get-togethers; pushing occupied armchairs around the patio, legs akimbo, shrieking, yelling, spilling drink; as men do…’ She tuts, sighs and shakes her head. Such antics still do puzzle her.

“I used to sit in the lounge talking to Roy Wood. He was a quiet, gentle man. Very shy. I suppose that’s why he wore all that make-up on stage, it was his mask, his disguise. That way he could cope.

“Other times we would pop round and find Jeff in one of his creative moments, sitting with a guitar, the floor covered with open books. I don’t think he was reading them, just looking for lyrical inspiration.”

For a few enviable months, Jeff and his beautiful schoolteacher wife Rosemary, together with Cliff and Pat, were the nucleus of a little coterie of musicians—including ex-Move-ers and ELO-ists Roy and drummer Bev Bevan—who met and used The Bell as their fountain. Original Cruiser drummer Roger Bowen, with whom Cliff and Pat had maintained their friendship, remembers one night particularly well:

“There was quite a gang of us, just drinking—as you could in those days—and at the end of the night, Cliff asked us all back to his place. We’d just met up at The Bell, as we did every Friday. Gill and I had driven over from Ombersley, met up with Pat and Cliff, then gone back to Lower Hollin, as was the norm. We were a bit surprised at the size of the crowd back at the house; Cliff’s kitchen was full to overflowing. ‘Rog,’ he said, pulling me to one side, ‘there’s somebody really famous in the lounge. Go and have a look.’ So I did. I recognized Jeff, Bev, of course, but nobody else. ‘There,’ he nodded, ‘the guy in the middle.’ Well, of course, as always, you imagine your heroes are ten feet tall. I stared at this little guy, standing (well, I think he was standing…) in animated conversation, with a strong American accent. I seemed to recognize the face, but no…, I just couldn’t place it.

'It's De-e-el Sha-a-annon,' laughed Cliff, in his best Kidderminster accent. 'Bloody 'ell,' I gasped. And just for one split second, what I remembered more than anything was the ten thousand times we'd rehearsed that bloody song ['Runaway'] back in the Cruisers days. And *still* not got it right! But there he was, drinking and joking with the rest of us. He was staying with his wife Sandra, at Jeff's place. The night peaked with Jeff and Del at Cliff's piano, singing their heads off. Wish somebody had've taped it, worth a bob or two now…!"

Lower Hollin also made the headlines in the local press following a flying visit—literally—from society photographer Patrick Lichfield, lording it in his helicopter. Booked to do some promotion pictures, he flew up to Worcestershire, misread the A-Z and landed on the local golf course, way over par. When he did eventually reach Clifford's house, by chauffeur-driven limousine, the ensuing session was equally hectic.
"He was all over the place," tuts Cliff, "tripping over the rug, knocking over a side-table, spilling coffee. He was a big man. He sat on one of our little benches and it collapsed, spraying his Gauloises all over the floor. Idjyat."
Nevertheless, the subsequent photographs bear testimony to Lichfield's fine reputation. Some lovely, reflective pictures were taken and used for forthcoming publicity shots, capturing Clifford in his casually attired, country-squired mode (the rare picture of Clifford and Pat in this book is one such shot), the copyrights of which Patrick generously waived for a recent fund-raising auction.

There were always people dropping in, passing by, staying over. Everyone who called was given the full Ward hospitality, including a young actress friend from London, whom Cliff had taught during his time at Bromsgrove High.
"She was a fairly ambitious lady," remembers Pat. "After leaving school she went down to London, found an agent—a *good* agent—and began working in theatre immediately. When she came up to visit her parents at Stoke Prior, she often called in to see us, sometimes staying over.
"She was a wonderful mimic, a good actress in fact, and could do a convincing French accent—to anyone who wasn't French…We had a young lad from the village, doing odd jobs on the house, a lovely, friendly country boy. He took a real shine to her, and when we told him she was coming to stay as our *au pair*, he went out and bought a huge box of chocolates, almost professing his undying love. It really went a bit too far, got a bit serious. When we told him the truth, he was somewhat embarrassed, but he eventually saw the funny side of it."
There is a bit of a Sting in the tale here. The girl was Trudie Styler.

"I think our friendship—or *her* friendship with Cliff—took a serious blow when Cliff overheard her talking to some London friends on the telephone. She made some remark about '...having a nice, jolly weekend, up here in the country with a famous pop star and his family...' To Cliff, who hates pretentiousness of any kind, well, that was too much. He really tore into Trudie, and the journey taking her back to the station was quite fraught. He actually reduced her to tears."

Enough.
Let us not forget our two intrepid heroes, Peter and Eileen Grogan.
Peter recollects it all so well:
"Following the wonderful night at RTE in Dublin, and Clifford's equally wonderful open invitation to visit, we came over in the summer of '75, with the one intention, I swear, of just taking a picture of the house, and, okay, if anyone was around—which we very much doubted, being the 'world-famous-always-travelling-musician' (as we then thought, ha-ha...)—well, we would say a brief hello and then move on.
"We hadn't a car at that time, so we'd caught a train to Kidderminster then made it to The Hundred House. It was that really hot summer. Everywhere looked parched, yellow. We started walking up through Abberley, young Irish fools that we were...but after about a mile, Eileen [she says Peter...] started thumbing it. No sooner the deed, than a white van pulled up and in we jumped. The man was a teacher and straightaway he says that we can stay with him if we have trouble getting back, Straightaway. Y'know, jeez, this is the British people, aloof, quiet, minding their own business, it's *us*, the Irish that are the gregarious ones. Even by that stage, the generosity we'd found was amazing. Here we were, complete strangers in what was, supposedly, a strange land.
"Anyway, he dropped us off right outside the house. We crept around the front and there, surrounded by hair and cement, was the man himself, building a wall. He looked up and straightaway said, pointing at us with the trowel, 'Dublin.' He couldn't believe it. Well, neither could we! Anyway, he made us feel incredibly welcome, took us into the house and introduced us to his daughter Debbie—who I stupidly hadn't realized was the 'girl in the wheelchair' from *Mantle Pieces*—then a little while later, in came the lovely Pat, who'd been next door looking after the elderly lady. We chatted, had a few cups of tea, then he asked us where we were staying. I told him probably in The Hundred House. He said something like, 'That's crazy. If you've not paid a deposit (which we hadn't) then you're staying here.' We ended up—not by design, but by sheer insistence from y'man—staying for five nights. That was Clifford T. Ward."

While Eileen and Pat were in the kitchen, Peter was in heaven, helping Clifford with his building work. They were installing a swimming pool, just up from the front of the house, after having re-routed the overhead electricity cables and heightened the surrounding walls. The patriarchal in-laws dropped by, mucking in; Pat's gentle, capable father, Cliff's strong, no-nonsense dad. "I'm 'appy for Cliff, lad," he told Peter. "He's a stubborn one…"

"Actually I was a bit affronted, him saying that about my idol. But as I got to know Cliff better, I realized how true it was. He had a mind of his own all right," and Peter shook his head in despair.

Oh, he had a mind of his own all right. Sometimes.

For the last three months he'd been in conflict with the Metropolitan Police who had impounded his car during a visit to London.

He'd replaced the Reliant Scimitar; Pat recalls him coming back from Bev Pegg's house in a fluster.

"We've got to get rid of that car. Bev says it's only made of fibreglass and if I have a bump it'll crumble to pieces."

He might have ruled the roost whilst recording, but, in the world outside, his naïveté led him to believe anything, so he had traded it in for a Volvo tank and whilst finalizing some detail in London, had overstayed his welcome in a SW side street. The heavies had been called in to tow it away and had damaged the steering lock in the process. Cliff really went for the jugular, and to his credit, received full reimbursement for the repair costs, though, in true paper-tiger tradition, was refused the cost of *all* the relevant telephone charges; a sum of *90 pence* being deducted from his final demand of £118.78. He claimed train and taxi fares, car hire charges, even telephone calls to Southwark Police Station and Scotland Yard (wonderful…) and tried including the cost of a tin of black spray paint…which was refused; ahem, '…as this does not appear to be a charge directly attributable to the repairing of your steering lock…'

It is amusing, but quite sad, even pathetic to read these petty little authoritative letters refuting, contradicting, demanding; attempting feebly to maintain the *status quo*, trying keeping the law in order, fighting for little victories against trifling misdemeanours and to realize, all these years later, that nothing really matters after all…

But even taking the British idiosyncrasies into account, it was becoming a mad world out there. Back in March, Roger and Gill Bowen and Pat accompanied Clifford to Belgium for some media appearances. Cliff, in his wonderful wheeling-dealing way, had exchanged the flight arrangements and costs for cash enough to cover a driving break, whereby they took the Volvo across on the ferry, stayed in a small hotel overnight and turned up at the studios for the show; it was to be a pleasant experience, or so Roger thought.

"We got there in plenty of time and were sitting around waiting for Cliff to go on. Cliff was trying to translate the newspapers for us, as we drank some coffee in the foyer. Suddenly, there was a helluva hullabaloo and the whole building filled up with gangs of student-types, carrying banners, charging up and down the corridors. Cliff looked at me, I looked at him and we all ran off—in the opposite direction, naturally! They saw us running and decided it was a good idea to chase us. Like something out of a '*Carry On...'* film. We managed to get up some stairs and crashed into an empty office, slamming the door shut as they charged past. I slumped against the door, bloody breathless. Cliff couldn't believe what was happening. Gill and Pat were in hysterics, as always, seeing the funny side of life, but Cliff was very uptight...

"They weren't protesting at *Cliff*, mind you. It was just our misfortune to be there when it happened. Something political. North American Indians or something," and he laughs. "The TV people were very apologetic. Cliff did his bit, we drove home. Mad. I'm surprised a song didn't come out of that..."

The Volvo was a marked car, it seems. Two months later, in June, 1975, he was disqualified from driving for three months by Chippenham magistrates, following a fourth speeding offence on his way home from a Radio Brighton interview. And it wouldn't be the last time...

"He was always getting caught," Pat tells me. "He loved driving, and he loved driving fast. He also totally ignored yellow lines, parking restrictions, authority in fact; he just had to get caught sometime..."

Sounds just like somebody else I know.

He couldn't drive the Volvo, so, in his logical mind, it was superfluous. He gave it, in lieu of payment, to Frank, the builder who had helped install the pool and who, on numerous occasions, had cast an avaricious eye over the big red saloon.

Pat now had her own car, so transport wasn't a problem. In November 1974, in a moment of bewildering generosity—though obviously enjoying the newly acquired kudos of fame and fortune—he had written out a cheque for £650 to their local garage for a 1972 blaze-coloured Mini 1000, allowing her mobile independence for the first time in her life. Pat even began making visits to the studio with the boys during school holidays, but recalls the ongoing sessions as being "...so *bor*ing, sitting around going over and over the same thing, again and again. I took Sam and Martin down the road to the park..."

Yet even purchasing that second car had been traumatic:

"Cliff had been driving back from Chipping Norton. There's a small garage, just outside the town. He saw a Renault 4 on the forecourt, on sale at about £200. He went in, did some talking and decided to buy it for me. Next day, my dad drove us all the way down to the garage—Cliff's car was due in for service—to collect the Renault. When we got there, it wasn't quite ready, so Dad left us to wait—it would be about half-an-hour—and made his way home. Eventually we started back, me driving, with that funny little dashboard gear-stick. We'd gone about three miles when the thing just died on us. Cliff went spare. Cussing and shouting, as if it was my fault. He went to a phone-box, but he didn't call the garage, he called my dad, who had to drive all the way back down from Kidderminster, arriving about an hour later, to pick us up. As soon as we were home, Cliff was on the phone to the garage, cussing and shouting again, telling them that the car was there, by the roadside waiting to be collected and that the sale was cancelled. He'd stopped his cheque. We heard nothing else and he later bought me a car from a place a bit closer to home."

When Clifford's licence was reinstated, he chose a Lancia Beta, which, despite their emerging reputation as rust-prone and unreliable, proved—in this case—a worthy purchase. He drove Lancias for the rest of his time on the road, even, at one point—despite his apparent dislike for publicity—acquiring a personalised number plate, 17 CTW, which he eventually sold, with the car attached, to son Martin, who in turn sold it on to someone else, no doubt for a heavy profit.

The contentment at home, however, belied the unease he must have surely felt regarding his musical career. Though money from his Charisma albums was coming in thick and fast, he was now without a recording contract, without the friendship and invaluable assistance of Ken Wright and, until such times as a next album, he was only as financially secure as his brief success would allow. Unfounded and totally absurd—to those who knew better—rumours that he would appear at the Reading Festival that year, together with announcements that he was writing 13 songs for a Granada TV special, appeared in the corners of a few trade papers, but the actualities—past royalties and no live work, apart from sporadic radio or daytime television spots—meant that the money they were spending on Lower Hollin would soon diminish their healthy bank account.

Clive was his only hope, and thankfully, against all better instincts, he persevered. As always, he eventually found success. Clifford was offered a contract by Philips and the wheels, once again, were in motion.

The album *No More Rock'n'Roll*, recorded at the well-tried R. G. Jones Studios in Wimbledon, and released in December, 1975, was the fifth

Clifford T. Ward album and, though again inconsistent in mood and content, it did produce what is probably his finest qualified moment as a songwriter.

Other songs elsewhere in his back catalogue were arguably as good, but the ethereal 'Up In The World' caught the imagination of several internationally established artistes, beginning with Cliff Richard's vibrato-mannered version on his best-selling 1977 album, *Every Face Tells A Story*,

And I remember that song only too well…

Jim Little was a drinking friend of mine. Having originally met in the Freemason's Arms, a Kidderminster hostelry, we soon found we shared another common interest in tennis, and during the late 70s spent many balmy summer evenings playing at Brintons sports ground, or the beautiful pre-war courts at Summerfield Teacher Training College, before retiring to the Mare & Colt or the Freemason's for a jar. Or two.

Jim was also a music enthusiast; concerts, records, the lot, though his tastes were somewhat alien to mine: John Denver, Richard Harris, Jack Jones. He was continually recommending albums, which he would then lend me, and which I would never play. The covers were enough.

At the time I was just about getting over Clifford's success, Jim came around with a new Cliff Richard album, and the news that he'd just been to see Jack Jones in concert, and that Jack had sung 'Home Thoughts From Abroad', giving it a most affectionate introduction. Continuing in that almost *schadenfreude* way, he pressed the album into my hand, telling me it contained a Clifford T. Ward song. Thanks Jim, just what I needed…

A couple of days later Carole and I were going out somewhere. I'd changed my shirt and was waiting patiently downstairs. It would be another forty minutes at least…so I decided to play some music. I flicked through my record collection and then saw Jim's album winking at me. Reluctantly I picked up *Every Face Tells A Story* and decided to give it a try. I wasn't a great Cliff Richard fan, but at least he couldn't be any worse than Richard Harris. So on it went. Not straight to the song I didn't *really* want to hear, but straight from the beginning. Listen and judge in context, David.

My wife and I had never agreed on music. She considered my sentimental twaddle to be, well, sentimental twaddle, and over the years had learned not to say anything that would hurt my 'artistic sensitivity'. She could hear this music upstairs—it was not a big house—but I wasn't trying to convert, I was just passing time. The needle followed the groove. There was Harry's mechanical voice, breathing and warbling to perfection; bubbly and bland. Two or three fairly ordinary songs, then it all went quiet. Gradually, a string section rose until it filled the room—holding that same note for a few seconds—and he began:

You've gone up in the world...

I listened in amazement to a song the like of which I'd never heard before, and as it finished Carole put her head round the door and shouted down, "That was absolutely beautiful, Dave. Really nice." There was no possible way she could have known the provenance of that song. She had simply acknowledged hearing something quite special.

I muttered a curse, then went and sat in the cupboard beneath the stairs, adopting the foetal position and chewing at my knuckles...

That song then began a long journey, progressing—albeit sometime later—to Art Garfunkel's sugar-coated rendition on *Scissors Cut*, his 1981 CBS release. Irish legend Colm Wilkinson, world stage star of *Les Miserables* and *Evita*, also issued a limited-release version in May 1979—one which Clifford himself reckons the best interpretation—but once again, on listening to them all, the supremacy of the original is unquestionable.

There is also another footnote, for what it's worth, that Clifford T. Ward, Songwriter, had made his mark amongst the established music fraternity. On his 1976 album, *Rotogravure*, the luckiest drummer in the world decided, for some reason known only to himself and co-writer Vini Poncia, to plunder *No More Rock'n'Roll.* Taking the song 'Birmingham'—Clifford's quirky tribute to the big city of his teenage years—they rename it 'Lady Gaye' and change the first line of each verse to suit. It is an awful attempt at the exploitation of a well-respected songwriter, not helped one iota by the stellar line-up of Harry Nilsson's backing vocals, Klaus Voorman's bass, Danny Kortchmar's guitar and Dr John's piano. Whether Clifford was consulted or not is incidental—you don't say no to a Beatle—but I'm certain he would have disliked the end result, and, on the strength of the rest of the album, it is unlikely the royalties would have amounted to much.

The *Home Thoughts* trio—Ken, Derek and Terry—is noticeably and sadly absent on 11/12ths of *No More Rock'n'Roll.* The irony is not to be missed here. Bev Pegg recalls, as far back as May 1973, Ken dropping in at his home in Kinver, obviously as messenger, suggesting they recruit 'real professional' studio musicians for the forthcoming sessions. It seems that even then, Cliff, despite the triumphant release of *Home Thoughts*, with its flawless, innovative performances from all involved, was still dissatisfied.

And sure enough, two years down the line they have all gone, making only a brief 'filler' appearance on a re-mix of the star-trekked 'Jayne...', strangely included, as it was Clifford's penultimate Charisma single. It is the noted session musicians Chris Spedding, Andrew Steele and B. J. Cole—brought together by Richard Hewson's 'muso-fixer' Tony Gilbert—who, despite their noble talents, take the album, as a whole, away from that pure Englishness that had made Clifford's career such an initial success.

It had all started to become a bit patchy, a bit hit-and-miss. Charisma, under Stratton-Smith's directive, had issued 'Jayne...' way back in August '74, following it up in March '75—as part of their promise to Clive—with a real CTW stab at the pop charts, the 4/4 summer-sounding 'Jigsaw Girl', which combined his English-stringness with solid undertones of the earlier CBS Secrets' singles. A *Mantle Pieces* reject, 'Cellophane', was the flipside of this contender, but the public were quite unimpressed.

Confidant Leon Tipler, back at Radio G-LTK, remembers Clifford complaining about pressure being applied from the record company to 'come up with this up-tempo single,' writing to order, so to speak, '...which he never wanted to do...' But 'Jigsaw Girl' was a catchy, credible attempt. It received considerable air play, stepped onto *Escalator*, and that was that. Goodbye, Charisma.

As a trailer to the new album, Philips put out the haunting, working-class observation, the title-track, 'No More Rock'n'Roll', in November, but for some peculiar reason—in which record companies become a law unto themselves—backed it with the totally out-of-context (even on the album) 'Gandalf', from Clifford's ongoing Tolkien project. It was all up-against-the-wall stuff; if it sticks, fine, if it doesn't...well, maybe there's something by someone else that will...

The following spring, dear old Charisma had one last shot, reissuing 'Home Thoughts...' and 'Where Would That Leave Me?' as their final Clifford T. single. An admirable coupling—in Browning's April—it reminded the few who heard how beautiful it all had once been, only three years ago, when the accolades had poured like silver upon the shoulders of the singing-schoolmaster.

So, *was* he developing, changing, or was he indeed beginning to struggle as a writer?

Besides the Tolkien idea, Clifford's draft submission for the BBC *Play For Today* series, entitled—and subsequently inspiring—'Up In The World', had failed to materialize, despite his collaborating with Herefordshire writer Alick Roe (though Clifford's framework for this project would surface much later as the *Both Of Us* album in 1984 and on a 'Collector's Only' cassette, in 1993). Therefore, apart from the album itself, there is little else to consider. He was certainly *attempting* to branch out into other fields of work, but nothing was forthcoming; his album was currently his all.

On *No More Rock'n'Roll* there is a noticeably greater mid-Atlantic feel than anything previous. The songs are still gentle and rhythmic, but there is a subtle but unnecessary reverb on the voice, more blatant instrumentation and, one has to say, more 'easy-resolution' to some of the lyrics. Arranger Richard Hewson is given co-production credit here, as if to acknowledge his definitive work on the earlier albums, and the mellow sleeve, with its Coppelia-like model propped against a Wurlitzer 1050 juke-box, beautifully echoes the sadness of the title-track. But Clifford's desperation—the cover versions were still a few years ahead—must have been increasing, ironically just as his studio-obsessed attitudes were lessening. The album was completed very quickly. In terms of financial outlay, it should have made money. It *would* have made money, if only it had sold…

Back in Dublin, Peter Grogan, after overcoming his initial shock at the warm welcome he'd received from Clifford and Pat, set about using his charm and nerve on the Irish broadcasting icons. He was surprised at the initial reaction.

"It was really nothing to do with me," he maintains. "I know over in the UK it's y'managers who have to do the work—and that's what they're paid for—but over in Ireland, Cliff's name was so well respected I would just have to ring up, say, the Late, Late Show, and speak to researcher Tony Bolam and, after ascertaining that I was *not* in the music business but that I *was* reliable, he would just say, 'Clifford T. Ward? Yes. What date would suit him?' And, if needs be, they would bring their schedule forward to suit, or record it for a later date. All of them. I could give you lots of such examples. It was that easy. Nothing to do with me, or my powers of persuasion, only that Clifford would arrange to stay with me for a weekend, and I would get the work for him as needs be. His image, the family, no drugs, no booze, was so honourable over here. That's partly the reason Eileen and I were attracted to him in the first place. I mean, my father died when I was very young, seven or eight, and I suppose, in a way, I began to look upon Cliff as a surrogate father, a very *young* surrogate father…!" he laughs, "but his whole life-style was something I looked up to, there was no bullshit. Even the odd occasion when, say, Philips or whoever *did* book him into some posh hotel, he'd have none of it. He'd rather stay with us, and *some*times—I have to say—to my frustration, 'cos we'd miss out on some good nights. I'd want to go along for the sheer razzmatazz of it, but no, he'd rather go home."

But, whatever work he did do via Peter served him well. He became virtually a household name in Ireland, with successful appearances on every one of the country's top media programmes, including a memorable spot on Tony Johnson's 'Roll Over Beethoven' show, on 6th April, 1975, where he had given a warm, modest interview before singing his then current single, 'Jigsaw Girl'. Back home, however, in his own country, he continued renovating his Georgian farmhouse.

He was coaxed back into the studio for his second and final album for Philips, which would see release in November, 1976, entitled *Waves*. Clive had secured a massive £20,000 advance for the album, but most of this was already accounted for in back-dated recording costs and current bank overdrafts. Nothing is ever that simple. Reverting to the friendly Chipping Norton Studios, where Cliff had produced his finest moments, Clive again bought in John Mealing to arrange most of the tracks, Richard Hewson, due to other work commitments, only contributing his talents to the complicated 'Avenue Dreams' and 'Susan'. The orchestrations, mainly synthesized, give the impression of a somewhat lack-lustre affair, punctuated with vacuous instrumental passages and a pointless, uncomfortable reinterpretation of 'Not Waving—Drowning' from *Mantle Pieces*, noticeable if only for his slipping into the vernacular over the line, '...would not miss *yer* if you did not come.'

But as always, there are some worthy tracks—with a propensity of first-person love songs among just the eight new numbers—but also a lot of wasted groove-time. The up-tempo 'Everything Goes Out The Window' reminds us of Clifford's aptitude with a pop song: wonderfully tight, funky almost, those barely discernible harmonies, a great vocal and an infectious hook; but this farrago of an album was helped in no way by the bizarre air-brush illustration of Clifford T. Gandalf on the cover.

According to executive producer Clive Selwood, the sleeve was a *fait accompli*:

"We were presented with it by the company, and, after we expressed our total horror, and I *mean* horror—Cliff *hated* it—all agreed that if a hit single came off it, then we would re-do the sleeve."

John Mealing has none of the unpleasant memories other musicians associate with the making of a Clifford T. Ward album, though it was suggested that, apart from Derek and Terry—sadly playing their last goodbyes—Clifford maybe felt the contributions of industry session musicians were more difficult to question; that 'professionalism', so to speak, carried its own currency. John does, however, acknowledge that valuable time was wasted by indecision.

"Clifford ruled the roost. Very quietly, there was no shouting, no argument. He knew exactly what he wanted to do, except...," and he smiles slowly here, "he would then change his mind, and the *next* thing was exactly what he wanted to do."

We are both laughing.

"Does that sound right?" he asks. "Confidence, indecision, self-doubt. That's how it went. Clifford did so much soul-searching. He changed his mind so many times, and every time he did, he was convinced that he was right. That's why we moved on to Wimbledon to finish the album; we'd run out of time at Chipping Norton. What he really needed was a sympathetic, but strong-willed producer, but he wouldn't consider it."

So, despite these mandatory moments of 'unnecessary repetition', it was finished without trauma. A hit single was the answer, but was there one in there?

Well, of course, hit singles were a thing of the past for Clifford. With no heavy promotion, no live appearances, it was scarcely worth the trouble. But they played the game. Inexplicably overlooking the superb and more confident '…Window', with Pete King's blistering sax solo, a modified version of the opening track, 'Ocean Of Love', sneaked out in September, preceding *Waves* by two months. It waved, then sneaked back again, completely unnoticed. Mixed reviews for the album's November release, often citing the incongruous cover, more or less sealed its fate.

It was not looking good.

However, during this wilderness period, Phonogram, who, under their collective umbrella, owned various other labels—including Philips and Mercury—did succeed in bringing Clifford T. Ward to give the only true, live public performance of his career.

In a concert arranged principally to promote Mercury's new signing, model-turned-singer Twiggy, they asked Clifford—plus The Rochdale Cowboy, comedian Mike Harding—to support her in a prestigious concert at London's Queen Elizabeth Hall, on July 20th, 1976, where she would top the bill, launching her eponymous debut album. It was to be a glittering occasion; the media would flock to see the fashion face of the 1960s thrust herself into a second career, and many would be surprised at her success in doing so. Tickets were prized and priced accordingly. It was to be no mere pop concert, more a showbiz gala. With a sound system loaned by A&M stars Gallagher and Lyle, currently riding the crest of their wave, all proceeds were to go to the Music Therapy Charity.

Oh dear. Even so, after a few nail-biting days, Clifford agreed, but there would need to be much preparation…

They spent weeks rehearsing his short spot; it had to be absolutely perfect, this was live. Clifford hired Kyre Hall, near Tenbury Wells, a beautiful, ancient country home, then run as a school for children with special needs, and hours over days were spent practising the songs. John Mealing, who had now assumed the role of Musical Director in Clifford's line-up, drove up from London, with *Waves* musician Paul

Keogh, a gentle, talented Irishman, who had forged a solid reputation as a session guitarist amongst the London studio coterie, following his appearance on Carly Simon's debut album, *No Secrets*.

John and Paul stayed at Lower Hollin for three nights.

"They were so welcoming," remembers John. "Pat really fussed around us, feeding us and ensuring that we were comfortable. It was such a beautiful house, dotted with antiques and children, a real oasis from the city life. Our bedrooms looked out over glorious farmland, and [but unfortunately as it happened] also the farm. There we were, sleeping peacefully after a long drive and a strenuous afternoon's run-through—oh, and a few brandies—when we were woken at about six o'clock by the most horrendous noise, nothing like I'd ever heard before. It was feeding time for the pigs. I'm not kidding you, David, I leapt out of my bed in sheer terror. It was almost as if they'd been switched on..."

So that was why Pat was always up at the crack of dawn, doing the housework...

Pigs.

Many times, Cliff told me later, when he was working in his music room, the farmyard porkers insisted on hogging the limelight. Inquisitive piglets up at the fence, sniffing, foraging, poking their snouts through the railing.

"I often used to call for Pat [...] telling her one of them had got its head stuck. There was I, sitting at my piano, trying to write so-o-ngs"—he deliberately slurs the word—"and all I could hear was this awful squealing, which was, as you might well i-*maaag*-ine, ex-cruc-iat-ing. And it weren't my music...Huh."

Back to John:

"The rehearsals were extremely wearing. He was such a perfectionist, and yet, of course, it wasn't like recording; it would only ever be as good as it was played on the night. Keith [Smart, borrowed from The Barron Knights] managed to bring some levity into the proceedings, but otherwise..."

Derek Thomas and Terry Edwards, the two remaining members from the glorious past, complemented the group, and for the few songs he was to perform, Clifford kept them at it for almost four days.

But, the concert seemed to have paid off. With John Mealing fronting a string quartet, Clifford sang 'Up In The World', 'Home Thoughts...' and a couple of other songs from his catalogue. According to most who were there, it was a great success, though to Ken Wright, who had attended incognito, as a paying member of the audience, Clifford seemed 'extremely nervous' and that the string section was 'a little scrappy'. Ken hadn't seen or heard from Clifford since their acrimonious parting, but as he was still working in London, it was the ideal occasion to satisfy his curiosity as to how Clifford was developing. No contact was made. As he entered the foyer, however, he was more than a little surprised to see Pat stepping out of a taxi…

She had gone down with Roger and Gill Bowen, by train, though that had not been the original plan.

Roger had recently acquired a Mercedes convertible from his neighbour, in exchange for a piece of surplus land—this was country life, remember—and the three of them, Roger, Gill and Pat had started out from Pensax, full of the joys of the open road. At Great Witley, six miles down the open road, the car had died. Clifford would never believe them…

A rather hasty, tasty telephone call back to the neighbour saw them picked up and taken, post-haste, to the station, where, thankfully [and I would say incredibly, in light of modern day rail-travel], they were able to make a connection to Paddington and then on to the Festival Hall, in time for the concert.

Though the evening had gone well, it was here that the seeds were sown for it all to finally go wrong, and Clive Selwood, reluctantly, would finally step out of the picture.

Initially—and following the concert—the partnership was still in force. The record had done nothing, so it was up to Clive to find someone else. All is never lost…

"The options weren't taken up, so I did the rounds again and finally landed a deal with Mercury, who were *very* pleased to get Clifford T. Ward. We got a great advance from them, but after a while it became obvious that no new songs were forthcoming, so they suggested we took Clifford to America, away from his *milieu*, hoping a change of routine would spark the muse.

"Y'see David, Cliff had started to get *very* lazy. He never really came to terms with stardom. He really felt that when you're a star, things happen for you. He chose to ignore the essential hard work that goes into being a star, and…," here he takes a long deep breath, "Cliff just didn't work; it really is as simple as that. He wouldn't do *any* live work, saying that his piano playing wasn't good enough, which was just bullshit. I told him that people wouldn't come to hear his piano playing, they would come to hear Clifford T. Ward sing his beautiful songs, but no, he wouldn't have it. We could have secured him a really good living, going out for at least £500 a night, playing mid-price venues, but he just wouldn't get off his backside, and even on the few occasions he did, and I mean few…he was never happy. We did a Mike Read TV show in Southampton. Shurley and I, everybody, thought he was wonderful. We watched the recording later and Cliff just pulled himself to pieces. And it wasn't false modesty, he *really* hated it."

"Why wouldn't he play live? He'd spent years singing with pop groups, he couldn't have been nervous." I mentioned the 'Old Grey Whistle Test' appearance, a line-up that could have given a truly faithful, artistic reproduction on stage.

"He just didn't want to expose himself," Clive responded. "It was like the recordings, once he'd let go, they were up for grabs and people could make their judgements. You literally had to prise them out of his hand—that final mix—he was like a terrier, holding on."

"But he couldn't have felt insecure..."

"Let me put it this way," said Clive resignedly. "I think Cliff was pretty well secure about his talent, but he just didn't think the rest of the world was quite up to it..."

We laughed. Not in a derogatory way, but in a gentle, knowing acceptance of the man.

He continued:

"Then one morning *he* called *me*, sounding very excited. 'Clive, you've got to come up, there's something I want to discuss with you.' I'm sitting in my office at Pye Records.

"Well, what is it, Cliff? Can't we talk about it on the phone?"

In all this time, Cliff had never been a full time job for Clive. He had been headhunted by most of the major record companies, and had held a line of very prestigious posts, from Elektra to Marketing Director at CBS and now to the board at Pye Records.

"'No, you've gotta come up, today, if you can. It's very important.'

"So, I cancel all my appointments, collect Shurley and we drive all the way up to Worcestershire." He raises his eyebrows, throws his head back.

"We get to the house mid-afternoon. Lower Hollin, it must have been. He greets us, makes us welcome, cup of tea. By this time I'm a bit frazzled.

"'Well, what is it Cliff?' I ask, apprehensively. 'New songs?'"

"'No. It's *this,*' he says, shoving a piece of paper into my hand. It's a picture of a house."

"'It's a house,' I say, observantly. (I was in the cubs, y' know...) 'What about it?'"

"'What I want you to do is tell Phonogram that instead of sending me to America, if they buy me this house, I'll write them some *great* songs.'"

"I just couldn't believe my ears. Can you imagine me going back to Phonogram with that suggestion? I'd be laughed out of town. But he was serious, and to make matters worse," he speaks these last few words more slowly, emphasizing the point, "he couldn't see the senselessness of it all. I just got up and left the room, went for a walk to cool off. Shurley tried to explain, even to put the stupidity of his proposition into some kind of perspective, but he was unrepentant. We drove home angry, bemused, perplexed, feeling quite insulted. It was all going terribly wrong."

So America it was.

And this was a strange move. It wasn't the change itself, but the scale of it. American producer Bill Halverson was brought in to oversee the recording, using a group of indigenous musicians who, quite coincidentally, worked under the name of Waves. The idea was to take Clifford away from his 'nonsense in the studio', his diminishing but still possible studio-control-mania, and hopefully provide—and concentrate on—the new material. But, supposedly to protect the record company's interest, Justin de Villeneuve, who had somehow inveigled his way into the position of Promotion Manager for Phonogram, also went along.

The die was cast…

They moved into Long View Farm, North Brookfield, Massachusetts. Boasting state-of-the-art facilities, only 30 minutes by air from the Big Apple, it was an idyllic New England retreat, surrounded by alder, birch and aspen woodlands, low, white fences and, straight out of Robert Frost, a 'West-Running Brook'. To all intents and purposes, a home from home…but where were the songs?

"We got over there and my worst fears were realized," sighed Clive, lighting a cigar. "All the advances became quickly swallowed up wasting time writing—or trying to write—songs in the studio. I got so bored, so angry, I would skip off to the public library in town. It dragged on and on, with no apparent focus. A couple of the half-baked songs were finished off by the musicians themselves, and Cliff even recorded a song without *any* of Clifford T. in it [Tim Moore's 'I Got Lost Tonight'], so things were not looking good. We…persevered."

But there was room to manoeuvre.

Justin, in his soon-to-become-apparent manner of dealing, had suggested Long View Farm because it was run by his American brother-in-law, so that between them, a deal was contrived where 'family-favourable' recording costs could be billed to the recording company at going industry rates…they were into something good.

With this open expense account, for Clifford's trademark orchestrations, they flew right across the country to The Record Plant, Los Angeles, where they enlisted Jimmy 'Bridge Over Troubled Waters' Haskell to write some costly string arrangements—another no-expenses-spared outing—in the hope of adding credibility to what was being seen as a fairly lack-lustre album. It was fun, but it didn't save the hour, whilst back home, adding a touch of incredible irony, Clifford's orchestrator *par excellence*, Richard Hewson, was riding high in the charts with his very own Rah Band instrumental, 'The Crunch'.

Clive, by this time, had returned to England. It had all been too much—and not enough—to warrant a longer stay. He left Justin in charge, a move he was soon to regret, although most probably he could sense a change in the wind, and wanted time out to think it all over.

The recording was completed, with Justin overseeing final production and costings. He was forever watching the purse, ensuring that he, and occasionally his client (when it suited), received the best deal and were the beneficiaries of any spare change.

"He was always thinking money. Money, money, money," nods Cliff, and here he recounts an incident that, even without the wonderful Ward embellishments, has gone down in family folklore as a salutary reminder of the Justin Days.

"We were flying back to New York, after the sessions were finished. Justin had hired a private plane, a four-seater thing that Americans seem to use like taxis. We were up there above the clouds, bouncing along, high over America, when somebody, either Justin or the pilot, said something…wrong. It certainly wasn't *me*," and he gives that gruff, one-syllable laugh.

"Next thing David, they were shouting at each other, insults began to hurl across the deck.. From what I could make out, the pilot was asking Justin for some money he was owed. It got really heated, until, with me sitting there a little nervous—to say the least—they started exchanging blows. Justin took a swipe at the pilot, who naturally retaliated, until they were locked in combat. The bla-wd-y plane was rocking back-wuds and fore-wuds [his burr becomes quite pronounced], as I desperately tried to calm things down. For a couple of awfully long minutes nobody…was…driving…the bla-wd-y…thing. Huh…" He takes a long draw on his cigarette. "Don't mention Justin to me," and you know, even though his eyes are hidden behind the sunglasses, he is angry.

New England Days, released in October 1977, was the first Clifford T. Ward album produced by someone other than the artiste, and, rather than giving a new dimension to his work, it reduces the work to true AOR-America, in sound and mood, even down to the pseudo-horseman cover—Clifford had never ridden a horse in his life. It can be argued, of course, that the songs themselves weren't up to scratch, but in taking the heart of England to the hip-coast of America, replacing sincerity with slickness, it made Clifford T. Ward's music seem more like musak.

All concerned had evidently enjoyed making the record, as photographs taken along the way suggest. Besides buying Clifford his first camera,

Waves presented him with a copy of their recent album, signed by each member, with glowing testimonies to his qualities both as a musician and as 'a warm, wonderful human being'.

But that there *are* no outstanding songs on the album to lift Clifford above it all, suggests that maybe—just maybe—the fountain was beginning to run dry. There *were* more songs to come, but from here on, it all started to get a wee bit dodgy...

Justin was on the prowl.

Clifford had first met Justin de Villeneuve after his Royal Festival Hall concert. They were all celebrating at the *après*-concert dinner, held at the fashionable Mr Chow's in Knightsbridge—with David Frost and actor Ronald Fraser amongst the celebrity diners—and it was there during the wine-soaked celebrations that Justin began to circle Clifford like a basking shark...

A one-time boxer from the East End, before achieving celebrity status via his handling of the waif-like Lesley 'Twiggy' Hornby, Nigel Davies had renamed himself and cultivated a suave, irresistible persona, utterly charming, sartorially elegant, using his dandy-like veneer to conceal a man of serious ambition. He was, in fact, now managing the 'former' model, steering her into what would ultimately become a fairly successful, though short-lived, singing career. He had approached Clifford, suggesting his services in management and, feeling his career had lost momentum somewhat, Clifford, whilst mentioning his arrangement with Clive Selwood, had implied an interest, before leaving the 'boring showbiz' party and driving back up to Worcester with Pat, leaving his four-star hotel room to Roger and Gill, who were having a ball.

Justin then had met up with Clifford again on the American jaunt and, noticing Clive's increasing dissatisfaction, had made a mental note...

Upon completion of the album, he moved fast. He had to. He wanted his name on the cover and not just as the photographer. He continually telephoned Clifford, speculating on his plans, whispering in his ear like a temptress, 'Come with me, come with me...'

After yet another mention of Justin's name, Clive had put the ball firmly back in Clifford's court:

"Well, do you *want* him to manage you?..."

"Oh no, no," Clifford had replied, "it's just that he keeps on pestering me..."

And indeed he was.

"...oh, and Justin's just said ...," Clifford, *en passant*, "...and Justin can help me..."

It went on until finally Clive telephoned Justin. They agreed to meet for lunch.

"It was a fairly exotic restaurant, as you might imagine," Clive tells me. "I can't recall exactly where, but Justin did about half-an-hour of table-hopping before we actually sat down and then proceeded to inform me, quite matter-of-factly, that he'd like to take over Clifford's management. So I asked him the obvious. 'But Justin, what can you do for him that *I* can't?' 'Well, [film director] Ken Russell's a friend of mine and I can get some of Clifford's music in one of his films.' 'Well, that's great, Justin. Do that and we'll sort out a percentage. All fair and above board,' I replied. 'No, it's got to be all or nothing,' he said, almost defiantly. 'Well that's *bollocks* Justin,' I laughed. 'You might as well go up to Robert Plant and say to him, "I can get your songs in a Ken Russell film, but I want the complete management of Led Zeppelin."'

"I just got up and walked out. But, he kept on at Clifford, until finally, Cliff said he wanted to give it a try. We—Shurley and I—were *very* upset. We were dumped just like that." He snaps his fingers. "After all we'd done for him, all the money and time we'd invested, and there was a lot of *both*, he just walked out on us. But, there was no legal agreement, it had all been done on trust…"

There was an uncomfortable silence. It's an oft heard tale. Artistes are always looking for the better deal, the bigger advance, the best manager, and in such a fragile, untrusting, ego-ridden business, with so much at stake, advice often stays just that. So many creative people, reaching a hiatus in what they see as a 'career-in-flight', have changed horses mid-stream; some have chosen wisely, others have indeed, fallen from fame to obscurity. The sale racks in record stalls world-wide are littered with them, but, at the time, who can possibly tell?

Clive Selwood had talked openly to me about his role in this story, but now we had reached the point where he was to bow out.

We talked of many other things, of cabbages and kings, before I realized that the night was closing upon us. It was 9.30. We'd been talking for a long, long time. I rose to go, walking out into the courtyard. Clive was still talking. I'd mention a name, he knew a story, or, if he didn't, he'd graciously listen to mine. A light rain started to fall, the bats started diving across the sky, riding the invisible airwaves. There was a genuine remorse in his voice as he, and Shurley, tried to reason with what had been, and what had gone, and I felt it too. Here I was, a complete stranger to them, stirring up memories of a time when, more than twenty-five years ago, they had taken a star contender under their wing and nurtured his talent, encouraged his ambition and then lost him, way, way before the rest of the world did.

They hadn't seen him once in all those years. In their mind's eye he was probably still the slim, blond-haired, wholesome country boy; bursting with ideas, the quintessential English dreamer. For a brief, sad moment I thought of the time, only a few days earlier, when I'd called—on impulse—at the bungalow near Tenbury, *en route* to yet another tiresome gig. No-one had answered the door. I had checked the garage, there was no car, but I felt maybe, just maybe someone was at home. I rang the bell again. I heard Cliff's voice. "Whoisit?" he shouted. "Dave Cartwright," I answered.

"Holonaminute, Day-vid!," he called, and so I stood by the frosted-glass front door and waited. I saw a blurred mass come crawling along the hall floor and slowly reach up to undo the lock. I stepped in and looked down at him. It was a hot afternoon, really hot. He was on the floor curled up against the corner of the hallway, like a big St Bernard. Exhausted. His once golden mane was matted thin with sweat, his swollen face red, almost purple with the heat, his blurred eyes masked by sunglasses, and his bare, useless legs, the skin-sored knees, curled under him. But he was laughing.

"You don't have to gen-u-flect to me, Cliff," I teased.

"Ar day," he slurred, in his best Tom Crite accent, "Ar fell ovewr the bla-awd-y cat," and we both started laughing. Laughing at the absurdity of it all, the sheer helplessness and hopelessness of the situation. I sat down on the carpet beside him, and we conducted a bizarre conversation only occasionally interrupted by his deep, heavy sighs.

"Oh, Day-vidd," he groaned, and breathed a mild curse. I could truly feel his frustration rising to the surface, but he held it back. I tried to imagine what was going through his head.

But such moments would be over in a flash, as we gooned and giggled together. About ten minutes later Pat walked in, back from her shopping, and made some remark about silly little schoolboys…

They could never imagine that scene. No-one could. Life throws up some terrible wrongs, and this was one of them.

I told Clive how Cliff had haunted me for years. Everywhere I went his name was there, seemingly up in the world, and yet I'd never really known the man. So here I was, trying desperately to form an impression of him from those who had. I felt an intruder into a sad and distant past.

The rain wet my skin. I had to go. We shook hands, best wishes were exchanged, I turned on the ignition, lighting Shurley in my headlamps as she sheltered in one of the barns. The wipers skimmed the diamonds from my windscreen and I swept out into the crepuscular lanes of West Sussex… where I soon got lost. Again.

TIME, THE MAGICIAN

Confusion now hath made his masterpiece! Macbeth: II.iii

Justin immediately went to work. Well under his spell, Clifford had already followed earlier advice and cut his hair. The corn-yellow mane—a photogenic trademark since his teaching days—was now cropped collar length, and appeared as such on the cover of *New England Days*.

But despite—or probably because of—all this supposed change of direction, the album hadn't taken off, and, in what seemed to be an increasingly common occurrence in Clifford's one-album deals, Phonogram let the option lapse. There followed a brief and worrying hiatus, prompting many visits to Castle Weir by Justin.

Castle Weir…?

Oh, yes. My apologies.

The house Clifford asked Phonogram to buy in exchange for some songs? Well, as stubborn as ever, he went ahead alone.

"Cliff was determined to get that house," Pat told me. "The owner had died, and her son—who lived in London—wasn't interested. It had been on the market for some time before we spotted it, and, after Clive had removed himself and Phonogram from negotiations, Cliff went straight to the building society and sweet-talked them—*really* sweet-talked them—into putting up the money.

"He then took his solicitor down to London to talk to, or rather *listen* to, the son, a rather pompous army officer, and after a lot of over-the-table haggling, reading through countless aged documents, deeds and such, he made his offer. £45,000. It needed a lot of work, but structurally it was sound, They wanted £53,000, but Cliff stayed his ground, and won. It was an absolute bargain."

Clifford's enthusiasm, together with his innate ability to charm and convince those who mattered, crunched into overdrive, and within a few weeks the purchase was complete. They also bought much of the furniture—the 'bits and pieces' that hadn't already been seconded by the heirs. On a day when the heavens seemed to be emptying, these two somewhat bewildered working-class people walked through the echoing oak-panelled rooms, with the rain crashing against the French windows and hissing on the gravelled drive, as the Major specified items for sale and prices to pay. At last, when everything was agreed, they became the new owners of a country estate.

For the first time in their lives, they moved out of their beloved Worcestershire to neighbouring Herefordshire, to a place near the Welsh border. Just five miles from Hergest Ridge—immortalized by Mike Oldfield three years previously, in his follow-up to *Tubular Bells*—Castle Weir stood at the head of Lyonshall village, on the beautiful A44 road winding on to historic Kington. This pretty town, with its narrow streets, its bookshops and antiques, once provided refuge for Lord Byron in 1812, his first year of glory. Here, at the Oxford Arms, a grey, rambling building once the country seat to the Earl of Oxford, Byron had found solace in the bed-chamber of Jane Elizabeth, the earl's beautiful free-thinking wife, after fleeing the pleasurable but potentially destructive attentions of London society—the tiresome (eventually) obsession of Lady Caroline Lamb.

Castle Weir had been empty for a couple of years, following the death of the Talbot-Rice family matriarch, but in its days of genteel glory, it had boasted 11 gardeners, a couple of butlers, kitchen maids and a moat, with sheep safely grazing its sixteen acres. A Frith picture-postcard, in sad old sepia dating from the mid-twenties, shows the 14-bedroomed ivy-clad mansion nestling between broad oaks and sloping lawns, a tranquil scene from the English heartland, long before the days of tourist traffic and television, 'to send you fast asleep'.

And so, the Wards moved house yet again, in Spring, 1977, the day before Clifford flew off to America to record his seventh album...

But that was Pat's concern and so, naturally, she got on with it:

"It was difficult, being so far away from anyone we knew. I recall just sitting there, as the boys clattered around this mausoleum, thinking, 'Well, it's all very nice, but who's going to see it?' I got on the phone to Roger and Gill [Bowen] and asked them to come across as soon as they could—like, '...tomorrow?'"

Though all the family had been very happy at Lower Hollin, Clifford's continual desire to move on, his need for change of surroundings—at whatever cost to others—meant a constant stream of estate agent brochures pouring through the letter box, and, when he saw Castle Weir, it was love at first sight. But he had plans this time. With the huge accommodation facilities, the extensive grounds, it would even make an ideal holiday home for disabled children, for others like Debbie and her friends. That, apparently, was his grand design, but all that would come later...

It was a house of great feudal tradition—the manor house of this pretty, ancient village set off winding lanes deep in the countryside. Newcomers were, indeed, outsiders; foreign…
Pat confirms as much:
"When the agent showed us around, on the first occasion, we had Martin and Sam with us, it must have been the Easter holidays. Cliff and I were talking at the front door, when Martin began tugging at my dress. 'Mom, there's a man watching us through the hedge.' Cliff strode across and put *his* face up to the privet, and out came this shambling, gentle giant, who introduced himself as Bert, the last of the Castle Weir gardening dynasty. He was almost bowing and scraping to us, but Cliff soon put him at ease. Bert Bayliss was ex-army, impregnated with the English class system, and loved his job on the land, with its country estate feudalism. He had a tied cottage over the hill and was understandably concerned at the fate of his beloved gardens. He'd been tending them even though the house itself had been empty for some time. We became good friends, even though we didn't—well, *couldn't*, despite our apparent wealth—employ him."

Cliff hoped Castle Weir would bring new solace to what had become unsettling times. Living the life he had always tried to live, with his own little family unit, surrounded by peace and tranquillity, he became the country squire, the world outside became secondary, but only almost. The business of records and recording continued unabated.
To all concerned, it was the next album. It was always the next album…
And so it had been America, and the awful business of trying to change the leopard's spots. Clifford had dug in his heels, fought and screamed and succumbed; the album was completed and he returned home to his wife and family.
Though costs and time had escalated way beyond budget, Phonogram seemed prepared, at first, to put a little more money into promotion. A beautiful cassette box-set, folding outwards to reveal Clifford's handwritten lyrics, was issued, but once again, the generally low-key release—and reaction—of *New England Days*, in October, only made him more determined to pursue the house-dream. Christmas 1977 saw them as lord and lady, rattling around the huge building, sanding down the painted doors, polishing the oak-planked floors, scrubbing the tiles. If only it could have continued.
Initially, and as if a new desperation had seized his previous record companies, three singles had been issued within the nine months following the move to Castle Weir, yet no-one could have possibly foreseen the wilderness years that were to come.

Cliff Richard's cover version of 'Up In The World', though not released as a single, had prompted Mercury to give Clifford's original rendering a chance on the market. March, 1977 saw the seven-inch—coupled with the badly revisited 'Not Waving—Drowning'—pitted against Abba, Showaddywaddy and Berni Flint (oh, so there was room...but only with maximum exposure, which was not at hand). Then, come September, in a bizarre 'see-what-happens-here' move, they put out the first ever Clifford T. Ward single not written by him, Tim Moore's 'I Got Lost Tonight', from *New England Days*. Tim, a young, versatile musician from the Woodstock camp, was probably the nearest America ever got to the pastoral feel of Worcestershire; in a 1974 Mooncrest (another B&C subsidiary) release, Clifford's influence is quite noticeable. The song used for the single however, is noticeable for its Adult Orientated Ordinariness. It could be a Chicago C-side (and that is not a misprint...). Only that pure English vocal—though double-tracked and almost transatlantic at times—manages to give the track any credibility. What this would have done for Clifford's confidence, should it have scored, one can only imagine, but, it had absolutely no chance. It got lost all right...

For Valentine's Day, 1978, a strangely conceived, gorilla-sleeved, 'Someone I Know', from the same album, was launched, corner-page reviewed, picked up a few radio plays, but that was all, and of course, it wasn't enough.

There was even a re-release of 'Gaye' b/w 'Scullery', on the mysterious Old Gold label, but these were all futile gestures, or obligatory nods to the artiste. The pop scene, never static, was now charging along, open to all and sundry, but generally being won by those who, like Clifford way back in 1973, had media-influenced attention. Television actors, Eurovision winners, spangle-sequinned dancers were all being heavily marketed; it was not getting any easier.

It was to be almost seven years before Clifford T. Ward would release a complete album again. Seven long years.

"Scuse me, I'm after Cliff Ward."

"Never heard of him."

"Well I've been told he lives here and wants some work doin'."

"No. You must have the wrong house," but then came that slow, enigmatic smile.

Ron Bridges stepped into the hall of Castle Weir a little bit puzzled at his reception; his open, country ways not used to such subtleties.

"I'd been sent to the house by a mate of mine, Cecil Taylor, who'd been doing some building work for Cliff, but they'd had a slight falling out...," and Ron gives a quick, corner-eye look. I nod. "He told me there was this pop star who'd just bought Castle Weir, who was looking for a painter-decorator, but he warned me that the bloke was a bit...well contrary...That didn't bother me. I was after work, so I tootled on down. Had no idea what he looked like. I'd heard 'Gaye' all those years ago, think I even bought a copy, but when he answered the door, it could have been anybody as far as I was concerned. But I didn't like being teased, bloody impudence...," he laughs.

Ron was born in the Forest of Dean, and speaks with that fast, rolling, guttural burr that makes even profanities sound friendly. A ruddy-faced, bespectacled, wiry-haired man, with a sturdy frame, active and amiable, he recalls the days at the Ward household with great fondness, though, as seems to be the case, there were many moments of sheer exasperation.

"He took me on as virtually permanent. Not out of necessity, mind you, he just continually changed his mind. About everything. I did the whole house, from top to bottom. At least twice."

"On your own?"

"Yes. Cliff tried to help, but he ended up being more of a hindrance than a help. Always bloody fussing around, checking things I'd done, or was doing, even before they were finished. 'You're not getting on with it very fast,' he'd say, 'I'd better come and give you a hand.' Course, he'd end up with paint all over the place, hands, face, hair. Hopeless. Tried to use a mole wrench once, to get a nail out of a window frame. Stood there for half-an-hour meddling about with it, like a caveman looking at a microphone. In the end he threw it down and went out in to the garage for some pliers. Did I laugh. But, then, we had our rows. He wound me up something rotten. I said, many times, 'Right. That's it Clifford. You can stick your job up your bloody arse, I'm finished,' and I'd pick up my dust sheets and walk out. He'd come after me, apologizing, so I'd start again, bloody seething, boiling up inside, as he pandered around, smoking—he always walked about with a packet of fags in his hand, even in his own house—talking as if nothing had happened. Then he'd start up again next day, after he'd had chance to look at things, think it over. On and on and on. Always changing his mind. He had this thing about white, everything had to be white. All the window frames, the skirting, any colour as long as it was white. He did get adventurous one time though, got me to do one room in green, then, when I'd finished it, he told me he wanted it white again! That's one of the times I lost my rag. *Bloody* mad I was." But Ron was laughing.

"But everything got done. The door knobs, escutcheons, finger plates; all the brass was dipped in nitric acid, then re-lacquered, everything had to be just right. Then he got me doing some re-roofing, the summer house, the stables. He'd be standing at the bottom of the bloody ladder, talking up at me, or talking as I went up and down, talk, talk, bloody talk. Watching everything I did." He shakes his head.

There was a long pause, as if he was thinking of something quite important.

He speaks slowly:

"Do you know David, Clifford T. Ward was the only bloke I ever knew who used to wipe his feet to go outside." We roared. "'Strue. He had this thing about wiping his feet. I had a go at him once about it. He saw the funny side as well, but then, he'd have to. Stood there at the kitchen door, wiping his feet, and he'd walk straight outside. I nearly wet myself. Bloody fool."

Cliff's explanation is equally as funny.

In his dry, precise manner, choosing his words, wasting nothing, he tells me:

"It was Pa-a-at. She brainwashed me so much, David, into...wiping my feet, that absolutely every time I saw a mat, which*ever* direction I was pointing, I...wiped...my...feet. Huh."

I came across a similar tale, from Sam Ward a little while later, recalled from his childhood way back at the Oaklands. A patterned rug lay in the middle of the small lounge. Obviously Pat's pride and joy, it was hoovered every day. Even after six months, a year, and a house full of children, it was still pristine, because '...we all treated it like a patch of wet tarmac. We daredn't step on it. It was there to walk round, not to use...'

Ron Bridges holds Clifford in great affection. This warm, rustic man, who reads about the world, the government and the pop star life-style—the drugs, the parties, the jet-setting—in the tabloids, found his employer a complete contradiction, with his family home, his non-socializing, his solitude.

"Don't think he ever went to the pub. Sometimes he'd be seen in the village, or Fred Price would get a visit from him at the timber yard, but that was it. No sides to Cliff, unassuming, up-front, a good man. Kept himself to himself."

"Did he ever talk about his music?"

"When I started there, he'd just come back from America, and he wasn't very happy, said they hadn't done exactly what he wanted," and he raises his eye-brows resignedly. "And he didn't like the set-up over there, on about drugs and such, but apart from that not really very much. He would play me his records as he made them, y'know, when he came back from a session, and seemed genuinely interested in my opinion. I liked most of his stuff. But he hated my radio. I had it on all the time I was working and he hated that. Probably if I'd had a tape playing of his stuff it would've been okay! And sometimes he'd talk about his teaching days, his pupils—the good ones and the bad ones—in a favourable way. He seemed quite proud of those days. But he never spoke about his family, in fact I didn't know he *had* any brothers or a sister until years later, at his fiftieth birthday. Never mentioned his mother and father, though he talked affectionately about Pat's father, Charlie, who was often over at Castle Weir, building a bench or something. Lovely bloke, Charlie.

"He'd tease me something rotten about my accent. 'Why don't you learn to talk properly, Ron? I'll teach you,' he'd say, as we were—well as *he* was—splashing the paint on. Then he'd drop out a word, something like 'onomatopoeic', asking me if I knew what it meant. Bloody nonsense. What did I want to use words like that for? I was a painter not a teacher. We had some good laughs about it.

"I remember meeting that Justin de Vinnue [*sic*], whatever his bloody name was. Poncey little git. A short-arsed little guy. He came out one day in a tweed suit, carrying a silver-topped cane, like bloody lord of the manor—and somebody *else's* manor, mark you!—waltzing up the garden. I felt like asking him if he was going mushroom picking."

I told Ron that Justin had been the only person who refused to be interviewed for this book.

"I'm not surprised. I took an instant dislike to that guy. I told Cliff to leave him alone. I told him, 'That bloke's gonna bloody rob you Cliff, black and blue.' Was I right? Bloody maggot."

"What did Cliff say to that?"

"'No, no-o, Ron,' he said, 'he's a bloody good bloke. He's gonna get me a big deal. He's got some plans for K-Tel to do a big marketing job, TV advertising, on my next album…' Quite convinced he was, really impressed, and I suppose if that had've worked he would have had enough money to go ahead with his plans for Castle Weir."

"So Clifford had a lot of faith in Justin?"

"Yes, at the beginning. But Cliff was like that. He could never, ever see harm, bad, in anyone, until it was too late."

We started going through Ron's meticulous time-sheets from all those years ago.

"I kept these time sheets 'cos I was paid by the hour, weakly—sorry *weekly*—and then Pat took over and started logging my times. *Very* efficient she was. To the quarter-hour. 'You didn't get here till 8.45,' or 'You left at 4.45.' Honest. I didn't make much out of those days. I'd get in the van, drive off, thinking I could be making more money somewhere else, and in cash. She, not Cliff, paid me by cheque every Friday, no cash, always a cheque…She was certainly the business side of the marriage. Cliff left her to see to everything, he was the musician. Even when he and I came to loggerheads about a colour scheme, he'd shout for Pat, and she would come in to sort it out. Whatever she said, he went along with, so I had no chance then. Outvoted. And even when she *wasn't* there, you always had the feeling she was watching. Cliff would be serious about something for a few minutes, then he'd start his nonsense, we'd be giggling away—he was just like a child sometimes—then he'd say, 'Shhh, Pat's coming...' so we'd just get back to whatever it was he was supposed to be serious about...Quiet, demure, but, The Boss...Bloody hard as nails. She gave me an LP once, though. A present. For Christmas. One of his mind you!"

But all this is recounted with great affection.

"Getting back to tantrums, I remember him showing me around the place one time, saying he wanted this doing, that doing, taking ages, and I casually reminded him that I was charging him for all this time, walking around. He went bloody spare. 'I'm not paying you for walking around my house!!' Right off the deep end, he went. What a bloke.

"And that time where they'd gone out, into Hereford. I was left painting the Forth Bridge...and the phone rang. I didn't answer it at first, wasn't my house, but it was a bit persistent and when I did, it was him, Cliff. They'd broken down at Dinmore, in his new Lancia. I went out and towed them back in my 1952 Hillman Husky. And I made a point of going back right through the village, the long way round, to let everybody see. I didn't half tease *him* about that. We got back and he spent the rest of the day huffing and puffing, striding around the house, talking, muttering, smoking...I used to wonder what the 'ell was the matter with this feller. Always irate, wound up about something. Why doesn't he just relax? There was always something there, at the back of his mind, niggling away. He would *just* about cope with everyday life until this 'thing' would spark it all off, and he'd blow his top. Always on such a short fuse.

"He was so intense, believe anything. Took everything at face value. Sometimes I'd get my own back. He was a great bird-watcher, always had been, since a kid apparently. His favourite bird was the spotted fly-catcher and he asked me early one spring whether I'd seen it yet. I told him I'd never heard of it, wouldn't know a spotted fly-hatcher from an eagle. 'Fly-*catcher*!' he shouted. 'Bloody 'ell, don't you country bumpkins know *anything*!?' and off he'd go, ranting and raving. Course I knew it, know all the birds, I'm a secret twitcher," and he giggles into his single-malt.

"I never saw much of the boys, I suppose they were at school by the time I got there, and when they came back they'd probably get lost raiding the pantry for an hour. Debbie used to come home weekends. Always laughing she was. She tried walking up the stairs once, getting me to help her, on her crutches, but we ended up going in different directions, so I just picked her up and slung her over my shoulder. She really enjoyed that. Laughed her head off. A great kid she was.

"And it must have been a great place to come home to. In the summer, those acres of daffodils, the trees, the lovely driveway, the lily-pond, which, sadly, the boys and Cliff filled in when Polly was born. The house was so well built. I suppose it was Georgian, maybe Regency, with Victorian extensions. Y'know, David, up in the roof, under the tiles, it was all tongue-and-groove panelling. Marvellous. Cliff certainly made the right choice. For once…" Again, he laughs.

"But I *did* like him, we both did [referring to his wife, Sandra]. When Polly was born and Cliff went off to America again, Sandra used to go round and help Pat, do some shopping and all that, but I also had a laugh that time, just as he was about to leave for America. I didn't know he was leaving that *minute* and I told him we needed some more paint. 'More paint! I'm just off to bloody America, Ron, I haven't time to get any more bloody paint!'

"But he did. He had to, else it wouldn't have got done till he got back. He supplied everything, y'see. I just turned up with the brush. He got all the paint and stuff from Kidderminster—probably 'cos it was trade discount, about half-a-crown cheaper—although it was an eighty-mile round trip…"

And so Ron continued his work on the house, watching with amusement and puzzlement the comings and goings of Clifford, Justin and various other drifting musicians, out for a spin in the country, calling in to see whoever was at home. Even Waves' drummer Marc Singer came to stay for a few days, hanging around '…in his brash American way,' recalls Pat. 'I baked a cake as a kind of welcome. He ate the lot…'

Karl Hyde, training for Underworld whilst studying at Cardiff, still maintained contact with his erstwhile teacher, and, when he could get the time, would persuade one or two of his fellow students to drive him up to see his hero, living the pop star-in-the-country existence to which he, as ever, aspired.

"The house was a dream. Every young man's ideal. The driveway, the lawns, the bedrooms, the space. We'd get there, say, three or four of us. Pat would answer the door, ever welcoming […] and show us into the lounge, sometimes with the proclamation that Cliff was in his music room, working, and that he wouldn't be out until, I dunno, 6.15. We'd sit there, small-talking, noticing the books of Wordsworth, Browning and so on, strategically placed within eye-view, a bit pretentiously, we thought. And definitely out of time. We were all into Kerouac, Ginsberg…

"At the appointed hour, out he would come. Always glad to see us. He showed us into his work-place. I remember thinking how sterile it seemed. Just a piano, in the middle of this huge room, standing on a piece of underfelt, surrounded by velvet-draped French windows. Like the 'Imagine' video. A tad out of date…

"To me, it was completely void of any stimulation. Nothing to spark the creative process. Okay, we all have different ways of writing, maybe Cliff needed the silence, the enforced frugality, but I just thought, 'This guy's beating himself to death with an image.'

"If I mentioned it, which I obviously did, he'd react by saying that I was lucky, I could write songs when I wanted to; *he* had to get up each day and write for so many hours, that was his job. And of course, on my last visit to Castle Weir, he had the trump card. This time he was off to America. And that shut me up. Really impressed me. That was the land of Paul Simon, The Doors, Patti Smith. [Buffalo Bill…]."

Indeed, America it was. Again. Justin was keen to get on with the next, the *big* album. Clifford was writing some great songs. Wasn't he?

Pat, even while she was pregnant with Polly—ten years after she had convinced Wyre Forest Council that she was infertile—remembers it all so well:

"Justin and his then business partner, the *other* Ken Bruce (a former Polygram press officer and *World Pop News* editor), used to drive up to Castle Weir to listen to the 'new songs' that Cliff had insisted were in hand. When he heard their car coming up the drive, Cliff would place a few lines of lyric—any old line or two—on the piano and walk out into the back garden, knowing that, after the initial greetings, Justin would wander into the music room, see the half-finished masterpiece and feel happy at the progress…"

Only Pat would know the truth.

"Was he actually writing, was he just getting lazy, or…?"

"I think he was drying up," she answered. "He hadn't written anything from scratch for ages. All the supposedly new stuff was rehashed from previously discarded songs that he wouldn't have even considered ten years earlier."

I suggested that maybe, even then, in the last years of that decade, the illness was taking a grip of Clifford's creative *and* emotional spirit, even that maybe it had *always* been there…

"Well, nothing was said. He could have kept things—small things—to himself, but I would have noticed eventually. When the illness *was* diagnosed, some years later, I was there, and I knew. I knew everything, of course I did, I'd been married to him for nearly twenty years…"

Yet life at Castle Weir continued, outwardly at peace. The newcomers opened their home to the village for the church fêtes; Cliff, instantly recognisable as the 'squire', welcoming the congregation; Pat, in her deliberate anonymity, enjoying mingling with the crowds, listening to comments about the alterations, the decorations, that the pop star and his wife were doing to the house, watching them press noses up to the French windows, shading their eyes to get a view of the interior. The life of the country gentleman suited Clifford's temperament perfectly, though it soon became apparent—but to Pat only—that they had maybe outstretched themselves financially.

"He really didn't want to know about anything financial, unless it was incoming," she says. "It got to a point where I used to dread the morning post, wondering what was next. I hid bank statements, building society letters, final demands...It was wrong, I know. We should have talked it through, but with Cliff... well, you just couldn't...He had such a temper."

Even small things that would have caused him to angrily question her abilities as a wife and 'financial manager', were dealt with efficiently and, thankfully, without his knowledge. He assumed, quite wrongly, and—if he'd thought about it—quite impossibly, that they were living well within their means.

Whilst he was in London, a speeding fine, paid for by cheque, was returned...in the hands of a local police officer, who, quite legally, had come to arrest Clifford.

"My parents were visiting, so I ushered the policeman into the kitchen where I convinced him [as she would...] that it had been an oversight. While he sat there, drinking a cuppa, looking through the windows at this beautiful mansion with its beautiful gardens, I was on the phone to the bank, pleading with them to allow me to draw out some cash to settle the fine."

They eventually agreed, she drove into Kington—about five miles—where the arrangement had been authorized, then to the police station, where, amid great confusion and embarrassment, it was all cleared up.

Even approaching Christmas, whilst she was lying in hospital, waiting to give birth, she was worrying about the building society's letters concerning defaults on their repayments, praying to God that no-one would call at the house until she got back home.

However, in the first week of that cold December, 1979, bringing a wonderful, beautiful relief to such incidentals, their second daughter, Polly, was born.

Pat was happy, naturally:

"I'd done my last shopping expedition before going into hospital, ensuring that there was at least a box of chocolates for Cliff to bring me when he came to visit the ward. To save face...He turned up, empty handed. 'Where are my chocolates?' I asked him. 'Oh, I ate those last night, watching the late-night movie.'

"So much for grand gestures," Pat smiles, weakly...

But Polly came into their world, and Clifford, for a while, came alive.

Meanwhile, Justin had eventually managed to secure a wonderful publishing deal with Warner Bros, coaxing a lovely advance out of them—after doing some of his 'tap-dancing' as he told a naïve, puzzled Clifford ('…we've got to do a bit of tap-dancing…')—then taking an equally lovely 60 per cent chunk for himself before organizing some more recording in Massachusetts, continuing the previous arrangement, though with a somewhat different line-up.

Derek Thomas, whose role in Clifford's story has been greatly overlooked, though no longer playing on his records due to work commitments elsewhere, had often stumbled across local bands who were able to provide backing tracks for demos at relatively cheap rates, and one such group was led by a friend of his, Pete Bennet, who led a four-piece, featuring keyboardist Mark Tibenham [later to become a pop star himself, co-writing The Maisonettes 1983 Top Twenty hit, 'Heartache Avenue'] at that time playing bass. After meeting them during some work at Muff Murfin's Kempsey studio, Derek recommended them to Clifford, who subsequently enlisted them to record various demos at Tony Rook's small, home-based studio in Stourport.

I spoke to Mark. We were sitting on a bench outside a little hostelry on historic Richmond Hill, overlooking the glorious River Thames as she curved rightwards toward Twickenham. It was one of those late summer mornings, bright and still warm, when London seems to come alive, when the buildings seem to shine with pride, and the air actually feels fresh. To our left was a huge Victorian folly, its grounds sloping down towards the river. 'And he says he can't get no satisfaction…,' I thought. Behind that, in a superb Georgian mansion lived you know Who…; he *hadn't* died before he got old, and was probably enjoying every minute of it. Up on the Hill itself, in an equally beautiful terraced house, lived—only occasionally no doubt—Catwoman, though for popping out to the shops she would presumably wear something a little less conspicuous.

"Much as I hate this city, I could live *here*…," I mused. But then, who couldn't?

Mark began, in his low, lugubrious manner:

"We tried a few songs with Cliff, but he wasn't too impressed with the band. Then he found out that, although I was playing bass, I could also play piano, and better than he could. So I went over to Castle Weir and began learning some of his new songs. I actually didn't know any of his stuff at that time. I knew the name, of course, but, well, everybody was caught up in their own little world in the late seventies. We all wanted to be our own star. Doing covers was a bit passé. Pete Bennet was a good singer-songwriter himself, but as a band we weren't really up to much.

"Anyway, so Cliff got a good—*very* good—rate with Tony Rook, and we went in to do these demos, me playing piano, overdubbing synthesized strings—which Cliff was very fond of—on an old eight-track. We did about 12 or 13 numbers altogether.

"Clive had gone by this time, and Justin was on the scene. He was—and still is—an extremely dazzling, charming person. Very charismatic, which always struck me as odd, the wrong way round, rather weird, to have a manager who is more charismatic than the artiste...

"Clifford was *very* struck by Justin. He told me that he was getting this massive deal with Warner Bros, where they would put out singles and K-Tel, in an extraordinary piece of negotiating, would push his albums, backed by their extensive television advertising. Well, that seemed extraordinary to me. But that's what Justin had told Cliff, and *he'd* believed it, so why shouldn't I? I wanted to, because the talk was that I'd get 10 per cent. I never saw anything. In fact I didn't make much at all out of my time and my work with Cliff [though, in fairness, Pat's meticulous accounts show considerable payments to Mark over 1981-82...]. He actually paid me once, after a long weekend's work, with a Victorian chair. I've still got it, and I'm not saying it wasn't worth what I was owed, but bartering isn't the norm in the music business...," and he made a sound that wasn't quite a laugh.

"So, following the master plan, Justin, Clifford and I flew to Massachusetts, to Long View Farm, to start on the second American album. It was January, 1980. We hired a New York session band, good musicians, as you would expect and we started recording. Immediately, in my view, it began to go wrong. One of the guys raised doubts about my ability on the piano, which I admit, in those days...well, I've come on a great deal since then...but, although I knew Clifford's songs and could understand the harmonic structures, I wasn't exactly a free improviser, not by New York standards anyway. Well, Clifford took this comment a little too seriously and began debating about sending me back home and bringing somebody else out. It got to one point where he actually reduced me to tears. I mean, I had really studied his songs, note for note. It was a big chance, career-wise, for me. I'd never even flown before all this, so I'd treated my role very professionally. Because he was self-taught, Clifford had developed a most peculiar chord-structure, three finger shapes, which gave some lovely inversions, and which he, naturally, insisted be kept. I'd spent days learning them, and here I was being brought to task. My confidence was reduced to zero. I've never had it done, before or since. So little disregard for the person.

"But we battled on, It was such a gorgeous place, maybe the

surroundings helped to calm things. There were horses available, though I wasn't allowed to ride. Justin would say, in his pseudo-Oxbridge accent, 'My dear boy, we can't have you falling off and breaking your wrist..., just after they'd spent a fortnight questioning my playing."
"And Cliff, did he ride?"
"Er, no. He was too busy elsewhere...but I beat him on *that* one, much to his chagrin...," and his voice hangs in the crisp air, with a slow smile spreading across his face, recalling a pleasant dalliance from those far-off days...

They proceeded to put down whatever Clifford had pulled out of the hat, under a somewhat cloudy sky, then came home. However, upon his return, Clifford decided that the salad needed some dressing, so a hastily conceived session was arranged at Jerry Boys's archaic Sawmill Studios in Cornwall.
"We then took the tapes to this dreadfully shabby studio, with an equally shabby 24-track machine, purloined from somewhere—probably an old Sound Techniques cast-off, the rubber bands kept breaking—you know, that sort of thing...and the accommodation was less than salubrious, dingy little huts in a dingy little valley somewhere, and you couldn't reach the studio by road...you had to load all the equipment, tapes, luggage, onto a barge and sail up the river into this cove...A smugglers' paradise. Typical bloody Cornwall. Cornwall. I hate the place..." And he means it. He drags on his cigarette, recalling *not* so pleasant a time.
"A few new guitar overdubs were recorded, using a house band that was hanging around [Big Al Hodge] and Clifford added some vocal bits, but it was still not good enough. Former group front-man Dave Dee, who was then head of A&R at Warners, expressed *his* dislike, in a none too uncertain a manner, so Clifford, in true, artistic, temperamental style, just upped and went, heading back to his beloved Worcestershire. Justin, realizing what was at stake and still safely covered by Clifford's advance, then brought in Hugh Murphy."

I had worked with Hugh—a charming, extremely successful and respected freelance producer—during the wonderful hot summer of 1976, recording my fourth album.
He had first stepped onto the rocky road as a roadie for Southend's very own Kursaal Flyers, before moving into production and taking the one-hit Ozzie, Gary Shearston, and his wonderfully nostalgic cocktail-lounge rendition of 'I Get A Kick Out Of You'—on Charisma—into the Top 10 in November, 1974, Clifford's 'Jayne (From Andromeda Spiral)' year.

But Hugh had been there, from the start, with ex-Humblebum/Stealer's Wheel-er Gerry Rafferty, producing his extraordinary debut album, *Can I Have My Money Back?* and eventually hitting the jackpot co-producing *City to City*, which spawned the multi-million selling single, 'Baker Street', in 1978. It was following this, in 1980, and whilst at his commercial peak, that he had been approached by Justin…
Mark took a drink of his Becks, I took a swig of Theakstons, and we both took a break, looking around, savouring the view, the place, the people. A woman, obviously a tourist, was walking up from the river and enjoying the panorama so much that she was stepping up the hill backwards. And it was nowhere near Christmas…
Mark continued:
"Hugh brought in his girlfriend, an American pianist, but Clifford insisted that I stay on the project because of my knowledge of his chord inversions…so I had to write out all these weird chord shapes for *her*, whilst I was demoted to bass guitar. And not just bass, Hugh wanted fretless bass, which I'd never played in my life. We found one, went into some little studio in Birmingham for a run through, and there I was, playing this £2000 instrument, for the first time in my life, with the producer of 'Baker Street' up in the control box, his lady sitting at the piano, feeling *extremely* awkward.
"Things still didn't work out right. So a bit of subterfuge ensued. Somehow, behind Clifford's back, they got hold of the multi-tracks. Justin crossed the Atlantic *again*, with Hugh *and* his girlfriend—for another working vacation—to add some more expensive overdubs. But the album, though it was finished, as far as I'm aware, was never released?" and he looks at me for confirmation.

When he *did* hear about the re-mixes—whether he liked them or not would have been irrelevant—he was so angry at such deceit that he telephoned Justin and told him that, as far as *he* was concerned the management agreement was terminated, and that in no way would he agree to any more work. To alter Clifford's work, in any way, especially without consent, revealed the true extent of Justin's ignorance of the man and deviousness of the perpetrator. When the fertilizer hit the cooling blades he desperately tried to persuade Clifford it been done in the singer's best interest. Realizing the implications, and true to form, he jumped straight in his car and drove all the way up to Castle Weir. They spent all evening discussing the project before retiring, and without coming to any conclusion, and went off to supposedly 'sleep on it'. Over a frosty breakfast next morning, Justin asked Cliff to pass the orange juice, '…oh, and by the way…'. Clifford anticipated what was coming, left the table and went for a long walk in the woods, across to the 'Ram', Castle Weir's medieval watering hole, way down in the valley. Once again he passing the responsibility onto Pat, who, in her soft, yet authoritative, 'no-messing' manner told Justin—still pleading and pouring out his charm—to leave. 'I think you'd better just go…'

He did. And he never came back, or ever re-established contact.

Mark was correct, the recordings were not released collectively as an LP, though some of the 'America - Part 2' songs did find their way onto subsequent releases. WEA released three singles from those sessions: in July 1980 came 'Convertible' b/w 'Taking The Long Way Round' (in its original form a great, confident song; here, though somewhat enhanced, still a solid track); and in April 1981, the delightful 'Contrary' b/w 'Climate Of Her Favour'. But sandwiched in between, for January of that year, came Clifford's most beautiful new song—and arguably his best double side for years—'The Best Is Yet To Come' and 'Lost Again'. If he had been drying up, then these two songs must have been written much earlier, or maybe, even in times of darkness, he had still managed to find that spark of genius, and in Mark, of course, he found the musician to interpret his thoughts.

The remainder of the tracks, kept in cold storage for that rainy day, would appear as the backbone for the *Both Of Us* album, issued by Philips, Ireland many years later, but still obviously under copyright—and accountable—to Warner Bros. Music, which by then had become swallowed up by Intersong Music Ltd. This take-over, almost becoming an everyday occurrence in the music business, would, in the complicated nether world of royalty distribution, cost Clifford dearly in the years to come.

Mark suggests that with Justin and Clifford, it was a case—a prime case—of the blind leading the blind. He hints that Clifford even tried approaching other producers behind Justin's back, or at least that's what he *heard*; but they really were not good to—or *for*—each other.

"They ended up both accusing the other of sabotage. *I* found Clifford to be extremely paranoid. His paranoias were all embracing. Even going back to Long View Farm, when my abilities were being put under the microscope, I felt as if I wasn't getting any support from him, that he would have done anything for an easy solution, a quick route to getting things done to his satisfaction. Faithless would be too strong a word, but loyalty wasn't his greatest forte… But then, again, that's the music business. They're all fucked-up-egocentric-no-faith-in-anyone tossers. And whether they appear self-confident or not, just bring *anything* into question, let anything go wrong, and if it's their gob on the recordings, their mush that's on the cover, then you can bet your life somebody else gets the blame."

Of course, by this time, I'm almost rolling about the grassy bank in hysterics at such outpourings. Mark is not a bitter man, but his deadpan delivery creases me. And of course, the truth being delivered so vehemently, whilst he is holding a half-full glass of beer and a cigarette, in bright sunlight, surrounded by sightseers, on Richmond Hill.

"But Cliff's humour, which I find so acute. Did you never see any of that?"

"Oh, yeah. Especially when Justin was around. In spite of all the rancour they managed to develop between themselves, they could be *hilarious* at times. They bounced off each other, with these imaginary alter-egos. Justin became this super, or quasi-Noel Coward character and Cliff would play the country bumpkin, the wonderful Kidderminster yokel [Tom Crite rides again…]. It was really funny. *Really* funny."

We walked up to the pub for a second pint. The landlord noticed my tape-machine.

"You a reporter then?" he smiled, in a broad Scots accent.

"No, I'm writing a book. About a musician," pre-empting his next question.

He didn't give up.

"Anybody I might know?"

"Oh, I doubt it. A bit before your time, mid-seventies," I said, trying to be cool. This was London.

"Jeez, I was about nine. Try me."

I tried him.

"'Gaye'!" he exclaimed. "One of me mam's favourites! Whatever happened to him?"

"I'll send you a copy of the book," I joked.

"Great!" handing me the drinks. "That's £4.47, thanks."

But *he* wasn't joking…

Back down the hill again, Mark continued:

"This may sound like jilted-musician talk, but Clifford was not generous. Well, he was extremely *un*generous with songwriting credits. A sort of egotistical blindness seemed to put any such considerations out of court. Unselfishness wasn't a natural trait. I put a lot of shaping, chord reworking, an extra bar here and there, into a lot of those songs. 'Lost In The Flow of Your Love' [which he worked on for the *Sometime Next Year* album, for Tembo, in 1986] was almost rewritten, structurally. The lyrics of that song have got *so* much magic, there's a feel about it, and, okay, it could be just me thinking, 'well, hold on a minute, *I* put that bit in…'; me trying to gild my own lily. But when I worked with Lol [Mason, 'Heartache Avenue'] it was Lol's lyric, his basic melody, yet when *we'd* dressed it up and recorded it, he gave me

50 per cent co-writer credit. Cliff didn't *ever* credit close musicians with their input. Enlightened self-interest would have prompted him to think, 'This guy's doing a lot for me, I'll give him 2/12ths,' or some such figure, to give a greater incentive. As it was, well, he ended up working completely alone, and I think his work suffered because of it."

I then put to him the perennial question; that Clifford's illness was germinating for longer than anyone realized.

"Yes." He was quite adamant there. "With the wonderful power of hindsight. I noticed that his nerves were completely shot towards the end of the period I was working with him. He was chain smoking like crazy, way too many; he had a slight tremor in the hands and his train of thought wasn't terribly good. He'd repeat himself quite often. This was about 1980-81. I played piano for him on Noel Edmonds's 'Dingley Dell' in February, and various other radio/television shows about that time and he was, literally, a bag of nerves."

I remember hearing that Radio 1 programme.

I'd been working abroad, doing the Middle East circuit—live work in Britain had been virtually decimated overnight by the disco craze—and must have just returned home. I was sitting in my kitchen, contemplating attacking the February wilderness around my front—and back—door, but must have thought better of it, so I turned the radio on. After all, it was Sunday.

What was that I said earlier, about Clifford T. Ward haunting me?

Of all the shows, in every day, on every station, I had to pick that one... Clifford was brilliant, playing the clown to Noel Edmonds's ringmaster, but never letting his artistry become second best. In Dickens's—and subsequently Edmonds's—Dingley Dell, that fictitious piece of Olde England, all was well with the world. Tom Crite would have led the cricket team and there would have been honey for tea; but as soon as he began to sing, Clifford T. Ward was in a world of his own. He sang 'Home Thoughts From Abroad' and then his current single, 'The Best Is Yet To Come', before sliding into the lovely opening line, 'Gentle is the rain that falls on me, and gentle too, the raging sea...', the opening track from *No More Rock'n'Roll.* A somewhat throwaway version of 'Gaye', preceded by an almost Goon-ish repartee, with voices off and footsteps approaching the microphone, finished the set, and he was gone. I kicked the dog and moped out into the garden, wondering why on earth the man wasn't a superstar.

Mark continues to elaborate on Clifford's anxieties:

"Like everyone else, *including* the medical profession, I don't know very much about MS, but I think it's a disease [*sic*] that can be exacerbated by stressful situations. And Clifford was forever—even at the very beginning—in a stressful situation. He was difficult, and it was in his nature to make even the most normal of projects become stressful. If that makes sense…?

"But then, it seems to be the nature of the beast. After Clifford, I became a recording engineer at Zella Studios and I dealt with a lot of other artistes who were absolute bloody tossers. Totally and utterly screwed up. A lot of it was drugs, of course, but in Clifford's case he never touched the stuff, didn't go near it, or near anyone that did."

[He actually sacked at least three session musicians for smoking 'dope'.]

"So what kept you working with him? You say the money wasn't brilliant, and the atmosphere was not exactly 'Round The Horne'…"

"Oh, the music. I adored it. Some of it was very twee, very parochial, but then he'd come up with something that would just blow me away. Send the hairs shooting up on the back of my neck. His sense of melody and harmony was extreme, and that strange way he played piano, well, for his music, it was exactly right, and I had to emulate it, bring it into a contemporary structure. It was all in his head, which, because he had no training, made it completely unique. I still, to this day, use what I learned from Clifford, which, in fact was *un*learning, if you follow me."

I did. Absolutely.

"His music was the one thing that kept me there. Nothing else. I remember one time, during those horrendous American sessions, he'd been struggling all day with the vocal to 'Contrary', and we'd got into a really late session. Maybe he'd had a couple of brandies, but he insisted on giving it one last try. He went in and did a vocal, a complete take, from beginning to end, that was absolutely stunning. We all just looked around in wonder. He had a truly astonishing voice. Especially when a tune was pitched probably at the top of his range and he'd go for a note and *just* get it. That tension, you could hear it. It was breathtaking in its beauty. Those times made up for all the arguing, the angst."

I also remember such an instance. Not that I was there, but I recently saw a video recording of the 17th Castlebar Song Contest, in October, 1982. An annual event, held, yes, in Castlebar, Northern Ireland, at which Clifford was asked to perform a short set, as guest artiste. He was quite plainly feeling the early effects of an illness that had not yet been diagnosed. Together with Mark as his accompanist, he had driven across—well, the ferry had taken them part of the way—and, after a hilarious [in Mark's view, but not in Clifford's…] altercation with the customs, which had entailed completely unloading the car, they had arrived at the television studios leaving very little time to rehearse with the twenty-piece orchestra… and it was to be televised. Live.

Clifford had not even taken a change of clothing. He appears on camera in his travelling clothes; a beige sports jacket, blue jeans and white shoes, sitting at a keyboard. Following a warm welcome from the MC,

the man himself, without so much as, 'Hello', goes into a very clumsy version of 'Gaye'.
Mark confirms the situation:
"The monitoring on the first song was rather shaky. I don't think Clifford could hear himself properly. I've never seen anyone so nervous. I was playing acoustic guitar, in the orchestra, and I was thinking, 'Don't cough, don't anybody make a wrong sound; sneeze, nothing, 'cos he'll go into a spin...The slightest thing and he'll lose it...'"
After 'Gaye' he leaves the piano, walks centre stage, again without a word, and visibly hanging onto the microphone stand for support, his knuckles white with fright, glued to the spot, he gives a quite spine-chilling rendering of 'Up In The World' [popularized in Ireland by Colm Wilkinson] which brings a spontaneous burst of applause over the first line—Tony Bennett-like—from the audience, before they lapse into complete silence for the remainder of the song. Then, over the subsequent cheering, with just a brief, 'Thank you, and here's one I wrote for the missus,' he drops straight into 'Home Thoughts From Abroad'.
He is scared, absolutely terrified, petrified. Even the unflattering camera-work—zooming in, dropping back, then panning the crowd—can't detract from the white-knuckle intensity. It is electrifying. His voice soaring and sweeping, unenhanced; without affectation, false vibrato or cloyed emotion, and he without a trace of a smile. That slight crack in purity and the perfect, perfect pitch. The result is, to use Mark's word, stunning. Positively stunning. This isn't a man showing off. It is a man singing on the very edge—yet from the very depths—of his soul.
If anyone ever questions Clifford T. Ward as a contender, let them see that clip. Ten minutes of an artiste equal to anyone. And I mean anyone.

If only...If only...

Mark saw a lot of family life during his visits to Castle Weir and subsequent houses. I asked him how he saw Pat's role in all this.
"Pat, to my mind, was very strong, down to earth, Cliff's crutch, feet-on-the-ground woman, shrewd and quite hard at times."
"To whom?"
"Mmmm." he hesitates, searching for the right way to say something.
"I got the impression—I don't know for certain—that she kept a close eye on the money and if Cliff was up to paying somebody £100, it would end up being £50. As I say, I don't know that for certain, maybe that was Cliff's way of working, auto-suggestion kind of thing, so's he

wouldn't come out the bad boy...but she managed all the moves, all the houses, wore the trousers, so to speak. When Justin left, she ended up managing him. Mind you, behind the scenes, she probably always had...

"Actually," and he gives a sharp intake of breath, looking positively sheepish...for half-a-second. "I *really* fancied her. Cliff seemed to take her very much for granted, he was almost ignorant of her. Well, they had been married quite a few years..."

But things were changing both inside and out, and not for the better.

He had begun to experience a blurring of vision—only now and then—and a loss of balance, again, only now and then, and it was put down to stress, as it always is. But the whole situation was going terribly wrong. The dream of Castle Weir had turned sour.

There was not enough money coming in to maintain the mansion, let alone to fulfil Clifford's ambition and set up a home for disabled children. He and Pat began selling off precious antiques they had collected over the years; a burr-walnut Davenport, a linen press, a set of Georgian dining-chairs, all lovingly purchased, but then, quite disposable. Easy come, easy go.

And again, when things were not going well, boredom would set in, and they would decide—though probably in this instance out of necessity—to move home.

Castle Weir was put on the market, and quickly sold. There were no regrets, no tears at leaving a place of such beauty, and in autumn 1981, they moved back into Worcestershire, to a house called Thresholds, in Trimpley, not so very far from the Park Attwood Hotel, where Cliff Ward and the Cruisers had begun their short career almost twenty long years earlier.

In the final years at Lyonshall, as if bizarrely fulfilling some of Justin's promises to Clifford, there had been, apart from the singles, a flurry of album activity on the music side—though only as compilation tracks—with one of the American songs, an out-take of 'Lost Again', appearing on K-Tel's *The Love Album*, in 1980. 'Gaye', 'Wherewithal', 'Home Thoughts from Abroad' and 'Up In The World' were also reissued, on two Tellydisc collections in 1981, and 'The Best Is Yet To Come', his most beautiful new song—having failed to impact as a single—would appear on the K-Tel *Dreaming Vol. 1* collection in 1982. This was the year after they had returned to Worcestershire, and the year when Clifford T. Ward found himself without recording, publishing or management deals, in an increasingly parlous financial situation and slowly, frighteningly, in a questionable state of health.

Justin de Villeneuve had gone from their lives, and the promises of fame and glory, shared over late night brandies or morning walks in the dew-soaked fields, had gone with him.

Clifford was now on his own, with just his songs and his own faith, and, of course, the only constant thing in his life, his wife. So much seemed to have happened and yet so little seemed to have been achieved, since those heady days, when the world was celebrating his talent and believing that the best, indeed, was yet to come.

Clive Selwood said something to me about how, during his life in the music business, he had seen so many similar career situations:

"I dunno, Dave," and he gives his long, heavy sigh. "It's not an unusual tale, by any means. There are so many factors that make up success. Talent, for sure, is one of them, but my experience is that talent is never more than…maximum 25 per cent It takes character, total commitment, a huge amount of luck, a big machine behind you, and timing. We got the first bit right, with 'Gaye', but Cliff didn't really hold up his end of the bargain. I feel that he really could have gone on to be something very special, but well, nobody deliberately shoots themselves in the foot. Fear, exposure to extreme public scrutiny, self-doubt, I don't know what it is. Some people get *so* near…," and he mentioned two or three artistes he also dealt with who *did* get that close.

"Clifford had his taste with 'Gaye', but he just didn't grasp it, hold on to it. A great shame."

And Justin?

I tried to get Justin to put his side of the story, but he repeated only what he had said in his own book some years ago, that Clifford T. Ward had been 'unmanageable'; other than that, he '…couldn't think of anything positive to say, so he'd rather say nothing.' This last quote came, ironically, via Mark Tibenham, who happened upon Justin at a small dinner party in London, and where anecdotes apparently flew fast and furious about those days in America. But he wouldn't be quoted, not Justin. As was also said, by someone else who wouldn't be quoted, Justin was not with Clifford for his music, he had never been that keen on it…

Despite all this, Pat remembers Justin, in her pragmatic way, with great affection:

"He was always polite, well-dressed—to the point of being ostentatious—and forever looking for the quick or easy way to make money, but, a charming chancer. He stayed with us many times, both at Lower Hollin, when he came up *en route* to somewhere—anywhere—and then more so at Castle Weir. He had stayed in the area as an evacuee, with J. B. Priestley's family on some farm close by, and remembered being ‘crocodiled’ through the village by the lady of the household. Nice memories, I would think. If we went down to the George in Lyonshall for meals, he thought it was paradise. Little incidents come back, like the time he complimented the landlord following a trout supper, only to be told that Martin and Sam had caught the fish that very day, in one of the Lyonshall pools. Martin, an early learner, had sold it to the pub. To Justin that was just magical. Country life.

“I would take him a cup of tea in the morning, and there he would be, sitting up in bed, Harrods nightshirt, hair immaculate [no nightcap?!] ready for another day. But, you know, in all those times, he only ever paid me one compliment.

One evening at Castle Weir, the men were sitting at the table, and I was doing my Betsy the serving-maid bit, dashing and dishing up the meal. As they started eating, Justin leaned back in his dining-chair, knife in one hand, fork in the other, looked at me and said, “Mmmm, now *this* is how I like my sprouts…”

AUTUMN

CRISIS

The sickening pang of hope deferr'd.
Sir Walter Scott: *Lady of the Lake*, III

It was late autumn, 1981.
Cats had been previewed at the New London Theatre; Salman Rushdie had published *Midnight's Children*; the film of John Fowles's remarkable novel *The French Lieutenant's Woman* had been released; Human League were singing 'Don't You Want Me (Baby)' and Clifford T. Ward was 37 years old, in yet another house, and reeling from his own inertia…
As his life seemed to be stagnating, the world of music was about to undergo its greatest change since Edison's phonograph. IBM had launched the first personal computer, and the compact disc was about to be launched on the domestic market. Soon, with microchips all over the shop, recording facilities would be available to all, and the record companies would see a back-catalogue spending spree that would pull most of them from the brink of insolvency, as Joe Public rushed out to renew favourite vinyl albums in this supposedly indestructible format.

Thresholds is a solid, between-the-wars house, set back along the lane that winds over Trimpley hill and down through extensive woodland into the shady groves of Habberley Valley, a beauty spot synonymous for years with lovers and parked cars.
Considerably smaller—by about ten bedrooms—than Castle Weir, Thresholds was a move made out of desperation as much as desire.
It had become painfully obvious that they would never furnish and maintain Castle Weir to their dream-expectations. After Justin, Cliff wanted to exorcize the whole spectre of failure and mistrust; he couldn't live in a house constantly reminding him of such times. Pat, a martyr to the cause, had constantly refused to take in help for the cleaning, let alone anything else, and the continual demands of stone floors and rooms by the dozen had virtually killed her love of the place; what little she ever had. So, smaller, manageable and cheaper was an obvious solution, though they were still at the mercy of the building society and the bank. What little profit they had made from the move

was soon drained by their overdraft. Once again, Pat was monitoring calls—and callers—as the financial institutions tightened their grip, but, once again, they spent whatever money *was* coming in renovating Thresholds, which was in a sorry state of repair.

It also meant another change of school for Martin, now at the sensitive age of 17 and embarking on his A-levels, and Sam, 14 years old, embarking on his first love affair whilst beginning to notice the unease clouding his family life. Debbie was in University at Coventry, literally rolling through her life with the same joy and energy she had shown as a child. three-year-old Polly grew sweeter by the day.

Cliff sorted out a room for his studio. That, as ever, was the first priority, but he was finding inspiration difficult. Despite Pat urging him on, he could see little point; there was no incentive any more, he felt drained, shattered, disillusioned, lost, and something wasn't quite right inside…

Ireland, however, still held his music in great esteem, and Peter Grogan was in no small way responsible for helping keep Clifford's name in the limelight over there, though even unaware of the *real* truth, he was beginning to worry about certain traits in y'man's character.

Like everyone else, he had never managed to persuade Clifford to perform live, in concert, though he knew there were opportunities a-plenty waiting.

"I kept on at him. There were promoters over there that could have sold out just by putting his name on a poster, or in the newspaper. But he'd get so angry. Maybe because he realized the truth of it—that he had to get out there—and that he didn't feel he was up to it. 'I'm no fucking Billy Jo-el or Elton John [as if that was a criterion…],' he'd shout, and I'd try to tell him that he didn't have to be an all-singing, all-dancing entertainer, his songs were what people wanted to hear. Not some slick, wise-cracking showman. But he wouldn't have it."

Still, Peter continued to organize radio and television spots whenever he could, spurred on by his incredible enthusiasm, guileless bravado and, indeed, knack for being in the right place at the right time.

"We were walking down Oxford Street, myself and Eileen, one summer, about 1977-78, when I saw Tim Rice coming towards us. [See what I mean?] I went up to him, said 'How y're Tim, I've met a good friend of yours in Ireland, Colm Wilkinson [*Jesus Christ - Superstar*, *Les Miserables*, etc.] and I'm hoping that he will record a song ['Up In The World'] by a friend of *mine*, Clifford T. Ward.' Tim knew of Clifford's work, and after exchanging a few pleasantries, wished me well and went his merry way.

"A few years later—after Colm *had* recorded the song, incidentally—" and he gives a nod of smug satisfaction, "it was November, 1984, I helped secure Clifford a spot on the 'Davis At Large Show', an RTE programme with a vast following. I went with Clifford to the studio, Derek [Davis] made us welcome in his usual warm, pleasant way and showed us to the dressing room. We went along and there, up on the door was 'Tim Rice and Clifford T. Ward'. It was pure coincidence that Tim and Cliff were doing the same show.

"He saw the names on the door and he just wanted to go home. He said, 'Jesus, no, I'm not going in there.' It wasn't that he didn't want to share a dressing room with Tim Rice, what he was saying to me was, 'I'm not going to be able to handle this...' Well I bloody well told him that he was going in. 'To hell with you Cliff, *I'm* meeting Tim Rice. He's an old friend...' And I had to jokingly say, 'He might not recognize *you*, but he'll bloody well recognize *me,* 'cos I met him in Oxford Street.' So I literally insisted that he stay in that dressing room. Now as such, we didn't meet up there, 'cos Tim was doing his spot on air at that time. Cliff went ahead with his bit, he sang 'Messenger', and that was fine. Later, we were all in the Green Room chatting away, and Tim Rice—unfortunately—didn't recognize me, but he did recognize Cliff." We both laugh. "I'll never forgive him for that. Gobshite!! Anyway, he came up and he shook hands with Cliff and he said, 'You are one of the few people whose songwriting has affected me.' Now you might think this is trite, whatever, but the man was absolutely genuine, and *then* he said, 'I think your song 'The Best Is Yet To Come', has to be one of the best songs ever written. It is the ultimate tear-jerker.'

"Clifford thanked him, in that husky, almost embarrassed way, and that was that. And of course, they were going on somewhere, and of course we were invited, but of course, Cliff just wanted to go home, well, back to our place.

"Now I'm not criticizing Cliff here, but I definitely think, in retrospect, that about this time, the MS, nervous disorder—call it what you will—was certainly taking hold. I mean, Cliff has always been shy, diffident, in *public* (in his own surroundings he could be as truculent and opinionated as the next man); that in itself can be charming, but he began to back off in such a way that it began to work against him.

"But he *loved* that incident, and he retold it on countless occasions over here and in Ireland. He was thrilled that Tim Rice had come up to him and acknowledged his talent, and he thereafter referred to Tim Rice as 'a gentleman'. That was Cliff's highest social accolade. But y'see, that's what I, and everybody else couldn't seem to get *across* to him; that he *was* up there with these people, in terms of talent. He was one of *them.* And also, if he hadn't met Tim, seen that side of it all, then I'm sure that Cliff would have gone through life referring to him as part of the 'gin-and-tonic' pop brigade, the showbiz crowd, which he hated. There must have been many similar times in England—when I wasn't with him—where he would have walked away, fought shy, and it militated against him. Okay, he was a bit reclusive, that's fine, leave him be, but if he'd just played the game a bit, mixed a little more with these people, then I'm sure he would have got more cover versions, for instance, which would have been a great insurance policy for now. But you have to be *out* there.

"I spoke to Vince Hill once, doing cabaret in Malahide, when he was doing really well. Again, a lovely man. Okay, not your major league guy, but he sold an awful lot of records. He assumed Cliff had retired after *Home Thoughts* and gone back to teaching.

"And Colm Wilkinson, when he was at his peak with *Les Miserables* in London, made a wonderful observation. He visited Cliff at Castle Weir, had a most enjoyable time there, as everyone did; the Ward hospitality was, *is*, legendary. When he got back to Ireland he called to thank me for giving him Cliff's address, and we talked, obviously, about Clifford. Colm said, quite matter-of-fact, that Cliff was '...just too close to his music. Every song,' he said, 'was like having a baby to him...'

"Cliff wasn't interested in the music business, point number one. Point number two, he wasn't *part* of it, until he had to be, and then he would work himself to death for two months—be it writing, be it recording—and it would absolutely drain him. At times when we visited him, he was either really uptight, going in, or he was completely drained, having just come out. I would see his temples throbbing, when he got a letter from his publishers or record company, and I used to think, 'Jeez, why is he getting so uptight?' Wisdom after the event, I suppose, but that kind of thinking, reaction, whatever, can't be good for the soul *or* the career.

"Cliff's mother—with that maternal intuition inbred in all mothers—I remember her saying that she always knew Cliff didn't have the right personality for the music business. And that was true. He really was his own worst enemy.

"We have a saying in Ireland," and he flows into that wonderful language of the Gaels, the romantic tongue of the poets of Erin, except that he then translated it thus: "If you've only a pup-goat, be in the middle of the fair."

I laugh again. Wonderful.

He elucidates further:

"Y'know, 'If you haven't got much make sure people can see you. No matter what you've got to sell, be available.' And Cliff had a damn sight more than a pup-goat, but he certainly hid his light under a bushel, there's no doubt about that. He had the bones for five really strong albums and at least ten excellent singles, but the world only knows him for 'Gaye'."

Peter is quite correct. Although 'Gaye' contains, to my mind, one of the most enchanting couplets in Clifford's works:

Locarno title defenders 1964. Trevor wears a 'Bottom' head, Terry wears a pig-mask, for Big Dee Irwin's 'Swinging On A Star'. Fashion note: not a bald head in sight...

Hotel Launoy, Fontainebleau

Le Deauville, St Dizier

Martin Raynor & The Secrets: 'Candy To Me'

The Secrets: 'I Suppose'

Early demos in Bev Pegg's studio

Bev Pegg, 1972

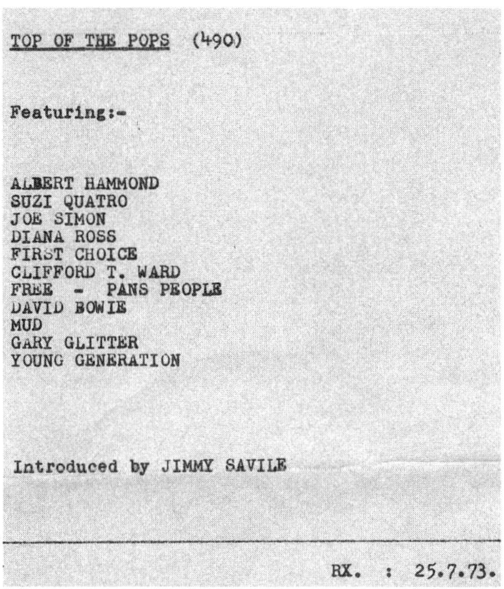

TOP OF THE POPS (490)

Featuring:-

ALBERT HAMMOND
SUZI QUATRO
JOE SIMON
DIANA ROSS
FIRST CHOICE
CLIFFORD T. WARD
FREE - PANS PEOPLE
DAVID BOWIE
MUD
GARY GLITTER
YOUNG GENERATION

Introduced by JIMMY SAVILE

RX. : 25.7.73.

Top Of The Pops camera script for 'Gaye'

Island Music, 1973

Derek Thomas

Ken Wright

Terry Edwards

Counting the royalties at The Spinney.
Pat, Martin, Sam, Cliff and Debbie

At Pensax, photographed by Lichfield

Castle Weir

Long View Farm, Massachusetts. The studio is the building on the right

Castle Weir, at 1.57pm, and twenty seconds

Pretty Polly, *Both of Us* cover girl

Debbie's wedding, Upper Norchard, May 1985.
Cliff's symptoms are apparent

The last official publicity shot, for Tembo
Records, August 1985

MS claims life of 'sixties musician

Tragic: Rodney Simmonds.

Second member of group hit by disease

TRAGEDY has struck a 'sixties band which was once a musical institution in Wyre Forest.

Rodney Simmonds, a former member of Stourport band Cliff Ward and the Cruisers, has died of the crippling disease multiple sclerosis at the age of 49.

Former Stourport High School pupil Clifford T Ward, lead singer and founder of the band, has also got the tragic illness.

Cliff Ward and the Cruisers was probably the most well-known local rock group of that era.

When Cliff left the group to pursue a solo career, Rodney and the remaining musicians formed The Reflections.

They had great success around the Wyre Forest area.

Meanwhile Cliff, as Clifford T Ward, had a top-ten hit in the 1970s with *Gaye*.

Rodney, originally from Kidderminster, was stricken with multiple

Rodney's death makes headlines in the Midlands'
largest evening newspaper, the Express & Star

Pat on her 53rd birthday

Ireland, 1992

> You're the tray of nice things I upset yesterday,
> The display of bright rings, I let slip away...

there are other songs hidden like nuggets in the river-bed; songs that—in the flow of his labours—have lain almost untouched, sparkling with originality and beauty, only to be discovered by those who have truly mined the seam. They stand equal to the two, maybe three, that *are* known; some surpass, but all of them glow, all of them are unmistakable in their origin.

There are many from which to choose; maybe you should sit down and listen to some of these gems, discover or re-assess, the haunting beauty, so sadly neglected by a world that seems to have lost its way:

'Home Thoughts From Abroad' is a song of apparent simplicity yet astonishingly complex in its presentation and structure, which will always be Clifford's *tour de force*. Forget about it being the only love song to mention Worcestershire—a beautiful county, deservedly mentioned—it must surely be the only love song with 'cistern' in it, and yet the word doesn't leap out in shock-horror or embarrassment, it is sung with such matter-of-fact reference that it becomes, rightly so, part of the thoughts of home. The prose-poetry, sung with that astonishing English purity, without affectation and stretched over a breathtakingly simple melody, is complemented by a sublime, neo-classical string section, with that very last phrase soaring like Wordsworth's skylark, to hang in the air...

'Up In The World' begins with the suspense of the unknown, and develops into a song of magnificent sadness. I can't think of another single British songwriter that has written a piece as lucid yet as powerful as this, and any other singer who surpasses this, the original. No hip-mannerism, just a pure and simple *cri de coeur*. Its melody fuses Anglican roots, classical form and operatic modulation. It whispers, it soars, and it stings...

Stunning.

'Open University', with its enticing first line: 'Let me tell you 'bout a girl who's breaking my heart...' draws the listener straight into confessional mode. The husky, precise vox humana underscored by sighing harmonies; the temperate jazz band, and the totally original concept—education, passion, and the lover who learns—lock this little gem forever into the mind.

'Coathanger', though probably not an accurate chronological pointer, is the true demarcation line between Cliff Ward, aspiring pop writer and

Clifford T. Ward, singer-songwriter. Though both this song and 'Carrie', its precursor (and blueprint for 'Gaye'), were taken from the same album, there is a marked difference in both quality and approach. 'Carrie' could have been written by any competent tunesmith, whereas 'Coathanger', with its quirky lyric and extended metre, is pure Clifford T. Ward. Infectious to the point of irritation, this was the first amalgamation of his pop and neo-classical styles. Using his wonderfully effective falsetto to impose the distinctive pop melody, and singing words that no-one else would even consider to express love and desire, the song is subtly enhanced by Richard Hewson's cello-based accompaniment. This should have been a hit.

'Wherewithal' is the most neglected classic, a mature 'Coathanger', with all of Clifford's trademarks in one song: that end-of-line leap, the extra bar, and scholarly lyric. Totally irresistible, with tambourine doubling rhythm over the verse, and oboe used with great effect (Hewson's nod to Brazilian composer Antonio Carlos Jobim) to 'attract your attention', Derek's remarkable guitar solo, and the paired chorus vocals emphasizing that fluid voice.

'Where Would That Leave Me?' carries a lyric that says what we've all wanted to say, many times. 'Why don't you tell me you love me?...' opens this gentle, pleading love-song, with its swaying, 'Elizabethan Serenade' instrumentation, and Clifford, using his all-too-infrequent cracked-voice intonation, on the line, 'Aah, you know that I could...'; sounding warmly sexual. Beautiful.

'The Way Of Love' uses another basic three-chord melody that no-one else could possibly have written, and yet was always there, waiting to be plucked from the air. A song that would fit in any musical, and stop it dead. Here, in one fell swoop, the untrained musician—raised on rock'n'roll, pop and soul—brings his classical, symphonic, *majestic* instincts to their peak. Simply exquisite, and again, despite its simplicity, startlingly original.

'A Day To Myself' is awesome. The gentle title draws you to a subject you would normally avoid. As in D. M. Thomas's terrifying novel, *The White Hotel*, you are enticed by skilfully seductive writing, only to find yourself unwilling witness to the horrors of war. Here, Clifford begins the song in typical 'Home Thoughts...'style, gentle piano, 'missing-you' lyric, then, following an almost casual mention of his visit to a battlefield cemetery, it develops a hymn-like magnificence, with the words forming a powerful juxtaposition, as he views the sadness of his temporary absence from home as selfish, futile, compared to that of the

young war-dead, and their final resting place in the green fields of a foreign land.
Besides being one of the most popular songs amongst his followers, this is also Cliff's own favourite.

'Time, The Magician', a phrase borrowed out of Hardy's *Far From The Madding Crowd*, is used to great effect in this gorgeous lyric, a celebration of togetherness through the years, with a 4/4 melody—instantly memorable—sung in that smoky, effortless Ward manner, hung on Beatle-counterpoint harmonies and high-strung guitar backing. Summers of love.

'Where's It Going To End?' is one of *Home Thoughts*' most underrated tracks. Using the love-motor car metaphor, Richard Hewson's astute orchestration—and Terry Edwards's sliding bass-line—conjure up wonderful images: the motorway heat, the car-horns, the stop-start journey; all weaving around the unpredictability of Clifford's long, shuddering vocal breaks, his last top note screaming frustration at the 'stream of endless traffic', the resolving first verse, and the slow, plunging realization of it all…

'For Debbie And Her Friends' begins in a playground, children talking, as Derek's rippling acoustic guitar leads Clifford's stainless voice into a lyric and melody, which, though it may subconsciously borrow the first eighteen bars of 'Ruby Tuesday', develops into a simply stunning song, dealing with a subject of unquestionable delicacy—to those who patronize disability. Only with his first-hand experience, and with his mastery of meiosis, could this release of taboo emotion be executed so well.

'The Best Is Yet To Come' is the most understated of all his songs. A solo piano accompaniment—with the CTW trademark chord inversions painstakingly interpreted by Mark Tibenham—enriches yet another haunting melody that sounds as if it must have flowed from head to hand in pure inspiration.
Two verses, a bridge, a third verse, finish. Other artistes would have repeated the bridge and last verse, but Clifford, as ever exercising restraint, says all there is to say, and leaves the stage. The words tell his own story, almost prophetically—considering it was written before the onset of MS—but speak of promise, misfortune, tragedy and despair in such a way that they could relate to any failing marriage.
It has the sad beauty of a sunset.

There are others as good and as popular, mostly in demo form and known only within the sacred circle, and it is wrong. It has to change. Where this style came from is locked—forever—in his own mind. Cliff told me, during one of our radio interviews, that he realized the need to adopt a new sound, to get away from the '...run-of-the-mill pop writing that seemed to permeate music at the time...', but this doesn't explain where or when his approach became so distinctive.

The nearest I can get to a similar sound is Barry Mann's 'Come Back Silly Girl', recorded by The Lettermen on Capitol in 1962. The introduction—arpeggio piano and sweeping strings—leading a strong but simple melody, with pure vocals and perfect diction, could very easily be an early Clifford T. Ward song.

He certainly knew that record. A Cruisers set list from the French tour of US bases shows the song on the agenda, and Cliff used to sing it. No, I'm not suggesting he copied their format, but subconsciously it may have influenced him during his search for a new direction. Cliff's erudite lyrics take the formula up a few notches, his melodies are more beautiful, but there is a pointer there.

Kevin Gammond, one of only three people who collaborated with Cliff (Graham Drew and Martie Echito being the others), speaks also of his musical stoicism:

"Clifford's approach was very precise, very Germanic in its structure. At that time [the Bronco days], we were all experimenting with diminished 9ths, augmented 6ths, whatever, but Cliff stuck to his self-taught and very basic piano style—he found some incredible inversions now and then—but it was mainly just three or four chords. Yet he got some wonderful, beautiful melodies out of those few simple chords, tunes no-one else would have found, ever."

Yes, once again, Peter Grogan was right. There was much more there than the world knew about, and Clifford must have realized that in many ways, down the years, he had been his own worst enemy. As Clive Selwood acknowledged, success is that old ABC; ability, breaks and courage. Cliff, even before his illness began to manifest itself, had run out of courage. He had told them all to '...sod off'; he was interested only in the ultimate prize of success—to be able to live his life in his own way—and that had not been possible. Now, in desperation he was trying to make amends.

When the poet Stevie Smith wrote about 'not waving but drowning' she conveyed the feelings of all frustrated artistes. Years later, Clifford T. Ward, after tasting the ripe fruits of success and after artistically extending that same plea, was also locked in his 'shuttered room', quietly shouting for help.

His music in England—despite the release of the two new singles and a 'Pebblemill At One' spot, the video of which shows a serious, camera-shy performer walking alongside the Pebblemill stream, singing the haunting 'Contrary'—was now suffering even more in the wake of the 'in-ya-face' punk explosion, so Ireland, in that sad year of 1981, must have brought *some* solace. It seemed that whatever the trends, he would always be in demand over there, still commanding respect in the land of his ancestors, appearing again on RTE television in Gay Byrne's 'Late, Late Show' and doing various acclaimed radio spots.

In one such interview, hosted by Jerry Byrne way back at the beginning of February, before Cliff had finally terminated his relationship with Justin and the depression had set in, he had been remarkably upbeat, his voice light, somewhat mannered, but spirited, talking of his desire to be recognized as a songwriter. He expressed his love of the Irish and American people, "...because they wear their heart on their sleeve...I've always been aware of reluctance towards the emotional-type love song—my type of music—in England. It is more difficult to achieve success [with such material] than it is in America or Ireland."

Jerry asks him about his attitude to writing, in that he has to write about "...his experiences..." Doesn't it embarrass him?

"It's a problem I know, and that's what I mean...Can I write about this? Can I reveal this? This is very personal."

He continues: "But, you know, to hell. If you're gonna be sincere to your craft, whether it's the pop song, or whether you're trying to create something with much more literary merit, then I think you have to be honest. And that's what I hope I am.

"I want to write songs that people will still be singing in 50 years time, and still be shedding a tear for in 50 years time. If I can do that, I shall be delighted.

"We all crave for commercial success...to get into the national charts, but if I had the choice of a record that's in the top five one week and forgotten in a month's time, or a song that's gonna be played in ten, twenty, thirty, forty years time, I'd go for the latter every time. That to me is what it's all about."

Jerry plays Colm Wilkinson's operatic version of 'Up In The World', which Cliff praises highly, speaking of his pleasure in hearing other artistes singing his works.

"It was always my original intention to be a songwriter rather than a performer, 'cos I don't think I've got the...wherewithal to be a great, dynamic performer. Writing is really my first love."

Jerry then asks the perennial question:

"Does that mean that you don't want to tour any more, you don't want to tour at *all*?"

"No, I wouldn't be that dogmatic about it, because I mean, we are in fact now—my management and myself—in the...[and here, back in 1981, he makes a very rare stumble over a word] ...pre-lim-in-ary stage of planning a tour. I think if you make records...then you have a responsibility to go out and promote the records. I'm actually looking forward to it now. I've grown a bit fed up with renovating our house [Castle Weir] and all the other things we've been doing. I would actually like that, to go out and do a tour."

"It would be very, very different from when you were out on the road before though. Things have changed." Jerry reminds him that it's been a long, long time. "Everything's become so bizarre. How do you feel about that?"

"Yeah, I know. All those kids with green hair," Cliff laughs. "But hopefully there are still suckers for sentimental love songs...If the venues were right—we'd have to choose the right venues—nice comfortable places where people could come out for the evening, bring their wives or girlfriends, maybe where there's a bar, have a drink. I'm very keen to go."

Considering all he'd said and *not* done before, this was a revealing conversation, a great contradiction of all he had implied through the years, to Clive to Peter, even to Pat. Cliff was either saying what he thought people wanted to hear, or Justin, prior to their break-up, had been *that* close to changing the leopard's spots...

"There's some funny buggers out there, Roger. You keep by my side, and keep your eyes on the crowd."

Stourport Carnival, August, 1981, and Clifford T. Ward was guest of honour, to declare the event open, and to crown the Carnival Queen, Alison Freeman. Roger Bowen, big, beefy (sorry, brawny...but he *is* a butcher), looking every inch the part, was asked along by Cliff as his minder. I kid you not. With Pat and Polly at his side, they sailed on the river floats, waving at the crowd on shore, posed for photographs with Clifford in his new outfit and superstar sun-glasses, as Roger stood over them, right hand strategically placed inside his jacket, hand on his water pistol...

Never being the exhibitionist pop music demands, it had taken three, maybe four years to get him to appear in his home town, as guest of honour. Pat knows that he felt 'awkward, self-conscious'; he didn't want anyone to think he'd grown 'arrogant, or conceited with his fame...', despite the fact that he had recently given away his gold disc for the 1980 K-Tel compilation—on which his song 'Lost Again' featured—to a local charity; not, methinks, the action of a man too full of himself.

But she did try to get him to wear a suit. He insisted on sports jacket and jeans.

"It don't matter what you wear, who you are," he joked to Chris and Wendy Jones, their Lyonshall friends, "there's always some bugger who will say he knew you when y'r arse was 'angin owt y'r trousers."
The *Stourport Courier*, now amalgamated with the *Kidderminster Shuttle*, featured a picture of him leaning against a tree in the Castle Weir orchard, short-haired and serious, the accompanying article reminding its readers that Clifford was 'a son of the town', and that he was '...giving his time entirely free'.
It was a great success, a brief moment of glory, harking back to the days when his name had been on everyone's lips as the local hero, the boy who had made it in the big, wide world, without any Faustian deals. Yet, back home, away from the cheers and the fireworks, in the silence of his room, Cliff felt the cloak of depression around his shoulders. Whatever it seemed to the world outside, inwardly he was struggling to come to terms with his professional hiatus.
Socially, Cliff and Pat were as marooned as ever, but that was how they seemed to want to be. Gill Bowen was still cutting Cliff's hair, maintaining the shorter style he had adopted for the American fiasco, and the Wards and Bowens visited each other in turn, Roger still working in the family business, but by now anticipating a welcome retirement, to concentrate on—or maintain, as Gill would insist—his lovely home in Ombersley, or—as Roger would suggest—his golf.
But his gradual change in fortune had seemingly made Cliff more reflective on such occasions. Roger recalls one night when they came over to Ombersley. Cliff, in a rare moment, opened up to him, about music and about his children.
"The only time I saw Cliff relaxed was sitting down here." He points to the large, sumptuous sofa in the centre of their lounge. "He loved a glass of red wine, and we'd sit and listen to music. It was always *his* music, mind! But I loved it. And I realize now, that, considering all the criticism he showered on his musicians, all the demands he made of them, those note-for-note, roll-for-roll instructions, well, nothing else would have fitted. The only musician *I'm* aware of who ever met his expectations—that he ever expressed satisfaction with—was the Irish-American drummer chap [Marc Singer] who played those wonderful fills on 'Before The World Was Round' [*New England Days*, part 2].

"He also confided in me on one of these occasions. Maybe Pat and Gill were in another room, I dunno, but we were a little bit, well, shall we say, red wine-ish, talking generally, and he started to open up, something quite rare in Cliff. He was a very private person. But he told me that he'd never really appreciated his kids. He'd been too young, too busy, too ambitious, and had never taken the time to get to know them properly, despite his family image. When Polly came along, he seemed to dote on his daughter, and to us, he and Pat seemed to become much closer."

Polly had indeed been doted on by Cliff. Pat remembers his possessiveness almost as an obsession. He fussed and protected her, cocooned in her special bedroom at the top of the house, away from germ-spreading visitors and the noises of everyday life. They were almost inseparable: riding the tractor-mower together, walking the orchards together, digging their way out of the snowdrifts 'together', during that wonderful, unforgettable, winter of 1980, when the whole country—and especially the Castle Weir central heating system—seemed to grind to a halt, for a real Victorian Christmas.

But that had been the last festive season in such surroundings. By the spring Pat and Cliff were talking houses. By autumn they were at Trimpley, and the children, once again, were almost incidental to his state of mind.

Well, parents. We all do things wrong, we all feel we could have done things better.

But what was it *really* like having a father so eminently portrayed as a loving, family man, yet who was at the mercy of inner demons and, because of his profession, outer 'demonics'?

I spoke to third child Sam, born in 1967, christened Simon, and who is now a father himself, living in Denmark with Hanné, his lovely wife. He was over here visiting his parents, proudly showing off their newly born son, Jack, who lay sleeping contentedly in Hanné's arms.

Sam and I sat in the garden of his father's house. Initially, I found it hard to accept this handsome, mature adult as the young child who stared so knowingly out from the cover of *Home Thoughts*—even though it was many, many years ago—but as he began talking, his shy, gentle manner seemed to evoke the very essence of that Englishness we have all now so sadly lost.

I wasn't, however, prepared for the bitterness.

He spoke freely, willingly, without prompting, raising his voice only occasionally above the sound of dogs barking in the distance, or stopping as we listened to the autumn bird-song.

As is normal, most recent and traumatic events spring to the fore, but, in doing so, they automatically trigger incidents and emotions from deep down in the growing years.

"Dad was always at odds with something or someone. One of my most vivid memories is of when we were living at Dunley [their house from 1983 to 1989]. He physically attacked the workmen, who were converting one of the barns into a recording studio. Something had gone wrong—or was not going well—and an argument started. He picked up a large piece of wood and began hitting the ground with it and screaming at them. He then went for one of the men pushing him away, almost onto the ground, shouting, telling them all to get off his land. They did. They ran to the car and shot off down the drive, leaving most of their tools behind."

"Do you think that the illness was at work then, even way before he had been diagnosed?"

"Oh yes," nodded Sam. "I'm sure that he was so stressed by the work, being the perfectionist that he is—or was—that, coupled with whatever was happening inside him, of which no-one else seemed to be aware, he just snapped. During the building work, he would get up in the middle of the night to nail up pieces of plaster board; it was always on his mind."

"Well," I remarked, "about that time, things weren't going too well. He'd been a few years without management, someone had said, after the event, that he had been, literally, 'unmanageable'. Awkward. Cussed."

"Yes, but even before then, in fact, always, as a dad, he was awkward. Going back to when we lived at Trimpley, I used to dread coming back from school. If he was at home, sitting in the lounge or in his studio, I used to try and creep past him and run up the stairs, rather than get into conversation.

"He was so difficult, terrible, in those days. He'd always been a bit like that, but he got worse, trying to put me down, making me feel so small. I don't think it was intentional, I just think he was trying to compensate for his own insecurities, and in doing so he'd turn on the people nearest to him. I mean, Mom as well. She had to put up with so much crap, and I'd watch her doing the washing up, pretending, as if nothing was going on. There always seemed to be an...atmosphere. Consequently, my relationship with *her* suffered at that time, 'cos whenever I tried to speak to her, he was always there, in the background, rubbishing whatever we said.

"On Boxing Day one year, we were all sitting in the lounge, the whole family, grandparents, plus my girlfriend, Vanessa. There must have been about ten of us. Mom and I were having a quiet conversation together, in a corner of the room. Someone said something like 'Oh, look at those two in a world of their own', just an innocent, jokey remark. Dad went spare, bringing up Oedipus and his complex, saying how unnatural it was for us to be so close. We just couldn't believe it. It was so ridiculous. Well, ridiculous is too mild a word, I mean he was my dad, and yet he seemed jealous or threatened by a normal, loving relationship. It just ruined the whole day, and the whole holiday. I just couldn't speak to him. He wasn't drunk, nothing like that. Nothing as *simple* as that. It was just him and his neuroses.

"If he picked me up from school, which I used to dread, he'd go spare when I told him what I'd been learning; as if it was in my power to choose. Really, very negative. Never any encouragement whatsoever, which at that age is exactly what you need. But then, from what I hear, or can remember, I got off rather lighter than Martin. Until Pol came along, I think he favoured me, which in itself is wrong, you don't have—or shouldn't show—favouritism with your children. I think he loved the idea of having kids, the family, but he never saw himself as being part of it, as if it was beyond him or…

"Saying all that, he played games with us which, on the rare occasions they *did* occur, were great fun. Crawling into the bedroom, which Martin and I shared, after the lights were out, making animal noises and scaring us to death, which we loved. Sometimes he'd play football with us—the normal dad things—but only when *he* felt like it; everything was always on *his* terms. This was all when he was at the height of his success. When things started to fade and he began looking back at the glory days, then family life became *really* strained. When we moved to Castle Weir, Martin and I would sometimes come back on the school bus to find the house completely locked up, no key to get in, even in winter. There was no trust shown, no key under the doormat. We had to stand around for ages, waiting for them to get back. Dark and cold. Dad didn't want us in there messing with things—or it was probably Mom, scared that we'd get in and mess up the kitchen…" He laughs. "She's always been a bit particular…

"No, Mom was great. She always seemed to compensate for any lack of loving. Everything, basically was left to her. And I don't say that Dad wasn't loving, he just never showed it. I'm not into cuddles, that kind of thing, but there was no encouragement. We were told to do our share of the gardening, all those massive lawns and flower beds we always had; so as soon as we got back from school, out with the watering cans….raking up the leaves. I moaned about it once and Mom told me to make out a list of the hours we spent and they would pay us so much an hour. So of course, I went at it all summer, working and noting down my times. I clocked up loads of hours and I never got a penny for it… There was a time I wanted to get a part-time job, like some of my friends, but his attitude was that there was enough work to do at home, he wouldn't have us working for anybody else. We never got pocket-money. I'm not saying we went without, we certainly didn't, but it would have been more productive to pay us *some*thing, so we could've learned how to handle money."

"Did you ever have friends round, parties and such?"

"Yeah," he shrugs, "sometimes, but again, it was always questions, or putting on some act, trying to 'entertain' them with something totally unfunny. Most of my friends thought he was strange. It was a bit embarrassing…"

This all sounds terribly sad, but, dare I say it, a typical reaction by teenagers to their parents…

"I dunno. I've got very mixed feelings," Sam continues. I look at him, sitting on the wall. Still with his shock of straw-blond hair, but his gentle face now adorned with a thick, ginger beard. His gaze continually wandering around the garden, his long, artistic fingers idly picking at faded flower-heads and yellowed grass-stalks.

"Through my teenage years, I think he viewed me as a threat. He seemed jealous. You hear about these things. I mean, his life perhaps wasn't going anywhere, whereas mine was just beginning, and he felt threatened. There was one time, I was about 17 [1984], we had this stand-up row where he stated, quite categorically, that intellectually, he was far superior to me, and he said it in such a way that I actually thought he was going to hit me. I just backed off. There was never any point in arguing or contradicting him, he always managed to belittle me. I could never get anywhere. I always froze inside and I ended up by avoiding contact whenever I could."

I suppose any father-son, parent-child relationship can identify with *some* of these incidents, though Clifford was certainly more Victorian in his family attitudes than most; frighteningly strict and certainly not one to display love by emotion. He was never a social animal. Even in his childhood he had been a loner, and one can only assume that—despite outward appearances—as his world continued to develop, it became such a private, personal, judgmental place that he began to lose control. And who can possibly say exactly how long his illness lay there, tormenting him, waiting to break out and surface? Sam certainly suffered the consequences in his later years.

He looked at me:

"When he began to be successful, my friends used to question me, wondering what it was like, but to me it was just as always. Other people changed toward *us*, if anything, but I suppose that's normal as well. I was told to get my hair cut by the headmaster, when I was about seven, as I'd been picked for the swimming gala. It was either that or wear a bathing hat…I was in the barber's next day.

"When I was about four, maybe five, Mom called us into the room and said that Dad had sold a lot of records—or maybe he'd signed a deal—so she was going to take us into town and we could choose one present each…Off we went—to Woolworths in Kidderminster," he laughs. "Deb picked a jigsaw puzzle, Martin chose a fishing rod and I grabbed a plastic space-gun—which was broken by someone across the road next day. Hmm. We certainly weren't spoiled. There was also an amusing incident—and this has really got nothing to do with Dad—when Martin and I walked down to Pensax Stores to buy some Christmas presents. We bought a car-cloth for Dad," then laughing at the absurdity, "some bird-nuts for Deb…and a bottle of bleach for Mom…to put in her bath…We thought it would smell nice…

"But nothing really changed, apart from the moving of houses, which puzzled me. I loved Pensax, the swimming pool at Lower Hollin…I didn't want to move.

"Music was a no-go area. Again, we weren't encouraged to play instruments [though elder brother Martin is now a professional drummer], and Dad never talked to us about his work."

"Were you surprised when the illness was diagnosed?"

"Not really," he shrugged. "I always thought that his strangeness was him. I never ever stood back and looked at him objectively. Other people noticed; my friends' parents would ask what was wrong with my dad, but to me it was just how he'd always been, only probably worse…

"When he told me, well, he was still my father…It didn't make anything different I suppose, besides which, none of us really knew what MS *was*."

All very sorrowful. Maybe I caught Sam on a bad day. I know there *were* good times, but with Cliff's ever increasing health worries, maybe it was difficult to have a normal father-son relationship anyway. They went out jogging over the hills and lanes when Sam was full of the joys of his first romance—though who ran faster depends on who tells the tale—but of course Cliff would have felt the side-effects of any such exertions, and would have been unable to identify the causes or express his concern to anyone.

But at that time, in Trimpley, no-one really suspected anything so serious…did they?

Artistes suffer by the very nature of their being creative. The American farmer-poet Robert Frost, forever feeling his output restricted by his domesticity, once stated that '…no artiste should have a family…', but Cliff's family had never knowingly intruded upon his thought processes—quite the opposite—yet they were now beginning to feel the backlash of his current lack of success and subsequent low self-esteem.

The years were beginning to fly by without any new offers or developments forthcoming. Cliff tried to write, but invariably found himself reverting to half-finished songs, started in happier times. He became even more withdrawn and, as Sam pointed out, less tolerant. Even eldest son Martin, then studying for his 'A' levels, found himself, on more than one occasion, reduced to tears by his father's attitude and criticisms, though he wouldn't elaborate on the incidents when I met him in London. (However, I did find out that years earlier, Cliff, who was vehemently opposed to 'elitist' education, had prevented Martin taking his rightful place at grammer school, despite a truly exceptional 11-plus result.)

As 1981 drew to a close, bringing in another cold, harsh winter, it seemed to Pat—trying hard to maintain family unity—that all the years of devotion, forbearance, subjugation, call it what you will, were being eroded by the fears of a man losing control of his life.
The songs were not forthcoming. Occasionally he would drive into town to see old G-LTK himself, Leon Tipler, maintaining the friendship that *could* have drifted as Cliff and his family had drifted away, across the border, into deepest Herefordshire. But fame had never affected Cliff and his attitude to people, and Leon was always keen to recreate the old days; to him also, nothing had changed. Gloria Bosom might have moved on, but dear old Rodney was still around; a bit heavier, a little less hair, but still willing to play the guitar, or the upper-class fool as they gooned around, for their ears only…
There were, however still the unreleased 'American' songs, so Cliff thought that perhaps he could fuse these together with an idea that had germinated ten years previous, an aborted project for the BBC's 'Play For Today' series, the love story set in the now declining carpet factories of Kidderminster. Because of his continuing popularity in, and affinity with, Ireland—underlined by the forthcoming guest appearance at the Castlebar Song Contest—he decided to move the play's location to Dublin, introducing *very* Irish references, interspersing the story line with poetry and some of the unreleased songs. After working on the revision for most of that summer, *Both Of Us* became the new title, and though the *idea* was not entirely new, he felt confident with its newly-dressed situation. Upon completion he was certain that RTE, Ireland's television station, would be only too pleased to consider it for production.

He drove over to Castelbar with Mark, in October, giving the vocal performance of his life to the Irish glitterati, and upon return booked into R. G. Lamb Recording Studios in Birmingham to decorate the unreleased American tracks, using Mark's developing talents to overlay his existing keyboard work—done so long ago and oh, so far away—adding extra subtleties to 'Messenger', 'Watchin' The T.V. News' and the apocalyptic 'Twenty Minutes', songs which were now being shuffled into position for the album of the play…
By spring, 1983, the recordings were complete. To all intents and purposes, this was the second American album that had never seen the light of day, and feeling sure he had a viable product to hand, Clifford began the heavy trawl of the London record companies. All through the long, hot summer he met and talked to old acquaintances, to new A&R 'boys' [known under the collective sobriquet 'Um-and-Ah men'…], who eight years ago would have been star-struck in his presence, to *anyone*, whatever contact he could now make in such a transient

business, but it was always the same; to their blinkered eyes, he had not moved with the times. Charisma were still up there, enjoying a brief chart success, but it was with punk Svengali Malcolm McLaren's 'Double Dutch', Polydor had Paul Weller's Style Council and WEA were selling Howard Jones's synthesized singles by the bucketful. From a writer who had not enjoyed chart success for ten years they were '...good songs, Clifford, but we need something more up-front, more dance-orientated...Beat, rhythm, groove...' But there was, of course, a little more to it than that. The songs were still not free. He was trying to sell an album which consisted solely of material that was already under contract, to WEA publishing, now known as Intersong Ltd. The recording arm of WEA were no longer interested in Clifford T. Ward as an artiste, and no other company could see the business sense in signing an 'old name' without publishing rights being available. The reaction was relentless in its consistency. He came home, time and again, a disillusioned man. Who could he turn to, where could he go?

It had to be Ireland. And so, in October, after a complicated, protracted agreement had been negotiated and drawn up, thanks mainly to the efforts of John Woods, managing director of Polygram Ireland, WEA/Intersong agreed to lease the masters—which they contractually owned—to the Irish label, whilst Clifford arranged the cover artwork (using cousin Gordon Ward's Thresholds photographs), the test pressings, final cut, publicity handout and prints, and submitted the finished product to Polygram for pressing, labelling and distribution. Not exactly cottage industry, but a highly commendable attempt at self-help. It had considerable drawbacks, however. There was no facility in the contract to market the album in the UK and so, for the many fans who had been waiting almost *seven* years for another Clifford T. Ward album, it became available on import only, via IMS in London, an extraordinary situation. Releasing it in March, 1984, to their credit, Polygram did a promotional mailout, low-key but efficient; I found a copy in my post at Radio Wyvern, at that time in its very infancy (as was I...) but, because of the budget—or lack of one—there could be no press advertising, no media blitz, it had to be word of mouth. The die-hard fans would find satisfaction, but there was no way it would sell outside the inner circle.

However, securing some kind of record deal had persuaded RTE to go ahead with the play, or, as the contract describes it, the 'dramatico-musical' work. An agreement was signed on 21st March, 1984, coinciding with the album's release, stipulating television production of a 60-minute work, to be transmitted twice within a five-year period following completion, which was to be no later than 31st March, 1986. That is called forward planning...

The BBC, as ever in those days, was keen to promote Clifford T. Ward, especially when new product was available, though jubilation at the new deal for *Both Of Us* was tempered by a slight *contretemps* with David Vercoe, then producer of Brian Matthew's delightful 'Round Midnight' programme, which I often listened to whilst driving back on my own from dark, gloomy gigs in the Welsh heartlands.
Clifford had been invited down to London on 20th March to record a 10-minute interview with Brian—promoting his new album—but which was subsequently removed from Radio 2 transmission schedules, though he was paid the nominal £20 appearance fee. This, of course was not good enough. He wrote to David Vercoe requesting an explanation.
On April 18th, he received a reply stating that, in their opinion, they [the BBC] had been '...slightly misled by your record company [this refers to IMC, the importers of *Both Of Us*, who had been working hard on Clifford's behalf; *not* Polygram, Ireland] who did not make it clear that the LP was not available through the normal UK retail outlets, or that the [RTE] film in which you were involved had not actually been scheduled for transmission ...' continuing to say that they had '... been offered a wealth of good material during that period...and as I felt that the justification for your interview ... [was unfounded]...I decided not to use it.'
The usual apology follows, and so does Clifford's reaction, ten days later, confirming availability of the album in Boots, Virgin, HMV, but also stressing that at no time had scheduling of the play been mentioned, '...as the work had not yet gone into production.'
Then in a beautifully concise rejoinder, he concludes:

> I'm sorry if you still feel you've been misled. Perhaps you'll find some consolation in that I was misled too, 'cause I was the one who made the round trip of three hundred and twenty miles to appear on your programme.

Hmmm. One doesn't do that to the Beeb. They have long memories. I too, have been there, and look where it got me...
But elsewhere, things had begun to look good, well, better. Cover versions of 'The Best Is Yet To Come' (now the closing track on *Both Of Us*), one by the enigmatic Judy Collins—on Clive Selwood's one-time baby, the Elektra label—another by Swedish crooner Göran Folkestad, on CBS, were released; Matt Monro and Mary O'Hara had both expressed interest in 'Messenger'—the second track on the Irish album—so maybe after the wilderness years, yonder light was becoming brighter, or less ominous.

But no. There was still not enough income to satisfy their borrowings, and so, in May of that year, Thresholds went up for sale. Martin, now 18, decided that this was his chance to break away, so he moved into a flat in George Street, Kidderminster, and started working, in those easy days when work was plentiful. Never interested in the academic side of life, he began a career of job changing and self-employment, becoming quietly but happily independent.

All the restoration work Cliff and Pat had done on Thresholds enabled a quick and agreeable sale and within little time at all they had moved into Upper Norchard Farm in Dunley, the beautiful whitewashed converted farmhouse, balancing on the side of a hill, with a view straight out of New England.

"This will be it," he said, "this will be my Innisfree. I will build my studio over there in the small barn. Here I can walk the sunlit valley, watch the songbirds nesting in the rafters, and breathe inspiration to write my songs and my plays. Life will be good. This is the fulfilment of my dream. This pressure within me will vanish, my nerves will calm, my vision will sharpen and I will be at rest. I will be steady."

Work on the studio began almost immediately. He hired a local firm of builders to reinforce and soundproof the walls, giving explicit instructions as to how it should be done, and watched from the kitchen as they laughed and fooled around, drinking coffee, taking too many breaks…

At night, when they had gone, he would inspect and criticize. Sam remembers, so does Pat. He would not rest. Lying in bed at night, he would be worrying about the next day's work; he would even dress and go into the barn to alter or continue the job in hand, he just could not relax. In the end, it was all too much and, as Sam recalled, he flew at them in a rage, threatening them with a broken plank. They left. At once.

It meant, of course, that he would have to finish the work himself. He spent the next two months shaping the room, nailing up the large pieces of plasterboard, his neck twisted up at the rafters, his mind racing with anger and doubt…

There was something wrong. His health was unstable. He was experiencing tremors, tingling sensations and loss of balance on a more frequent and pronounced level. This was not stress. Maybe something simple, such as an ear infection, could account for his balance problems, but the spasms, the shaking, though still sporadic, well, that was an indication of something more…

Pat persuaded him to seek advice:

"He went to see the local GP, who was new to us, as we'd just moved into the area. At first Cliff maintained that it was a middle-ear infection, but the GP suggested we visit someone in Worcester, privately, as he found the symptoms, to use his words, '… most interesting'. We drove to the residence, somewhere in Bath Road, a big, impressive Georgian house. For some reason, I sat outside in the car, whilst Cliff went in. He was there for about forty minutes. He reappeared, leaned in the car and told me to come and have a word with the specialist. The man asked if we knew anything about an illness called multiple sclerosis. We'd both heard of it, but knew nothing of its symptoms, its causes or its effects. 'Well,' he said to Cliff, almost casually, 'I think that is what you have. All the tests I've done, and your own experiences, seem to confirm the early stages of multiple sclerosis.' And then, 'Are you able to drive?'

"Cliff replied that he could, but occasionally had to close one eye, because of the double vision. The specialist advised that he would have to report such a 'disability' to the DVLA, and that Cliff shouldn't continue driving, at least until further tests were made. (Actually, we never heard from the DVLA—in fact, Cliff still has a licence…)

"We were then referred to a neurologist in Birmingham, who, after an extensive examination confirmed the worst. Cliff's immediate reaction was, 'Well, now I know what I've got, how do I get rid of it?'…He was, *we* were, that naïve."

Pat drove them home. Their solidarity, honed over the past 22 years together, had initially given strength and hope. It was to become a hopeless situation. Cliff wanted the cure, Pat wanted time to think, but as they reached the lane and turned up into the long, sweeping drive, pushing the five-bar gate gently open with the front of the car, the hill seemed to rise up menacingly ahead. She felt a great darkness come over her and began to sob, uncontrollably.

They sat down at the pine kitchen table.

"Pat, it's…all…right. I'll get better. It's only an infection." But his Mr Micawber attitude, maintained throughout their life with great resolution and often greater result, seemed to pale against Pat's realism. She heard the song, deep inside her head, and it wouldn't go away:

> What did we do wrong?
> We had all the magic to put us on our way,
> And all the tragedy we ever wanted to see…

The words, suddenly, had become so portentous. But there was no more time for tears. Life, as always, must carry on, just as it had done so many years ago, when they had been teenagers with their first child.

The telephone rang.

She jumped up, lifted the receiver and began talking animatedly to her mother, just as if everything was fine.

HOME THOUGHTS

Vaunting aloud, but racked with deep despair.
John Milton: *Paradise Lost*

Summer, and the rolling hills shone with the joys of life.
Though he was unsteady at times, Clifford's mind was still as active as ever. It would always be so—such is the tragedy of multiple sclerosis—and he once again plunged into the murky waters of music. They needed money, perhaps now more than ever, if he was to complete the studio and continue writing.
On July 2nd he received a letter from Bruno Kretchmar, the managing director of Intersong Ltd, in effect exercising the first option of the publishing contract Justin had negotiated with WEA, but, as no royalties whatsoever had been earned to offset the enormous advance—and indeed, how could they be, without having a product in the marketplace—no new monies were forthcoming.
Clifford saw an opportunity here, and went for the jugular…
After what must have been great deliberation—as his margin notes on the original contract show—he wrote back to Bruno, in a letter sent by recorded delivery, dated 15th July, 1984.
On first name terms, he refers to Bruno's letter and states that:

> … I am not prepared to accept any extension of the contract … and subject to legal advice … I regard the agreement at an end … I would [however] be happy to negotiate a new contract [and a new advance…] with you.

He continues:

> Firstly I believe you are in default … of the contract.

Here he stipulates those clauses in dispute, then says:

> …When my career had reached a complete stalemate, it was through my own professional and financial efforts that I was able to complete an album which I licensed to Polygram

> Ireland and which now gives you the opportunity of earning monies from my songs. Polygram UK, of which, I understand Intersong is a member company, have rejected … my album … thus preventing you and I of extending earnings on the album … a 'Catch 22' situation which I am not prepared to accept.

This, of course, is all very true. Er, in parts. The *Both Of Us* album *had* been put together solely under Clifford's initiative, although the WEA advance had virtually financed it. They had indeed rejected the option of releasing it, despite the huge amount still unrecouped on the publishing deal, and yet it could—as Clifford maintains—have helped reimburse some of their outlay had it been taken on. And so it *was* a 'bit of a Heller.' Who was going to capitulate?
But continuing, he may have gone a middle-eight too far:

> …I believe it is relevant to point out, though best forgotten in view of the traumas created at the time, that my signing the contract initially negotiated by you and Justin de Villeneuve was during a period when I, and certainly you, were misguided by him. You, to the extent that you allowed him office in Intersong's building and paid him directly £7000 of the £15,000 advance you [now] debit my account with. However, I wish to make nothing of this and put it all down to experience.

Clifford then expresses his desire to negotiate a new contract, indicating that John Woods, in Ireland, is happy with the sales of *Both Of Us*, and is keen to make a second album as per their recording agreement.
But *then* he demands a modification of a standard publishing condition, which gives the publisher right to choose which of the compositions submitted are, or are not, 'suitable for commercial exploitation', and *finally*, a change in percentage of royalties, from 50/50, 'to the normal division under the Performing Rights Society's rules.'
He concludes:

> I trust you will be able to approach my letter in the sincere and positive spirit in which it is written, with the firm hope of being able to work together for a more prosperous and productive future.

Well, that was truly a shot across the bows.

Bruno didn't reply straight away—Clifford actually telephoned him at home a week later—but when he did write, on the 25th July he delicately suggested that:

> … [as] the contents of your letter make no sense … it appears to me … once again [that] you are going through a counter-productive emotional period and strictly, contractually speaking, Intersong Music is well within its rights to act as we have done. Once again I need to say that, creatively speaking, we are totally committed to you as a songwriter … I have recently had tentative discussions with the well known [Womble] producer Mike Batt, concerning possible collaborations with you—a matter we can further discuss if you are inclined to do so.

Bear in mind that Clifford had not mentioned his diagnosis to anyone at this time, and in fact it would be a while before he would do so, and then only when it was impossible to disguise the symptoms any longer. So, stand back, me hearties.

On July 31st, Pat typed a reply to Bruno, dictated by Clifford and again sent recorded delivery, showing every indication that the combined stress of finances and health were gnawing away, as he tried desperately to find a way out of this mire of confusion and fear.

Reiterating his previous comments, he also states:

> … my company [Clifford T. Ward Associates] does not find relevant or need such comments as 'counter-productive and emotional period …'

but then, after threatening legal action, continues :

> … if you need further product from me I need an advance of £8000 [no less…]. This will secure you a minimum of twelve new songs which will contain my best endeavours and for which my company will strive to obtain a recording release in the UK and Ireland.

Once again he demands amendment of the clause specifying the publisher's right to pick and choose submitted material, citing the tracks 'Both Of Us' and 'Watchin' The T.V. News' as having been accepted as part of his forthcoming RTE play, despite Bruno's rejection of both songs (though to be fair, Bruno had no say in the content of the Irish programme, or indeed the *Both Of Us* album).

He then reverts to the split of royalties, quoting the PRS standard of 60/40 in favour of the writer, before concluding, 'I await your comments and please avoid any personal and inevitably inaccurate observations.'

Ouch.

Bruno's reply was tactful but firm. They were, after all, socially acquainted—inasmuch as anyone in the music business could become an acquaintance of Cliff's—and it was obvious that any tempering of the situation would have to come from Intersong.

He maintains the company's legal position in terms of the Agreement, and then expresses the obvious surprise at Clifford's request for a further advance:

> … in view of the outstanding unearned balance of … £15,000. You did, of course, at the time … instruct Intersong, in writing, that a proportion [he does not say what proportion] … should be paid to your then current manager, Justin de Villeneuve … we only complied with your instruction. In view of the slow progress in securing activity with your songs … [we rightfully extended the contract].

Acting as a 'gesture of good faith', Bruno then agrees to amend the wording in the agreement to allow any further compositions submitted to be deemed acceptable without 'evaluation [by Intersong] as to their commerciality,' stating that this [fairly standard] clause was only enforced due to the content of Clifford's songs often being 'tailor made [by him, for him] as a recording artiste, and not exploitable … with other artistes.'

Good songs they might be, but 'Waiting For The Garda' and 'Twenty Minutes' were patently non-commercial. This was a generous move, and would—hopefully—confirm Intersong's commitment, encouraging Clifford to continue writing in his own singular style, and without pressure to deliver commercial works.

Bruno adamantly refuses any further advance or amendment to the contract, and endeavours, in signing off, to calm the situation:

> I hope you find this further 'olive-branch' satisfactory … to confirm the … continuing good and close creative working relationship between [us].
> I look forward to hearing from you very soon.

Oh dear.

12th August, 1984, Bruno does indeed hear:

> Whilst I find one aspect of your letter positive, unfortunately I cannot support my family on 'olive-branches', so unless you

> are able to offer something more substantial in return for new work from me I must go elsewhere to earn my living.

No reply acknowledging this broadside came for some time. A further statement of account was churned out, showing no reduction whatsoever in the £15,000 debit. A *billet-doux* was received from Bruno mentioning Mary O'Hara's performance of 'Messenger' on her 19th August TV show, with which she opened the programme and credited the writer, the letter also indicating that Mary's management has been approached with a view to guesting Clifford on the show…but no mention of The Contract.

And so Clifford tried again, but in a less formidable tone, as if he realized that maybe he had overstepped the mark. Bruno was apparently vetting calls, and not returning them, so on October 23rd, Cliff, in a handwritten letter, suggested a compromise—a financial one—but nonetheless a compromise.

He stated his desire to remain within the framework of friendly and professional expectations, then detailed, briefly, his recent and intended expenditures, saying:

> … I have recently completed the … restoration of the barn … I have spent slightly under £4000 … and am about to invest in some 8-track studio equipment [at a cost] of £8000, … with a view to creating master quality recordings.
>
> As … you can appreciate, nothing can be more ideal in our creative medium [than] to work from your own studio in the exact relaxed atmosphere essential for the best results.
>
> Now, I would ask you, if it within your ability, to contribute … £4000 towards the cost … which will alleviate some of the burden of debt I've incurred on the project.
>
> I can assure you of some, dare I say it, fine material in the near future and my complete co-operation … [in] a new contract term…

Meanwhile he had heard from John Woods that, after the impetus of the initial sales, *Both Of Us* had slowed down considerably. It had not even reached 5000 units, and, because of the peculiar 'pay-as-we-sell' contract [the only way Polygram Ireland could afford to work] no more money was available. John mentions Chris De Burgh having four sell-out concerts at Ireland's RDS Hall in October, citing Clifford as an equal—if not greater—in terms of broad appeal, and hinting at the need for concert work to increase sales. He also asks the progress of the RTE drama project and briefly queries Clifford's preparations for a new LP.

Cliff made a mental note to visit Dublin as soon as he could, maybe an

appearance on Gay Byrne's 'Late, Late Show' could be arranged, but firstly he had to raise some money, and so to Bruno.
But even before a response—not that one was to come for many a month—Clifford, breaking the law again, but this time not for speeding, just for driving (his precarious physical condition now made even this everyday task illegal), went down to London and bought an Otari-MS2 1" tape machine and mixing desk. The bank were still backing him.
Pat recalls:
"He hired one of those big estate things because the equipment he'd ordered wouldn't fit in the Lancia. He was very shaky on his feet, but his mind was completely focused on the studio, getting it up and running. You could never reason with Cliff, and now it was even more of a lost cause. He seemed to sense the urgency, even though he would never admit to there being any; to him, it was just a means to an end. He wanted his product out on the market, and, I suppose, he felt Bruno would comply with his request for money."
But Bruno, it turned out, had other ideas, and, purely by circumstance rather than by intent, the Intersong fiasco would eventually dissolve into confusion, and cost Clifford T. Ward dearly in the years to come…
Christmas 1984 saw Frankie, Madonna and McCartney battling it out with Band Aid and Wham! for the silly season's number one. There *were* good songs around—well, in comparison with a few years ago—but getting them on board the music machine was becoming increasingly difficult. Suddenly the world was obsessed with the word 'mega', and the media were awash with mega-lomania…
Peter Grogan, dependable as ever, secured a 'Late, Late Show' for December, during which visit to Dublin Cliff managed to meet John Woods and prise a few more punts out of his friendly hand, also intimating that he was looking forward to the next album, and a workable budget, to which John diplomatically replied that the option would be gladly taken up in the New Year, '…assuming we can keep recording costs to a minimum without sacrificing quality…'
Silk purses and sows' ears come to mind.

Never mind, it's Christmas.
It was spent, as always, with Pat cooking for the whole clan and enjoying every minute of it. [Well, that's what it says here…] The house was decorated and welcoming; visitors were given the wonderful Ward hospitality and shown around the new studio, with its glistening machinery, waiting, through that bewildering medium of audio-science, to transfer thought into sound. Cliff was now confident that his illness had peaked. He had appeared on Irish television, talking and singing as if nothing was wrong, met his Irish record manager, discussed the future with confidence and humour, and could now spend his time

creating master quality recordings just across the yard from the kitchen. RTE had gone strangely quiet on the drama front. Christmas always takes a couple of months out of the year, media-wise; that's a foregone conclusion, but their silence was somewhat unsettling. A lot depended on the success of this project. Clifford had written to Peter Gormley, Cliff Richard's long time manager, with a view to involving the singer in his play, but, in a nicely worded reply, the standard rejection term 'very heavy commitments' leaps from the page, although Peter was gracious enough to enthuse about the music.

Clifford celebrated his 41st birthday in February, and as spring crept over the hillside, Martin, living a few miles away, celebrated his 21st year with a few friends, in his own mysterious way, whilst daughter Debbie, still fiercely independent, and attending college in Coventry, announced her engagement. Sam-Simon, having now reached the grand old age of 18, was still deeply entrenched in that first grand love affair, taking his heart and his artistic talents to Goldsmiths' College, where, despite the evident distractions, he would complete a Fine Arts degree, with honours. Polly now had the run of the house; a six-year-old charmer, with friends all over the hills and vales.

Once again, it was all there, but all suspended. So much seemed able to happen, but no-one would commit themselves to Clifford T. Ward, or, in the case of Intersong, agree to his ideas of 'commitment'.

The October plea for a further advance, albeit now down to £4000, had fallen on deaf ears, and so on 5th March, Pat, in her role as Director of C. T. Ward Ass. Ltd, wrote to Bruno stating quite emphatically that unless they comply with the request '...we are unable to accept the option...and ...regard the contract...at an end.'

Sales of *Both Of Us* in Ireland had finally peaked, prompting John Woods to indicate little chance of a second album. So Pat concluded '...Cliff now has to seek in earnest a new outlet for his material and will need to offer his publishing as an incentive to any...interested party. If you intend to oppose this, I would ask you to make it clear, in writing, within the next five days.'

Well, Bruno's lack of response was explained. Without reference to anything that had passed between them, in a letter dated 14th March, he announced his immediate resignation from Intersong and subsequent appointment as Managing Director of Chrysalis Music, wishing Clifford '...every success for the future'.

The future came in the form of a letter the very next day from the Legal and Business Affairs Department of Chappell-Intersong Music Group rejecting all lawful right to any claim for a further advance, stating—and quite correctly—that the writer was not open to demand change, or reject terms, of [a] contract. They quote the receipt of only six songs, *since 1981*, towards the contractual stipulation of *twelve* per term, saying that the company had shown great tolerance in waiving exact terms of contract, and taking up options only to counteract such a shortfall. They were, in law, perfectly entitled to continue to extend the agreement until an acceptable number of songs was received, and/or '...demand immediate repayment of the last preceding advance...[of] £15,000. You will be notified of our election at the relevant time. Until then, the Agreement continues in full force and...Clifford remains exclusively contractually bound to this company and we will maintain claims to all of his songs falling within the ambit of the Agreement. Any attempts to place his publishing rights with a third party would be in breach...' Blah, bloody blah.

Then, just to show that they are human [ha, bloody ha...] the writer concludes:

> If you wish to make any realistic proposals for Clifford's release from his exclusive contractual obligations ... we would be pleased to discuss them.

This is the old 'dog in the manger' syndrome that appears in all business dealings, notably so in the music industry, where, because the generosity of an advance is suddenly called into question, creative spirit becomes stifled by strict interpretation of law. Ask any composer, ask *me*...! Music publishers are notorious for putting contracted songs into a 'bottom drawer', allowing no coverable activity whatsoever, as the poor old songsmith eats away his advance with little prospect of further earnings elsewhere until the damned contract expires. Some writers have been strong enough, financially or mentally, to take such cases to court, and win, but in Clifford's case, financially he didn't have a chance; mentally well...

At the risk of becoming tedious, I will quote most of his 24th March reply. It is wonderful in its defiance and subsequently gave him a noble David-type victory over the Intersong Goliath.

Following his acknowledgement and admission to weariness of the whole situation, he continues:

> ... I would ask you to consider the contents of my [previous] letters to Bruno Kretchmar ... where there can be no doubt my objections to your company's lack of promotion and exploitation of my work are entirely well-founded ... If you wish to recoup ... the initial advance ... [why don't you] make an effort, as I have done and am doing, to promote the fourteen songs I delivered to your company at a ... cost ... of £7000, and not the six songs you refer to. That Bruno Kretchmar decided ... to reject many of them points not to any inadequacy

> in the material but to the futility of [the clause in dispute; that the publisher has the final say] for many of the songs he rejected … I secured commercial release for, together with a number of songs owned by WEA … and in which you have an interest as sub-publisher … on my current Both Of Us album, which I financed, negotiated release for, and licensed to Polygram, Ireland … I reject, therefore and despise your mention of possible demand for repayment of the advance … having given you the opportunity [to recoup some of these monies] solely through my own efforts and those of John Woods [Polygram, Ireland] … otherwise the material would be lying idle in your offices.

Clifford then draws attention to Clause 12, which allows the writer to provide suitable demos, at the publisher's costs [albeit on prior and written approval, which was not given…] and the '…reasonable and conciliatory letter of October 23rd … [where he reduced his advance request to a mere £4000] then, sticking his head truly above the parapet, proclaims:

> Now, if you insist on retaining your bullying stance, you are clearly preventing me from earning my living, and I will not allow you to do that.

Well. Not exactly High Court syntax, but a beautiful combination of stubbornness, determination and British Bulldogism.

On 25th March, a circular from Intersong announced promotion manager Chas de Whalley's appointment as Bruno's successor and, in a show of good intent, Chas wrote to Clifford on 16th April.

That must have been a worrying four weeks. Anything could have landed on the doormat at Dunley; a solicitor's letter, a demand for repayment, a High Court judgement…But the reply from Intersong was strangely subdued, and, with a little consideration tucked away between the lines, the outcome was that, subject to the deliverance of a further four titles [*without publisher evaluation*], or that the next two titles Clifford recorded, under his, or any other name [?] will be credited to Intersong, then all relevant option periods and product commitments will be considered fulfilled, and he would be free to seek publishing elsewhere. An extraordinary capitulation.

He had won the day. He had taken on the might of the mighty and beaten them, albeit with a great deal of understanding and sympathy from Chas de Whalley.

Cliff sent—post-haste—four obscure titles, and, in a letter dated 26th April, he was released from his contract, with a warm goodbye from

Chas, someone obviously on his side, but unable to help:

> ... To strike a final note, however, I would like to say I regard you as an intelligent and thought-provoking writer and I regret that we never enjoyed the kind of creative dialogue which might have helped you maximize your considerable potential in the modern marketplace.
> I wish you the very best of luck.

In a final, legal note, on 3rd May, Reg Bonney of Intersong listed the twenty-four songs '...which we consider to be those we control for the life of copyright.'
Mysteriously—and I'm sure to Clifford's amusement and gratitude at the time—it contained only five titles from *Both Of Us*.
But it was here that one song in particular, already one of his most covered numbers—and indeed now acknowledged as one of his finest—began its strange existence in the shadowlands.
As Cliff and Pat became hopelessly preoccupied with personal problems, the world of music publishing grew increasingly unstable. Amidst the turmoil of takeovers, mergers, and liquidations, the song seemed to take on a life of its own, appearing and disappearing almost at will, and the mechanical (record sales) royalties followed suit. Some were paid, some were not, and those that weren't—considerable sums of money—disappeared forever, lost in the void, became 'unaccountable'. And no-one today will accept responsibility. The song's title proclaimed a sad irony: 'The Best Is Yet To Come', indeed.

But he was free of Intersong. That, at least, was settled, though it must have seemed a somewhat pyrrhic victory; there was no lump sum to cover his recent outgoings, and the bank were beginning to doubt the wisdom of their lending.
And above all this there still loomed the spectre of multiple sclerosis. Despite Clifford's eternal optimism, his refusal to accept the reality, he was worsening. Pat was under oath not to mention it to anyone, not even their own family and, for a while, it worked, but for how much longer?
Those who remembered him, in the world outside, possibly assumed he had retired from the business, gone back to teaching, or, if they did know of his continuing attempts to secure new deals, would never have any reason to suspect anything was wrong. Why should they?
On 24th April, 1985, after a brief pre-emptive telephone call, Clifford had received a telemessage from researcher David Nicholson, regarding Noel Edmonds's television show, 'The Time Of Your Life'.

In the message David refers to his preparing a programme based on '...events and personalities prominent in August, 1973.'
He continues:

> I think 'Gaye' is one of those rare British classics that are of particular interest because they became popular at a time when the chart was infested by raucous and mindless glitter.
> I would be very grateful if you would consider re-recording the song and performing it on [the show]. Yours would be the only music item in the programme...

Clifford's handwritten answer, which shows a noticeable deterioration in his once elegant style, was later typed into a more fluid and less angry form by Pat, and went as follows:

> No.
> Would not do the show justice and more selfishly would not do myself justice.
> Do not like that kind of nostalgia-reminiscence in the pop context. It does tend to inevitably portray the artist as 'finished', 'washed up'—where I am still battling on working as a writer and would not wish to be viewed in that context.
> That type of programme, to me, tends to come across in a rather sad way—I'm not for looking back—but for looking forward. I am not living in a reclusive lap of luxury on a farm as you seemed to suggest on the phone. I am continuing struggling making a living as a writer.
> If I may suggest—if you really want to include the song 'Gaye' why not just use the record and insert [it] at some pertinent point in the film in relation to Adam Faith [not sure of the reference there...] as a background to some action?
> That way, you are portraying chronological 'pop' accuracy and by not having me on the show and talking, unkind assumptions and conclusions about me are avoided.
> I would rather, for the many who do not follow my career, have them say 'I wonder what happened to him?', rather than have them say, 'Oh *that's* what happened to him!' [a piece of logic rarely voiced in such a business...]
> In my view that would be the fairest way to me that you should do it. Failing that, I would have to decline and suggest you get someone else.

Nowhere in this refusal is Clifford referring to—or indicating—his illness, or that maybe his career is finished. His words are chosen to indicate a determination to continue re-establishing his name as a *contemporary* writer and that he has not 'retired', even though he must have been more than aware, at the time, of the doubts as to his future.

Leon Tipler, at Kidderminster's mythical G-LTK, noticed something was wrong. Despite having lost direction, or, most certainly, control, Cliff was still popping round, still playing the fool in that tiny, airless room that had offered some respite down the years to the pressures of...well, life. Even back in the lost winter of 1983, when he must have realized the futility of his situation, resorting to an Ireland-only recording deal, he had spent four hours doing a 'live' Christmas Eve Special with Jack Powdermonkey, Arthur Bantock, Hugh St John-Stevas, Tom Crite and the cast of a thousand idiots, as Pat dashed around the shops, stocking up Thresholds for the festive invasion.

But now, in the summer of 1985, the atmosphere was not quite as carefree as it had been down the years. Rodney Simmonds, his rhythm guitarist from those far-off Cruiser-nights, also a vital ingredient in Cliff's demo and dialogue days, here in this very room, was sadly, no longer around. He had been under treatment for some while now; a strange, debilitating illness which none of them, at the time of Rodney's initial diagnosis, had known much about, something called multiple sclerosis...

In what was to be Tom Crite's last appearance, thus drawing the curtain on one of the world's best kept secrets, on the evening of June 10th, 1985, he joined fellow-gooner John Davies in another hour of nonsense, playing, for the final time—with what must have been a touch of sad realization—the slurred, drunken doom-merchant of Kidderminster.

Cliff sat at the desk, reading the entries for 'The Poetry Competition'. Ceremoniously presented to him by the master of ceremonies in sealed envelopes, he opened them, one by one, reading Leon's fictitious, crazed rhyme-wanderings. He giggled and guffawed his way through the show, pretending that all was well... But Leon was not fooled. He couldn't be. He had spent almost twenty years recording that voice, in all its guises, and this time there was something not quite right...

It was another beautiful summer. Bruce Springsteen was setting the world on fire, bringing his power-house stage show to the stadiums, and his seven previous albums back to the charts. Bob Geldof was about to step into the Wembley Arena and host the most successful live concert ever, raising £50 million for famine relief, and monumental record sales for all those involved...

Dance re-mixes in their hundreds hit the shops; even Richard Hewson's Rah Band, after eight long years, had a second glorious, but brief, return to the charts.

John Woods had been unable to make any further payments against the *Both Of Us* deal as sales were now non-existent. He advised, in a letter dated 26th July, that only concert work and television would rekindle interest, a suggestion made in the sad ignorance of Clifford's plight.
Was there really anybody out there who would still see potential in the new songs of Clifford T. Ward?
I met Ian Summers in Buccis Wine Bar, sunny Goodge Street, after squeezing out of the tube I'd caught from East Acton, my first such London journey for many years. Yes, maybe I do live a sheltered, Luddite-ish life up here in Worcestershire, but how do people down there tolerate such daily discomforts? Stifling, swaying, clutching handgrabs and possessions, staring vacantly ahead, avoiding eye contact. Grim, dull, menacing…
I leapt up onto the pavement, desperate to gulp in some air, some sunlight. It still has a buzz, London, but it has even more cars…and lorries…and taxis…
I found the meeting place, after being given one or two surprisingly friendly directions, and ordered a Perrier. What a good boy. After about twenty minutes, Ian walked in. I'd been told to expect—by someone who hadn't seen him for two years—a large, overweight bear of a man. That's why I ignored the solid, genial guy, ordering coffee at the counter, until he looked over and greeted me. I expressed surprise at being recognized by someone who didn't know me.
"It's the rock'n'roll hair," he joked.
Thank God, he can't see the join.

Ian is a lovely man. One of the old school. Dark, temple-grey hair, bright, beady eyes twinkling out from a rugged face, a long, firm handshake, Arfur Daley accent, gold necklace, cigar, black coffee (it was only 10.50 a.m.) and genuine eye-to-eye contact. Straight in.
"I was head of promotions for K-Tel Records. About 1980, we did a big TV shot for Roger Whittaker, all his hits, which obviously went mega. I presented him with a gold disc at this function, and *he* presented *me* with a solid-gold lighter, engraved with my initials. In all my years previous, at CBS, and other similar such presentations, that was the first time an artiste had ever given *me* something. He told me I was the best promotions man he'd ever worked with, and that he was about to start his own label up, and wanted me to be involved.
"I thought no more of it, until I received a phone call about three years later. By that time, I'd left K-Tel, and was running my own promotions company, handling Irish stuff, rock'n'roll, even Chas & Dave. Anyway, it was Roger. He said that he'd just completed an album about his Kenyan days, an environmental look at the world, and could I get an English deal? He'd already set it up in Canada and Scandinavia. I got a

Polygram arm to handle it and it did really well. *Then* he really went for it. He started Tembo Records, ('tembo' is Swahili for 'elephant'... Not many people know that...) and put me in charge. Just me. I was Tembo. First thing I did was re-record all his hits, with me producing, which again went mega. Then I suggested he broaden his artiste base...there was only him. What would happen to Tembo if he was trampled by an elephant...? This was late '84, and in the following summer, right out of the blue, we received this tape from Clifford T. Ward, whom we both remembered, of course, from his mid-seventies success. We liked the songs and so a deal was suggested. I was fairly surprised that he hadn't got a deal—hadn't had one for some *time*—but that's the music business. I went up to their house in Dunley, met the lovely Pat and daughter Polly—a gorgeous little kid—and set about setting it up. We went ahead, paying some good advances on the publishing. Because they were demos—albeit master quality—but with synthesized strings, I intended to record it all again, with a proper orchestra, but, in view of subsequent development, it wasn't possible."

Cliff was once again experiencing throat problems, and was still convinced, because his hearing was also affected, that some lowly virus was contributing to the worsening of his other symptoms. In a valiant attempt to halt further deterioration, on August 5th he booked into an Edgbaston nursing home to have his sinuses drained, an awful undertaking...After about two days, as he lay there well and truly drilled and padded, he learned that the specialist in charge had gone away for the weekend, and that there was no-one to consult regarding progress. That was red rag to a bull to someone like Cliff. He tore off the bandages, the drips, the whole lot, and discharged himself.

Pat believes that act of recklessness contributed greatly to the speed with which he worsened:

"From then on, it was relentless. I watched helplessly as a strong, healthy man, full of life and humour, began to waste away in front of my eyes."

She recalls going down to London to sign the contract:

"Cliff didn't want *anybody* to know, for obvious reasons. We sat in the Tembo office, close together, *very* close, because Cliff's symptoms, the shaking, the involuntary spasms, his general unsteadiness, were now beginning to develop noticeably. Ian must have suspected something, though I'm sure MS was the *last* thing he considered; musician, booze, drugs, you know, that would have been the train of thought. But the signing was successful, we went ahead."

The collection of demos, with ex-Maisonette Mark Tibenham again having contributed all the piano, bass, guitar and synthesized parts, thus became the *Sometime Next Year* album, which Tembo would release in July, 1986.

Some of the tracks had been recorded at Dunley, and they were to be the last studio songs that Cliff would complete. Mark hadn't been aware of the diagnosis, but within a very short time it would be common knowledge. In show business, you have to be on show…

Music Week covered the signing in their October 17th edition, with a picture of Ian and Clifford announcing the deal, and the following week Clifford T. Ward made a return visit to the very popular Gloria Hunniford programme, on good old Radio 2.

It was here that the truth became apparent.

Ian continues:

"We got a lot of media interest but that Gloria Hunniford Show, considering how many times he'd done things like that before, was very sad. It was too much for him, his speech was slurred and he actually dried up, and, of course it was live radio. Gloria, bless her, diplomatically played another record, but it was then I realized there was something seriously wrong, and because of whatever it was, there was little point in getting him any television work, which I could have done, quite easily. I'd just produced 'Skye Boat Song' with Roger and Des O'Connor—*don't larf*, it became a monster hit in '86—so Des's show would have been an easy, and very powerful promotion spot."

Ian eventually telephoned Clifford, confronting him about his state of health. Though inwardly fearing the worst, Clifford expressed his optimism, insisting that it was only a 'mild' form of this mysterious illness. Nevertheless, within the week, Ian came up to see him at Dunley. There followed a "strictly business…further investment…it's necessary…you understand?" confrontation, which hurt Ian as much as, if not more than, anyone. "I recognized at that time, though I don't think Clifford did, what the future held, in terms of his illness," Ian remarks. In a sad, humiliating, scene, he asked Clifford to simply walk across the room. He rose, stood, stumbled and despairingly slumped into the nearest chair. He was defeated. It was all over, though for him *and* the lady who had been his real strength over the past 24 years, the worst was yet to come. He was 42 years old.

"It was all very, very sad. I knew that Clifford could write songs about anything, inanimate objects, that chair, your ear-ring [?], whatever, and so I said to him, once the bad news was confirmed—by Pat, incidentally—'Well now you've got something really powerful to write about.' Not being ruthless, but just trying to encourage him into, well, continuing…

"We were committed to the release of *Sometime Next Year*, sometime next year…but it was obvious there was no future career for Clifford.

"What *really* angers me is that, *because* of his niceness, his trust, his naïveté, he's been shat on, had some bloody rough recording deals. The

WEA set-up was quite unethical. From what I can gather, it was what we call 'cross-collateralized', which basically means that advances go into recording costs, obviously, but that until such costs are recouped, then everything else, *including* air play and publishing, goes towards reimbursing such costs. On the second American album, which was never released, there were lovely songs, including 'The Best Is Yet To Come' and 'Lost Again', so with no release, there was no way Clifford could make any impact on the bottom line, and by the time they did come out, in bits and drabs, it was too late. Nowadays, that wouldn't be allowed. Totally immoral, *illegal.* A songwriter should always be allowed to earn *some*thing from his songs... Terrible."

And, naturally, many other ears heard that fateful show on October 26th.

Remember Clive Selwood?

"A few years after the Justin saga, when it had all gone down the tubes, Cliff telephoned me and, after a few pleasantries, asked me if I would consider taking him on again, picking up the pieces, so to speak. Well, I just couldn't. His career was in a real mess, but apart from that, I didn't want to get involved with him again, which was a great shame 'cos I really liked the bloke and I had believed in him. But not any more; it was too late. Too much had been said and done. He knew he'd made the wrong decision. He hadn't had any success whatsoever since he'd walked out on us, and now it was all too late. I wasn't gloating; it was just too painful for us to consider.

"Then a while after that I heard him being interviewed on Radio 2, 'The Gloria Hunniford Show' and I thought he was drunk. But I knew Cliff would never do that, drink before an interview—not that I considered him a drinker anyhow—so I immediately telephoned Ken Wright. 'Haven't you heard,' he said, 'Cliff's got MS.'

"Well that was a blow. I just felt so sad. I'd been considering re-releasing *Singer-Songwriter* for some time, on my Strange Fruit label, and this shock more or less galvanized me into action, mainly to see if I could do something for him; but as the news filtered through, from various sources, I realized just how serious it all was and that maybe I should back off for a while. You know how people jump to conclusions..."

It would be a few years before Clive would be able to help, and then only in a small way, but as for the here and now, autumn 1985, Clifford T Ward found his world crumbling around him. Unless this monster within was halted in its tracks, there would be no more deals, no more media performances and, worst of all, no more songs...

The morning of the Hunniford show, Pat received another response from Polygram, Ireland, saying how quiet things still were, and again suggesting some live work from Clifford to give a much needed shot in the arm to *Both Of Us*, until which time, no further royalty payment could be made.

Cliff returned home late afternoon, with his friend Dennis Lee, who had driven him down to London and provided moral support. He sunk into his chair, more angry than embarrassed. Pat knew it had been wrong to even think he could carry the pretence through, though she had gone along with Cliff's bidding. She had sat on the edge of her chair, alone in that beautiful house on the hill, and heard that once lucid, articulate voice stumble and slur its way through a ten-minute interview, suggesting, to each and every listener, the beginning of a dreadful decline. Gloria had done her best, and as Ian said, had worked it professionally. Clifford had done *his* best, but had failed, rather than admit to anything, and now the phone would start ringing, and people would express concern, and offer to help…

It was the beginning of the end. Clifford T. Ward would not be taking the spotlight again. Peter Grogan, his manager-designate in Ireland, cried openly when he was told by Pat, in a late evening telephone conversation.

Peter, exasperated at his idol's reluctance to step out onto a stage, had called frequently over the years, suggesting this, that, feeling the water, tempting him, hoping against hope.

"Since meeting him, my greatest ambition had been to walk out onto an Irish stage, to what I *know* would have been a capacity audience, and say, 'Ladies and gentlemen, will you please welcome Clifford T. Ward.' I would have died a happy man."

He shakes his head:

"When Pat broke the news—apart from the dreadful sadness I felt for them both, the almost disbe*lief* that such a thing could happen to someone like Clifford—I knew, of course, that my dream was gone, and that Ireland had been robbed forever of what could have been a night of magic."

There was still hope, however, that Cliff's music would reach a far greater audience than a packed theatre in Ireland.

RTE, whilst they were planning their schedule and the forthcoming production of the *Both Of Us* play, had suggested to Cliff that Channel 4 might be interested in taking on the UK rights. A nod was as good…and so he had written to Mike Boland—the then commissioning editor at Charlotte Street—way back in March, whilst reloading his rifle for another pot at Bruno Kretchmar.

But, it was not to be. As if the gods were conspiring, in a reply referring to '… numerous telephone calls from … Pat, and no small frustration on your behalf …', on 11th December, Seamus Cassidy, Assistant Entertainment Editor at Channel 4, wrote:

> I'm sorry that you've had to wait so long for a reply, but we've been swamped with scripts …
> I regret to say that we aren't in a position to do Both of Us. I think it's a charming story, though I was less happy with the dialogue, which dragged for me in places. That's always something that can be fixed, though, so I wouldn't be discouraged.
> To be honest, though, we felt that the mix of poetry, music, and quite serious drama was not something which we could tackle: it's just not very Channel 4.
> I'm sorry since I enjoyed reading this. Sorry to be the bearer of bad tidings
> All the best.

So what was really wrong with the play?
I have it here before me, it in its original format, painstakingly written in that flowing longhand, with alterations crossed out and replaced, stage directions, camera angles, music fades, visionary scenarios, and it is, quite literally, charming. Seamus was right. But I also see everything that Cliff saw. I see the plot unfold with all his gentle nuances, his experienced eye recalling the excitement and frustration of days on the road with a band, his perfect portrayal of the young child—daughter Polly was undoubtedly the role model for Fionella—and her reaction of bewilderment and eventual resignation to her parents' break-up, brought on, in this instance, by the success of her mother's career. It is almost autobiographical, and because of that, it is real.
Wonderfully sentimental, but it has no bite. This was 1984. There was no room for romance. Here again Seamus was right.
Even biblical references and Yeats's poetry, fused between Clifford's utopian storyline, whilst lending the perfect Irish allusions, tend to soften, rather than lift, the impact of the play. It is romantic and beautiful, as are the songs, cleverly woven into the text, but to the media, relishing their newly acquired 'in-your-face' doctrines, it lacked impact, controversy, sex-appeal, and therfore potential ratings…
In his simple, modest, naïve way, Clifford was '…wish[ing] for the cloths of heaven…'
He was speaking through Yeats:
'I have spread my dreams under your feet.'
But that was not enough.
And Yeats's poem concludes as if written specifically for him:
'Tread softly because you tread on my dreams.'

A dismal end to a terrible year. Even the world was in disarray. A hole in the ozone layer, the sinking of Rainbow Warrior by the French and the subsequent trial farce; Heysel Stadium, the race riots in Handsworth, Brixton and Tottenham, and as if all that wasn't bad enough, something called Eastenders began on BBC 1…

Only Ted Hughes and Boris Becker must have enjoyed 1985, oh, and Dire Straits with their *Brothers in Arms*, but for Clifford T. Ward it had been a year of highly-charged emotion.

There was, possibly, just one more chance to reclaim his position in the world of song—with the forthcoming Tembo release, scheduled for June, 1986. The RTE production of *Both Of Us* was somewhere on the horizon, but, here and now, away from public scrutiny, as the rain came in sheets across the dark valley and the north wind swung the farm gate wide and back with a crash of steel, he lurched across the yard to his studio, fumbled at the controls of his tape machine, sat down at the keyboard and began to write, and he thought about Jesus on the cross…

COLD WIND BLOWING

Finish, good lady; the bright day is done,
And we are for the dark. Anthony and Cleopatra

The schoolwork would have to wait. He could do the marking if he rose early tomorrow, but—and he turned slowly to look—there was quite a pile…

No. This is too good an idea to leave: Robert Browning, April, England.

He played a few notes and thought back to Fontainebleau; the woods, the bird-song, his loneliness.

Martin and Sam shouted goodnight and ran upstairs, laughing in anticipation of tomorrow's sports day. He shouted a reply without turning his head, as Pat 'shushed' them on, not even daring to glance into the lounge where he sat, his long, flaxen hair hanging over the keys.

Those customary G major-A minor-D major inversions tumbled out.

'I would be a millionaire … a song to make you laugh …' Yes, that worked. 'How is it back home?' No, that was too obvious. 'How is…Worcestershire?…'

"What a racket," giggled Martin, putting his hands over his ears, as the two boys fell into bed. "I wish we'd got a record player up here. Mom says she'll buy that Benny Hill record on Saturday," and they both started singing, as loud as they dared. "'Ernie, Ernie, he drove the fastest milkcart in the West.'"

"Oi, you two, off to sleep !!" she shouted up the stairs. "C'mon Deb, time for a bath. Say goodnight to your dad."

Cliff stood up this time and walked across to them both, Pat carrying the child, almost as big as herself.

"Here, let me take her upstairs," he offered.

"No, it's all right. You carry on with your work."

He gave his daughter a fond kiss, as she hung there, wrapped around her mother.

"'Night, Deb, see you in the morning."

He walked back to the piano, passing the overloaded bookcase in the alcove, glancing at the names across the top row. Larkin, Keats,

Betjeman, Wordsworth. Sitting down again, he played what he could remember of his half-melody, and more words came into his head.

'...William Wordsworth, Keats and Robert Browning, they all say ... the way I feel ...', and gradually, as he chopped and changed, something began to take shape, something quite beautiful...

Pat wasn't working tonight. It was a relief not to have to clock in with the other women for yet one more twilight shift. She enjoyed the badinage—what chance she got, above the roar of the loom—but the dirt, dust and sheer physical effort required to stand feeding that great steel machine four hours every night of the week dampened any pleasure she felt from hearing small-town talk.

Maybe, just maybe, Cliff's record would take off. He seemed pleased, there was a single coming out after the school holidays. In her own secretive way, she felt something might just happen this time.

And even if it didn't, he now had a good job. The school seemed to like his work, his drama classes, the students thought well of him. Maybe the music thing would die a natural death. The milkman, the butcher, the postman; they all once had such dreams; for a while. Boys grow up, don't they...?

She bathed Debbie, marvelling at the child's continual high spirits. She didn't feel sad, sentimental, regretful about the twists of fate, but knew her daughter wouldn't find growing up such fun in the coming years. Teenagers and wheelchairs are a tender combination, and Deb wouldn't tolerate sympathy, she was too independent for that. It would be important to have the right kind of friends. When she had been at school with Martin, *he* had been her legs. She'd spurred him on—much of the time against his will—just to bask in the glory of winning, by proxy. She was a bright, clever child. She'd been top of her class at primary, but this new place, it wasn't right for her...

Hauling Debbie out of the bath, a quick thorough drying, and then carrying her into the back bedroom, she lifted the towels, said a long goodnight and then went back downstairs to get things ready for tomorrow. It was Sam's first year and he was a little apprehensive at the prospect of competing with his classmates.

She cleared the ironing board away, then started polishing the shoes, half-listening to the notes, the gentle voice, replaying a sequence, halting, then moving on:

'...How's your broken heart? Mine's broken too...'

A stop, then a small moan, then again, '...How's your broken heart, is that mended too? I miss you, yes I do. I-miss-you...'

After about half-an-hour, with a flourish of two heavy block-chords and the piano lid closing softly, he came into the kitchen.

"Well, that's a bit different, innit? I think I'm gonna slow down. There's too many people writing that there pop stuff." For a minute he was almost Tom Crite. He smiled to himself, shrugged his shoulders, poured some coffee in the cup, lit a cigarette up, and went off to mark twenty-four essays on the Roman Empire.

She turned on the television, and yes, it sent her fast asleep…

The rain woke her. It was late and she was cold. The heating had gone off, and the gate was still creaking in the yard. Where was Cliff? Surely not in the studio, it must be freezing at this time of night. She went to the window. The barn light was on, so he *was* still working. Good Lord. She put on her long coat and ran out and across, pushing the door open. There he was, hunched over the tape recorder, laughing to himself.

"Cliff! You must be freezing! Come on, you'd better get to bed." She was angry.

He flicked a switch:

'Here's BILL Giles *with* the *wea*—ther…' And a voice echoed, fast, slow; Bluebottle slurs, Chipmunk giggles…

"Oh God, you're not fooling around with that machine. I thought you were writing some songs. Forget that Leon nonsense, Cliff. Come on…"

But he just laughed again, quietly, before rising to his feet.

He fell backwards against the desk; his cigarettes shot across the cold stone floor, his lighter fell. A metallic clunk. It spun, then slowly came to a halt.

Pat rushed across and grabbed his arm to steady him further. For a brief moment they stood there, looking at each other, frightened. It could have been tears, real tears, but all Cliff could say, in a croaked whisper, was, "Bla-w-dy hell, Pat. What's happening to me? What's going on?"

Although the news was 'out', still nobody knew. For certain, that is. It was never mentioned at home, only that Cliff—Dad—was ill, the old ear-infection story.

Christmas rolled around again, and the whole clan descended on Dunley, Debbie bringing her fiancé across for the inquisition by turkey, which he passed admirably. Pat fed and watered them all, managing as always to confound the statistics of supply and demand, and soon it was all over.

The New Year came in, and the business of earning, or finding, money began its relentless assault.

On 14th January 1985, Pat wrote to Niall McCarthy at RTE, requesting confirmation that *Both Of Us* was still scheduled for production, as the contract, signed way back in 1984, was due to expire 31st March.

In a reply dated 20th January, Niall confirmed the worst:

> … We have been unsuccessful in attracting co-production

> finance or interest in *Both Of Us*. We also failed to interest Cliff Richard's manager. As the only hope of making this venture artistically good and viable was to have been successful in both of the above, I am afraid the prospects are now bleak. Please do not lose contact...

And that was it. A simple letter, as they always are. Sympathetic but unyielding.

After all this time, and especially at *such* a time, the dream of having his words and music up there on the screen, beaming into every home in the Irish nation, had failed, gone.

Ironically, in the very same week, John Woods sent a further royalty cheque, expressing pleasure at the Christmas sales of the album in Ireland, but they both knew this would have no impact on an already irrevocable decision at RTE.

The only hope, therefore, was the Tembo release, but that, more than ever, needed personal appearances, and that, of course, was out of the question. Cliff insisted on hiding it from the world, as far as visuals were concerned. If it was known, then so be it, but he wanted no-one to see his condition first-hand.

In retrospect, Pat knows this was wrong:

"I told him continually that it was nothing to be ashamed of. People would be sympathetic, encouraging, they would admire his efforts. But Cliff wanted no part in sympathy, and if there was to be any admiration, it had to be for his talent, not for his ability to fight an illness."

Peter and Eileen Grogan, friends for so many years, even they, on their annual visit, were fobbed off with some tale about overwork.

Peter tells me:

"I had recently read an article about Ray Kennedy, the footballer. He had been diagnosed with Parkinson's disease, an illness very similar to multiple sclerosis, in that it attacks the nervous system.

"I had been there [Cliff's house] for only ten minutes before I realized something was wrong. The involuntary shaking of the head, the hand tremors. Even though they were slight, and infrequent, it wasn't the Clifford T. Ward I knew.

"'What's wrong, Cliff?'" I said, with my usual Irish candour.

"'Oh, Pet-er, it's all the work I've been doing, fitting out that bloody studio,' he said dismissively. But I knew. I'd read that article and I'd read other pieces subsequently, and I recognized the same symptoms. But would he admit it? Jeez, he would not. He came over to do Jim O'Neil's radio show sometime later, and Jim's assistant met us in the lobby at RTE. Even she noticed, asked me what was wrong with Clifford, as he held on to me for dear life, his fingers gripping my hand, almost digging into my flesh, both in gratitude for my silence and for my physical support. If only he'd have come out with it, maybe on that particular programme, lifted the burden for once and for all, 'Look, actually I've got multiple sclerosis,' then he could have got on with it. Instead, the hiding of it became as important as, if not *more* important than, his music.

"He felt, obviously, that having MS was a sign of weakness. That's how he'd been about his shyness, which to me, and everyone else, was endearing. He'd watch videos of his performances and squirm, whereas we all thought they were wonderful. His enormous level of self-criticism led to his equally enormous lack of self-confidence, and that, in turn, he considered as a sign of weakness. Catch 22. So he backed off. Then, when the MS came along, he couldn't bring himself to admit to what he considered to be *another* weakness."

But, the wheels keep turning. Following the low-key release of his Tembo out-take single—the tropical 'Cricket', backed with the topical 'Computer'—Ian Summers came up to visit Cliff in March, bringing his associate from Tembo, Brian Dunham, to discuss what could be done to further promote the album now scheduled for July. Ian remembers it as a lovely day, and being made as welcome as ever. He knew of course, but he saw the deterioration, and was surprised at its speed, yet still Cliff insisted that he would overcome. There was special treatment lined up, he would be going down to London soon to see a specialist and that would be the end of all this cursed nonsense.

Debbie was married in May, the reception held at Upper Norchard. Cliff didn't want anybody to suspect the worst, even though he must have realized they would. His balance was poor and sitting down was the only possible way to disguise it, so, as the guests assembled outside, on the field sloping down from the front of the house, he was spotted sitting under the trees on his beloved tractor-mower, dressed up for the wedding, but supposedly waiting to mow the lawn. He actually believed that it would appear normal—or be socially acceptable—to cut the grass on his daughter's wedding day. After some cajoling, possibly a few mildly uttered threats, he staggered at Pat's side, prompting his mother to remark rather loudly, and in front of the assembled revellers—in complete innocence—"Look at our Cliff, he's drunk already!..."

He still hadn't told anyone; only Pat's folks knew, as, in some peculiar way, he'd always been closer to them.

The photographs leap out from the book in triumphant colour, now marred only by the sadness of hindsight. We see daughter and father, outside the barn; Debbie looking radiant in blue silk, clasping a lilac and lily-of-the-valley bouquet (picked from the garden and assembled by Pat that morning), Cliff standing behind her, leaning on the chair, in a cream jacket and dark trousers, with that broad, enigmatic smile, his eyebrows raised in a heartbreaking shrug of surrender, his head to one side. It speaks volumes. The daughter who so defiantly fought her disability—spurred on in no small measure by her strong-willed father—looking out at the world with her eternal optimism and pride, as he stands, unfocused, uncertain, inwardly fearing the future.

About forty guests enjoyed the reception-buffet, held in one of the barns that afternoon, after which Deb, husband and her friends retreated to the Sutton Arms in Kidderminster for the obligatory disco. Pat, Cliff, and Peter and Eileen Grogan joined them later, but it was a bad mistake.

Cliff, by this time, was in a foul mood. Whether he was unwell, or angry at the day, he made the evening as unpleasant as possible for them all. Pat wanted to stay, but knew the consequences and decided the only recourse was to retreat. Eileen was enjoying herself so much that Peter saw no reason for her to leave, but thought it best he should go back to the house; he was astute enough to see Pat would need help. What he didn't expect was for Cliff to turn on *him*:

"How can you leave Eileen there dancing the night away? She should be with you, Peter. She's your *wife*," he complained.

"Aaah, she's fine, Cliff, it's good to see her enjoying herself. She'll be all right."

"But she's pregnant, you shouldn't leave her there," he continued.

"Cliff, Eileen is fine. She's pregnant, not *ill*, and she's happy. Leave her be."

They drove home in silence, apart from occasional, but unsuccessful attempts by Peter to lighten the atmosphere.

Back at Dunley, Cliff went into overdrive, moaning, criticizing, complaining, concluding that '…it had been a dreadful day…'

He went off to bed; Peter said he'd keep Pat company until Eileen returned. She sneaked in around midnight, with Sam. They said an uncomfortable goodnight, retiring to the stable-flat, Sam to the studio-flat, across the yard, as the lights were turned off and peace—though not of mind—descended on Upper Norchard.

Next morning, at the crack of dawn, Pat rose, went into the barn and cleared everything away, sweeping every sign of yesterday's celebration into bin bags. She wanted no reminder of a day that had been so methodically ruined. It was all best forgotten. Later in the morning, when Cliff appeared—in a foretaste of a behavioural pattern that was to develop—he acted as if nothing had happened, even asking why he'd not been woken earlier to lend a hand.

Peter and Eileen said their goodbyes in the late afternoon, leaving Sam as the only remaining guest. After a somewhat fraught evening meal,

Cliff disappeared into the studio. Sam, up from Goldsmiths', and Polly were left to provide whatever comfort or companionship for Pat. Sam, though he had long since accepted his father's moods, felt now that something else was at work, and so, after Little Sis had been coaxed into bed, he sat down with his mother.

Pat was obviously in an emotional state, happy that her eldest daughter had found love and security in such a tough old world, but now torn apart, for just as it seemed everything was working out fine…

"But what is it, Mom? Dad keeps telling me it's a middle-ear infection. This has been going on for ages now. Can't he get something done about it? What did the specialist say last time you went down?"

"He doesn't want me to discuss it with anybody, Sam. You know your dad, he's a very private person. He doesn't want to feel as if he's beholden to anyone…"

"But I'm his *son*. He'd never have to feel that way with *me*… If I don't know, I can't help…"

"Sam, he doesn't want help. Cliff says he'll beat this thing on his own terms."

"What *thing*?"

She really couldn't see the point any longer. All their married life, 24 years, she had obeyed and conformed; instructions, demands, but…now, well, Sam was *her* son too.

She told him the diagnosis. And the prognosis.

There was a brief, but uncomfortable silence. He felt as sorry for his mother as he did for Cliff. It was not a future to look forward to any more, and he knew, although MS was an unknown quantity for all of them, that, once again, his mother would eventually have to bear most of the burden.

Sam thought quickly. He suggested they all went on holiday. Vanessa, his long-standing girlfriend, wanted to go to France during the summer break. Why not all pile into the Renault and share the cost? Pat and Cliff had never, in all those years together, taken a holiday. Really. A few working weekends, but that was all. Here was an ideal opportunity, and, 'Yes,' she said, they would talk tomorrow… but, sleeping on it, Pat realized, with her accustomed sweet surrender, that she would be the only one able to drive…

"It was a disaster," she recalls. "I drove over 1000 miles, with Cliff constantly moaning away in the front seat, and Sam, Vanessa and little old Pol crammed in the back of our red Renault 5. Nothing I did was right. We stayed in a gîte near St Malo and played the game of happy families, but Cliff was so awkward, obtuse, *difficult*, to put it mildly, that the whole atmosphere was grey, leaden. Frankly, I was glad to get back, to turn up that drive, though I knew—we all did—that it would be exactly the same even back home. But at least we wouldn't be crammed together quite so incestuously… Mention France to me and I go make a cup of tea."

Sometime Next Year was released on schedule, but there was no promotional angle to work on. Cliff adamantly refused to allow Tembo to 'exploit' his illness, still believing that he would make a full recovery and—perhaps understandably—not wanting to be the object of public sympathy.

A few reviews crept out, but it had all been too long, it was all too late; the songs, without a doubt, had lost their immediacy, their accessibility, their appeal. The Tin Pan Alley-Hollywood publicity yardstick, 'Don't read it, measure it', with, in Clifford's case, three lines in a bottom left-hand column, and no personal appearances, only a tiring trawl of local radio stations, with Pat driving, resulted in little reward for a still-worthy contender.

The irony of Chris De Burgh, whom he had unknowingly inspired so many years earlier, now topping the charts for the very first time, as Clifford himself struggled equally with failure both in profession and health, is tragic in its timing. It is certain that if Chris had known the extent—or even known, *period*—of the situation, he would have done everything in his power to help (as he was to do, in an act of extraordinary kindness, many years later).

And if Clifford had even thought about Chris's success, or even known then about being his early inspiration, the feeling of frustration would have been unavoidable, but it wouldn't have fired him with envy; it wasn't in his nature, as Peter Grogan takes great pains to point out:

"He never grudged anyone anything, and was always ready to help or give what advice he could, though I wish he'd have taken some of the advice himself, that he dished out to others…" he remarks, in exasperation, and he comes back to that one concert, that *one* chance, that if Cliff had taken, would have given his career the boost to lift it up where it belonged:

"Okay, he did the Twiggy thing, and it went well—though I wasn't there, I've heard the comments—but he should have tried for that Clifford T. Ward Concert. You know, of *course* you do. It's like riding your first roller-coaster. You do it, and it's 'Jeez, is that all there is to it? Let's have another one.' But he wouldn't step out onto the track. I know he could perform, he spent years in pop groups, whooping his way through Eddie Cochran and the Four Tops. Of course he could do it."

I put it to Peter that apart from the arrogance, the impetuosity of youth, and of course the sheer buzz of those days, maybe Cliff felt easier because those songs had already been accepted; that they were already—even after such a short life—standards in most singers' repertoire, whereas, Cliff singing his own songs…well, maybe his confidence, for whatever reason, and known only to himself, just wasn't strong enough.

"I talked and told him, but no, he wouldn't accept the love we had for his music as being justification for him baring his soul, putting himself up to be analysed, scrutinized, criticized. Something held him back. It wasn't his music, that's for sure. It was in his mind. The demons in his mind..."

But Ian Summers still believed he could do something with the songs. They had sorted out the publishing—or so it seemed—and, being the tenacious breed that he is, he started the rounds, putting Cliff's Tembo catalogue into every pair of hands possible. He also mentioned that *maybe* they could do something with *Both Of Us*, but agreed it needed some rewriting, so Cliff got to work once again on his manuscript.

Back in town, the bank manager, checking statements regularly, watched the outcome of *Sometime Next Year* with an agreeable tolerance. He knew, from years of experience, that royalties took a circuitous route, but advised, '...there could be no more financial outlay until the overdraft was considerably reduced...' Few people at that time, apart from Cliff and Pat—both holding on for dear life—were in much doubt that it would be...

The shifting of power between them was hard for him to accept. He had always held the outdated belief that the husband was the provider; the wife had her role as home-maker, mother and comforter. This is how it had been from the beginning of their marriage, and Pat had fulfilled her duties far beyond the call, as he had followed his profession. But now, losing the control he had always believed he had...together with the unrelenting onset of MS, it was all too much.

No more the 'soul-mate' situation; the jokes—sometimes even the admonishments—about not doing something quite right to his satisfaction or invariably high expectations. Now, whenever he tried to prove to himself that he *could* still write, or sing, he frequently lashed out at the inanimate, illuminated machinery that surrounded him; the gentle hum of 'standby', the whirr of the capstan wheel, the meters, ready to leap in response. He sat, bewildered, angry, terrified as his life slowly lost its meaning.

"He had depended on Pat for everything outside his music, and that was his romantic vision of how a marriage should be," confirms Peter Grogan. "We saw it so many times, and Pat took his often unjustified and unnecessary scoldings remarkably well. In fact, she never contradicted, answered back, questioned anything. If his mind was preoccupied, say with a forthcoming session, or the seeds of a song, he would fly off the handle at any peccadillo that the poor girl committed.

Jeez, call it artistic temperament if you will, but she was a very tolerant lady in the face of it all.

"That time, remember," he says, glancing across at his wife Eileen, "we'd come across for the first visit. I didn't drive then, you did." She nods. "So I knew nothing about cars, nothing. We were sitting in the back, Pat and Cliff in the front, him driving. Something started to niggle him, and I heard the phrase 'shock absorbers' thrown across at Pat. Eileen was whispering to me, patting my hand in sympathy at my ignorance, 'Yes, Peter, *I* know what they are…' Now me, in my utter stupidity, I hadn't a clue. Honest. They—or it—could have been a sexual device for all I knew at the time…but anyhow, it transpired that Cliff was giving Pat an earful because she hadn't seen to the faulty shock absorbers. The car was *her* domain, he was a musician. Such humdrum things were *her* department.

"He even suggested, when Eileen was taking maternity leave, that, instead of following her highly respectable PA job in the government, she should stay at home and be what he termed, 'a proper mother'. Okay, maybe he was being a bit tongue-in-cheek at the time, but it was his idea of an ideal.

"Saying all that, when things were off the boil, musically speaking—which, Cliff being the person he is, tended to be most of the time, ha-ha—" and Peter rolls his eyes heavenwards, "he mucked in, played games, relaxed, and was a man of enormous warmth. But even then, mention that gobshite Margaret Thatcher and you *would* need a good set of shock absorbers…In all the years I have known him, I don't think I've ever seen such contempt in his feelings towards *anybody* as there was in his loathing for that woman, and the 'survival of the fittest' doctrine that she stood for, and endorsed. That was his upbringing, his Labour ethic [as perfectly exemplified in his political hymn 'Sweetness and Light'], his abhorrence of injustice."

"His songs are sprinkled with religious allegory. Was he a religious person?"

"Well, I can't say whether he believed, but, again I used to wind him up, insisting that I was a practising Catholic, especially when I discovered—to my amazement—that Cliff wasn't aware that his *father* was a Catholic until the poor man died, in 1982, and the priest was called in to say the last rites. That really astonished me. When Cliff told me, I remarked, jokingly of course, that I always knew there was some good in him, in Cliff…He took the bait, hook line and sinker, and we had a terrific…er…discussion for the next two hours. Pat and Eileen hid behind the sideboard…"

"Look, it's *easy*, Peter. All you've got to do is reverse it through that gap in the hedge. Line it up, then put the *mower* into reverse, let your foot off the clutch…"

"Yes, I know how the friggin' thing works, thank you, Clifford T. friggin' Ward," simmered Peter, jaw set firm, eyes sparked with fire. A reprimanded schoolboy.

Cliff had that tone of humour in his voice; measured, warm, light, but with a touch of relish. He was enjoying this one.

Castle Weir, its lights blazing onto the velvet lawns, the crunch of washed pebble underfoot, the tall evergreens waving in an early evening breeze, the voices rising, shouting, cheering for her, or him, or them. This was bliss. But Peter was two-one down. He'd *thrashed* this upstart Englishman at badminton, only to be soundly beaten at bowls (a ladies' game…) but he'd never come across 'Mower-Reversing', for God's sake, on any other sports field; wasn't Clifford taking advantage of his daily domestic duties a little, here?

He climbed aboard. Eileen cheered him on:

"C'mon Pe-d-er, c'mon Pe-d-er."

Throttle, clutch, reverse. Slowly, slowly…Jeez, it's going all over the place!

Straight into the privet.

"I guess I win," grinned Cliff, stepping forward to unhook the trailer from the hedge. Then as if to rub salt in the wound, "Three games to one."

"That was bloody unfair," shouted Peter, fair loser that he is… "You must do that all the time, when you're not making dem bloody records…"

They shook hands and walked back into the house, laughing at the stupidity of it all; men will be boys.

Pat was cooking, Sam was laying the table. Martin was nowhere to be seen, but then, the television was in the lounge.

"Deb's coming home tomorrow, Pete. She asked on the phone if you'd still be around for the weekend."

"Oh, I'll be here, if only to beat that gobshite husband of yours at 'Mower-Reversing'." He rattled the paper open to the sports page.

Cliff had just signed the new—big new—deal with WEA, and things were looking rosy, after so many years of frustration. He'd told Peter over breakfast about his plans for Castle Weir, how he saw it as an ideal place for children like Debbie and her friends. Some of them had already been up and stayed overnight, sometimes for the weekend, camping out on the back lawn. They loved the adventure. He'd come back late at night, driving from London, or from a radio spot, or even from Leon's, and he'd find them there, gathered together singing on some beat up old guitar, or swopping ghost stories. Castle Weir was the perfect place.

Peter remembered the first time he'd seen Debbie, when he and Eileen had crossed over from Dublin to pay homage to their hero. They'd arrived at Lower Hollin, been welcomed into the house and were just sitting down when she appeared at the top of the stairs, laughing, as always, and began sliding down on her backside, step by step. Bump, bump, bump. Peter had leapt to his feet to offer help, but Cliff had held him back, saying quietly, "Let her do it herself, Peter. She'll manage."

And indeed she did. And she went right through life managing, becoming fiercely independent, her own woman. Disability was nothing more than an inconvenience to Deb, and Cliff had taught her that.

After supper, they sat in the lounge and began the crack. Peter baiting Clifford, he, in turn, teasing the Irishman about his teaching aspirations, suggesting pop management as a more exciting lifestyle.

"And good money too. Look at Justin, what he's doing for me, just by being able to talk to a few people, convince them I'm worth the money, and we all come out happy and rich. Surely that's better than teaching?"

Peter, pragmatic as ever, accepted the facts, but expressed concern at the uncertainty of such a business, and then broached his favourite subject.

"When are you going to come over to Ireland and do a friggin' concert? I could sell you out a hundred times over. The Concert Hall, the Festival Theatre, they wouldn't even need to advertise it, apart from an announcement in the [*Irish*]*Times*."

And Cliff responded, as he always did, and always would, with an excuse or a reason, and always with a firm "No".

Peter poured himself another brandy. 'Twas hopeless.

"So, Cliff. You're writing lots of good songs for this new album?..."

Peter's voice; a phone call just this evening. He walked across to the keyboard, supporting himself against the mixer as he slumped onto the stool. His eyes were bad again tonight, but the tremors were less noticeable; maybe he could get something on tape.

Pat was alone in the house. Polly had gone to stay with Kate, down in the valley, she wouldn't be back until Sunday afternoon.

What was going to happen to them all? Cliff was booked in to see another specialist on Thursday, a few more tests perhaps, a new prescription perhaps, but no cure, for certain. They'd been told, only last week, that it seemed to be a particularly severe strain of multiple sclerosis; remission would seem to be, in his case, noticeable by its absence. In plain English, he would become increasingly disorientated. It could only get worse…

She went to the bureau, pulled out an envelope and laid the contents on the table.

Three final demands, a letter from the building society—received last week—confirming arrangements that their five months arrears '…would be bought up to date within seven working days'; a statement from the bank, with the covering '…no more…' missive; a solicitor's letter on behalf of the builders Cliff had dismissed 18 months ago; it was all there, waiting to explode. And he knew—or wanted to know—nothing about it.

She couldn't tell anyone about this, no-one would believe her. They had been living this fairy-tale existence for so long, almost since the days he had first been successful. The money had poured in all right, but not as quickly as the money had been pouring out. Cliff always assumed it would continue on a high, and, of course, she had gone along with it. Even the times when warning bells started ringing and she had tried to pull on the reins, her fear of his reaction—of him sensing the reality of it all—had made her retreat into that silent acceptance.

It became quite clear to her, sitting there alone in a house that was worth much more than they could afford, that once again they would have to sell up, and move down. This time it wouldn't be Cliff's boredom, but his condition, his illness, that could be used as the reason. It wouldn't be too long before he would be unable to climb the stairs; so they would have to look for a good-sized bungalow, local, of course.

The phone rang. It was Roger Bowen, calling to see how things were. He chatted about his latest group, now fully ensconced in the burgeoning country-and-western scene, "…even wearing a Stetson now," he laughed.

"We played the Mitre Oak last night. Remember that time when Rodney came along…?"

She remembered it all right. Roger wasn't being tactless, or vindictive, far from it. He had a mordant wit, and sometimes, in his exuberance, he became a little, well, careless, unthinking.

It had been in the very early days, when Roger was still a Cruiser. Rodney Simmonds had long since departed from the ranks, going off to play in various other local groups, but they'd heard on the grapevine that he'd contracted something called multiple sclerosis, '…whatever the bloody 'ell that was.'

They'd been playing along to a fairly enthusiastic crowd, shaking the acorns from the rafters, when Rodney had walked in. Smiles all around, and, come the interval, he came over and shook hands. He was visibly unsteady, but as keen as ever to get up and do a song or two. There was a sharp intake of breath all round.

"Oooh, I dunno, Rodney. You can't be up to it, surely?" Cliff said, but Rodney persisted and, trying hard to control his uncontrollable tremors, he'd invariably made a mess of things, much to Cliff's discernible annoyance. Whether out of youthful insensitivity, or embarrassment for his own image, he teased him, '...mocked him on stage...', made an obvious scene of Rodney's incompetence. Rodney had been deeply hurt. It was an uncomfortable incident—that insensitive combination of youth and ignorance—and was only saved by the band launching into a blistering version of Marv Johnson's 'You've Got What It Takes'.

And then Roger recounted a similar but not so uncomfortable incident that had occurred a couple of years later, when he had left the Cruisers and was drumming for a country group called Woodfield. They were playing at the good old Mare & Colt when Rodney shuffled in. Despite his condition, his spirit was still unbroken, and he tried once again to recapture the past, to get up on stage and play. He failed dismally, but this time there was genuine concern and sympathy from the other musicians.

Roger went up to see Rodney when the extent of his illness had taken on a new and final twist. His wife had left him, and he was now living with his brother in Edinburgh, his daily routine dictated by visiting nurses, who washed and cleaned his wasting body.

"He lay there, his guitar by his side, and all he wanted to do was talk about the Cruisers, the good old days. 'Remember when ... Rog. Remember when we ...'"

"Gill'll pop round on Saturday to cut Cliff's hair. I can take him for a ride somewhere later, if that's okay," Roger continued, quite unaware of the reaction his recollections had stirred.

"Yeah, that's fine," answered Pat. "He'll look forward to that. I'll get something in for tea, you bring the wine. A good one, remember, none of that supermarket rubbish! See ya, then, Rog," and he was gone.

She put the papers back in the envelope and made herself a coffee. Cliff came in and, without saying very much, slowly climbed the stairs, leaving her once again alone.

She would mention it tomorrow. Not tonight, she was tired. Tomorrow.

A grand scheme was hatched. After great deliberation, an agreeable compromise was reached; that they should divide the farm, put a fence right across the yard, cutting off the house from the outbuildings and courtyard, and put these buildings up for sale as one lot, keeping the house for themselves. Cliff was still convinced that he would beat his

illness, and that the stairs would present no greater threat, his mobility would not deteriorate further, that they were all wrong. He knew best.
There was the studio and flat, the converted stables, and a listed barn, full of hay—but that could soon be cleared; a fair-sized property. The planning officer was called in to inspect and approve, but he rejected it…
With its general state of disrepair, the ancient beams and earthen floor, it would be impossible to even consider planning permission, they were told. But Cliff had other ideas. Behind the studio barn were hundreds of house bricks; gnarled, brown, aged teeth from the original building, stored there over the years, waiting. With Sam and Martin reluctantly seconded in to help—with promises, invariably, of huge reward—they cleared the hay and laid the bricks as flooring. It took a long time, and a lot of sufferance, but it worked, it looked good, and the three buildings and courtyard, thoughtfully renamed Upper Norchard Barn, went up for sale, though without full planning permission, for £100,000.
This time they weren't selling up, they were selling off, and with house prices at an all time high, if they got the asking price, all their borrowing would be repaid, with maybe even some to spare. There was no shortage of viewers, a couple of pop music notables drove up the long, winding track to look over the buildings, one even made an offer for the whole farm, but Cliff was adamant that they were staying there, in the small house, so no sale. It was a gamble, they held out, and it worked. Within six weeks, a local builder, able to see enormous potential despite the lack of planning authority approval, paid the asking price and so, following the time it takes to complete contracts, and breathing a collective sigh of financial relief, Cliff, Pat and the bank were on speaking terms once again. They were solvent at least and at last, though no-one gave a second thought to how long it would last…

"That's nice. Have they got it in any other colours?" he asked her, drawing the cigarette to his mouth, shaking noticeably. The flowered smock reflected in his sun-glasses as she stood nervously parading before him.
She half-turned to the assistant.
"There's a moss green, cornflower blue and the one you're wearing, oatmeal, I think it is. That's all we have in at the moment," the girl smiled back, cold-eyed. "I think there are two other shades. Let me have a look at the catalogue."
She flicked the pages, quickly finding the display.
"Yes, these two, but we don't stock them here. They'll have them in

our Cheltenham branch. Would you like me to telephone them, just to check?"

She did, and they had.

"Oh, I dunno. Which one, Cliff?"

"Get them all, all three of them," he ordered, casually but positively.

"But Cliff, they're £47.00 each," she whispered, leaning towards him.

"Pat. Get…them…*all*."

That slow, precise manner, which meant, quite simply, 'Don't argue'.

They left the shop, Pat loaded up with three dresses, a wide-brimmed felt hat, a table lamp, oh, and a pair of leather boots he'd noticed in the window. He held her arm tightly, for support, as they crossed the road and slowly made their way to the car-park. He was unsteady, but in good spirits, and she knew why.

He swung into his seat.

"Now. What time is it? Right. Let's go to Cheltenham and get the other two."

"Whaa-aat?" she gasped, but again, he gave that soft, low, casual instruction.

"Let's …go…to…Cheltenham and get the other two."

Since the Barn had been sold, a new 'entertainment' had entered his life. Shopping for clothes. It was a diversion that had slowly become an obsession, and she—don't call her irresponsible—was going along with it.

"He was unwell, but he needed to exercise the control he had always assumed; to maintain his authority, power, call it what you will, and this was his way of doing it," she tells me, in a voice trembling with confessional emotion. "Yes, I know. So what woman wouldn't enjoy spending the waking hours buying clothes, even furnishings? But to me, this was nothing short of mental abuse—the driving, the choosing, the parading, the orders—knowing I didn't want them, didn't need them, and that I would never wear most of them again. If I protested, he would fly off into a rage, and boy, could he rage… No-one could ever understand the horror, the sickening, of what would be a pleasurable experience—to anyone else. For me, it was nothing more than a way of keeping him sweet, tolerable, bearable."

They would spend days, and miles, travelling from Dunley, to Worcester, Stratford, Solihull, Birmingham, Cheltenham, Shrewsbury; up and down motorways, weaving through lunchtime traffic, finding somewhere to park, ambling across town to the Laura Ashley store, where Cliff would claim a seat in the corner, light up a cigarette and watch her try on dress after dress, hat after hat.

"At that rate, it didn't take long to build up another overdraft," says Pat, despairingly. "We were—or I was—buying possibly three dresses a *week*. It was all Cliff wanted to do. We'd get home from a spree and I'd then have to model them all for him, one by one, as he sat there, taking pictures. We even bought a video camera for the occasion. It was the Laura Ashley Show. My wardrobe overflowed with smocks, skirts, blouses, boots, more smocks…"

The world outside, meanwhile, carried on in its own sweet way. It woke up, went to work, then went back to sleep, or that's how it seemed. The visitors were less frequent. It seemed that not many people could handle the situation. They would telephone, maybe even write, but, towards the end of the Greed Decade, Cliff and Pat found themselves, for the greater part, drifting, very much alone in their world of make-believe.

In August, 1987, Ian Summers and Brian Dunham paid a final visit to Dunley. Pat collected then from the station, fed them and watered them in her wonderful manner, as they discussed *Both Of Us.* It wasn't going to work, in fact, it never would; but Cliff thanked them. They had given it fair consideration. A shame.

Being the disciple he was, Ian didn't just leave it at that, though there was little else he could do regarding Tembo. Plugging away in his own supreme manner, he quickly recorded as many of Clifford's songs as was financially possible, using session singers to give them a less personal feel; hence the version of 'Who Cares?' doing the rounds under the 'Pat Ward: vocals' misnomer. "One of Cliff's little jokes," shrugs Pat. "I mean, really, can you seriously imagine me standing in front of a microphone? I can't sing a note. But these people, they believe anything he says, they believe what they want to believe. It was not me. Not on your life."

Ian's efforts paid off. He secured a cover of 'Lost Again' by Ireland's new country-songstress Ann Breen, much later, in 1994, which received tremendous radio coverage—a so-called air play hit—but which didn't chart, though it did provide some welcome PRS income for a now destitute writer.

"That was the last time I saw him," Ian sighs. "I took the record up to his house, went into his little studio room and put it on. He cried. Said it was wonderful and just cried. I can understand that. I loved Clifford. He was one of the most honest, upfront guys I'd ever met in the business. We hit it off from day one, and I *still* feel there is something inside, he is such a talent. If only we could find a way to transmit his thoughts onto paper or better still onto a keyboard. I really feel for him and I *really* feel for Pat. She has to live through it very day, every *hour* of the day—and night. She is such a strong woman."

Karl Hyde also came by to see him. He'd lost touch over the years since Castle Weir, steadfastly following his burning ambition to crack the world of pop music, alongside completing his fine arts degree at Cardiff.

"Because we'd disagreed a few times too many—my teenage years fuelled my ever-changing opinions—I kept my distance for a while. I still kept contact with my schoolmates who were living in Bewdley. A couple of them were car mechanics, and one weekend when I was back home, over a drink or two, Cliff's name came up. Somebody mentioned that he'd been in the garage recently with his wife, to collect a car after it'd been serviced, and that he was acting a bit strange. They even joked about him being on drugs, and not for medication…

"I didn't believe that for one minute, so I got his number, and gave Cliff a ring. Pat answered. She sounded decidedly odd, not the Pat I knew, but she asked me over. So me and another mate went over to see them. I could see the change straightaway. I knew he wasn't drugged up, and, if the past was anything to go by, it was too early for a drink, Pat would never have allowed it… But he tried to pretend there was nothing wrong and I, we, went along with it. Yes, we talked about music, and he asked, as he always did, whether what I was doing had integrity, whether I really believed in it, and was I enjoying it. 'If you're gonna do this', he would say, 'you've got to tackle these issues…take it seriously, work it as a craft.' He certainly sold that to me. He never belittled me.

"I'd grown a bit more confident by that time and inevitably it came around to his songs, his music. I said he'd grown irrelevant, out of touch, virtually implied he was past it. He didn't defend, he went straight into the attack, quoting lines, playing tracks, dissecting phrases here and there, which, to be honest, I'd never noticed before. Subtleties, humour, social comment, always understated, but, to my amazement, always there. And I'd missed them.

"The only comment I feel I was justified in, was that his production had become very sloppy. This was the eighties, and here he was, stuck in the seventies. Sadly, I didn't know the reason why, of course; that he was recording under severe financial restrictions and increasingly poor health. But he still wouldn't have any of it. He always stuck to his beliefs, wrote straight from the heart, he never saw the need to adapt. As opinionated, cocksure as ever.

"But he liked it when I told him that if it hadn't have been for those early days at Bewdley, if he'd been sent to some other school for teaching practice, I doubt whether I'd have been doing music at all. He inspired me as a schoolboy, and he inspired me *then*, even while we were arguing at Dunley, and even when we were arguing at Castle Weir. To me he was the local hero. Okay, there were many others from around the area that had made it, some made it much bigger of course, but Cliff had been *my* personal champion. He was somebody who, for a long time, I aspired to be. I admired his eloquence, his tranquillity, and I was desperate for just one *ounce* of the success he'd enjoyed. I always came away from seeing him, fired with enthusiasm, determined to do something, and do it better and better. Not so's I could stick my fingers up at him, but to *please* him…

"As we left, he gave me a tape, a kind of *Best Of Clifford T. Ward*, which he'd put together. That was a nice gesture, but I never thought it would affect me the way it did. I put it on the Walkman and played it as I sat looking out at backyard Britain on the old Inter-City.

"I've always loved coming back to Worcestershire. No matter what my mood is when I leave London, by the time I reach here, home, I'm feeling better. Conversely, when I'm going back, I'm the opposite. My heart gets heavy. I played that cassette all the way down to London, and by the time I reached Paddington, I was crying. I was homesick. And I'm tough, man!" he laughs, self-conscious at showing his emotions.

"Do you think his songs stand up over the years?"

"Whenever I recall those visits to Cliff's house, I can see that he refused to move with the times. From those early days at the Oaklands, when I was still at school, and he had his Revox and his piano, all the way down the years, nearly a quarter of a century later, he still had the same set-up, the same approach. It was if he had this image of, well, it was like Tin Pan Alley, the artisan, working at his job, locked away, and that was it.

"I was experiencing life. Cliff never socialized outside his close, very close circle; he never saw the changes, he was forever stuck in the past. Yes, okay; love, the home, the family…"

He stopped:

"Well, no, actually, I was about to say these things *never* change, but of course the family did, and drastically so, but he wouldn't tackle the thorny side of life. Yet he still wrote some *cracking* songs. His sense of melody was astonishing, some of the notes he stuck in that were way off the scale, but they worked. Even now, when I'm writing, I think of what Cliff would have done here and there, and I do just that, put in a note that throws it, gives an extra dimension."

The treble Cliff…

"But saying all that, I would never *dream* of sitting down and playing him any of my stuff, what we're doing today, 'cos I know he just would not understand it, even though I feel that I am at my peak as a songwriter."

He acknowledges my surprise at that last remark, though at that time I honestly didn't know anything by or about Underworld. Luddite, *moi*?…

"Yes, honestly. I am more convinced of my work now than I have ever been. All my heart and soul is in there, more than it has ever been. I suppose you could say it's poetry more than songwriting—we are very technical, *techno*—but to me, it's what I have been working towards, a fulfilment. I stand by it totally, and I don't think Cliff would see that, would admit to accepting the worthiness of my music. But there is no denying he was my driving force. And I miss his voice, his incredible voice. Singing or speaking, it had that honeyed warmth, that timbre."

From *Home Thoughts* to *Trainspotting*. That's quite a journey.

Mark Tibenham, now married and living in London, eventually heard the news and was deeply shocked.

"I was very upset. I knew nothing about multiple sclerosis, other than it was life threatening, and that was enough to upset me. Since that time, well, of course, it's been better publicised—if better's the right word—and I know a lot of people try to use it as an excuse if they're busted...' Oh, I'm just getting it for a friend who's got MS...' he jokes in a mock-crim voice.

"All those days in America, all those hours in the studio at Dunley. It suddenly seemed to fall into perspective, seemed to give his personality some justification. But that's it. If he'd just taken a few spliffs, just relaxed, things might have been different. He was such a bag of nerves, *all* the time. I don't mean nervous. He was wound up so tightly, a coiled spring, a volcano, waiting to erupt. The idea of putting up *now*, with what I did *then*, well, I'd never have done it. Apart from what I've said about the wonderful music, and, of course the promise of money—I was very ambitious at that time, and when Justin was around, all that talk of huge amounts of money kept me chuntering along; I mean £25,000 was mentioned at one time, for *me*—apart from all that, I'd never have taken what Clifford dished out to me.

"But this was such a tragedy. We hadn't exactly parted on the best of terms. I'd never seen a copy of *Sometime Next Year*, still haven't, but I'm pleasantly surprised—from what you told me—that he actually had the grace to give me a credit—albeit as Mark T—on the sleeve. At long last!

"I promised myself to go up and see him as soon as I could, but at that particular time I was running a hectic life pattern myself, everything was happening, some good, some bad, but I was busy. Very busy."

And producer Hugh Murphy?

Though no more recording deals were forthcoming for me—I'd completely lost interest in the business, and the business had certainly lost interest in me—I maintained some contact with him. Unusual for me. But I thought a lot of Hugh.

When I last visited him, in 1991, he was living in a lovely hideaway tucked behind a small copse of evergreens in deepest Buckinghamshire.

Despite his enviable track record, the music business had moved so fast over the last ten years that even Hugh was feeling out of it. To relieve the boredom of telephone-sitting, he had taken to the canvas. He showed me some of his beautiful paintings, done in naïve art style; I was very impressed, surprised even. (I actually ordered one, but never received it; Hugh being Hugh, bless him, well he probably sold it to some sweet young thing for half the price, or for payment in kind…)
We chatted about old times, opened a few cans of Theakstons, and he cooked me a mushroom omelette, just as he had done all those years ago when I had stayed at his house in Wandsworth during recording dates.
Hugh leaps around when he talks. He's a great mover, even when he cooks, gesticulating, emphasizing, sometimes tripping over telephone wires, rugs, dogs, his expression always that enigmatic half-smile, a lovable, enthusiastic Londoner, who did do well, for a time, in a very difficult business.
Again, inevitably, talk got around to Clifford T. Ward. He knew of Cliff's condition, but didn't seem at all surprised by it… He recounted the Justin débâcle and how nothing had been good enough for Cliff. How time after time they had changed, altered, re-mixed, re-recorded, and *still*…no, no…
He jumped up to his sadly burdened bookshelf:
"It's all in here. Diseases, illnesses, causes, potential victims." He had pulled down a huge, multi-coloured book, decorated with herbs, star signs, and cosmic cartoons. Hmmm… "Here you are. 'Multiple Sclerosis … cause unknown, but most certainly more prevalent in persons with a highly-strung temperament, of a nervous or irritable disposition …' He was a prime candidate," Hugh remarked, slamming the pages shut. "Doesn't surprise me a bit. He just could not rel-*ax*. Always on *edge*, always looking for something wrong, always nit-picking. Even his *own* work…Nothing was ever *good* enough…"

I looked it up myself, in one or two more orthodox publications, and in a way I could see the reason for such thinking; the homeopathic attitude towards illness, the cause-and-effect rationale, but I honestly can't accept that it's quite as simple as that:

> Multiple Sclerosis, a disease of the central nervous system in which myelin, the white, fatty substance that sheathes nerve fibres, is gradually destroyed, and multiple lesions develop in the brain and spinal cord. The cause of the disease, which chiefly attacks individuals between the ages of 20 and 40, is unknown. Symptoms vary according to the sites of the lesions in the nervous system; the commonest symptoms are blurring

> of vision, loss of vision or double vision, tremor of the hands, weakness of the extremities, sensory changes such as numbness, tingling, or pain, slurring of speech, and loss of control over the urinary and anal sphincters. The disease is intermittent in most cases; the initial symptoms are usually transient and may last only several hours or a few days. They generally disappear after the first attack, leaving the person symptom-free, often for many years, only to recur and disappear again, fully or partly. This waxing and waning of symptoms, which may vary from relapse to relapse, may occur repeatedly over many years, leaving few after effects at first but eventually producing permanent disabilities. Thus the person often becomes clumsy and progressively weaker. Occasionally, the disease is slowly progressive. It is rarely present as an acute or subacute condition running a progressive course of only weeks or months. Multiple sclerosis is in most cases eventually fatal; and no specific cure has been found. Physical and occupational therapy and several drugs may provide symptomatic improvement.
>
> Louis J. Vorhaus
> ©1994 Funk & Wagnall's Corporation.

I found a further entry, in another medical publication, under the sub-heading 'Disseminated Sclerosis':

> Incurable chronic disease of the central nervous system, occurring in young or middle adulthood. Most prevalent in temperate zones, it affects more women than men. It is characterized by degeneration of the myelin sheath that surrounds nerves in the brain and spinal cord. Depending on where the demyelination occurs—which nerves are affected—the symptoms of MS can mimic almost any neurological disorder. Typically seen are unsteadiness, ataxia (loss of muscular coordination), weakness, speech difficulties, and rapid involuntary movements of the eyes. The course of the disease is episodic, with frequent intervals of remission. Its cause is unknown, but it may be initiated in childhood by some environmental factor, such as infection, in genetically susceptible people. In 1993 interferon beta 1b became the first drug to be approved in the United States for treating MS. It reduces the number and severity of relapses, and slows the formation of brain lesions giving hope that it may slow down the progression of the disease.

All very informative, scientific, precise, except that such explanations invariably avoid—are quite unable to give—any indication of the cause. It is 'unknown'.

And then, in the process of writing this book, I came across an amazing, indeed alarming, number of people who had suffered—who are still suffering—in varying degrees, from multiple sclerosis:

First and foremost of course, Rodney Simmonds. Following his argument with Cliff, Rodney had left The Cruisers to join his brother in The Simonals, before moving on to The Reflections. An MS sufferer since his teenage years, he had married, fathered two sons, then split from his wife, before meeting Val Nichols, who *herself* later contracted the illness. Rodney was eventually to die, at the age of 49, from a derivative stroke. His funeral, in West Lothian, where he had moved to live with his brother Ian and family, was attended by Trevor Jones, Roger Bowen and Graham Drew, who travelled the 600-mile round trip together, to show their respects. Cliff, of course, was unable to attend.

Rodney's girlfriend Val is now confined to a wheelchair, being cared for by her elderly parents.

In 1978, Clifford was asked to open a fête at Bewdley High School, where Sam, his youngest son, was a pupil. One of the teachers there introduced Cliff to a girl called Alison, who had recently been diagnosed as being in the initial stages of MS. In a bizarre act of hero-worship, she began calling herself Gaye, after Cliff's song. She is now in her late 30s, still quite mentally alert, but residing in an old folks home in Stourport, her aged parents being unable to cope.

Cliff's mentor, Clive Selwood, had a daughter Samantha, by his first marriage, who did some vocals on one of the Charisma albums. She was diagnosed with a mild form of MS in 1979.

Ann and Denis Lee, great Clifford T. Ward fans. Three years after Cliff's diagnosis in 1983, Ann herself developed MS, though she is bravely fighting the effects, and seems 'fortunate' in experiencing bouts of remission.

And probably the most amazing and puzzling tale, which I haven't had chance to authenticate: Sally, the wife of ex-Free keyboard player John Bundrick, herself a Clifford T. Ward devotee, told Pat that a friend of theirs, a sculptress, who had been confined to a wheelchair with multiple sclerosis, literally woke up one morning completely cured. All her symptoms had disappeared, overnight.

Cliff, sadly, sees no such cure, no remission. Technically known as 'chronic progressive', his strain of MS is relentless. There are no 'better days'; only perhaps an easier few hours—for all concerned—on the odd occasion when the sun is upon his face and the birds are singing.

It seems that, despite these many sufferers living silently amongst us, the general ignorance shown towards MS is quite astonishing. The illness only reaches any kind of public perception level during 'awareness weeks' organized by the Multiple Sclerosis Society, or when a celebrity is diagnosed or indeed dies from one of the many associated complications.

Some years ago, the Radio 1 and 208 disc-jockey Stuart Henry was congratulated for his valiant attempts to highlight the torment endured by patient and family, though the current film based on the tragedy of Jacqueline du Pré shows little progress has been made to heighten such understanding. The film may deal with her many personal attributes and the initial side effects of her sickness, but no-one, it seems, dares to portray the true anguish and discomfort inflicted on all within that immediate circle.

And of course, there was dear old Ronnie Lane.

I played Birmingham Town Hall in January 1974, as a nervous support to Slim Chance, Ronnie's terrific post-Faces group. Originally booked for 30 minutes, I had to extend for over an hour because '...Ronnie was late.' He eventually came on stage swigging from a bottle of Newcastle Brown. To all intents and purposes he was drunk. He was brilliant, but he was drunk. Except that he wasn't really drunk. It was a grandiose performance calculated to conceal those sickening, uncontrollable symptoms.

Diagnosed around the same time as Jacqueline, Ronnie Lane also fought MS, for over twenty years. But despite his talent and bravura, despite the best treatment his wealthy friends could provide, he died 3000 miles from home, yet another victim of this 'mysterious illness' that seems to come out of nowhere, to attack and destroy the very qualities such people have in abundance, in fact their very reason for living.

And Molly, wife of Alan Holden, Cliff's head of department way back in the teaching years that preceded his rise to fame.

Alan had been quite correct. In the thirty years since his wife had been diagnosed with the illness, and the ten since she had died, there had been no positive progress in identifying the cause, and most certainly not the cure.

Despite the enormous amount of time and money poured into research, the risk of contracting multiple sclerosis seems destined to remain determined by nothing more than fickle chance, hazard, the roll of the dice...

It was the moment she'd been dreading.

A letter from the bank expressing concern at the mounting overdraft, with no regular payments going in. It was merely a formality, but it showed they were keeping a close watch this time around. And it ended with that loaded invitation: '...Would you be kind enough to make an appointment as soon as possible to discuss the situation?'

Why do these damn letters always drop through the letterbox on Saturday mornings, usually when you're feeling fairly relaxed, and invariably when the sun is shining?

They spent the whole of Saturday driving around Laura Ashley-Land buying dresses, curtains and cushions, her heart leaping at the sound of the till, stuffing the receipt into her new handbag, filling the petrol tank, buying the groceries; the credit cards shining with the friction, before she collapsed exhausted in front of the television. She couldn't sleep so easily these days, and it wasn't because the programme quality was any better...

Nancy and Charlie came around for Sunday lunch, Cliff insisting that Pat show off her new purchases, which she did; the smile, this time, never quite reaching her eyes.

"No, we're fine, Mom," she insisted, over the washing up, as Charlie read the *Sunday Mercury*. Cliff was upstairs resting. The cigarette smoke permeated down through the old oak flooring.

"Well, if there's anything we can do, you must let us know," whispered Nancy, looking down across the valley. Then, straight at Pat:

"Where is all this money coming from? Has Cliff signed another deal?"

Mothers. They always know when something is wrong.

Monday morning, 9.45, Pat phoned the bank. Cliff was outside, on the mower. That bloody mower. That's all he did these days, apart from when they were shopping. Riding around the front lawn, chain-smoking, getting stuck in the mud, calling for her to come and push him out. Sometimes she felt like pushing him over...

She spoke to the manager.

An appointment was made for one of his deputies to come up to the house and have a chat on Thursday morning. That was fine. She could handle him. Cliff would have to keep out of the way, pretend he was 'working'. She didn't want him to get involved. He had never bothered in the past, or whenever he did, it usually went wrong, so keep him clear.

It was Wednesday afternoon, and he was right on time.

'He doesn't look old enough to be driving, let alone deputizing,' she thought, as he stepped out of his red Escort.

He slipped on his jacket, quickly took in the property with what he hoped seemed an experienced eye, flattened down his hair and knocked the door.

She welcomed him, smiled that melting smile, sat him down, made a coffee and began to talk to him, almost like a mother…

As he stood up to leave, he seemed almost embarrassed, nervous. She showed him to the door, and out onto the yard, where they both stood for a while. He remarked on the beautiful property, looking out across the rolling hills. The house-martins screeched and swooped between the ancient eaves, the orchards shimmered in the distant heat. She watched a blue van bounce across the top road, heard the gentle purr of the engine.
Only then, turning back almost casually, did he mention the overdraft.
They both smiled.
"Oh," she told him, "Don't worry. Everything's under control, it's just a matter of cash flow, rather than cash shortage…"
"Of course."
They shook hands, and he strode off to his car, slipping his jacket over that dreadful nylon shirt. He bumped off down the track, piping his twin horns in farewell.
'No problem there,' she thought.
For the moment anyway.

Cliff came in for something to eat about midday. He didn't even enquire how it went, but she mentioned, in passing, that maybe they should sell the house and find somewhere a bit more 'on the level'.
To her surprise he agreed, but it was clear that truthfully, he didn't really care. And who could blame him?
There was nothing to care about any more. Piece by piece, step by insidious step, their life had been chipped away, slowly sinking to the depths of despair. Though brought on by unavoidable circumstances, the situation had been exacerbated by pride, stoicism and stubbornness.

And here, again, I recall Alan Holden. When he spoke to me about Clifford and the awful tragedy that had occurred, he was talking from the very heart of experience. Alan's wife Molly had suffered for twenty long years from the very same illness, and they too had seen the effects, both on themselves and on their acquaintances; the slow but noticeable decline in health and, subsequently, in friends. But perhaps to them it had been all the more acute because of their wide circle of social activity.
Cliff and Pat had never been great socialites. Yet sometimes, late at night, as she lay there dreading the dawn and all it would bring, she would let out that silent scream of nightmares, crying for help from anyone.
There was a cold wind was blowing, and, in their different ways, they

both could feel it, all around, just as Alan and Molly Holden must have felt it, all those years ago.

An accomplished poet, Molly had written of her experience many times over those twenty years of suffering, but in one particular poem, from her collection *Air & Chill Earth*, published by Chatto & Windus in 1971, she draws a haunting, harrowing picture.

In a desperate attempt to convey her symptoms and her helplessness to those of us outside, she draws upon familiar images from childhood, nature and her surrounding world; and yet whilst describing her emotions, she also seems to imply that something—some indefinable thing—had always set her apart; had always been there, nestling within, waiting.

'Illness' by Molly Holden

Poetic justice is imperfectly exemplified in me
who, as a child, as a girl, was persuaded that
I felt as earth feels, the furrows in my flesh,

buttercups curdling from my shoulder blades,
was what I saw. The rain would fall as pertinent on me
as on the lichens on the flint-embedded wall.

I had always a skin too few, identified
with sun-hot blossom on the far side of the road,
felt beneath my own warm envelope of flesh;

the foreign winter that calcined the delicate
bones of the organ-grinder's shuddering monkey.
A ploughed field poniarded my chest.

So now it seems a wry desert that youthful
ecstasies, my earthly husks of joy,
should be so turned about by this disease

that feels like mist upon my fingers, like
a cold wind for ever against my body, and
air and chill earth eternally about my bones.

WINTER

WHERE'S IT GOING TO END?

This is my last message to you: in sorrow seek happiness.

Dostoyevsky

Upper Norchard was put on the market in the autumn of 1988, and, not surprisingly, interest in the beamed, creamed cottage was high. The bank drew back a little, following yet more wordy correspondence relating to the size of the overdraft. The young manager, despite her obvious charm, had not been quite so gullible, for quickly on the heels of his visit, further borrowings were curtailed.

"These damn letters," she cursed. "All my life I've opened letters about money; the lack of it..."

That wasn't strictly true, of course, but it seemed that way right now, as leaves twisted and tossed around the garden, and long shadows stretched ominously across the yard. Another birthday, another year, another winter waiting to chill the bones.

Cliff wasn't empty of ideas. He was finding it difficult to play, and worst of all, impossible to sing, but he could—with great concentration and when the blood flowed freely—put pen to paper, and his ideas were still as original, obscure, quirky...

'Panacea' (Dummy Run)

Not many people know this
But Jesus and a few of his disciples
Turned up last week at Thames Television
But the team there thought it was a bit heavy for them and sent them to the BBC.
Now the team there put there heads together and felt they could sell this/it to America
And asked them if they would start to/by re-enact/ing throwing the money-lenders out of the temple.
James and John were learning quickly, and trying to appease Jesus' increasing anger said, "Let's try Channel 4."

> It coincided with Peter Jay's 'Week In Politics' [this line crossed out]
> So they went along there and were shown into The Video Box
> And this is what was said:-
> Jesus: "You [say] we will reach many people."
> Producer: "And so you will. Just speak into the microphone."
> Jesus: "But I can't see anyone."
> Producer: "But they'll be able to see you."
> Jesus: "Are you for or against my father? "
> Producer: "I don't know. Who is your father."
> Peter: "Lord, this is trickery, let's leave."
> James: "No, no, it's their science. The people will be able to watch and listen to Jesus from a box in their houses."
> Jesus: "What if there are people without a box?"
> Producer: "Everyone has a box, I mean, a television, and they [always] watch it."
> Jesus (turning to the others): "Then we must do this properly, according to Scripture…and confound the box."
> At this he turned and left, followed by the others; Simon, Peter, James and John.
> And the producer stood, shaking his head, with a perplexed and disbelieving smile [crossed out] grin.
>
> I await the Panacea …the real thing.

She found this filed amongst some old lyrics he had left on the bureau. It was undated, but she knew from the writing that it was recent. His once stylish, flowing hand was now child-like, even the spelling was inconsistent, as if he was in a hurry, trying to prove that he could still call upon the creative spirit.
But this kind of stuff was of no use at all. The world was full of scriptwriters; the world was full of *song*writers, but at least Cliff had a track record. Songs were all that mattered, and, as it slowly became clear that there would be no more new ones, she would have to concentrate on the back catalogue.

The 'Sold' sticker was pasted across the sign outside Upper Norchard before they had chance to look for somewhere else, but this time even the oaken beams seemed to join in the sighs of relief.
There would be no more houses of grandeur, no more renovations, no more rock'n'roll. Whatever they could find—within the price bracket this last move would afford them—would have to be a compromise. Cliff was still able to walk, but only short distances, and certainly

wouldn't be able to cope with stairs for much longer, so, maybe a bungalow.

"We were driving around every day, everywhere within the area, through January 1989," Pat told me. "The contract had been signed, we didn't want to lose the sale, but we had nowhere to go. This was before the Misrepresentations Act, and those lovely, cuddly houses in the photographs turned out to be sited next to all manner of things; garages, workshops, pubs, even refuse-tips. I spent days, weeks, driving about Worcestershire, the car littered with brochures, stopping at call-boxes, questioning cyclists, running across to school-kids; trying to find some—unbeknown to me—tatty bungalow hidden behind a cowshed, or tucked at the back of a coal yard.

"To Cliff it was all a huge joke. He sat there, smoking away, winding me up, as we rushed around, knowing we'd have to get back to collect Pol, but knowing also that each day was one day less before we would be out on the street."

They were lucky to get Cherry Hill. They had already viewed it and put in an offer, only to be gazumped by a couple of, well...let's call them speculators. Then, one morning in town, her head spinning with trepidation, Pat bumped into agent Andrew Grant, who told her that the house was now back on the market. A quick rallying of the troops and they put in another offer, which was accepted immediately.

It was ideal for their requirements, though perched somewhat precariously on the edge of a narrow, winding lane dividing quaint Victorian cottages and incongruous modern chalet-style dwellings. Originally built in the early 70s, a rather questionable extension a few years later had resulted in a spacious five-bedroomed, three-bathroomed residence, overlooking the Teme Valley, though almost as Beachy Head precariously overlooks the English Channel.

For house owners in 1989, the price war was raging, at a peak never to be seen again,. totally out of control, fuelled by a government promoting the doctrine of affluence and acquisition. A deal could be struck without question, guided only by the nerve of the seller and the blind acceptance of the buyer. The sale of Upper Norchard, minus overdraft and fees, bought Cherry Hill for cash. It was as easy as that. They cleared everything and borrowed nothing, the house was theirs. All they had to do now was stay afloat, and try to make some capital.

With just Cliff, Pat and Polly, the house was large enough for each of them to find their own patch and build their own nest. Cliff took over one of the back bedrooms for his studio, setting up the Otari 8-track, the mixing desk and the DX-7 keyboard to face onto the garden and its spectacular view over the valley.

From the dining area, there were two manageable steps, the only ones inside the whole building, down into the huge lounge. Here, the glass sliding doors allowed a panorama stretching across the River Teme into the blue hills beyond, and on a perfect day, the mystic Black Mountains of the border country.

In the sloping garden, a neglected cherry tree stood as a sad token of the days when the fruit-laden orchards had leaned down the side of the hill; when the whitewashed Methodist chapel next door, joined at the hip to the former New Inn public house, had been the bustling centre of a bucolic village life, unchanged for aeons.

"Life and coincidences," smiles Pat. "Cliff and I came all the way out here for a drink when we were newly-weds. The landlord of the New Inn was also her collections agent for Pearl Assurance—Mr Morris, my mother called him—so we drove over one night to say hello. He was pleased to see us. No wonder. We seemed to be his only customers. I'm sure he was sleeping behind the bar when we walked in. A peculiar place, all fishing nets, coloured glass baubles and stuffed animals.

"Little did we know… But of course it was right out in the country then, long before they started knocking up retirement bungalows. It's a wonder he lasted as long as he did. Ironically, with all the new homes that appeared after he closed down, he'd probably have managed all right. But he just couldn't hang on. And that was years before drink-driving laws came in. A strange part of the world then, I'd say."

After a short period settling in, Cliff got to work on ideas that didn't involve him recording, but though he wrote to various old contacts, there was little response, so, out of sheer desperation—for it meant swallowing his enormous pride—he dictated a letter to Clive Selwood, now running his own eclectic Strange Fruit label.

Considering that *he* approached *them*, and was offering back catalogue, the sheer audacity makes me smile:

> Dear Clive,
>
> Please find enclosed my suggestion for a new Clifford T. Ward album on your label. Most of the songs are free of any recording and publishing commitment so you may own all if you wish.
>
> For the tracks as you hear them and for ownership of publishing and recording and for my commitment I would need an advance of £10,000.
>
> I hope you will be interested,
>
> Best wishes,
>
> Cliff.

There must have been some telephone conversation preceding this note; no-one, not even Cliff, would deliver such an arrogant proposition out of the blue, and there is no mention of exactly what he was submitting song-wise, but in his reply, Clive mentions, in passing, the poor quality of the cassette copy, hoping that masters still exist, then agrees to the idea of re-releasing the *Singer-Songwriter* album, from their Dandelion days, plus the Irish album, *Both Of Us*, on a double CD, and confirms the royalty they would be prepared to pay.

He concludes, quite truthfully, that, '...we simply do not have £10,000 to advance. We do reasonably well with our catalogue, but are not in a position to pay advances to anybody!

'I hope you are improving. We think of you a lot.'

Under the working title of *Clifford T. Ward - Now and Then*, they corresponded over the next few days, finalizing with Clive's letter of 15th August, 1989, in which he confirmed agreed royalties and enclosed a letter contract, copy of which Clifford was to sign and return.

But, as the Beatle said, 'Life is the thing that gets in the way when you're making plans', and as his illness became noticeably worse, the project gathered dust, and was eventually swept under the carpet.

Another visit to see the specialist in London was imminent, and Pat was desperate for some assistance; Cliff was becoming intolerable. Come back, Ron Bridges...

"I can't remember them actually leaving Castle Weir, I'd finished working for them some time earlier. We had the occasional chat on the telephone, probably exchanged cards at Christmas, that was about it, after such an intense working relationship. I did go up to Trimpley once, up to Thresholds, just passing through. Cliff was quite happy, he played me a demonstration record of one of his new songs, 'Contrary', which I thought was lovely. That's what I liked about him, David, there was no side to him. I was just a painter-decorator, yet he considered my opinion was worth something...

"After that we just drifted apart. I didn't hear anything about them for three or four years, until one day Sandra saw Cliff, Pat and Polly in Hereford. They had a chat, she gave Sandra their new number and that was that. Sandra was convinced that something was wrong with Cliff. Then one of the women in the village, a doctor's wife, told Sandra that Cliff had been seen drunk in Kidderminster. Well, I knew that couldn't be right, so I telephoned them, asking if we could come over. I wasn't being nosy, I was genuinely concerned. Pat didn't say anything about MS, but she did warn me not to expect to see the Clifford T. Ward I used to know. So, we came over to Cherry Hill [their present house] to where they'd just moved from Dunley, to this large bungalow and realized it was because Cliff was unable to walk unsupported, he certainly couldn't manage stairs. It was 1989, on Polly's 10th birthday. It really shook me, and how quickly it had all happened. All that had happened in just a couple of short years.

"But I came round again, brought Bert [the gardener from Castle Weir] and his wife Mary. It was all very sad. Very sad. But y'know, he still made us laugh. Then we came over to a party, met Roger Bowen and the gang—I think you were there—and this time we maintained contact. Later on, Cliff was referred to the National, in Queen Square, London, to see a neurologist, so I offered to take him down. My mistake…

"Sandra, my daughter Tina, and me, took him down the first time, left him there overnight [by arrangement…Ken Wright, who had re-established contact, brought him back the next day, after tests had been carried out], although he protested. 'Take me home, Ron. Phone Pat,' he was saying. 'I don't wanna stay in this bloody awful place.' I can understand it. Terrible, depressing, it was. Iron bars on the windows, about ten inches between the beds, and Cliff was left at the top of this long room, on his own. God, it was like an asylum."

Pat stayed there once, but never again:

"They gave me this tiny fold-up bed, tucked away in a corner, in a room that people were walking through all night. I didn't sleep a wink."

Ron continues:

"Then I took him down again. That was a…bit more fun… He was still difficult, except more so, ordering me about like a lackey and I'd *offered* to do this! It was a boiling hot day and when we got there, with Cliff in a wheelchair, I pushed him up this bloody great slope to the reception. When we checked in, they didn't know who we were and who we wanted. I showed the girl Cliff's appointment letter and she sent us all the way back down and around the other side of the block. When we got *there*, same thing again. Cliff was at the end of his tether, I was sweating like a pig. He's a big weight, Cliff. He was just telling me to take him home when—and only by chance—some nurse walked past and overheard him moaning. I told her I was looking for this consultant that nobody else seemed to have heard of, and she just pointed us straight across the corridor to his office. There it was. Name on the door. The very person that nobody else seemed to think existed. Including us. He took Cliff in, gave him a thorough check over; very concerned about his swallowing, checked his movement, speech, hearing, then sent me all the way up three flights of stairs (the bloody lifts were being serviced…) for some pills for Cliff to take. Then we had to go and see somebody *else,* by which time he was really on a moan. Kept on asking for a 'f-a-a-g', so I had to take him outside. Then he'd got no matches, so I had to ask a workman. He got talking to Cliff, after I'd told him who he was, y'know—'That's Clifford T. Ward, famous singer-songwriter'… 'Oh, I've heard of him'… 'Well go and have a chat to him, while I go for a pee'… Give him his due, he was still talking when I got back. probably couldn't get away! But then, Cliff liked talking to people. He had a great affection for people, no matter who they were. Then we had to go back inside and he started up again. And I can understand it. Nobody seemed to know what they were doing. They wouldn't even give me a coffee! Gave Cliff one, but said I'd have to get mine from a machine somewhere, probably on the top floor!... It was like Fred Karno's army. All seemed a bloody waste of space to me." And then in his no-nonsense manner, " Or an exercise in staff training.

"Driving back we got lost. I should have known better than to believe Cliff when he said he knew the way. Lost in London, lost on the motorway. We ended up in Banbury. Banbury! He thought it was *funny*. Sitting there, hiding behind those bloody sunglasses, smoking his head off, that big moon-face smile."

But Ron, as ever, rolled with the punches and delivered his charge back to Cherry Hill, before riding off into the sunset, another thirty-five miles or so through the lanes and valleys of Herefordshire. A good man, a rare breed. And Cliff still continued, even at this late stage, in playing games, to those who didn't know the grim reality.

Ray Hume hadn't seen Cliff since his late teens. He'd heard of his success, of course, but even in such a small, thinly populated area, their paths had never crossed, ironically until the illness was taking its grip.

"The last time I saw Cliff was about 1989, Christmas time. I'd grown disillusioned with music; I was teaching guitar but felt unable to show the tolerance needed to accommodate tone-deaf pupils who had no sense of rhythm, well, no sense period...so I'd taken a position as part-time warehouseman at Marks & Spencers in Worcester.

"He came around the back of the shop to collect some goods they'd just bought. He recognized me straight away, which was encouraging, as I was feeling pretty well lost at that time. We chatted for a couple of minutes, until, in classic Ray Hume tradition, I put my foot in it by saying that I gathered he wasn't too well. He immediately went on the defensive, insisting that he was fine. I tried to compensate for my lack of subtlety, saying something like, '...oh ... is it your *wife* that's not very well.?' as I'd heard there'd just been some incident in the store where one of them had fallen over and the other had picked them up. It was one of those gossipy, third-hand tales that never quite come to you unadulterated. He was glad of the escape route and bluffed that his wife had indeed been ill..."

Well, not quite bluffed. Pat *had* been into hospital, but was now fully recovered. It was nothing serious, nothing that a woman can't handle...

Poor old Pat. This continual charade of having to lean on each other in public, rather than openly admit the problem, of never knowing when or where Cliff would lose his balance and collapse or stumble, of having to hold on for dear life to a sudden dead weight, twice her size. Strangers would assume the worst, that he was drunk or drugged, yet still he would not admit—or *show* to have admitted—his illness.

But this was only on home territory. In the Irish media he now openly discussed his condition, almost making himself a figurehead for multiple sclerosis, though again, he had initially tried to hide the symptoms.

Way back in August John McKenna's RTE radio series 'Tower Of Song' had featured Cliff and his music, which John had recorded some time earlier at Dunley, during a visit to the UK.

"He came up from London with a lady friend. I don't think he drove a car," Pat told me. "He and Cliff did the interview in the lounge while I looked after John's companion, showing her around the house and the garden. We gave them an hour or so before we came back, but they were still at it, so she and I went upstairs and sat in one of the bedrooms, twiddling our thumbs. I always remember her saying, as we discussed life, love etc., something that kind of took me aback, being the shy retiring person I was.

"She said that she thought women should marry women; that we really didn't need men at all."

'Tower Of Song' was followed a couple of years later by another RTE programme entitled 'Coming To Terms', John this time acting as producer and which he recorded at Cherry Hill, using Barbara Jordan as the interviewer. Here, at last, both Clifford and Pat talked candidly of the way their lives had been changed by the insidious advances of the illness. It was powerful radio, and produced an overwhelmingly sympathetic reaction from the Irish people. Yet he *would not* promote his condition at home. In his mind—nurtured by the manner in which his mother, and then his daughter, had surmounted disability—to acquiesce would be seen as a sign of weakness.

John McKenna was just one of the many figureheads of the Irish broadcasting network who considered Clifford T. Ward as being 'up there with the best of them', and is proud to have been able to contribute to his successful career in Ireland.

I spoke to him, asking when they met, and in that warm, eloquent Irish manner, with words flowing and eyes glowing, he recalled how it all began:

"How many times does the first hearing of a song lodge in your head so that you remember the exact moment and the exact place in which you heard it? And I mean exact.

"I can remember clearly—and few things are clear any more—where I was when I first heard 'Home Thoughts from Abroad'. I was driving towards Athy from my home in Castledermot, rounding the bend at Kilkea church, when it came on the radio. As soon as I cleared the bend, I pulled off the road, stopped the car and sat listening, entranced, overawed by its sheer beauty. Then I drove straight to the local record shop and they didn't have it in stock! It took them a week to get it!

"The song, the singer, the voice, they were so different. There was a simplicity about it that you only find in the greatest pieces of music, or poems, or novels.

"I was a teacher then, and I bought everything of Cliff's that I could find. I put his lyrics into hand-out form and the kids lapped them up. We played his music in class. Teenage boys and girls, teachers in the staff room, young lovers in the dance-halls; he and his music meant something to every one of them. He transcended all ages, backgrounds, beliefs.

"Years later I started working in radio, at RTE. Clifford came in to do one of his many interviews with Val Joyce. I was like a child, asking him to autograph all his albums that I'd brought with me that day. We chatted. His modesty and courtesy made a lasting impression upon me. Later still, through Peter Grogan, I made further contact and we recorded a programme for the 'Tower Of Song' series. Meeting him at his home in Worcestershire, getting to spend the day with his family, talking with him about the songs, was marvellous. And throughout, he'd keep asking me, 'What do *you* think of it?'

"What did *I* think? I wasn't thinking. I was just overjoyed to be in his company. Three things stick in my mind about that meeting. Cliff's genuine warmth and humility about his work; Pat's real welcome when we got to the house; and Cliff's oncoming illness, which he tried so hard to hide. The signs were obvious, but he ignored them. He was lost in his music and it was a privilege to be there, lost with him.

"The response to the programme was great. Ireland loves his songs, the voice and the care that shines through. It isn't ego, it isn't a front, it isn't a performance. It's real," and he takes a deep breath, half-turning to look over his shoulder, "unlike the 'friendliness' of some other songwriters I've met. But that's another story!

"The second time I visited Cliff and Pat was to record a 'Coming To Terms' programme. This series concerned people who were dealing with tragedy; the vicar in Hungerford; Jim Swire, whose daughter died at Lockerbie, and others. But amazingly there was no hint of tragedy about Cliff. Physically he was beginning to really suffer, yet we left the house lightened, warmed and, I have to say, well fed by Pat. *Very* well fed."

I sensed some spirituality in his approach, his comments.

"I don't know whether I believe in God—agnostic some days, somedays not—but I don't understand suffering. But then," and he gives a quiet laugh, "Cliff would probably explain it to me.

"What I *do* believe in is the power of words and music. There are so many songs of Cliff's I could say have made a difference to me, but there's one above all else that confronts tragedy on a grand scale, yet loss and loneliness on a personal level, for the writer *and* the listener. 'A Day To Myself '. If he never wrote another word or note, that would be such a phenomenal piece of work to have produced. Sheer beauty."

"Let's do a bunk, Ken," she whispered, looking straight into his face. But he knew she was teasing him, didn't he…?

The place was packed, another Friday night at Brintons canteen. Cliff was in the changing room, either lacquering his hair or retching with stage fright. Graham was tuning up, 'Clang…poing, clang…poing…'

"Come on, let's do a runner." She grabbed his arm, pulling him doorwards.

"Pat, don't be silly." He gave his forced, staccato laugh, and turned to the front of the stage, catching Terry's eye.

"Don't you fancy me any more?"

He looked sidewards at her, pretty as a picture, standing there. That look, even at twenty.

"Pat, I've got to set these drums up before Cliff comes out, or he'll throw a wobbly. I'll speak to you later. In the interval."

She'd had enough. She knew Cliff was seeing someone else, that he was in love, 'again'… He always had to justify his affairs by being 'in love'; the romantic ideal, hearts-a-beating, pulses racing, 'But, this is *love.*' That supposedly made it okay… The others laughed at him, or just took it for granted. Singers and girls, well, it's the norm. But he was *married* to *her*. But then, he was married to his music, and he kept the two quite separate. As if he was two different people.

Ken was keen, they were close, though they hadn't been *that* close… and she thought, well, why not? If other people do it.

She watched him drum his way through the first set, as she danced around the floor near the side of the stage. Cliff was off, on another planet: '24 Hours From Tulsa', 'Just Ask Your Heart', 'Bachelor Boy'; they were good, well rehearsed, and the girls shuffled around at his feet, trying hard to win a smile, a nod, a dedication. Ken pounded on, trying his best to maintain his dignity, knowing that she was there, staring right through the patina of his concentration, waiting.

Bloody hell. What was she going to say? Was she serious?

No, she wasn't. She was teasing him, but it was interesting how much she had thrown him, and she laughed when he jumped off the stage, hot and just a little bit concerned.

"Well you were keen enough on Tuesday. It's a good job it was your Mini we were in," she whispered, a touch too loudly for his liking.

"Couldn't keep your hands off me...," and she brushed his cheek with her lips.
"Pat! What if Cliff sees us?"
"Naw, he's too busy," she replied, half-turning to face the crowd of dancers.

Next day he called her. Could they meet?
Yes, they could.

She lay alone and almost lost, in her giant bed, listening to the house creaking at the end of another empty day, amazed at how long ago it all had been. Had that *really* been her?
She remembered everything so well, but remembered as if she'd been told, or seen it in a film; there was no feeling of experience, no touch, no smell that evoked *any*thing of those young, vibrant, living years. And now, here she was, almost in middle-age, and her life seemed to have gone full circle. Another birthday, gone, forgotten; another anniversary, forgotten, gone.
"It was always up to me—as I suppose it is in most marriages—to remember the children's birthdays, sort out Christmas and so on," Pat told me recently, "but in all the thirty-five years of our marriage, Cliff never acknowledged *one* anniversary or bought me a birthday present. Never. Ever. Oh, except for show, to impress. There was one instance, around 1973, when we were at The Spinney, he wrote me a cheque for £100—a lot of money in those days—in front of Martin and Sam and gave it to me with an off-hand flourish of public generosity, telling me to buy anything I wanted with it. The boys were absolutely knocked out, as he intended them to be. But I knew, as Cliff did, that there wasn't even *£20* in the account. It was an empty, but effective gesture, and I knew better than to raise the matter again. Even days afterwards, Sam was asking me what I'd bought, or what I was going to buy. 'A sweet occasion such as this...', indeed. That's a joke. What they call poetic licence I suppose...," and she shrugged, looking resignedly away across the room.

An invitation dropped through my letter box: Ken Wright's 50th birthday party; March 30th, 1990, Arley Village Hall.
Despite his incredibly long-standing relationship with Stourport's Maggie Hannaby, throughout the 'fame' years and times previous, he had—seemingly 'overnight'—married a London girl nearly two years

ago, almost bouncing the pointer off the local Richter scale—'How could he *do* that?'—and had recently become a father, his wife Vanessa giving birth to a son, christened James.

Ken had been up to see Cliff and Pat in their latest house, whether from curiosity or concern didn't really matter; it was good to see him after so long, almost 20 years in fact. He had never visited them at any of their 'posh' houses, Lower Hollin or Castle Weir, The Spinney or Upper Norchard, but now, as time, the healer, trifled old wounds, and as the sorcerer coped with new ones, there was every reason to let bygones be. It had been uncomfortable for a few minutes, naturally, but Cliff and Ken's sparkling, sparring repartee had lost none of its bite or wit over the years, and the tension soon lifted. The stay was brief, but the spell was broken. They sat around the lounge coffee table, sizing each other up over cups and cakes, making small talk about music, the children, the government, Salman Rushdie's *fatwa*, Ken's impending early retirement and, of course, Cliff's state of health.

Ken, like most others at the time, knew only the basic facts about multiple sclerosis, and Cliff was quick to assure him that specialist treatment was forthcoming, and would soon rid his body of the symptoms.

"I'm still recording and writing. I've got my own studio in the back there," he said, waving his hand in no particular direction. "I'm planning a new album this year, and it's going…to…be…*great*."

But he didn't say who with, he just drew on his cigarette. Ken looked across to Pat. Her gaze fell to the ground and she was silent.

That had been last autumn.

It was now 1990, and the last decade of the 20th century had begun a little confusingly, with Jason and Kylie representing the sorry state of pop music, and Nelson Mandela's release, after 27 years, bringing a spark of hope to the sorry state of the world.

Cliff had been down to London again, and they had poked and prodded him again, recommending yet more pills and procedures, to which he defiantly thumbed his nose. All indications were that things were never going to improve, but, he would keep on keeping on, irrespective. He would not pay lip service to their trials and suggestions, he would fight it *his* way, and, as time went on, Pat realized that his way was to ignore it, pretend it wasn't there; that any setback was just a bad hair day, tomorrow would be fine…

Arley is still a pretty village. Two approach routes, half-a-mile apart, twist down through tree-lined lanes from the A442, to the watercolour riverbank, where fishermen sit the days away, gazing across the silver Severn to the lush meadows opposite.

The rustic cottages, the Norman church, it will never change, because it is safe from traffic. This is a dead end, a precious jewelled cul-de-sac, hidden from the roar. Only the ferry has gone, superseded by a large, tubular framed footbridge, which, after a hard day's fishing, leads the thirsty anglers across to what is now the only hostelry within walking distance.

In 1990 however, on the village side, The Valencia was still trading as a hotel. A long, neo-Gothic building, with leaded windows and panelled stairways, overlooking the river, it had once been a popular meeting place during the boisterous, affluent sports car days of the sixties, but was now on its last legs, struggling to avert the fate of so many similar country inns hit by driving laws and fun pubs.

The beginning of the seventies saw Jess Roden's Bronco living out the hippie dream on a small farm off the beaten track, not a mile from here, where they had written and rehearsed their Island albums, concocting *Smoking Mixture* in their rented Country Home… But those days were gone, and here, now, in what was probably one of its last re-creations of such times, the guests who were staying over for Ken's party had booked in for the night, and were dressed up and ready to make their way to the village hall.

It was a gentle spring evening, the light fading into dusk as Carole and I drove into the car park across the road from the hall. We were feeling somewhat apprehensive, deliberating who would be there, and indeed surprised that we had even been asked; it had been a good many years since our social paths had crossed with anyone in this area.We had been safely hidden in the depths of the Herefordshire countryside for some 12 years. The invitation had come right out of the blue.

We popped into The Valencia for an early evening drink, hoping to see at least someone we knew, or have some indication of the mood of the crowd, but it had been fruitless. I recognized no-one, and was not exactly encouraged by what I did see, but, it had been a long drive, and despite a last minute deliberation outside the hall, we took a deep breath and walked in.

Ken made us particularly welcome as he strode towards us, proudly carrying his son, James. We were introduced to the lovely Vanessa, and after a brief exchange of pleasantries, headed straight for the bar area, far away from the quick-steppers and fox-trotters. If we were going to know anyone, that is where they would be. Sure enough, the celebrations and celebrities were already beginning to compete for attention, as old friends struggled to remember the names of even older friends. Carole and I spoke to Bev Pegg, Robert Plant, Stan Webb, Johnny Haynes and many other faces from the past, but, as the evening

wore on, and my courage became suitably Dutched, I left Carole talking to Diz and Harry Rowlands and made my way to the corner of the room, to a man sitting in a small group, somewhat distanced from the crowd, his long blond hair leaving little doubt as to his identity.
Here, after 28 years, I finally met up again with Clifford T. Ward.
And here also, after I had introduced myself and been agreeably surprised at his knowledge of my music, a vivacious, henna-haired woman, dressed in a Laura Ashley frock—returning to her husband with a glass of red wine—then smiled down at me as I sat talking. I stood up quickly, offering her seat back, holding out my hand to introduce myself.
There was no need. She pre-empted me, rather imperiously, I thought:
"I know. You must be Dave Cartwright..."
We'd never met, but I had formed impressions from the few pictures I'd seen. But this wasn't the meek, subdued woman standing shyly next to her partner on the *Home Thoughts* cover. Things had changed... Or we all had been wrong.
Pat had daughter Polly to attend to, so I continued talking to Cliff for a few more minutes, then rejoined the crowd.
After an hour or so, the inevitable musician roll-call began. Stan Webb leaped up on stage to join Bev and Ken, who were the nucleus of the house band (yes, even on his 50th birthday, Ken was setting the tempo for the evening) so, being the shy, retiring person I am, and suspecting my name would eventually be called out, I decided to say my goodbyes. As we reached the door, I turned to see Stan, in his element, giving, as ever, all he'd got, and thinking how strange and charming it all was. A village hall, with Formica tables and a commemorative plaque to the war dead, hidden deep in the heart of Worcestershire; a gathering of middle-aged musicians, some of whom had touched the stars, some of whom were still climbing, others who had played for the sheer love of it, and some who had tried, and failed. But, whatever the status, all those who had experienced the thrill, the pleasure, the magic, of performing, were indeed the lucky ones. No matter how fleeting the hour, it had always made up for in height what it lacked in length. It was good to be there.
We drove the dark roads home, reaching Ledbury in time to promenade the dog and scrape the cats off the radiators.
I made a mental note to telephone Cliff within a couple of days, but in fact I wrote to him, suggesting we meet up again. In a six-page Basildon-Bonded letter, I virtually poured my heart out to someone who was, in effect, a stranger.
I referred, acutely—but in retrospect a little sycophantically—to our spectacularly different careers:

> ...Still, we both bought pleasure to a lot of people, though yours is more enduring; good albums last an awful lot longer than one-night stands. You sold records and songs, I sold bums on seats; you can't file those away in alphabetical order for posterity ... there can't be a greater waste of a life than, night after night, year after year, playing to ecstatic yet anonymous pockets of people all over the world. Conversely, there can't be a greater reward than hearing your own songs sung by the great and respected. I congratulate you, sincerely...

and, referring to one of my most enduring memories of frustration:

> ...I distinctly remember eating fish'n'chips, (from the newspaper), car windows wide open, [parked] in a lay-by somewhere in Derbyshire, before a gig, thinking, 'Bloody 'ell, I bet Clifford T. Ward's not doing this...'

I wasn't too surprised that I didn't receive an immediate response; in fact it was almost three weeks later, by which time we had moved house. Pat had obviously put some detective work into finding our new ex-directory number.

Carole answered the telephone and passed me on to Cliff. The voice was slow, precise, husky, friendly. He thanked me for my letter, I made a few inane comments—to which he respectfully responded—then he asked Carole and me over for supper, '...as soon as you like...'

It was arranged for the following weekend, a Saturday evening late in May.

We took the Tenbury road from Worcester, where the cherry was 'hung with bloom along the bough', past the silhouetted clock tower at Abberley and through the slumbering hop-fields, eventually to reach the bungalow, almost hidden behind a row of giant leylandii, just as the light was beginning to fade, and the hills were blue shadows in the distance.

Pat introduced us to daughter Polly, and we all joined Cliff in the lounge. After we congratulated them both on becoming grandparents—first-born Debbie had recently given birth to a daughter, christened Ellie—the conversation soon got around to teaching. Carole was about to take up a position in London—her age and years of experience putting her too high on the salary scale for local schools—and Cliff was in fine form, polite, humorous and attentive. Pat hardly said a word the whole evening. She fetched and carried, but was noticeably silent, and there was little attempt to persuade us to stay when we at last decided to make a move. Cliff's interest had waned, he appeared tired—or

bored—and I'm sure everyone was relieved as we shook hands or kissed cheeks, and said goodnight.
On the way home, we pulled in at The Hundred House, that impressive, Georgian hotel standing in welcome at the busy junction leading to Stourport and Worcester, from Tenbury and Bromyard. At that moment, as I sat staring into my pint, I had no idea that this was one of the many venues Cliff Ward and The Cruisers had used for practice almost thirty years ago, when Bob Tansley was Mine Host and the world was still young. A few overweight, ruddy-faced gentlemen farmers stood around the bar guffawing, a party of five or six—a family maybe—sat in the large candlelit dining room finishing their main course, a couple of white-shirted businessmen, miles from home on a Saturday night, sat in the large bow-window, planning the weekend assault on the agricultural fair in Tenbury, and that was it. Life in the country. Life...In...The...Country.
I looked at Carole.
It had been a strange night. I couldn't quite put my finger on it, but something hadn't quite gelled. Not exactly a disaster, but towards the end of the evening it had grown uncomfortable, there had been too many silences. The invariable awkwardness of strangers hadn't lessened. It was hard to say why, but one thing Carole and I agreed on. Pat's silence had been deafening...

It was a few weeks again before I made contact.
I realized, in my role as a freelance presenter on Radio Wyvern, that the Clifford T. Ward story would most certainly make a good one-hour special, if I could catch him in the right mood. He was still a well-respected figure, if only in terms of local interest, and, without intending to capitalize on his illness, I was sure that many people who knew of him in the seventies were probably unaware of his predicament.
I popped over one afternoon, late summer. He was sitting out on the patio, dressed in shorts and a black tee-shirt, smoking. His skin was red from the sun. The air was warm, almost tropical. A couple of buzzards circled lazily overhead, a dog barked in the distance, a lawn mower rattled, a tractor roared down the lane. Peace in the valley...?
Pat poured me a glass of wine. We small-talked, and then, as if by telepathy, Cliff turned to me and said, "David, I think you should do a programme about me for your radio station."
"What a great idea," I laughed, and that was it. He was ready and more than willing. If I'd had my tape recorder with me, we could have started that very moment, but I was travelling light, as usual. No scoops for me...

But the plan was hatched, and two days later I went around again, suitably armed—or so I thought—for the Clifford T. Ward interview.

Radio Wyvern was possibly the last of the true local independent stations, based in the city of Worcester. It opened with a great flurry of excitement and much blowing of trumpets, in October 1982, and in July, 1984 I was asked to present a Tuesday evening folk programme to which I gladly agreed. Little did I know…

At that time I was still living in Ledbury. I had no experience whatsoever with broadcasting, other than doing the rounds of stations whenever a record of mine escaped. But I bluffed them into accepting that, well, a desk was a desk. I knew my way around a recording console, and anyway, I'd have a producer, wouldn't I?

Martin Henfield was the programme controller in those early days. We had met during my days performing on BBC TV's first daytime national magazine programme, 'Pebblemill At One', in the mid-seventies. He welcomed me to the Wyvern fold, told me the salary—with a decidedly embarrassed grin, saying that £10.00 per show was the going rate for all freelancers—and quickly showed me the studio, the toilets, and the Folk Library. This consisted of two Steeleye Span albums, one Jake Thackray collection, and a quite horrendous Scottish compilation, the cover of which depicted a dozen or so mad-looking Caledonian 'folk artistes'—of whom I knew perhaps two—dressed in kilts, shawls and bonnets, entitled *Welcome To McTavish's Kitchen.* Hmmm. Things were not looking good.

But, as usual, I went along with it. I turned up at 8.30 p.m. the following Tuesday, July 24th, carrying a dozen albums and a few notes, only to find that, yes, I was on air at 9.00 p.m. precisely, but that I was on my own in the studio, to play the records, talk the intros, take any telephone calls (as in police, fire, ambulance and nutters…) and insert the ads. Alone. Solo. One. Uno. The toilets were on the other side of the building. Welcome to the big-time… But that's another book.

Anyhow, things worked out fine. Seven years later, 1991, I was still running my own show, still virtually saying and playing whatever I wanted—but from my own collection—and bringing in live guests, musicians, poets, traffic wardens, in fact anybody I happened to bump into that seemed interesting, and without any interference whatsoever from the man upstairs; literally having a ball. Oh, and still on £10.00 a week…

So money—and therefore equipment—was not readily at one's disposal via Radio Wyvern. Cut-backs began from day one. The cleaners were asked not to walk in front of the managing director brushing the carpet (though he was *always* to be addressed as 'Sir' or 'Boss'…) and within the first five years the staff was not halved, but quartered. (We were to be hanged and drawn later…) News-room strikes, union-backed, brought no resolution to personnel disputes, and soon the station—at night in particular—took on the appearance of the Mary Celeste: dark, empty rooms, unmanned studios, unopened mail. And this was show business. Listeners, sitting in their red Fiestas, cosy council living rooms, or pool-room pubs, visualized the hustle-bustle of America-FM: hip jocks, efficient, sexy PAs and frantic news-room banter; the loosening of neckties, the scratching of heads, those dramatic moments of indecision. Not quite so. When I signed off at 10.03 p.m., I secured and closed the building, then ran hell-for-leather down the side passage—as I had done as a child, back from our outside toilet at the top of the yard—to the car-park, fearing someone would leap out of the darkness and force me back in and take over the airwaves. A *coup de radio*.

Thus, with such a low-key operation, outside broadcasts were, well almost non-existent. Oh, there was a portable tape recorder, a battery operated Scheur reel-to-reel, which worked fine, as long as you held the microphone at exactly 28 degrees and placed the machine on its end.

Well, that's the one I had to use. I sat on the floor of Cliff's bedroom, suitably angled, as he proceeded to relate his life; beautifully, succinctly and—in his own recherché manner—dramatically, embellishments by the dozen. And I fell for it hook, line and sinker. But that didn't matter. People will believe what they want to believe, and I was impressed by his sensibilities, his wonderful humour and apparent acceptance of his situation.

The recording, however, was a disaster. I won't say any more on the matter, but it was impossible to use. It was a good thing in a way—though explaining my incompetence to him wasn't—for it was decided that the best way to do this thing properly was for Muhammed to come to the Mountain. Pat agreed to bring Cliff into the studio on a Sunday afternoon, when all was quiet, and we would use the 'high-tech' Revox. Fortunately, it also gave me a chance to do a little more research into Clifford's music; to my shame, but I think understandably, I also knew him only for 'Gaye', 'Home Thoughts…' and a couple more. This would be much more professional interview—if Cliff was in the right frame of mind—which, Pat was at great pains to state, would be in the lap of the gods.

But the gods were kind, and I had a wonderful afternoon.

Pat drove up at the pre-arranged time, hitting the car-park, with it's pot-holed tarmac, at exactly 3.00 p.m. I watched in awe as this gamine figure manhandled her dead-weight husband into his wheelchair and rolled him into the studio, without so much as a puff of breath. Well, at least not from her…

He looked around, quickly taking everything in with one shaded glance. He was in a mischievous mood: "Er…what's this thing then, Day-vid?"

pointing at the yellow-capped studio microphone; and, looking at the Revox: "Is...dat...one...of....dem...tape-recorder things?" Pat gave a him short, sharp warning to behave, and he automatically obeyed.

It was a heart-warming and often hilarious interview.

Me: "Do you think romanticism is dead?"

He: "Ye-ea-h".

And about the craft of songwriting; me: "...so what do you think?"

He: "David, I...think...I...want...a...p-i-i-dd-le."

But slowly, and, as ever, fluently, told his story, though '...my....dear wife Pat...' sitting right at his side, refused—even when asked—to speak; her eyes throughout the two hours cast downwards at the floor. It was not, as she said later, her interview, though I felt that was a poor excuse.

However, despite his apparent openness, he was up to his tricks again. Here I encountered my first taste of Clifford T. Ward, the story-teller. He talked convincingly of a concert that he had on tape, and wanted me to include in the show. It had—he said—been recorded live in Boston, Massachusetts, during a break in the making of *New England Days*. He led me, by the nose, through into my introduction, emphatic in his statement that '...this was done with the wonderful American musicians at a local theatre on our night off...' and, without listening to it, I took the show home to edit into the programme.

It threw me into a slight quandary. As soon as I played the whimsically-titled *Boston Supper Party*, I knew that this was bogus. Oh, the songs were real enough, brilliant numbers I had never heard before, but I squirmed in disbelief at the canned and somewhat unconvincing applause; the fan shouting her 'lur-ve' for 'Cli-i-ff-o-rr-d'; and above all—though I had not heard him for many a year—I recognized the unmistakable 'American' voice of Kidderminster's very own G-LTK host, Mr Leon Tipler. This wasn't a Boston Supper Party, this was a 'bedroom supper party'.

For a moment or two, I was a bit insulted that Cliff expected me to embrace this bunkum. Whilst introducing the songs, his voice bore the full-throated slur of his illness, yet his singing was as pure and fluid as ever. But then, as time went on, I decided that the music was justification enough; with the inclusion of this 'concert', I could easily extend the programme to make a two-hour special, and—heavens above—I would hopefully get £20.00 for that...

So I spent the next two weeks editing at home on my newly-acquired Revox, checking with Pat that any amendments or inserts were in order, qualifying certain statements (or accepting them at face value as pure Clifford-isms), and putting the whole thing into shape.

It truly became a labour of love. Splicing analogue tape, to me, is one of the most stimulating of pastimes, getting everything just so. Listen,

rewind, chalk, cut, join; the purpose of precision, feeding the music in over the voice, fading out. Ah. 'Tis no wonder that everything today sounds so cold, so sterile, so what?-ish; with Digital Editing Suites shaping Digital Recordings sung by Digital Voices... It's all light years away from real music, from the...
Oi !!
Sorry.

I purposely included only songs from Clifford's first two albums for the musical links, letting the 'Boston concert' draw in any lesser known numbers, but I *did* include a few home demos Pat had passed on to me, especially three spoken-word pieces. These were nothing more than Cliff and his Otari, fooling around with Bill Giles, A Rat, and the Education of the Masses, all of which I thought hilarious, true to Tom Crite's sacred memory, but which, sadly, fell on many a deaf ear.

Considering how pleased everyone at Wyvern seemed to be with the finished product, the bizarre programme scheduling took me back a little: 2.00 p.m. on Christmas Day, 1991. Naturally, I protested. Naturally, I was ignored. Even my two-hour special with Robert Plant, something else I'd spent weeks putting together, was given the Christmas cold-turkey spot, 2.00 p.m. Boxing Day, but even so, the reaction to Clifford's broadcast took us all by surprise. Letters came in from all over the county, many of them asking for the show to be repeated, and on a more convenient listening date.

And it was repeated, but as a one-hour programme, with the concert, this time, held back in the wings. Not that anyone had objected to a bit of poetic licence by Cliff, the songs were what mattered, after all, but Wyvern had decided to enter the special for the Sony Radio Awards, and their rules for specialist category decreed a one-hour show.

In accordance with the plan of presentation, I wrote a letter of introduction to the judging panel—a brief précis of subject and content, to accompany the tape—and that was it. I heard nothing more. In fact, I'm still waiting, seven years later. Communication was not one of Radio Wyvern's stronger points, but they were good days. As long as you were on the outside.

The show, and its warm response, seemed to re-awaken Clifford's interest in publicity, but, as I began to visit the house more often, I realized that the old showbiz maxim, 'Don't read it, measure it', had, this time around, become Clifford T. Ward's *raison d'être*.

Within a month he handed me a tape of a play he had written, *Love Story In France*, purporting to be the true story behind 'Gaye', his hit single of long ago. We sat in the lounge listening; Cliff, Pat and I. It was all new to me, of course, but Pat must have heard it many times, and her glances at me across the room said as much.

Leon had supervised—and participated in—the recording, and Caroline Bovey, whom I knew from a few years back, played 'the French girl', Gaye. Once again, apart from the sheer beauty of the songs, it was terribly amateurish; corny, cloying, certainly not broadcasting standard—even for local radio—and I, quite uncharacteristically, told him so. He wasn't in the least offended, in fact he just shrugged, mumbled something that sounded suspiciously like '...Idjyat...', and we all had a nice cup of tea.

But a short while later, Pat told me that they had been approached by *Take-a-Break*, a weekly pond-life magazine, who wanted to feature the story—at the going rate—and that Cliff had agreed. A sharp intake of breath.

It was everything you would have expected from such a magazine, but the last thing you would have expected from such a respected public figure. Built around the cassette-story, the front page headlined 'I live with the guilt of my lover's death', whilst the article itself told of Clifford's 'anguish' at the suicide of his French girlfriend and how her parents had forgiven him for the tragedy caused by her unrequited love. But, to top it all, there, slap bang in the middle of the page was a picture of 'Gaye', with her bobbed, brown hair and halter-neck top, sitting on a spring-green lawn, smiling for her lover.

Pat, Castle Weir, 1976.

This was the greatest indicator yet of his escalating indifference to public reaction and personal feelings, of his loss of self-respect; Clifford T. Ward had decided to sell whatever he could; for whatever he could get.

"There never was any such girl," Pat confirms. "The story was a complete fabrication from start to finish, one of Cliff's little lies that got—quite literally in this case—out of hand, until he probably ended up believing it himself.

"And just in case people suggest I'm protecting my pride, the family unit, the image, let me say that there *were* other girls. He was a man, after all, in a business that attracted chancers. He'd had to get married, we were both very young, and he was out playing almost every night, somewhere, and there would always be someone. Ask any 'music widow'. Some girl even came all the way up from Tenby, knocking at our front door! Cliff had given her our address. Other little incidents: coming home at night stinking of perfume, letters, aborted telephone calls. I wasn't stupid. But to be absolutely honest, I wasn't particularly bothered either. There was nothing I could do about anything. I loved the children, and had nowhere to go; it was take it or leave it. And Cliff knew that. It only got serious once: a neighbour of ours on the Oaklands, she did actually leave her husband—with the children—over

Cliff. The husband came round to see me, quite distraught, as if I had any say in the matter. But the affair came to nothing. They moved away, to Devon I think, and a while later they had another child.

"Just after his record ['Gaye'] took off, when we moved to The Spinney, the money of course was still in the pipeline—royalties take six to nine months to come through—so Cliff was famous, but poor, and I got a job at the Riverboat, in Kidderminster, as a waitress. I would come home late at night and the house would reek of Estée Lauder. The lounge, the bathroom, and, yes, the bedroom. He didn't make any effort to hide a thing, almost flaunted his dalliances in my face.

"But the Gaye story. Let me lay that ghost, once and for all. The only 'Gaye' in Cliff's life was Marvin Gaye. Cliff dreamed all this 'girlfriend-suicide' nonsense up after his MS was diagnosed, a little story to shock his fans and amuse himself. *Réclame*? Is that the word? He didn't care about what it might do to his family. I had to keep my head down for a couple of weeks, dodging the gazes and interrogations on Stourport High Street. Cliff's mom, who was now a widow, was particularly hurt by the article. Those magazines feed on loneliness, despair and gullibility. 'Our Cliff,' she said, 'I'd never have thought that of him…' It was pointless me explaining. She believed what she read, they all did, and still do. He wouldn't do anything like that. Not Cliff.

Well, he certainly didn't do *that*…, but he also certainly wasn't pure as driven snow… So, we took the money, all £250.00 of it—wow—but we needed it. 'To hell with it,' I thought. Hung for a sheep as for a lamb, and so, for my sins, I condoned it…"

A paltry financial reward for such evident distress. This time Clifford had played the game to its full potential. When I asked him why he had stooped so low, he merely cracked open that enigmatic half-smile. I couldn't see his eyes, but I knew what he was saying. It had all been done to feed his ego, to break the monotony, to get attention; all in the cause of self-publicity.

Though not, certainly, in the best possible taste…

The publicity in this case was to stimulate interest in a limited pressing vinyl album of demos and out-takes, put together by two dedicated and highly motivated fans from High Wycombe, Andy Savin and Jeff Amor. Released in February '92 on their specially formed Ameless Records label, *Laugh It Off* was the last collection of completely original material we were to see from Clifford T. Ward, singer-songwriter, and though the local press ran articles from the 'discovery of archive material by pop star…' angle, and I played a couple of tracks on my show alongside other local radio coverage, Cliff was hungry for national interest.

The magazine piece, he insisted, was his only way of reaching the masses, regardless of the hurt and unease it caused to those around him. Frankly my dears, he didn't give a damn.

The album itself, however, despite its assumed air of desperation, was a lovely reminder of the man's talent, and well conceived, on such a limited budget.

The cover is a monochrome delight. There is a genuine, uncomplicated photograph on the front—albeit of a 30-year-old Clifford T. Ward—in his 'whatcha-lookin-at?' mode, sitting at the piano in Lower Hollin, whilst on the reverse, from those far-off halcyon days, is a snapshot of the two recently married young lovers, standing in front of the stage curtain at the GKN Club, gazing shyly into the lens.

Some fine, poignant sleeve notes from Andy and Jeff, a warm thank you to them both from Cliff, '...for giving me back my sense of purpose', and other brief acknowledgements are printed beneath an almost *Playboy*-type pose of his wife, which carries the peculiar dedication 'To Pat, thanks for the absolute lot'.

Inside, between the grooves, there is an enchanting collection of 'cast-offs'. Tembo had kindly allowed the use of five unreleased tracks—endorsing their commitment pledged by Ian Summers all those years ago—and the songs, that despite their frugal treatment could have graced many a singer-songwriter's album, at any point in time, range from the country feel of 'The Dancer', the pet-sound of 'Jackdaw', the dying thoughts of Jesus on the cross, in 'Water', to the sheer exuberance of 1960s pop in 'Marble Arch'. Clifford's bizarre, novel, simple ideas, always charmingly realized, are programmed perfectly together, with the penultimate track—the goonish Bill Giles: Weather Man spoof—reflecting an artiste obviously enjoying time alone with his machine, taking a break from the pressures of composing, and reminding everyone out there that life, love, music, even the elements, should always have some light relief. Where would we be without a little humour, the ability to laugh at ourselves, or indeed, to laugh it off?

And Pat, to the surprise of all those who knew her, was actually seen socializing, and laughing. Almost overnight she seemed to change from the shy, quiet, demure wife that had supported Cliff down the years, into a vibrant, outgoing personality. Off with the old, on with the new.

She began throwing parties at Cherry Hill, asking anyone and everyone along, dancing the night away, as Clifford sat in the corner of the room, legs outstretched, holding court; smoking, talking, watching, and, it seemed, enjoying the house so full of people.

Mark Tibenham was one such guest, and he was as amazed as anyone:

"When I went up to Cherry Hill in about 1993, I hadn't seen either of them for about five years. The first thing that shocked me was Pat, who seemed to have rewound the clock by about 20 years; coloured her hair blonde, wearing 'grunge' clothes, Doc Martens and black jeans, jiving about, looking like one of daughter Polly's contemporaries, which I found *terribly* incongruous at the time. That wasn't the Pat I knew, strait-laced, Laura Ashley, middle-of-the-road woman. She seemed to have found a second youth. Astonishing. But I fell for her all over again. Another woman."

"Were you surprised at Cliff's deterioration?"

"Well, yes, shocked. But even with somebody in that condition, I could still see the same character there. Still see that slightly deranged personality…I think, despite his unsociable image, he, paradoxically, liked people around him, but only if they came to *him*. He'd never go to *them*."

And Ron Bridges, who virtually became Pat's in-house dancing partner at these soirées, bopping around like a young feller at his time of life…

"I never really got to know Pat at Castle Weir; she was there, in the background, the silent partner. So when I see her now, it's like two different women. Can't believe it's the same person, so full of life and energy and such a beauty. She tells me she was always accountable to Cliff, she was the minion, that's why she was so hard on my time-keeping and why my hourly rate didn't change in all the years I was there, why she seemed so, well, 'hard as nails'. She had to be. He supervised by delegation, so to speak. But now, well, she's ballsy, extroverted, a joy to behold. Never stops laughing."

In June, 1992, Kidderminster College of Further Education staged a musical play based on the life of Clifford T. Ward, initiated by old conspirator Kevin Gammond. The college was one of the first in the country to offer a B.Tech. Diploma course on studio recording techniques, and Kevin had become part of a disparate but effective team teaching star-struck and precociously talented teenagers the rudiments of the new digital age.

Earlier in the year the college, under lecturer David Gaulkroger's guidance, had released a cassette of local artistes, with a great flurry of publicity, and rightly so. It was an impressive line-up. Entitled *In The Forest*, and with all artistes donating an archive track for college funds, it included Robert Plant's pre-Zep Band of Joy (with Kevin on guitar), Stan Webb's Chicken Shack, The Clippers, The Big Town Playboys, Dave Cartwright, Duncan Swift, Ricky Cool and of course, Clifford T. Ward singing 'Change Of Heart', so the natural progression was for Clifford's predicament to be highlighted in a term-work project. The musical *Shattered World* was widely publicized by the local media, rehearsals were shown on Midlands television, and Cliff attended both performances on 17th and 18th June as guest of honour, accepting his role graciously, delivering his warm, hesitant thanks and enjoying the attention, despite his wheelchair confinement.

All participants threw themselves wholeheartedly into the production, which to them was, after all, nothing more than a course project for their assessment. The show was colourful, dramatic and loud; an energetic end-of-term concert, and although the nod in his direction was duly acknowledged, to the predominantly middle-aged audience it was perhaps somewhat unsettling that the sensitivity of Clifford T. Ward's music was interpreted with so very little finesse. But then, times had changed. We had seen Thatcher's grab-greed days, and subsequently lost all the subtlety nurtured and honed from the love and peace of the sixties to the glamour and grin of the seventies. The eighties had turned the world on its head. Generosity and consideration were things of the past; 'large', 'loud' and 'in-yer-face!' were the key words now. The show was only following the flow of the stream. Soon, the usual rumours would abound, of records, television production, taking *Shattered World* on tour, but it came and it went.

There was no room for the romantic, except somewhere deep in the vaults of Virgin Records…

Some idle moment, some new boy in the office, trying to make his mark?

Whatever the explanation, July 1992 saw the eventual release of *Home Thoughts* and *Mantle Pieces* on CD. Not on one CD—which might have been more cost effective, considering their respective playing times of 42:29 and 40:29 precious minutes—but separately and at mid-price. So those treasured vinyl albums could at long last be safely stored away, if not already damaged beyond repair, and the remote control would zap us back to the summer of 1973. The recordings were not digitally re-mastered, and lose none of their charm, though the surprising intrusion of a police message 12 seconds into 'Home Thoughts…' emphasizes the vulnerability of those analogue days. The CDs attracted little media attention, lost as they were in the swamp of current releases, but did attract some revues…

In a corner slot, *Q* Magazine's Rob Beattie referred to '…Ward's weedy, English voice…', and here I have to take issue. In the distant past, I myself have suffered greatly at the hands of critics—and deservedly so—but to see such a description of something that is obviously so wrong makes me wonder exactly what is going on? If reviewers are employed, then it surely is the duty of the editor to ensure they report accurately. Beattie is not enamoured of the music, obviously, but his comments, apart from being quite incorrect, are nothing short of vindictive, spiteful, malicious. Whether or not he likes Ward's music is irrelevant; if he is too immature to consider anything outside his own preferences, what is he doing reviewing?

Such articles, however, couldn't damage an established reputation. The

CDs sold well, though sales would have surely been healthier were it not for the re-issue, within a fortnight, of a three-album compilation, *Gaye and Other Stories*. Originally released in February 1987 on the back of Clifford's Tembo album, Virgin were now offering this compilation CD, with one extra track and my sleeve notes. Bizarre timing. Alongside his solo albums, it didn't really make much sense in the market place. Another new boy?

Not surprisingly, within a year both album CDs were deleted, though the compilation went 'gold' with Virgin (Ireland) within two months of its September release, reaffirming the respect he still commanded over there.

Ron Bridges has good reason to remember the Irish launch of *Gaye and Other Stories:*

"Pat called me one evening. I'd just come back from holiday, so I needed a break… They'd asked Clifford to go over to Belfast to promote the album, and combine his visit with the launch of a new Multiple Sclerosis branch and public appeal. It was impossible for Pat to handle Cliff, his wheelchair and the flight, so she asked if I would do it. No problem. But again, I hadn't realized what I was letting myself in for. He was so bloody cussed throughout the whole trip, except, of course, when he was on show. Talk about Jekyll and Hyde. I walked out on him, couldn't stand his whinging, his continual mind-games. Changing every minute. I was doing this to *help* him, to help *Pat*; as a favour. But he was so-o…, well, so bloody awkward."

Ron means no harm, but his tolerance was sorely tested that weekend.

"After one incident I just cleared out, went for a walk, left him in the hotel room. 'Sod you, Clifford, I've had enough.' I was fuming. But, out in the coolness of the night, well, I realized how he must be feeling. Who would want something like that? *I'd* had enough, but I could walk out on whatever it was. He couldn't. One minute he'd had it all, next minute, *whoosh*; gone. I went back. He was sitting in his wheelchair, smoking. He turned round as I walked in. 'I'm so-o-ory, Ro-on,' he said, and he gave a great long sigh.

"Broke me up it did."

A year or so later, as December lights decorated the nervous Belfast streets, Pat did manage to summon every ounce of her strength and will power to take Clifford across for a BBC television appearance with 'Anderson On The Box', sharing the spotlight with fellow musician Justin Hayward, a great champion of Clifford T. Ward's music. *Gaye and Other Stories* had long since gone gold, and media interest was high once again.

Justin had recorded a live studio version of Clifford's 'hope-against-all-odds' anthem, 'The Best Is Yet To Come', way back in 1985, and the irony of this current situation couldn't have escaped him. Here he was, on Irish television, talking to the respected composer of a classic song relating the all-encompassing difficulties of love, but who was now in a position of total disability.

Money, success, fame; it all seemed of little consequence.

But they talked freely with their host about the early days of pop; the great British beat group days, until Clifford, whether out of devilment or confusion, recalled '…rushing home from school and catching the bus into Birmingham to see the Moody Blues play at the Town Hall…'

Even considering Justin's precocious success, the incident, with Cliff being at least a couple of years older than him, it wouldn't have been possible. But Justin accepted it as a compliment, that beatific smile spreading slowly over his face.

How could he take offence?

He had said, some time before and many times since, of the pleasure those wonderful songs had brought him:

"I love Clifford T. Ward. His music gives me feelings I get from nothing else. I can't remember the first time I heard him, but I knew that I had to hear everything he'd done, after that. His music brings out deep emotion. Other songwriters recognize the presence of someone who is that extra bit special, that Englishness that no-one else has managed to capture. I aimed high recording with Peter Knight in Studio 1 at Abbey Road; that fleeting moment of magic. I got as near as I possibly could to his own definitive version."

The bank manager turned up right on time. Pat showed him into the lounge where Cliff was sitting, staring out across the hills.

It was a passing visit, nothing serious, just to see how everything was at home.

Cliff was more than prepared.

Yes, he was still writing, but as he couldn't sing any more, he was getting other people to demo his songs.

"This is my wife Pat singing one of my new ones; I think it's great," he said. Solemn, straight, honest. He pressed the switch on his cassette player, the tape clicked and whirred and the track began. They sat there listening, Cliff ghosting the keyboard from his armchair, his shaded eyes flickering around the room. It ended. The banker seemed impressed. If he knew the truth, he didn't say anything. He drank his coffee, finished his biscuit and made small talk about the nice view, the weather, oh, and forthcoming PRS payments… and then left.

Pat was furious.

"What did you do that for?" she asked him, incredulously. "What if he knew it?"
"He wouldn't know that," Cliff flicked his hand. "They don't listen to pop music," and he gave a short laugh. "Huh."
To placate, impress, or, I suspect, to help relieve the ennui, he had just played a recording of Everything But The Girl singing Cyndi Lauper's 'Time After Time'.
"Oh, I give up," Pat groaned. She collected the plates and went to hide in the kitchen.

THE WAY OF LOVE

Seldom comes Glorie till a man be dead. Robert Herrick: *Glorie*

Roy Noble had started the Clifford T. Ward Appreciation Society as a warm-hearted gesture, after learning of his hero's plight way back in 1989.

He wrote to Cliff, from his home in Spalding, asking permission—in that lovely British manner—intending it to be a very low-key affair: a few small press adverts in *Record Collector*, some well-placed posters and one or two phone calls to those who were used to this kind of thing. Fan clubs were a whole new experience to Roy, but naïveté often works wonders; the reaction was encouraging and somewhat surprising, despite Clifford's obvious appeal. It had been a long, long time ago, in a notably ephemeral medium, but those early albums, once bought, were never forgotten. Many of those who responded were nevertheless quite shocked at the news of his illness, assuming the singer was enjoying that fabled life of wealth and contentment.

As momentum grew, it was only a matter of time before the byword 'convention' was mentioned... and although it was now apparent that Clifford would never be able to sing his songs again—despite his stentorian assurances to the contrary—there had miraculously appeared, from within the crowd, the perfect vehicle for his songs.

On that fateful October afternoon in 1986, when Dennis Lee had driven Clifford back from his aborted Gloria Hunniford interview, a young, dark-haired singer-guitarist named James Davey had turned his yellow sports car into the drive at Dunley, having made the 30-mile journey from his home in the Black Country with nothing more to work on than the media address 'Clifford T. Ward, Nr. Stourport, Worcestershire'.

James was given the Ward welcome, a nice cup of tea and an exceedingly good cake, although the atmosphere, for reasons unknown to him, was a little fraught. He was encouraged to talk about his own music, for about ten minutes... saying how he was a writer himself and had come seeking guidance from someone for whom he had great admiration. Searching for inspiration, he had spent many late nights struggling to translate those strange piano inversions into guitar tablature; those weird chord structures, the strange subject matter, the musical subtleties all underlying the apparent simplicity; he was, it seemed, the sorcerer's apprentice.

The visits grew more frequent over the next couple of years, until, when the first CTW Convention was eventually arranged, at the Country Hotel in Bromsgrove in 1990, James Davey volunteered to interpret the songs of Clifford T. Ward. And he did so with amazing dexterity and confidence, and clearly with full approval from the guest of honour.

The format was thus established, through fortunate timing and willing participation. There was now something solid to work on, a gathering of dedicated fans who could meet annually, chat and listen to the songs sung live by another seriously dedicated and fastidious performer. He was from Wolverhampton, but, hey, nobody's perfect...

The Society membership escalated, and with its new-found success came the problems that often beset many such operations. Roy found that the organization and documentation involved was becoming too much; he was also suffering with his health. It needed a new hand at the helm, and help came along in the guise of Clive Winstanley, an unassuming but highly industrious schoolteacher from Slyne, near Lancaster. With his articulate, no-nonsense approach, Clive and his scholarly fanzine, *Waves*, already running alongside Roy's society, took on the challenge and soon became the epicentre of the Clifford T. Ward appreciators. Between a busy family life and the demands of modern-day teaching, he managed to find time to construct a definitive discography from the maze-like career path of his subject. Pat's scrapbook gave his project a healthy kick-start, with an extensive collection of press cuttings, reviews and pictures; and record rarities—albums and singles of all denominations—tucked away in the antique pine bookcase for so many years, were taken out and given an airing. Life rose once again from the ashes of the past.

In 1995, the *Daily Mail* took a bold initiative and sent reporter Mary Greene along to Cherry Hill for an in-depth interview. Someone at the *Mail* had noticed renewed interest in Clifford's work; air plays were increasing, even new releases were being mentioned. How was this possible?

Again, it was one of those lovely coincidences that make the otherwise tacky world of showbiz worthwhile, and it all started with a record called 'Food For Thought', in April 1980:

> Ivory madonna, standing in the dust...

Remember the lolloping reggae-beat of UB40, permeating the very stream of your consciousness that spring? As 'Indie' music began to challenge the stranglehold of the majors—with Adam and his Ants topping the very first UK Indie LP chart—Bob Marley's laid-back sun-sound was taken and shaken by a group of Birmingham musicians led by Scottish folk-singer Ian Campbell's two sons, Robin and Ali. With vocals as smooth and smiling as the Caribbean itself—no mean feat considering their Brummie accents—the multi-racial UBs stormed into the charts at number three, on David Virr's Graduate Records.

A slight, friendly man, with twinkling eyes, and an on-off beard, David had started out as a DJ, before opening a record shop in Dudley, West Midlands in 1969, which, at the height of record-mania, soon blossomed into a chain of similar stores throughout the Midlands, under the name Graduate Records. In 1979, he took the plunge and formed his independent label, signing UB40 the following January.

The success took everyone by surprise. Graduate had entered the record books—literally—by being the first indie label to achieve such a feat without any involvement whatsoever from the majors, thus opening the floodgates for many other entrepreneurs. He could have fallen flat on his face, but by sensible reaction and shrewd business acumen, the success was maintained, and their wickedly-titled album, *Signing Off*, with its pertinent benefit card cover, followed the single into the charts, and stayed there for over 70 weeks.

Even I bought it. Took it home, played it, liked it and, a couple of months later saw their follow-up album in a little shop in Ledbury, my new home town. UB40 *In Dub*. I took it home, put it on, sat back with a Southern Comfort and relaxed...

"Bloody 'ell, that's a long intro..." I thought.

Another drink.

"Mmm, maybe they're trying a new format: instrumental, song, instrumental..." But of course, no song came along.

I was a professional musician, but incredibly out of touch with the 'here and now' of the early 1980s. When my son came in I asked him what was going on. He told me, with that look of disdain teenagers reserve for their parents, that 'In Dub' meant "...no vocals, Dad." I was a bit miffed.

I took the record straight back. I'm a words man, me. If I want instrumentals I buy Mantovani. She didn't want to change it, but I insisted, threatening to stop my cheque. (I can get quite angry sometimes...)

After a swift phone call to her boss, she offered an exchange. But, as I left the shop, clutching the Scottish blues of The Sensational Alex Harvey Band, I heard her. Oh, I heard her all right:

"What a plonker..."

So David Virr struck gold, and the group went on from strength to strength, so much so that they when it was clear things were becoming too much for David's virtual one-man set-up, they decided to form their own label, Dep Int. He retained control of the Graduate name—and a nice piece of the publishing—eventually licensing the early stuff out to Virgin for world-wide distribution, who safely gathered in five platinum discs for *The Best of…Vol 1*. A nice little earner.

After enjoying a well-earned rest, David then ploughed some of this capital into forming Ready Steady Go! records, for The Maisonettes, and their single, 'Heartache Avenue'—with ex-City Boy vocalist Lol Mason and Clifford's erstwhile musical amanuensis Mark Tibenham on keyboards—jumped into the lower Top Twenty in January, 1983, and hit the button across Europe, surfacing again only recently for a lucrative Ford cars advert in France.

But despite his apparent Midas touch, he decided to wind down the record business side of life; it was really becoming quite carnivorous out there, especially for a vegetarian. He opened a second-hand record/bookshop in Worcester, where he excelled with his book-search system, being the only person in the *country* to locate the three volumes of Lawrence Thompson's biography of Robert Frost for little old me. At a price, mind you…

Meanwhile Kevin Gammond, now fully immersed in his lecturing role at Kidderminster College, was building a roster of speakers for his music students, bringing in local professional talent to chat about all aspects of life in The Business. David, with his top-notch recording and publishing experience, was soon enlisted for these 'Celebrity Lectures' and it was here, over coffee in the canteen, that he learned about Clifford's situation. Though decidedly taking it easy, he couldn't resist the chance of lending a hand, via his Graduate company. After reading a local press report about 'Lost Gems Found', he spoke to Pat and was genuinely surprised at the quantity of out-takes, demos, whatevers, there seemed to be languishing in the vaults. James Davey, during one of his visits to the house, had discovered the reels, smouldering gently under the thin, grey coating of Rothmans ash, had patiently threaded them onto the Teac reel-to-reel, and, after a few muffled clicks, clangs and curses, out of the speakers had come that husky, poignant voice, singing previously unheard love songs and lullabies.

A compilation was put together, with kind assistance from Tembo, and Intersong (albeit still clinging to their copyrights), and February, 1995, saw the release of *Julia and Other New Stories*, Clifford T. Ward's eleventh album. Though only issued initially as a limited pressing, it brought his talent back into the public eye. It was honestly publicized as a demo-quality album, but nothing could detract from the charm of the songs. They would never reach mass audience because of the rigorous guidelines for digital-quality broadcasting in the nineties—brought about by the neuroses of the powers that be—though the inclusion of a spoken introduction by Cliff Richard helped to stimulate some media interest, occasionally for the wrong reasons...Chris Evans, then breakfasting on Radio One, chose to use the intro and not the musical content for a few cheap laughs. But, that's his prerogative; he is but a child.

So, along came the *Daily Mail.* The article was printed on September 23rd, 1995, under the sensitive caption, 'Heartbreak of the man they called the new McCartney'.

It was a good piece of writing, gently telling the tale that had taken 25 years to unfold in a thousand words, with a 'then' and 'now' picture topping and tailing the article. Pat's frustration almost came out, but her stoicism won through, though there couldn't have been many people who read that article who didn't read between the lines.

Meanwhile, deep in darkest Sussex, Clive Selwood was also enjoying semi-retirement, running his Strange Fruit label, but, remembering his promise to revive the CTW back catalogue after a befitting period of grace, he now decided the time was right. It had been some years since the revelation of Clifford's illness; no-one could accuse him of jumping on any bandwagon at this late stage.

"In 1992, I had motivated Virgin into re-releasing *Home Thoughts* and *Mantle Pieces*, which amazingly hadn't been put out on CD. Maybe a year or two passed before I sat down again, after receiving some 'newer' stuff from Cliff—basically home demos and such like—and we'd learned of their financial situation. Shurley had sent some money to them—against my better judgement," he whispered. "I was still embittered with our treatment by Clifford, but I thought maybe this unreleased stuff, and the Dandelion songs, would go together quite nicely, something along the lines *Clifford T. Ward —Then and Now*, and raise some money for them that way. But honestly, Dave, I found it had become all too emotional for me. Whenever I started to play those songs of love, family, separation, and knowing how ill he was, I just cracked up. I honestly couldn't do it. Then along came See-For-Miles; they took the pressure off by offering to reissue the entire Dandelion catalogue under licence, and it's good to see *Singer...* back in the shops."

He was more than a little surprised when I told him that Virgin had since deleted both the subsequent albums, one of them considered by many to be one of the classic albums of the seventies, though *Home Thoughts* has subsequently been reinstated into the mid-price catalogue. But, good news as it may seem, this digs up the old bone of contention for Pat, continually struggling with their finances. By way of some bizarre financial arrangement made, buried and certainly uncontested through the shadows of time, Clive Selwood still takes half of all royalties from those first—and best selling—albums. Virgin account directly to Clive, and fifty per cent is deducted at source by his Dandelion holding company. Even on the last royalty sheet I saw, in September, 1998, these amounted to a not inconsiderable sum.

"I'm not saying there is anything underhand, illegal, going on," insists Pat, "it's just that nothing has ever been fully explained, and we're certainly not in a position to legally contest whatever line Clive is working from. Yes, I know there was considerable outlay making those albums, but we're talking twenty-five years ago here. If it's a question of a 'pound of flesh', then I would think that has been more than settled. Clive should come up and see Cliff, see his deterioration, then maybe he would relax his seemingly revengeful attitude a little. A couple of thousand a year means a lot to us. How long can you hold a grudge? I'm sadly shocked. But then," she adds, "knowing the business, why should I be?"

Following the *Daily Mail* article, the visitors began once again dropping by, some using amazing powers of detection, bulldog grit and energy—considering the distance many of them travelled—to find the bungalow tucked away behind the seemingly impenetrable wall of leylandii.

And they came from all walks of life. Hoteliers from Guernsey, builders from Birmingham, students from Matlock, even missionaries from Manchester…

Peter Hickford, a handsome, amiable ex-priest working with the Society Of Missionaries For Africa told me of his introduction to the music, during a beer-break at a recent convention.

"I was about ten years old, 1973, doing the obligatory paper-round through the back streets of Blackpool. Not much has come out of the tower-town, musically speaking, apart from George Formby, and Ian 'Jethro Tull' Anderson, the Grammar School's most famous son.

"I heard this song, 'Wherewithal', on Radio Lancashire. I hadn't a clue what it meant, words and phrases that, to a child of such few years, were almost a foreign language. But I liked the sound, the voice, the tune. I made a note of the name. Clifford T. Ward. Next day, reporting for duty in the shop, hot, tired and black with newsprint, I heard the name again, and another song, something called 'Gaye'. Then I saw him on 'Top Of The Pops'. I persuaded my parents—with the incentive of some small contribution from my paper round earnings—to put up the money to buy the album. I went into Roberts Record Emporium and put my money on the counter. Not for me Slade, or the Bay City Rollers. I wanted Clifford T. Ward, *Home Thoughts*. I've bought every album since.

"Even in my missionary days, deep in the heart of Nigeria, miles away from electricity and the white man's so-called civilization, I've loaded batteries and tapes into my pack and sat there at night, by the flickering flame, and listened to those beautiful, inspiring, English songs."

It has been twenty-five years now, since 'Gaye' made the charts. A quarter of an incredible century, where life and living have changed far beyond anyone's expectations, yet it seems there will never be enough new talent to replace the old guard. Radio and television, record re-releases, magazines; all revert and refer to the golden age of pop, and if you were there, making a mark in those years—and here you can draw your own boundaries; I'm not getting involved in that one—then you will be remembered.

Despite Clifford's minor achievement in the record books, his impact has been far stronger, his appeal shown greater longevity, than the many who churned out hit after golden hit. Most probably because he was a writer of real, solid, structured songs, not merely a verse-and-chorus man. In a recent and badly-conceived record company handout, Clifford T. Ward was referred to as a '... folk-singer ...'. A misnomer if ever there was. Apart from the undeniable talents of Martin Carthy and Ralph McTell, and possibly one or two other performers who have stuck to their original beliefs—the world of folk, especially British folk, is, and always has been, perpetuated by bland, flat-voiced charlatans, singing boringly repetitive songs. Just when you think they have finished, they start up again.

Clifford T. fused true melody with honest thought. His songs are unpredictable, powerful, and above all, concise. No pontificating folk-singer he, sat behind a guitar.

Consequently, he struck a deep, everlasting chord in many a contemporary soul, some of whom rose to become figureheads in the media. Running concurrently with the writing of this book has been the wonderful support shown, for example, by those at BBC Radio 2. Hardly a week goes by without Terry Wogan, Ken Bruce or young Jimmy passing on their best wishes and playing a Clifford T. Ward track, or choosing one of the many cover versions from his peerless catalogue of 'left-handed love songs'.

Yet although much of this nod to a tragic talent has come voluntarily, through such indelible admiration, there has been a noticeable increase of late due to the sheer persistence of the Appreciation Society's indefatigable communications officer, Liz Williams.

Liz appeared quietly through the convention door some three years ago, after travelling the 200 miles from the Lake District by train, via Crewe and Birmingham, to pay her respects to the man who had given her so much musical pleasure over the years.

Within a very short while, she appointed herself organizer-in-chief—a position the society badly needed—and re-christened everyone The Friends Of Clifford T. Ward. Then, in her implacable manner, she commandeered IT assistance from her son, during his holidays from

university, to design the first CTW Web Site. There are now four.
Soon there was talk of major fund-raising, and today no-one in the field of entertainment seems beyond Liz's tactful but forceful approach. Terrier-like, she sniffs, makes contact and then refuses to let go until a response—negative or otherwise—is forthcoming. She has lifted the public awareness and financial necessity of the annual convention enormously over the period since she took the helm, and her enthusiasm has galvanized other similarly minded fans into offering support. There have been sponsored walks, vinyl-to-CD transfers, reunion concerts, CTW calendars using digitally enhanced photographs; all time and cost projects, and all done absolutely free of charge. For a recent auction, and purely as a direct result of Liz William's persistence, Sting donated a limited edition autographed Fender Precision Bass, Reggie Dwight a pair of authenticated spectacles, Paul Beatle—living in the middle of what we have since discovered was his own personal and tragic nightmare—found the time to forward a signed copy of his highly collectable *Paul McCartney, Songwriter-Artiste* book, together with a charming letter remembering Cliff's work '...with great fondness...', and Harry Webb sent a necktie.

Even so, throughout these hard times, there have been some wonderful acts of generosity that came without any prompting. Protocol prevents me actually naming names, much as I would dearly love to—in appreciation—but those individuals who have given have done so without asking and without condition. One performer rang up completely out of the blue, having met Clifford only once, many, many years down the line, and after talking to Pat, posted them a cheque for £10,000. Ten thousand pounds, period. Another friend—a devoted fan—on a very limited income, sent £500 in cash last Christmas. Other 'star-companies' and organizations have provided contracted funds, against collateral, but that's all right; at least they have helped, they are obviously business-minded people. Some have made lush promises and delivered nothing, but as Pat insists, no-one is under any obligation whatsoever; charity is an act of wanting, not of duty.
But maybe I *can* scotch a rumour here about the 'Wolverhampton Wanderer'. As could be expected, with his love of blues and Americana, he has never been a great fan of the music of Clifford T. Ward. When I told him I was writing this biography, his immediate reaction was to ask why I wasn't writing about Jess Roden. His opinion of Clifford?
He replied—to my great amusement—that he thought Cliff was 'a bit of a clarnit', a slice of Walsall patois even *I* hadn't come across in my Black Country childhood.
But he has somehow gained a reputation—amongst those who

obviously don't know otherwise—for his…er, frugality, which is, in my experience, totally and utterly without foundation.

When I interviewed him for my radio show some years ago, Clifford was mentioned, naturally; all local boys. I knew how desperate things were with them, so I told my guest. Within a week, he had set up a financial arrangement to assist them. Again, with no pre-conditions and despite his already formed—but yet to be expressed—verdict on the man's music.

Also, another instance, from a purely personal point of reference, exemplifying his generosity.

When I was at his house last year, browsing through his wonderfully catholic vinyl collection in the kitchen, I homed in on a honeydripping selection of Extended Play records: Ricky Nelson, Marty Robbins, Don Gibson, Johnny Burnette, when out pops *C'est Fab!*

Françoise Hardy 1964.

Now.

I had hitch-hiked all the way down the N7, to Bandol, near Saint-Tropez, way back in 1965, ostensibly to busk and burn. I couldn't speak French at all well, but 'Tous Les Garçons Et Les Filles' was there in my repertoire. I'd learned it parrot-fashion, should I need to impress the gendarmerie. I adored Françoise Hardy, her chic vulnerability, her *Sprechgesang* vocals, her mouth…, and found, via some amazing coincidence, she was performing there that very week. I couldn't believe my luck, but also, I couldn't afford a ticket. So, on a Riviera-hot Tuesday afternoon, I crept through a half-open door, from white sunlight into backdrop shadow, and sat for over an hour, watching her rehearse in a tiny theatre that faced the beach. I was too shy to approach her—honest, I was only twenty-four—but for me, it was a day to remember.

I couldn't control myself.

"I've been after this record for twenty years!" I shouted at him—probably a little too loudly. "Mine was 'lifted' from a house-warming."

"Well that ay it," he laughed, in his pseudo-Black Country accent, "unless yow was gooin' airt with Sally Matthews, 'cos 'er nairme's rit on the back…"

Then he waved his hand dismissively: "Tek it."

Was he serious?

"Go on, you can have it, I can always get another one."

And that was it. I took it home and stared again at that beautiful face on the cover. But I didn't play it. I knew I would be disappointed.

A little later on, when we were all relaxing, I related an incident that had occurred quite recently, during my research into this book, and something which I had found quite bizarre, surreal, and amusing, given the scale of things.

Kidderminster could never be quoted as England's home of the blues—even if there is such a place—though it does have a justifiable claim to producing and nurturing a few fine guitarists and vocalists, besides being the cradle of at least one supergroup. It was in the backroom of one of the many pubs that illuminate these shadowed streets, with the cliff-like walls of the carpet factories blocking out the sun, that local bassman and one-time jazz banjoist Andy Silvester introduced local vocalist Christine Perfect to local bluesman Stan Webb, which would lead to all sorts of things, Shacks and Macs amongst them. But just down past the Carpet Union Offices, over the canal bridge and now dwarfed by the towering Social Security block, stands a row of commercial offices, which no doubt once housed small family businesses—greengrocers, toy shops, confectioners—and above which, in the early sixties, Frank and Winnie Freeman held their weekly dancing classes. Ballroom dancing classes. However, just as John and Pattie had foreseen a need for teenage entertainment to supplement their classes in Stourport, so Frank and Winnie decided to promote live bands, only on a much larger, more ambitious scale.

It was in an ideal spot, almost smack-dab in the middle of town, well within staggering distance—fortunately, for the Freemans had no drinks licence—and it took but a very short while before they had built up an enviable venue reputation, based on the quality of the acts, and the gentle humour, affability and appreciation of the crowd. Frank himself was a personality *nonpareil*, his old-style, father-figure charm welcoming the youngsters who packed in every week, to sit, squat or lie in some soporific state at the feet of the bands.

"We had laid a brand new maple floor for the ballroom dancing," recalls Winnie, "and were careful to make sure that the pop drummers didn't try to nail their kit to the floor, as happened on one occasion…

"Frank was always puzzled why the kids didn't want to dance, why they seemed quite content just to lie all over the floor, listening, …"

And what bands they had. It is difficult these days to imagine such close-contact stardom, but following our conversation, she handed me a list of the groups that had appeared in that long, narrow room, with the soft-drinks bar and the rotating mirror-globe, the bands that had travelled miles, maybe stopping off at the Blue Boar oasis *en route*, then humped and bumped up and down the narrow steps, to play to a full house of maybe 100-150 people, without so much as a pinch of trouble. Yes, no doubt there were many similar places dotted throughout the country during the wondrous sixties, where bands were keen and fans were keener, but a 'dry' hall, run by two middle-aged ballroom dancers in the industrial outback, must have been somewhat unique. Winnie remembered them all. Bronco, with local hero Jess Roden, played their formative gigs there, as did the Yardbirds, *and* the New Yardbirds…, the Moody Blues, Chicken Shack, Captain Beefheart (recorded live by John Peel for his radio session spot), Rick Wakeman with The Strawbs ("…his synthesizer fused during an encore…"), Barclay James Harvest, Duster Bennett, Yes, Tim Rose, Marc Bolan ("…when he was doing that Indian stuff with those big instrument things, and a bloke called Steve something…"), Jethro Tull, even Ron Geesin, 'Poet and Humorist' (*I* can vouch for that description, but don't mention Aberystwyth to me…) Black Sabbath, Deep Purple, ELP, Spencer Davies, Jimmy Cliff, The Rockin' Berries, Peter Green's original Mac, and a shy John Peel came up just to DJ a couple of times. Members 7/6d, guests 8/6d.

"We had lots of all-nighters, starting at midnight until ten the next morning. There was no bar, so the police had no trouble. As simple as that," she smiled.

Unbelievable, and the *Shuttle* file confirms such glory days:

> Tyrannosaurus Rex, 'highly rated by D.J. John Peel', appear at an Easter Sunday all-niter … session starts at 8 p.m. and continues until 8 a.m. the following morning.

An 'all-niter'. Good times indeed. A roll-call of musical celebrity, never captured for the video-market, never recorded for posterity, and the likes of which will never be seen again.

The Cruisers, surprisingly, only played there once, on 31st July, 1966, in between their first single 'Candy To Me' and Clifford's first home-thought release, 'I Suppose' on CBS, so Winnie's contribution to his particular story is lost amongst her other glories. But for me, to be there in that building for just a couple of hours, one warm, late afternoon in July, looking through scrapbooks containing 'family gathering' snaps of Jess, Robert, Trevor Lucas (then an Electron, later a Fairporter and a Fotheringay), Peely, Stan the Man: young heads full of dreams, what Larkin calls the 'clear … sparkling armada of promises', and poring over faded handouts, once fly-posted in the early hours, now eagerly sought after by collectors at memorabilia auctions. Well, it was more than worth the visit.

Now in her late seventies, Winnie still leaps around with the energy of 'mine hostess' from all those years ago. She talked emotionally about '…the ruination of the town…', the pointless demolition of the Black Boy Coaching Inn and the Lion Hotel, the precarious plans still under consideration to remove what little remains of Kidderminster's architectural history. How there had been such a community spirit in those days; the markets, the Methodist Hall, the policeman directing traffic from his 'pulpit' at the bottom of Church Street—something that would most certainly be a tourist attraction today—they have all disappeared, along with everything else those faceless, unthinking, narrow-minded, pension-clad town planners deemed archaic, all too readily accepting the coin in exchange for the soul.

She misses Frank. Of course she does. He died in 1991 and the town and its many luminaries paid a heartfelt and respectful farewell to that unassuming celebrity. But she continues to instruct. "... I'd get bored stiff doing nothing."

She was actually welcoming some tango pupils just as I was leaving.

They came tripping up the narrow staircase. Two painted ball-gowned women, maybe in their late thirties, dressed up and raring to go. What they hadn't seen, and what no-one else would ever see—for the moment had now gone to join those countless other ghosts of the past that weave invisibly around the room—was 78-years-old Winnie Freeman, of all things, line-dancing, just for me. And to a little number she had discovered as an ideal line-dancing track. '29 Palms', by Robert Plant.

But today, I'm in a pensive mood. Another magazine article, another clutch of accolades for this neglected talent. I see the picture of Cliff, with his dark glasses, staring into some unfathomable future, and read the words—almost written as an afterthought—that speak again of his wife's 'unflagging devotion ... her tolerance ... her quiet suffering...' and I wonder, just *who* is the victim here?

Cliff always extends a warm welcome to guests, holding court as once before, either in the panoramic lounge or sometimes in his studio, now used solely for playback. His acolytes arrive in awe and leave with regret, sparked by this *bel esprit*; his appreciation, his courtesy. What they don't see, realize, even think about—why should they?—(and we are all guilty here, though not by intent...), is the after-effects, the reaction that takes hold, depending on his frame of mind, when once again alone. The house, for a while, falls ominously silent...

Pat lives her nightmare through every day:

"No-one has a clue what goes on here. They see me out shopping, socializing, speak to me on the phone and it all seems, to them, to be drifting along. There are sympathetic gestures, 'How's Cliff?' or, 'You look so well'; that kind of thing, and they mean no harm, of course they don't. But it's like asking someone in the street how *they* are. If you actually begin to tell the *truth*, they can't wait to get away; it's human nature. And Cliff, most of the time, when someone *does* call round, which again is getting less frequent—unless it's the bailiffs or the

MEB—well, he just perpetuates the 'everything-is-fine' line. Yes, so do most married couples. Four walls, etc., but the abuse and rudeness, the throwing down onto the floor of food I've cooked, the deliberate soiling—and before anyone questions that, it *is* deliberate—I've lived with it long enough to know the difference; all these things that visitors *don't* see... He shouts, bawls, blasphemes, inside the house and out, slams doors in the middle of the night, smokes in his bed, generally does his best to make my life as unpleasant as possible. It is hell on earth. Don't let anyone imagine differently.

"Even the children—though now fully grown adults—when they do visit, find it almost impossible to sustain any kind of conversation with their father. He shows little, perhaps no, interest in them or their lives. All Clifford T. Ward wants to talk about is Clifford T. Ward."

Can he be forgiven for this behaviour?

It is one of the many known side-effects of multiple sclerosis, this need to be centre of attention, the need to thus create a demanding situation. But the rudeness, the contempt shown for others. Is this a side-effect? Friends *have* made the effort, have sat there, at his feet, by his side, across the room, and tried to talk generalities—or as Cliff would probably put it: 'ba-*nal*-ities'—but, depending on his whim, they have often suffered for it and consequently felt unwilling to let the opportunity repeat itself. Yet he can be his old self, very, very occasionally, but Pat gets mad when she hears me laughing with him, when I occasionally say what great company he can be; such humour, such intellect...

Sitting in his lounge one afternoon, the two of us talking with one of Cliff's friends about canned beer, now his favourite tipple. Guinness, widgets, and then real ale was mentioned, and I, in a piece of childish word-play, quoted the opening lines of Keats's 'La Belle Dame sans Merci':

"'O, what can *ail* thee, knight-at-arms...'"

Quick as a flash, Cliff pointed at me—to indicate recognition of the words—then slowly continued:

"'Alone...and...palely...loitering...'"

He couldn't have heard—and certainly wouldn't have read—that poem in ten, maybe fifteen years, yet there was no hesitancy in his response. It seems that whatever multiple sclerosis *has* done to his memory—and he uses it to his convenience on many occasions—he can still remember such things as he deems necessary to stimulate a conversation (although, with Cliff's anarchic humour, and a word like 'widget' floating around, it quickly deteriorated...)

"That's what I mean," Pat remonstrates. "He's fine with you, or when somebody is here that he wants to impress, but just imagine it for a moment. I mean, I'm here, in the house. I've *got* to make conversation, it's our *home*, we live here together—alone…" The inference doesn't pass unnoticed. "I say a few words, he responds, initially, and then the discussion slowly worsens; he becomes sarcastic, then abusive, until, when he sees *my* frustration, he throws down his meal, all over the carpet, crawls and crashes across the room, purposely knocking over lamps or chairs and leaves me there, stunned into silence. There is *no* justification whatsoever for that.

"I *never* get a break. It's out of the question. Who can look after Cliff? If he won't tolerate me, he certainly won't tolerate anyone else. The Musicians Benevolent Fund have been really kind to us, but they can only make the gesture; it's up to us—or me—to cope with the result.

"Three, maybe four years ago, 1992-93, they offered us a week's holiday at Park House, on the Sandringham Estate in Norfolk, where Diana Spencer was born. It is now a nursing home.

"I weighed it up, *really* weighed it up, and, against my better judgement, decided to give it a try. Just Polly, Cliff and me. I drove all the way over there, right across country. Some journey. We were made really welcome, but within two days no-one would come near us. He was so obnoxious to the staff that everyone just kept their distance. He had made up his mind to ruin that holiday. We came home after three days. It was unbearable. There's a lot of water out that way. Anybody else would have pushed him into The Wash…

"He's not the man I knew," she continues, and then as if to define the obvious, "I don't just mean the illness. That's not his fault, of course it's not, and yes, it broke my heart. Slowly, it broke my heart. A long, slow torture. I watched the man I had been with all my life changing before my eyes, not just physically, but mentally; and yet his *mentality* is unimpaired. Why, therefore, should his attitude to me and to mine—to *ours*—be so cruel? I feel now as if I don't—as if I've *never* known this person… And I can't grieve, because I've not been *able* to grieve, to say goodbye. It's not like a death. It is a permanent, terrifying nightmare. And before anyone jumps in to say 'Cruel, heartless woman,' let them remember that, despite it all, I am still here…

"We've got terrific neighbours, Peter and Hazel, Johnny Knott; but when Cliff gets going, they can hear everything. He roars profanities at the top of his voice, getting in and out of the car, even in the hall or his studio, when he's a mind to, and they can hear everything. And they sympathize. With me…

"I'm the last person to feel sorry for my lot, but I have to say that no-one deserves this. I didn't even want the music, for God's sake. What a world that was, and probably is even more so nowadays. All that duplicity; people saying things, doing things that are totally false. Even Cliff hated it. Really. I would have been quite happy just having lots and lots of babies…"

And what of her baby? The daughter they both adored, and who for a while became Cliff's constant companion during his civilized, calming, industrious days as Lord of the Manor at Castle Weir.

Polly is now living with her boyfriend Matthew. He, strangely enough, is not unlike how I would imagine a young Clifford T. to have been. He certainly resembles him physically—it is quite uncanny—and, quietly polite, he possesses a quick humour and an inquiring mind. She is a vibrant, intelligent young lady, in her final year at college, studying graphic design. With her father's early charm, her mother's disarming pragmatism, and an amalgam of their mordant wit, she positively glows with *joie de vivre*. She is, of course, an aunt twice over, via sister Debbie's daughter and brother Sam's boy, Jack. There is quite an extended family around, yet none of them seem particularly impressed or affected by the legend of their leader, at least in public...

Martin, the enigmatic dark horse, living with his German girlfriend, Silka—and occasionally drumming—in London, scouring *Loot* every week for wheels and deals, often plays Dad's music to friends during late night soirées, and Debbie, as I found out first-hand, admits to still getting a thrill whenever she hears her father's music on the radio, despite her being a fan—since childhood days—of the more well, shall we say, progressive sounds of pop...

By a fortunate coincidence, I caught up with her whilst passing through Coventry on my way to a gig. I called in and she was only too pleased to contribute to the book, though I must admit, my pleasure at yet another aspect of life with the Wards was tempered by the knowledge—and brief experience—of Debbie's more than up front attitude. She is renowned for her no-nonsense approach to life, and I, occasionally, can be full of nonsense...

She lives, with her six-year-old daughter Eleanor—a precocious, positive child of the nineties—in a pleasant two-bedroomed bungalow, about one mile from the Jaguar factory. A maze of right turns, left turns, leafy lanes and semi-detached T-junctions leads up to her drive, where Ruth, one of her carers, answers the door and guides me into the lounge. Moons and stars, candles and beads vie for prominence with Teletubby and Peter Andre posters: mother and daughter are fiercely independent spirits.

Debbie, as always, laughs a welcome, though she seems, surprisingly, somewhat ill at ease, nervous even. I plug in the tape recorder. She calls for some wine, which we both accept, but it's me who takes the biggest sip. Ruth then wanders off into a bedroom to watch some television, leaving us alone to talk.

Cliff's eldest daughter, Pat's first baby, is now 35 years old. She is a picture of health. Dark-haired, a flawless complexion, that full Ward mouth surrounding a smile to die for, radiant, vivacious and absolutely confident. No shrinking violet, she.

Debbie moves her wheelchair up to the fire, then, when I position the microphone, back-wheels slightly. I check for levels, make a weak joke—I don't know any strong ones—until gradually she seems to relax:

"He always insisted that we call him and Mom by their Christian names, even before the fame thing, which was quite cool in those days. My friends, some of them, didn't even *know* their parents' first names, so they were well impressed. It was quite a contradiction really, 'cos in everything else, he was so Victorian. I suppose it was an extension of his belief that children should always act as grown-ups. He couldn't hack childish behaviour, especially from his own children...

"I was completely unfazed by his success. Probably 'cos I found his music a bit boring. I was well into David Bowie when 'Gaye' became a hit, and besides which, I'd heard the song in all its stages of development, around the house. *'Gay-ee, won't you let me have a say-ee...'* He was always plonking away on that green upright. Not making a great 'I'm composing and it's a serious business' thing about it, but, in such a small house, there was no escape. I knew those songs almost as well as he did.

"Uncle Ken [*re*ally...] was always around, and that guitarist, Derek. The house was forever full of musicians, but none of it rubbed off on me. My teachers had great expectations because I was Clifford T. Ward's daughter, trying to encourage my musical skills, but I wasn't interested. If I'd have been any good, then it would have been a different story," and she lets out her raucous laugh, only briefly catching my eye.

"Considering all that Martin and I—with less than a year between us—were exposed to: the studios, the fame, the recognition, it's quite a surprise that we are how we are. Or maybe it's *because* of all that...

"But as a father, Cliff was quite a taskmaster. We were all scared witless if we did something wrong; spilled a drink or broke a cup. He was so unpredictable. His reaction could be anything from a cautionary word to a screaming fit. There was no room for mistakes or under-achievement in his world. Even now, I find myself trying to please him, though I have given up a little over the past year or so, but life was forever us—and by that I mean *all* of us, Mom included—trying to please Dad, to get some favourable reaction, some words of praise. If Dad was in a good mood, we were *all* in a good mood, and life was good; if he wasn't, we kept out of his way...

"I wasn't particularly academic, I found exams a bit of a chore, so I was quite chuffed when I passed my O-levels, albeit with 'C' grades in five subjects.

"I was on holiday with Mom's parents when the results came through.

She telephoned me and said that they'd have a little celebration when I got home. And we did. We sat around the table, opened some fizzy stuff, and there in the process of celebrating, Dad said, quite matter-of-factly, '...but you could have got 'B's if you'd tried a bit harder...', and I was like, 'What is this...?' I could have just turned around and left the room, but I stayed and soldiered on through a fairly tense atmosphere.
"He tried to persuade me to re-take them at Hereford College after I'd left my residential school, but, by then I was becoming more my own person. I said no. And he accepted my decision.
"What about his parents, Frank and Kathleen? Did he look down on them?"
"No, not exactly look down on them, but he certainly believed he was a bit different from them, and from the rest of his family. Actually, I think he was more like his parents than he cared to admit: his attitudes, his socialist beliefs, and of course his approach towards my disability. Because of his mother's own disability, and her courage, he expected the same of me. Cliff really couldn't get his head around 'abnormalities', or illness. I can't remember him ever being ill, and subsequently he found it hard to tolerate in other people, so he pushed me into acting as if everything was 'normal'. Except that I had to spend two hours doing up my shoelaces before I could even *pretend* to be like the others."
"So if he was so positive towards your disability, why isn't he the same in his own situation?"
Deb's answer was given without a moment's hesitation:
"Because he doesn't consider himself disabled. He just maintains that he is ill, and that sooner or later, somebody or something will cure him. But there is no cure. Dad has the worst type of MS. There is no remission, it's a relentless, day in, day out assault on the body. He's angry and sad that he's suffering and expects everyone else to feel the same. Not to look for ways of helping, improving his way of life, but just to feel for him. And that just doesn't help anything—or anyone.
"He had great plans for Castle Weir. I thought it was a big, cold mausoleum when we first moved in, but the grounds were glorious, it was a beautiful house, but it needed so much upkeep.
"He offered it to my school for weekend camping breaks, but things were beginning to get a bit tight for him, financially—though I didn't know it at the time—and the whole thing just petered out, although we did manage a *couple* of expeditions up there. We took over the back room in the local pub, all my friends from the residential school, and there I began to cultivate the habit of a lifetime..." and she laughs. "Dad was pretty cool about it, me drinking. He came down one night when we were all supping—well on the way—and walked into the bar. There was this kind of Clint Eastwood tension as he strode across to

me. 'Hi, Deb. What's that you're drinking?' I told him it was just coke. He took a sip. The room went quiet, very quiet. 'Yeah. Coke, that's fine,' he said, and gave me that secret smile. I knew that he knew... I was well impressed with that.

"But I was also at the receiving end of his temper many, many times. Loads. He didn't single me out for preferential treatment in any way."

"How did Cliff's illness affect *you*?"

"I knew there was something wrong. I'd known it for a long time, probably because of my knowledge and experience with impairment. I thought it was either Parkinson's disease or MS. It didn't come as a surprise. He'd been very untogether at my wedding, didn't want to make a speech—despite the fact that it upset my husband's parents—and well, I'd seen the signs of something wrong for quite a while. He's always been nervy, highly strung, but this was something quite serious. I could see that. What really annoyed me was that I had to drag it out of them. Mom eventually told Cliff to tell me, and so, much against his will, he did."

I suggested that, for someone who'd always liked to be in control, such an event, and such a diagnosis, must have been terrifying.

She half-smiled at me. "Except that he never was in control. He liked to think he was, but he wasn't. Ever."

Debbie acknowledges her debt to Cliff's mother, the tenacity born out of being 'disadvantaged' and I can indeed see Kathleen's legendary strength in her character. She has the bonus of a good education, and has grown up refusing to accept anything other than equality. Pop concert promoters, publicans and hoteliers, employers, restaurateurs, transport managers: they have all felt her wrath at some time or another, for their inadequate provision of facilities. She gets results and consequently lives her life to the full.

And of course her life—and Martin's, and Sam's and Polly's—is now her own. The *Home Thoughts* children—and the still recognisable *Both Of Us* cover girl—have lived through the best and the worst of it all, lived and moved on, breaking away, leaving Cliff and Pat on their own, for the first time in thirty-five years of marriage, living off the remnants of an extraordinary but unfulfilled talent, and the generosity of a few concerned friends.

There is no doubt as to who had the gift, but how does talent mould into achievement? Can it really blossom alone, without stimulation, without input from elsewhere?

I don't know the answer. I'm just puzzled by the change in this partnership of a lifetime, where the meek has become mighty...

So what happened? What transformed this pretty, hushed, tea-cosy person, almost overnight, into the sexy, outgoing beauty that she is today? The woman who 'lights up every room she enters'; the woman who, though now in her fifties, appears to be 'someone still in bloom'.

"After Ken's birthday party at Arley, I realized that no good would come—either for Cliff or me—out of locking myself away for the rest of my life. Despite living in the same area for nearly fifty years, I could count my friends, acquaintances, on one hand. Here we were, heading into middle-age and living like hermits. I decided to throw a few parties, push the boat out for once. Cliff's illness was strangling *our* life, and there wouldn't be another one..."

So, the Cherry Hill hoe-downs began. Food, wine and music, deep into the night. Pat took a fashion leaf out of daughter Polly's book, whilst adding a few ideas of her own, and became the perfect society hostess; vivacious, energetic, captivating. It took everyone by surprise.

"Suddenly I had a circle of friends, and, as these friendships blossomed, I found that I was being allowed, for the first time in my life, to speak unsolicited, to express opinions, for God's sake, to socialize, to dress how *I* wanted, in fact, to be myself. And I was as surprised as *anyone* to see the kind of person I was! All those years of subjugation had made me believe I *was* a mouse, that my place in life *was* only to dress the kids, make the sandwiches, iron the shirts, do the hoovering. Born again sums it up. I was born again."

She has had to wait a long, long time to cast off the shackles of subservience.

"But," she continues, "before the shaking of heads, or the wagging, accusing fingers, let me repeat: I'm still here. Any other person would have left years ago. I couldn't walk out on him, I couldn't live with such an act of cowardice. But that's my generation, or at least, that's how my folks bought *me* up. Guilt—Obligation—Deference. That is my GOD.

"Cliff will not help himself. We have tried every known aid for the relief of his symptoms. He tries once, then refuses to have anything else to do with whatever it was. The flotation tank was '...a bore ... he couldn't smoke ... he wasn't like the others waiting in line,'; exercises are '... a waste of time ...'; even computer-based music programmes, for composition, are '.... for invalids...' We had a letter from a fan only last week, out of the blue, a musician also suffering from MS, who'd read about Cliff's plight in a magazine. He enclosed brochures giving full details of commercial products available for disabled users. Cliff just threw it in the bin. 'I don't need that stuff,' he said. 'I can still play and compose, at night, when I'm on my own, when I'm in remission.'

"I looked at him. 'Cliff, it's *me* you're talking to. It's no good lying to *me*. I *know* what you can and can't do.' He glanced up at me, slightly shocked, as if I'd spoilt the game. I'd brought him down to earth with a bump. But that's his trouble. He finds it hard to differentiate between truth and lies. And I don't mean to sound heartless by saying that. He's just refusing to accept the reality, and not in a strong way, saying 'Hey, I'm gonna beat this thing on my own terms', but by continuing this pretence that he can still function as before, and that, really, he doesn't *need* any help. He doesn't want to admit—or to be *seen* to admit—the enormity of his plight. The weakness thing. He mustn't show weakness."

But then, there are the strange occasions when he thrives on close-encounter displays of weakness and disability, as if trying to shock sympathy out of the observer, or again, maybe to relieve the boredom.

Liz Williams, continuing her single-minded crusade, sent a copy of Lichfield's photograph of Clifford daintily suspending a cat on its hind quarters, to the feline magazine *Cat*, sensing another opportunity for some free publicity for the Friends. It was used, with Liz's address underpinning a brief article. Within a matter of days, the ever-zealous *Daily Mail* were in contact, asking to do an article on Clifford and his battle with multiple sclerosis, for their weekly Health Page.

The date was set, a photographer commissioned for the accompanying pictures, and, after a couple of minor setbacks, journalist Lucy Shakeshaft appeared on the doorstep of Cherry Hill. Pat had given Clifford the usual behaviour lecture: '…no nonsense, no lies, no sarcasm…' and, for a while, with Pat sitting, literally, on the edge of her seat, he seemed to be doing fine. Then Lucy asked him about his immobility, his inability to walk around unaided.

Clifford stopped the conversation in mid-flight.

"Of course I can walk. Of course I can move around."

Lucy expressed surprise. "You can?"

Pat's heart sank.

"Watch this," he said. And, as wife and reporter looked on, he slowly, clumsily, and downright stubbornly, slipped out of his chair, onto the floor and proceeded to scrape around the room on his hands and knees, panting and grunting, his hair hanging lank over his red face, causing what he hoped would be maximum embarrassment to them both.

But Lucy showed great calmness during the whole episode.

"She was far less uncomfortable than I was," says Pat. "She was young, noticeably pregnant, but obviously more able to cope with such unexpected incidents than I would have thought. She continued her interview with great composure, which must have thrown Cliff a little. She had evidently done her homework on MS, and possibly from someone, somewhere, found out a little about the mind of Clifford T. Ward."

The article, however, did not appear as scheduled, and, at the time of writing, is still awaiting publication.

Cliff is visited regularly, on a weekly basis, by Clive Edwards, a hairdresser-musician from Pershore, that pretty Georgian market town in the Vale of Evesham. He came as a fan, and now spends many hours over at Cherry Hill, accepting it all in quiet tolerance: the mood swings, the silences, the sheer cussedness, the hot, smoke-filled studio, playing tapes and talking music, Clifford's music…

He mentions certain names now and then, 'in the business…', as if offering some credibility to his enigmatic life. His dedication is, says Pat, remarkable.

"They sit in that room for hours, and as he leaves, Clive asks is it all right to come along next week, and I tell him, fine, of course, and he turns up, and goes through it all again. Masochism," she laughs, "but he's a great help to Cliff's sanity. Nobody else does that, on such a scale."

But, after two years of companionship and habitual name-dropping, Clive has actually come up with something productive.

Through one of his mysterious contacts, Pat was approached by RPMedia, a small but enterprising recording company based in Hove, run by David Paramor, nephew of the late Norrie who was musical director and A&R manager for EMI throughout the rock'n'roll years, and is credited for launching the recording career of Sir HeathCliff of Esher…

Clive had passed on a tape to David's business associate—Kevin Holland-King—of some demos Cliff had recorded at Leon Tipler's house, good old Radio G-LTK, a long, long time before *Home Thoughts*, together with old sparring partner Rodney Simmonds. Leon, in his rare spare moments, still enjoyed putting together such compilations on cassette, purely for Cliff's pleasure, and this one seems to have made an impression.

Pat always shows remarkable calm over such responses. She has been there many times before and usually, after the initial approaches, when the financial implications are put on the table, such proposals come to nothing, but David Paramor's enthusiasm maintained an equilibrium that surprised her. He persisted, they spoke at last, and, in her words, '…he seemed to be genuine…' After a few verbal negotiations, a contract was drawn up, very much in Clifford's favour—in itself an indication of Paramor's integrity—and the wheels started to turn.

David was already a devotee of Clifford's work, and loved these early songs. He wanted to enhance the original recordings and release a CD, well within the possibilities of modern technology.

A running order was agreed, and the first step of the recording process was initiated. The original quarter-inch analogue masters, still carefully filed in the G-LTK library, needed to be digitized, i.e., transferred onto DAT, and the task was assigned, rightly so, to Leon.

During the process of becoming—for the first time in his career—a 'transfer engineer', he reminded me of his original set-up for these simple mid-sixties recordings; the huge mono Ferrographs, the home-built mixer ('...I improvised on the original kit, adding a few extra channels...'); the wonderfully luxurious square AKG-D12 microphone for the vocals ('...also recommended for the bass drum...you could give it some welly...'); oh, and the lack of space...

Indeed, that room, no bigger than, well, a single-bedroom—for that's what it is—accommodated guitars, musicians, even a drummer...; recording machines, a mixing desk, and Clifford T.

"One or two of the backing tracks, the rhythm section, were done at Bev's house, in his more spacious studio, but generally speaking, it was mostly put together up here," Leon tells me over the top of his glasses, tweaking away at the desk, like some nuclear physicist.

"Cliff wouldn't use headphones at first. He always sang his harmonies against the playback from the speakers, which added to the complications, as you can imagine. I'd be watching the VUs, whilst gauging the build-up of wow-and-flutter [the increase of distortion as each take, each 'generation', is layered onto its predecessor] 'cos despite having all those input channels, we still only had mono, two-track recorders to capture the sounds. But I think it all stands up very well. Rodney was there with his acoustic, the lovely full sound he managed to get, his brother Ian added a few instrumental breaks...," and the Clifford T. Ward Tabernacle Choir sang the songs.

It was record, bounce, record, bounce. Bounce, bounce, bounce, until they could bounce no more.

But today, in the here and now, the analogue tapes can be transferred to DAT, which miraculously prevents further loss in sound quality of the original recordings. They become digital 'information'; there is no more bouncing and consequent deterioration. No wow, no flutter. So new instrumentation—some percussion, some bass, perhaps a few electric guitar fills—is added in a professional studio, over a hectic two-day session. Some tracks are barely touched, apart from equalization adjustment; a credit to all concerned at their conception. Technology and chips, which we have all at sometime scorned, brings these thirty-year-old home-recordings up to modern commercial and broadcasting standard, and the songs once again float through the air, free as a bird.

The demos were all done between 1965—'...when we were all out of work...' Leon reminds me—and 1970, when Cliff was beginning to get *genuine* interest from the big boys down south. He must have been writing like a man possessed, and one can only wonder why, with all this ammunition, his career as a 'pop singer'—before he became a 'singer-songwriter'—failed so miserably.

There are 21 songs, hitherto unheard by the general public. *Hidden Treasures* will open many people's eyes and ears to the vibrant, quirky world of Cliff Ward, 1965-70. It is not for me to recommend or single out individual tracks, but there is one song, the breathtaking ballad, 'I'd Like To Take You Out Tonight', which, once and for all, destroys the absurd criticism that Clifford T. Ward had a weak, insipid voice.

Over a block-chord synthesizer, an unusually seductive vocal takes flight, from deep baritone to soaring tenor, until the bridge note in 'Cry, *Try…*' sliding from G to F# in such an unprincipled manner, makes you wonder how on earth he can possibly resolve the melody, by which time of course he has, and you are back safe in his pleading, honest world.

Throughout this book, I have purposely avoided too much song-by-song analysis, it can be too subjective; but why this one remained unmastered is quite beyond my comprehension.

However, *all* these songs, written in a time long before programming, sequencing and digitalia, do raise the issue, once more, of the man's *sui generis.*

Cliff Ward couldn't even strum the chord of E minor. There is only one picture of him holding a guitar, in an awkward left-handed pose, yet these songs are written around—and, in the main, for—that instrument. How on earth did he do it? Rodney's double-tracked 12-string drives the songs along as if Cliff were playing it. Every nuance is there, echoed or precipitated, no stumbles, no tangents. Hand in glove. An eerie keyboard says hello, an electric guitar plucks a counterpoint here and there, but throughout the demo-collection it is just Rodney and Cliff, plus, of course, those trademark warm, precise, three-part harmonies. Some intuitive spirit most certainly flowed between these two; something that must have bonded during those early practices in seedy Stourport cafés and at glittering Locarno gigs, something that continued almost metaphysically, even after their teenage back-garden brawl sent them, for a while, their own separate ways. When maturity and circumstance brought them back together, they fell into their respective roles with consummate ease, and Rodney became the first in a line of talented musicians—Derek Thomas, Richard Hewson, Mark Tibenham amongst them—that would help shape the gems waiting to surface from the mind of Clifford T. Ward.

But apart from the music, *Hidden Treasures* has a poignancy quite of its own.

Locked in that small room, creating the songs that you now hear so many years later, no-one could have foreseen that Rodney would eventually die—and that Clifford was destined to suffer—from the same mysterious illness. Time and circumstance cruelly linked them together once more, even as, in their prime, they had shared that other, more glorious, common bond of music.

And a delightful little addendum to the *Hidden Treasures* story:

Just as I thought the book was finally, *finally* finished, I went out for a New Year's drink with Robin Parker, a friend of many years' standing—many years. Robin has lived in Kidderminster, Bewdley and Stourport all his life, a bluff but extremely likeable, dependable man. A rock. He and his wife Helen once ran the Horsefair Café in that colourful corner of Kidderminster, opposite Cliff and Pat's first home, though it was a while after the Wards had moved to Habberley. A young Stan Webb and his father '... used to pop in—often three times a day—for a cup of tea...' Robin knew them all, and the league of music managers; Nigel Reece, Peter Phillips, Roger Rowe, Ray Northover, and Carl Hasdell. Surely he must have some little anecdote to contribute?

Naturally, he mentioned the Park Attwood. Everyone mentions the Park Attwood.

Then came a delightful little tale concerning guitars and early ignorance of same:

"You remember those pin-ball machines we had in the café. One of our customers spent every spare minute he had rattling those things [no it wasn't Terry Jones], and he needed some more 'tanners' [the pre-decimal sixpence] to feed into them. So he offered to sell me a guitar for ten shillings. He told me it was made of tin... Tin! Well, I wasn't interested in 'tin' guitars. They had to be wood to be good..."

Robin knows only too well what he missed. 'National' steel Resonator guitars are now worth their weight in gold, but back in the 1960s, way before the current almost insatiable demand for 'The Blues', they were considered valueless. And to salt the wound, anything that *was* around in those days would have undoubtedly been of much earlier origin, and thus even more collectable today. Ten shillings would have bought a mighty good insurance policy.

I told him about *Hidden Treasures*, the 1960s demos, and mentioned the lovely, full sound Rodney managed to achieve.

"That could only have come from an acoustic 12-string. I thought I had the only such type of guitar in the whole of the Midlands at that time."

"Well that's right." Robin lifted his Boddingtons. "You had that Harmony, my brother Nicky loved it, so *he* went out and bought one, a Hofner. I've still got it." And then, quite matter-of-factly, "That's the guitar Rodney used to come round and borrow for Cliff's demos."

Hidden Treasures is of that prime time, yet also out of it, for no-one else was writing about such normal aspects of life in such an idiosyncratic way, which lends a charm—an English charm—to these perfectly performed vignettes. And there are many others tucked away in the G-LTK vaults, if they can be found. Well, if you can get *at* them (see Chapter Three…), thanks to Leon, the quiet genius.

He is still there, after all these crazy years, in his airless room, surrounded by a million miles of tape. Every Saturday evening he puts together a delightful two-hour programme of pure nostalgia for Ludlow's tiny Sunshine Radio, 855 AM; perfectly edited, flowing seamlessly through the golden years of radio music, and presented by one of his many alter-egos. His horizons have extended by only a few miles, over the brooding, mysterious Clee Hills into Housman's Shropshire and the Welsh Marches, but he is a man happily—or sadly, depending on your point of view—unchanged by time; content with his lot.

Whenever I bemoan my circumstances, the thirteen years I spent with local Radio Wyvern, broadcasting to such a small catchment area, playing undiscovered gems to incredibly enthusiastic listeners, and unable to penetrate that invisible ring of national recognition, I think of Leon and his quiet genius. The fact-filled mind of what we disparagingly call an 'anorak', but possessing the multi-talents of a true audio professional *and* a coruscating wit; labouring with love in his solitary way, all this time, for so little reward or recognition.

His enterprise has enabled those who were outside that circle of musical friends, led by their imperious, ambitious ringmaster, to listen in and try to imagine just what went on inside the young head of Clifford T. Ward. Leon recorded *every*thing he possibly could, even when they thought they were safe…

1965. The scene: The front room of Terry Clarke's home, a large between-the-wars residence, with tongue-and-groove floorboards of polished oak, sumptuous sofas and velvet curtains. Four young musicians—and a drummer—are hard at work, running through 'Pretty Words (Like 'I Love You')'.

Lines of cables run from the sound equipment along the floor, down the oak-panelled corridor, to the library, where Leon sits hunched over his Teac reel-to-reel, headphones in place, VUs flickering.

They grind to a halt, badly out of tune, sloppy. Ken hits the snare, a rim-shot, a cymbal, the bass drum. B-boom. Drummers: they always have the last word.

Voices off. Mumblings and murmurs of discontent.

Then Cliff, gruff, throaty, in surprisingly heavy dialect:

"Oh cum *on*, wayke u-up."

Terry: "You're singing it too fast surely, anyway." [Easy *on*, Terry…]
He plays it, rippling the chords. Slower.
Cliff, loudly, sounding irritated:
"Look, I knew this would happen. I said last night. You'm so half-*soaked*. What's the *madder*?"
Ken taps the cymbals.
Terry, whining: "I'm all flu'd up to the bloody eyeballs. I can't blinkin' help it, can I? I feel bloody rough."
Cliff: "What toime you ged up?"
Terry: "Eleven o'clock."
Cliff: "And you feels rough?"
Ken, in a clipped, precise tone from the other side [stereo inquisition here]: "What time did you go to bed?"
Terry: "I dunno. Same time as you, I suppose. When I got home."
Plink-plonking of guitar strings. A bit of pouting bottom lip, one presumes…
Cliff: "Well I can't under*stand* it. All I can say is, you want to get down to one of them gym-*nas*-iums and get a bit of stuffin'."
Terry, whining again: "No I don't. I want a couple of weeks off work."
Ken snorts: "Naaaargh!"
Cliff: "…your body is completely out of…"
Terry, whining a little louder, his voice rising to a crescendo: "I know it is, 'cos whenever I have flu or anything, I can't have time off work like you lot do."
Cliff [across mic, obviously a tad annoyed…]: "Oh-OH. Ah-ha-ARGH. *Very* cutting, Terry. Very cutting in-*deed*."
Ken: "Well whose fault's that?"
Terry: "Well it's my fault."
Ken, in his nasal, authoritative tone: "Well there you are then. Do something about it. You have a responsibility."
Terry: "*Pardon*?"
Ken: "You have certain responsibilities to yourself."
Terry: "I'm not blaming *you*."
Ken: "No. *We're* blaming *you*."
Terry: "*What*?"
Ken: "For not looking after yourself." [Hits hi-hat twice. So there…]
Cliff: "You can't be bad, mate. If you'd got the flu…"
Terry: "If I had one day off work next week, my old man wouldn't let me come out with the group for the next three weeks." He coughs. [Bit chesty, that, Terry.]
Cliff: "If you're bad, you get a doctor's certificate, and when you're better [he] signs you off. That's what I did when I was bad. We couldn't do the gigs."
More discussions about Terry's 'nightwork' and his father's attitude.

Cliff then takes control, his Stourport burr noticeably vernacularizing: "Well, this is all irrelevant. For God's sake, let's all *broyton urp*. It's this lack of enth-*usi*-asm."

He then turns on poor, silent Graham, sitting astride his amplifier.

Cliff's speech quickens:

"Look at Graham, either [*sic*]. He's like a s-, he's like a s-, he's like a stupid little schoolboy, just because his guitar ain't come over right... He's had it now. He ain't gonna give a damn. Just like somebody's taken a packet of sweets off 'im." He again moves across the mic, giving a deep, gruff curse. "Ya bloody...silly...id-*yutt*. My voice ain't come over right at all so far, but *I* ain't moanin'. I just want to purr-*fect* it. I keeps on tryin' all the time. God *strewth*..."

Terry is heard moaning his misery.

Ken laughs. "Ha!"

They must get on with it. He calls out:

"Five seconds, Le-[on]."

Terry mumbles. Cliff picks up on it. His voice takes on a tone of menace:

"There's no need to be nasty, Terry... Grow *orp*. Threatening about packing up and switching the television on." His voice deepens, almost pointing a finger. "Don't you rile me, 'cos I'm telling you. Don't you rile me."

Terry squeaks something.

Cliff: "*Do* it then [pack up]. Do it *now* then, why don't you."

Terry: "All right then." Coughs. Moans.

Footsteps across the room. The click of his guitar lead and the mains being unplugged, then the long, ominous rumble of an amplifier being dragged across the wooden floor, to a complete verbal hush. He's taking his bat and ball away.

Footsteps fade. A door slams shut.

Ken taps his drums... He's restless. Now what?

He turns to Graham:

"Wanna fight, Grae? Wanna fight?"

Graham, in his dark, country drawl:

"You lot won't be told. That's your trouble. It's moy guitarr..."

A discussion then ensues on volume controls, and the lack of them for drummers.

Cliff is heard gently complaining in the background:

"...I've left my family for this [tonight]. I wanna get on and do something. I'm shocked about Terry..."

The tape ends.

Another gem, almost equal to The Troggs tape, and it survives because of Leon's meticulous diligence ever since that chance meeting years and years and years ago, helped in no small way by the insanity of tangents, the law of bastard, the world of retro. Because of all these things and more, we find the music—huh, and the words—of Clifford T. Ward with us once again, refusing, against all the odds, to lie down.

That's him over there; he's waving—not drowning.

WAVING, NOT DROWNING

… Sand, sand, a rusted anchor, broken glass;
The listless sediment of sparkling days ….

C. Day Lewis: *All Gone*

But there is someone else there as well, as there always has been. She sits quietly in the long shadows, showing her true spirit only to negotiate or defend, as people come once again to meet and talk to him about his life and his work. When they have gone, and Cliff has stumbled off to bed, she sits alone for a while, trying to remember and make sense of it all, sometimes wondering: what was it all about…?

Five homesick musicians stuck in a hotel bedroom in France. Bored and broke, bats and baguettes, waiting for the last gig and the first boat home.

Terry Clarke slumps on the bed, reading out a letter he's picked up at the poste restante that morning from his wife, Angela:

> … I met Pat today in Liptons. She had both the kids with her, in a double-pushchair. I don't know how she manages it, such a tiny girl pushing them all the way up that hill. Anyway, we had a nice chat and she sends her love to Cliff, says she'll be writing later on tonight…

"What day was that Terry?" comes Cliff's husky voice from the corner.

"Er, ninth, Wednesday it's dated. Why?"

"What's 'er bloody doin' in Liptons on a bloody Wednesday? That's what I'd like to know, Terry." His speech is rapid. He is 'flummoxed'. Or is there something else?

Terry takes up the story:

"He spent the next *two hours* trying to get hold of Angela on the phone. [The Wards were without a phone.] He was… well, absolutely consumed with suspicion, jealousy. He just couldn't understand what

Pat was doing in town mid-week and suspected…An Affair. Blimey, I'm sure she'd got enough on her plate. We really took the piss out of him that night, and he went for it. Cliff always took the bait…"

A long and winding road. Cliff is driving his brand new Reliant Scimitar. He has started to reap the rewards of all those years of struggle; advances, air play, recognition. It's all happening now.
Pat sits at his side. She's got on a new dress. She's arranged baby-sitters, cancelled the milk, fed the goldfish.
They're off to Weybridge. A party at Cliff Richard's house.
"Who'd believe it?" she is thinking. "Mom and Dad asked me to get his autograph, but, well, *he'd* [Clifford] go spare…Doesn't rate him. 'Cos he's English of course. Jimmy Webb, Randy Newman, now that's a bit different, but Cliff Richard…"
They reach Oxford and turn onto the new ring road. It was starting to rain, getting dark. Cliff flicked the wiper switch.
Whoosh, whoosh. The blades rubbed across the screen.
An ominous silence. She made a weak joke about 'Wet in Weybridge'.
Silence.
"Oh, I can't be bothered. Let's turn back," he suddenly moaned. "All that way just to see a bunch of showbiz pos-*eurs*." The inflected sarcasm of the last syllable hangs in the air.
It wasn't a question, a suggestion. He'd already made up his mind. Not for him the fawning, back-slapping career moves.
Half-a-mile down the road he pulled into a lay-by, checked his wing mirror and swung the long, brown car around, through the intersection and headed for home.
They reached the Oaklands in time for the nine o'clock news.

A knock at the door. She took off her rubber gloves and turned the latch. Nigel Reece. With a bunch of flowers.
"Cliff said you'd like these," he smiled. "I only got back this morning, but this was my priority. Orders from the captain."
She asked him in, made him a coffee and they chatted about France. He'd been over to see the boys, just for the weekend. Peter Phillips had gone with him. They were still trying hard on The Cruisers' behalf, though of course they were not directly responsible for the tour that had gone so very badly wrong.
"Well, they're carrying on, but a bit reluctantly. Problems with the money, and some of the gigs are a bit… well, tacky. Some of the

audiences seem to be a little...unappreciative... Soldiers, *American* soldiers." And he gave that.wide, toothy smile. "You know Cliff. If it isn't right, it isn't..."
"Right," she interrupted. That sidewards look. She knew exactly.
"We couldn't stay more than a couple of days, Peter's getting very busy, and I've got the garage to run. Agency work is quite difficult, despite what Cliff says about commission..." A thin smile. "But I'm glad we went over to see them. Maybe next time they can get it sorted a bit better, find a more reliable agent. They work a little differently to us..."
But that was a nice gesture. She loved flowers.
Cliff came home three days later, with a bottle of Chanel No.5 and his dirty washing. After dinner he spent twenty intense minutes quizzing her about Nigel's visit. What time of day—or night—did he call, how long had he stayed, what had he said, were they alone, did she make him a meal...?
She binned the flowers next morning, before he came down for breakfast.

They had returned Cliff's Mini. Pat hadn't learned to drive yet, so Maggie, Ken's girlfriend, had borrowed it while Cliff was in France, but now the payments were in arrears, so it had to go. Rodney had offered them his old banger as a deposit on another one. Cliff's got his eye on a Hillman Imp. It'll be a pedal-car next if things don't improve...
The trip had been a financial disaster, yet Cliff still wouldn't get a job. She felt a bit sick at being the poor relation. People mean well, but always she felt inferior. Maggie and Angela had taken them for a lovely picnic in Brintons Park, while Cliff was in France—her, Debbie and Martin—and brought a gigantic hamper along, as they would. But she felt so uncomfortable. Debbie and her baby brother had a great time, tucking in, but, oh for some financial independence.
They were still hoping to get a council house, especially now that Martin had come along. Maybe then things would start looking up. Maybe...

A party, somewhere. Maybe her parents' house. They were not long married, and the sexual revolution was in full swing. She was in the kitchen, Cliff was upstairs, in a bedroom with some floozy. They'd all been drinking, the music was playing, bodies all over the place; dancing, talking, smooching…

One of the musicians came in, moved a bit close. They started kissing.

Somebody else opened the door, peering through the half-light, then quickly disappeared. Pat pushed away.

"I bet they've gone to tell Cliff."

And indeed they had.

But Cliff didn't make the usual male confrontation. Yes he was guilty too, but who said anything about equality?

Within five minutes, there was an resounding crash on the verandah roof. Everybody rushed outside. There he was, in a state of disarray and obvious anger, climbing down the drainpipe onto the lawn. In a fit of outrage, and to cause the greatest commotion possible, he had leapt from the bedroom window.

And the days at Castle Weir, when the world began to slowly and secretly slip from their grasp.

She remembers the crop-spraying. The aeroplane buzzing low over the surrounding fields, the chemical trails hanging in the air before slowly and silently falling to coat the window sills, the cars, the lawn, with a thin, silver film. Nobody questioned it. No-one would dare question it. Farmers were always law unto themselves.

No, that would be too simple an explanation…

New Year's Day, 1978.

The post-festivity blues had set in, so Cliff decided to organize some activity. Mom and Dad were coming across, a few of Cliff's brothers and their families were bringing his ailing parents from Stourport—for The Big Meal, but there was an air of reluctance to celebrate, so Cliff took over. He organized a treasure hunt.

They were told to look for clues along the way; signs, names, trees, churches, pubs, and 'the teams' would be quizzed upon arrival at the house. Cliff went into schoolteacher mode, assembling them all in the lounge, reading out his questions, and handing out a prize or two to the winner. A sack of potatoes, or a joint of beef. It was good fun, captured in Kodachrome for posterity. One of the good times, but once again, feeding the five thousand, and anticipating any likely mood swing always took the edge off things.

She also remembers telephoning Cliff's mother from Castle Weir. It must have been late March, early April, 1979.

"Hi, Mom... Just phoning to tell you the good news. I'm pregnant again! The baby's due about the first week in December."

"Ooh, our Pat. You *naughty* girl..."

That's all she recalls of the conversation. In the prime of her life, joyously announcing another baby to her mother-in-law. Why can't these people be normal...?

Lower Hollin was their best time. Life was glorious then. That beautiful house, set in the delightful Worcestershire countryside they both loved. The pool, the studio, the gardens, the pub just a half-a-mile down the road.

Cliff's mom came screaming out of the house:

"Our Cliff !!! There's an old bloke asleep in your music room, snoring his head off, covered in mud and filth and stinking and..."

Harry Knott, local raconteur and drinker, someone who, despite his appearance and behaviour, Cliff had a lot of time for. Whenever they went down The Bell, no matter who was there, or who they were with, he always went over for a chat with Harry Knott, hunched up in the pipe-smoker's corner, white-haired and toothless, his stained collarless shirt, his ancient Harris Tweed jacket, his silver tankard, filled to overflowing with cloudy cider.

He'd be there, lunchtime and evening, holding court. Cussing, belching, chuckling, drinking, until it was time to go, and back over the fields he'd ramble, through the mud, the wet corn, the pig-swill, looking for somewhere to rest and sleep it all off.

He was always welcome at Lower Hollin. It was an open house to anyone and everyone, and the 'music room' was the perfect place to end a drinking session.

"It's only Harry Knott, Mom. He's all right. He'll sleep it off. It's only Harry Knott..."

Oh for sure, life—*anyone's* life—is a catalogue of memories. But here they are, 35 years down the line, drowning in debt and misery. The family silver has been sold, there is little else left. The sound of a car on the lane could mean anything. Her heart still leaps at an unexpected ring of the bell, she still dreads the post, and her health, not surprisingly, is beginning to give cause for concern.

But Pat won't let it show.

Her father is now frail and in constant need of professional attention, moving between home and nursing home on a weekly basis; her mother, still suffering from high blood pressure and the inherent side-

effects, bemoans the inconvenience of it all.
Yes, her parents have had a long, happy, secure marriage, but nothing prepares for the perils of old age, and she, being the only child, is constantly on call, scurrying back and forth to Kidderminster, Stourport and all points east, clocking up expensive excess miles in her Motability Peugeot.

"What will happen to us all?"
She is holding this whole family together, and nobody questions her ability to continue doing so, forever.

Sometimes, despite his bravado—or his anger—she catches him unawares. He is maybe sitting in the car, or alone in the suffocating heat and smoke of his studio. She walks in to take him into town for the ride, and he has been listening to a song on the radio. His face is wet., from crying, but her sudden appearance makes him react as he has always done: he...must...not...show...weakness. The sheer effort of holding back the tears distorts his bloated face even more and he looks away, but she sees it all. She knows him so well.
Clifford T. Ward changed her world.
He also changed—or certainly affected—the lives of those who listened to his music, *really* listened. He wasn't a cutting-edge revolutionary, but he was important, inspirational, and true to his beliefs; indeed, highly vulnerable because of them, and it has all been so very bittersweet.
Look again at that mysterious, poignant Tembo publicity picture.
No-one knows its true history. Liz Williams bought it via mail order from someone in Glasgow, advertising in *Record Collector*. It was most probably taken for the Tembo release in 1986, because it shows both sides of the man: his past and his future, in one bittersweet glance.
Cover Clifford's right eye with your hand. There you see a man approaching middle-age maturity: still ready to take on the world, still assured, proud, handsome, confident.
Now cover his left eye. There, you can discern the suspect signs of an illness that was about to devastate his life, that had taken root—who knows when? I maintain it was always there—but was now beginning to show. Hooded, lazy, dark, unfocused. The mirror of his soul.

Maybe I have offended you—or, God forbid, Clifford (though somehow I doubt I could offend him...)—in telling this story warts and all. But I didn't set out to write a hagiography. *I* knew he was only human, and that he was here, in between these pages, only because he had stories to tell and songs to sing. I would have preferred to leave it at that; embrace the music and the words—they speak well enough for him—and let his life, with its thorns and flowers, remain.

But what is one without the other? Inherent curiosity drives us to enquire, pushes us to dissect, criticize and judge those whom we admire, and there are very few who are without fault. Anyway, hagiographies are terribly boring.

Saint or sinner, the legacy of Clifford T. Ward will last way beyond his life, and ours.

His 'fall from grace'—though not entirely due to his work—ran almost parallel with the change in social attitude brought about by the punk revolution.

The first real shift since the rock'n'roll years, punk, despite its wonderful energy and infectious rhythms, heralded a new generation of writers and producers, critics and entrepreneurs who were, quite frankly, embarrassed by sentiment of any kind; pure romance became—almost overnight—uncool, and it has never really recovered. It is much easier to be 'in your face' than 'in your heart'.

America subsequently invented a fail-safe formula of dreadfully tortuous, tuneless, contrived love-duets: singers expressing cliché-ridden sentiments whilst battling it out with each other in vocal gymnastics, and found a dumbed-down niche with a host of 'Impossible Dream'-drivel songs, which sadly continues to this day.

It is certainly not fashionable any more to like the plain sentiment expressed in 'Home Thoughts From Abroad', or 'The Way Of Love', and so this music becomes less and less accessible. Re-releases are deleted almost as soon as they hit the shelves; marketing is the all-powerful road to success—now more than ever—and Clifford T. Ward is considered no longer marketable.

But let us hope that before he or we leave this mortal coil, his music *will* rise again, and spread like seeds upon the wind, and he will be seen for the remarkable talent he was. Don't ever say he wasn't important.

He was so different and yes, some expressions were, in pop terminology, odd, even awkward, to you and me, but it was not pretension or contrivance. That is how he was, how he still is. Lyrics were written as life was spoken. No clichés, no rhetoric, no falsehood. He didn't spend hours agonizing over the perfect rhyme: what he felt, he said.

Even now, though he struggles to enunciate, he doesn't compromise his choice of words: there is no extemporization. His speech is peppered with precision and knowledge, with a mastery of the language of poets. There is no hip phrasing, no slang, very little—public—blasphemy. He speaks from an eloquent past, from the days of respect and passion.

We need that now, more than ever, for as we approach the hyped-up political millennium, the world of pop music—singer-songwriters, musicians, records, audio-creativity—is becoming a spent force. The participants, the 'old guard', are slowly being replaced, just as they replaced the strict-rhythm bands, the ballroom dancers and the skip-jivers, all that time ago.

The change is less volatile, almost insidious in its stealth, and that such a joyous, collective emotion is being superseded by the sad, solitary pursuit of computerized virtual reality does not appear to give great cause for concern, but it should. Some call it progress, the inevitable advancement. The computer is the new television, and television didn't harm us, did it…?

No-one is reaching out anymore. We are all closing in on ourselves, working from home, shopping from home, cocooned in safe familiarity, the handshake replaced by the password.

And so we must end this story where we began. Two people—in what should have been the years of a gentle autumn—locked in a marriage racked by fear and disability, staring out at some grey horizon for that next tsunami that could either engulf them with more misery or lift them, for a while, onto a lighter plane. Nothing can never be right again, and because of that, mere existence is all too dependant on a world that really, as a whole, doesn't seem to care.

Life—with all its wonders, its spectacular beauty, its constant dance of the seasons, its sheer magnificence—is still unbearably sad. And I find, upon drawing this tale of love, talent, hardship, humour, success, failure, loss and unimaginable tragedy to a conclusion, that I am consumed by a great melancholy.

Time for some music, methinks.

I could be a millionaire, if I had the money,
I could own a mansion, no I don't think I'd like that.
But I might write a song to make you laugh, now that would be funny,
And you could tell your friends in England, you'd like that.
But now I've chosen aeroplanes and boats to come between us,
And a line or two on paper wouldn't go amiss.
How is Worcestershire? Is it still the same between us?
Do you still use television to send you fast asleep?
Can you last another week? Does the cistern still leak,
Or have you found a man to mend it?
Oh, and by the way, how's your broken heart,
Is that mended too?
I miss you, I miss you.
I really do.

I've been reading Browning, Keats and William Wordsworth,
And they all seem to be saying the same things for me.
Well I like the words they use, and I like the way they use them;
You know, 'Home Thoughts From Abroad' is such a beautiful poem.
And I know how Robert Browning must have felt,
'Cause I'm feeling the same way about you;
Wond'ring what you're doing, and if you need some help.
Do I still occupy your mind? Am I being so unkind?
Do you find it very lonely, or have you found someone to laugh with?
Oh, and by the way, are you laughing now?
'Cause I'm not.
I miss you, I miss you.
I really do.

Home Thoughts From Abroad   Clifford T. Ward

The Leading Players

Ken Wright: Eventually rose to become Director of BBC Enterprises, with its turnover of £400 million, before taking early retirement and buying a converted church in the Cotswolds, where he now lives with his wife Vanessa, and son James. He still drums whenever and wherever possible, and is as good as ever.

Derek Thomas: After recording those hauntingly beautiful guitar parts that adorn Cliff's early albums, Derek entered Goldsmiths' College, becoming a B.Mus., via Schoenberg and the classical guitar. He then abandoned music altogether, and eventually reverted to his original career in the press gang. He is now working for the *Independent on Sunday* (what does he do for the rest of the week?...), and has found a new interest, in jazz, no doubt conjuring equally original sounds from his 1960s Gibson Byrdland.

Terry Edwards: After Cliff's enforced change of direction, Terry moved on, joining Freddie Garrity's Dreamers for a short while, another experience he wouldn't have missed for the world, and one which fully utilized his hidden talents. He is now back in Bayton, deep in the heart of Worcestershire; still a friendly, unassuming man, whom you would pass in the street without ever realizing that his smooth, sonorous bass lines are preserved for posterity on those classic Clifford T. Ward albums. He now plays like the devil.

Bev Pegg: Despite increasingly cut-throat competition from the Far East, Bev still manages to secure business for his castings company, now employing over eighty workers and recently celebrating its seventy-five years of production. In his spare time he continues to gig wherever and whenever possible, jazz, folk, joke, rock'n'roll. As keen and as able as ever; an all-enduring enthusiast.

Recordings

Clifford T. Ward had a chequered career, both in terms of success and public persona. From as early as 1965, when he began recording, he assumed various collective and solo guises, until the release of the first album under his real name in 1972, which coincidentally marked the turning point in a long struggle for recognition.

In *Bittersweet*, I have deliberately avoided a too detailed analysis of Clifford's prodigious output. It really is not for me to comment on songs which mean so much to so many people in so many different ways, apart from remarking on their startling originality and consummate beauty. Those I consider the truly outstanding or important tracks are mentioned briefly within this book, whereas en masse I can confirm 29 singles, 10 vinyl albums and 7 CDs over the years. He also appears on 13 UK vinyl compilation albums and on one very rare cassette-only compilation, and we are still finding more songs…

For a full discography, details of out-takes, alternative mixes, demos and oddities, I recommend back numbers of Clive Winstanley's excellent *Waves* fanzine, wherein the 'master' sleuth has meticulously noted such findings, and, where possible, their availability.

To discover the rich diversity of Clifford's songwriting talents, two CDs in particular, *Gaye and Other Stories*—a compilation from his first three albums—and *Hidden Treasures*—the first of a series of subtly enhanced '60s demos—are a joy.

If you are without, go forth and buy them.

Contacts:
Friends Of Clifford T. Ward,
E. Williams,
Bramble Cottage,
High Leys, Rowrah,
Frizington, Cumbria.
CA26 3XT

Clive Winstanley,
Waves,
P.O. Box 59, Whitehaven,
CA26 3GA

Acknowledgements

This book would not have been possible without the many people who gave their time freely and willingly, and whose names are sprinkled throughout the pages.

Special mention must go to Ken Wright, who entrusted to me—without question—his exhaustive archives: diaries, press cuttings, ephemera, and who, together with his wife Vanessa, provided generous hospitality; to Pat Ward, who trawled her past with disarming modesty, honesty and humour, and who also freely allowed access to highly sensitive personal documents, accounts and photographs.

To Jimmy Page, for phoning *me*; to Jeff Lynne; to Chris De Burgh, who, despite my unthinkingly calling him at a sad time, spoke with affection and great recall; to Robert Plant, who always makes me laugh; and to Clive Selwood for an long and enjoyable session of anecdotes. To Karl Hyde, for making a sentimental journey; and to Leon Tipler, for always being there…

I am indebted to the ubiquitous John Tobler, and thank Debbie Ward in Coventry and Sam Ward in Denmark for opening their hearts, and Kath née Ward for her early memories and finding those pictures.

To the eloquent Peter Grogan, for an Irish perspective; to Ian Summers and Mark Tibenham: thanks for the crack and the drinks.

Extra special thanks must go to the genial Jeremy Humphries, an old friend with whom I share some happy memories from teenage years. We rekindled our friendship via the airwaves, thanks be to guitars and good music, and Jeremy stepped in at the eleventh hour to offer his superb editing skills. When I just could not face another word, he lifted my deeply darkening soul. Yea, verily.

He also advised me that there were certain rules I *must* adhere to, though the jury is still out on some of them…

I must also mention the many publishing houses who returned my original synopsis. Their rejection letters told me the subject matter was not a viable proposition. I therefore had no choice but to go ahead alone. For the first time in my life, I took the helm, to oversee complete control of my work, and along the way I met many like-minded spirits.

Not featured in the book, but for inadvertently providing encouragement and calm, I thank guitar historian, Tony Bacon.

Terry Clifford of Print & Design, Worcester, sat me down and offered friendly advice; Solutions, again of Worcester, repaired my cursed computer, just when I needed it most; and Phil Wilesmith of Action Print, Kingswinford, gave guidance without obligation.

Finally, I am eternally thankful to the dirty yellow van that didn't indicate, yet pointed me in the direction of Ebenezer Baylis & Son, Printers, of Worcester. There—after scouring the country—right on my doorstep I found an endangered species: a company that offers modern technology and yet retains those mythical values, fair play and honest service; Chris Humphries, you're a star.

Oh, but hold on.
I can't possibly close without saying 'Ta' to the man himself. He infuriates me, teases me, and inspires me, but Clifford T. Ward is also one of the most amusing men I have ever met.
He will sit through conversations, his legs outstretched, his hands forming the prayer triangle, listening intently behind those dark glasses. Suddenly he will stop the discussion with a raised forefinger and just the hint of a smile, and you know, you just know, that something quite silly is forthcoming.
"David." He struggles to speak, his throat full, his head shaking. "Tonight we'll go on first."
Or:
"David. I don't want to play that bla-wd-y place again."
This man, despite his condition, is not rambling. He is playing it strictly for laughs, and it works, for me, every time.

I showed him the cover of this book.
He gradually found focus, pushing the sunglasses up on his forehead and stared for a few seconds.
"That's a *great* picture," he croaked.
"I took that," feeling pleased quite with myself.
A silence, before he turned, with a puzzled expression:
"I mean the one of *me*."
Not to be beaten, I then—quite patronizingly—asked him if he recognized the view. Another few seconds.
"That's the view from The Spinney, over Pensax, to...wards...*Clent*," he declared, with a triumphant flourish on the last word.
Spot on.
But, again, just in case it was all getting too serious, he pointed to one of the sheep in the foreground of the picture.
"And that's our Vera."

His spirit—despite his form—is omnipotent. Here's to you, Cliff.
With love.